THE FIRST FARMERS OF EUROPE

Knowledge of the origin and spread of farming has been revolutionised in recent years by the application of new scientific techniques, especially the analysis of ancient DNA from human genomes. In this book, Stephen Shennan presents the latest research on the spread of farming by archaeologists, geneticists and other archaeological scientists. He shows that it resulted from a population expansion from present-day Turkey. Using ideas from the disciplines of human behavioural ecology and cultural evolution, he explains how this process took place. The expansion was not the result of 'population pressure' but of the opportunities for increased fertility by colonising new regions that farming offered. The knowledge and resources for the farming 'niche' were passed on from parents to their children. However, Shennan demonstrates that the demographic patterns associated with the spread of farming resulted in population booms and busts, not continuous expansion.

Stephen Shennan is Professor of Theoretical Archaeology at the UCL Institute of Archaeology, where he was Director from 2005–2014. His main interest is explaining stability and change in prehistory in the light of evolutionary ideas. He has published over 120 papers and books, including *Quantifying Archaeology* (2nd edition, 1997), *Genes, Memes and Human History* (2002) and *Pattern and Process in Cultural Evolution* (edited, 2009). He is a Fellow of the British Academy and a member of the Academia Europaea. He received the Rivers Medal of the Royal Anthropological Institute in 2010 and a Shanghai Archaeological Forum Research Award for his EUROEVOL project in 2015.

CAMBRIDGE WORLD ARCHAEOLOGY

SERIES EDITOR
NORMAN YOFFEE, UNIVERSITY OF MICHIGAN

The *Cambridge World Archaeology* series is addressed to students and professional archaeologists, and to academics in related disciplines. Most volumes present a survey of the archaeology of a region of the world, providing an up-to-date account of research and integrating recent findings with new concerns of interpretation. While the focus is on a specific region, broader cultural trends are discussed and the implications of regional findings for cross-cultural interpretations considered. The authors also bring anthropological and historical expertise to bear on archaeological problems and show how both new data and changing intellectual trends in archaeology shape inferences about the past. More recently, the series has expanded to include thematic volumes.

RECENT BOOKS IN THE SERIES

THE FIRST FARMERS OF EUROPE

An Evolutionary Perspective

STEPHEN SHENNAN

Institute of Archaeology, University College London

CAMBRIDGE
UNIVERSITY PRESS

CAMBRIDGE
UNIVERSITY PRESS

University Printing House, Cambridge CB2 8BS, United Kingdom

One Liberty Plaza, 20th Floor, New York, NY 10006, USA

477 Williamstown Road, Port Melbourne, VIC 3207, Australia

314–321, 3rd Floor, Plot 3, Splendor Forum, Jasola District Centre, New Delhi – 110025, India

79 Anson Road, #06-04/06, Singapore 079906

Cambridge University Press is part of the University of Cambridge.

It furthers the University's mission by disseminating knowledge in the pursuit of education, learning, and research at the highest international levels of excellence.

www.cambridge.org
Information on this title: www.cambridge.org/9781108422925
DOI: 10.1017/9781108386029

First published 2018

Printed in the United States of America by Sheridan Books, Inc.

A catalogue record for this publication is available from the British Library.

Library of Congress Cataloging-in-Publication Data
Names: Shennan, Stephen, author.
Title: The first farmers of Europe : an evolutionary perspective / Stephen Shennan, Institute of Archaeology, University of London.
Description: Cambridge, United Kingdom; New York, NY, USA: Cambridge University Press, [2018] | Series: Cambridge world archaeology | Includes bibliographical references and index.
Identifiers: LCCN 2017060366 | ISBN 9781108422925 (hardback) | ISBN 9781108435215 (paperback)
Subjects: LCSH: Agriculture, Prehistoric – Europe. | Neolithic period – Europe.
Classification: LCC GN803.S47 2018 | DDC 936–dc23
LC record available at https://lccn.loc.gov/2017060366

ISBN 978-1-108-42292-5 Hardback
ISBN 978-1-108-43521-5 Paperback

Para Lúcia, a luz da minha vida

CONTENTS

FIGURES

PREFACE AND ACKNOWLEDGEMENTS

The origins of this book go back to the late 1990s and it represents the tip of the iceberg of a vast amount of earlier work with numerous colleagues that has depended on generous support from grant-giving bodies. Prior to that time my main research interests had focussed on the beginnings of the European Bronze Age, but by 1995 I had published the report on my excavation of a Bronze Age site in the prehistoric copper-mining region of Austria and was free to devote more attention to my growing interest in cultural evolution and, linked to that, in prehistoric population patterns and their implications. My inaugural lecture at the UCL Institute of Archaeology in 1998, published in *Current Anthropology* two years later, was entitled, 'Population, culture history and the dynamics of culture change' and began to develop this topic, which I took forward again with my book, *Genes, Memes and Human History*, in 2002. I had also become much more interested in the idea of looking for broad regional and inter-regional patterns in prehistory than in the archaeology of individual sites and micro-regions and I felt that the potential for this was being neglected in the archaeological intellectual climate of the time, which had turned against 'grand narratives'. There seemed to be great scope for combining my evolutionary and 'big picture' interests by turning to the origins of the European Neolithic and the spread of farming into Europe. Fortunately this view was shared by funders, and later by journal editors, despite the claim by many grant and paper reviewers that 'noise' from factors affecting data recovery and survival would overwhelm any historical signal.

In 1999 James Steele and I were successful in obtaining a research grant from the UK Arts and Humanities Research Board (as it then was) for a project entitled 'Spatial and Chronological Patterns in the Neolithisation of Europe' that involved collating available sources of radiocarbon dates. This was the first in a series of grants from the Arts and Humanities Research Council (as it later became) that made it possible to develop this agenda. 'The origin and spread of Neolithic Plant Economies in the Near East and Europe' followed in 2001, with James Steele and James Conolly, and 'The origin and spread of stock-keeping in the Near East and Europe', with Keith Dobney and James Conolly, in 2007. In 2000 a group of colleagues, including Mark Collard, Mark Lake and James Steele, and I had been successful in obtaining a five-year Arts and Humanities Research Board Research Centre award for a 'Centre for the Evolutionary Analysis of Cultural Behaviour', which enabled a variety of theoretical and methodological research projects in cultural evolution to be carried out, and this continued with the award of a continuation of the Centre in 2006 as the 'Centre for the Evolution of Cultural Diversity', under the direction of James Steele. At the same time, grants from the Leverhulme Trust to Mark Lake and to me for the projects 'Strontium isotope analysis and multi-agent modelling' and 'Ceramic analysis and cultural process', the latter with Paolo Biagi, also focussed on Early Neolithic themes. All these developments culminated in 2010 when I obtained a European Research Council Advanced Grant for the project 'Cultural Evolution of Neolithic Europe' (EUROEVOL), 2010–2015. This made it possible to bring together and update previous data-gathering work as well as develop new analyses, in order to produce the basis for a new 'big picture' account of the arrival of farming in Europe and its impact, with a particular focus on the demographic dimension. It was Todd Whitelaw who, after reading the draft grant application, suggested that I should commit to producing a synthesis at the end of the project and not just a series of papers. My knowledge of a key region for understanding the spread of farming, western Anatolia, was then enormously enhanced when in 2012 I was kindly invited by Joachim Burger of Johannes Gutenberg University in Mainz to be a co-investigator on his Marie Curie Initial Training Network project 'Bridging the European and Anatolian Neolithic'. This enabled me to have a PhD student in this field, Beatrijs de Groot, as well as visit the area, get to know a new set of colleagues, and to contribute as a co-author to Joachim's important ancient DNA papers on the spread of farming. Since the end of the EUROEVOL project in 2015 I have been able to continue with very similar population and economy agendas by collaborating with Andy Bevan, Mike Parker Pearson, Tim Kerig, Neil Roberts and Ralph Fyfe, on two projects again funded by the Leverhulme Trust. Andy Bevan's data-mining work is now taking the potential for 'big picture' studies of prehistoric patterns to new levels.

It will be obvious that without the support of the funding bodies named above none of this would have happened. I am also extremely grateful to all those who have generously shared data with us over the years. Without data sharing large-scale projects would be impossible, and the growing expectation from journals that authors of papers make available the data on which they are based is one of the most important developments of the last few years, both in archaeology and more widely.

Of course, I have also incurred an enormous number of personal debts to the people I have worked with on these various projects and it is a pleasure to record them. My fellow investigators on the grant applications, who made them possible, have already been mentioned. Key to the success of these projects though has been a wonderful group of very talented post-docs with whom it has been a privilege to work. They include Alex Bentley (with whom I've continued to collaborate) and Michela Spataro, from the early days, as well as Barbara Stopp and Fiona Coward. Sue Colledge has been there virtually from the beginning, in 2001 with the Neolithic plant economies project, and has played an essential role in project organisation and data management through to the end of the EUROEVOL research, as well as in her specialist field of archaeobotany. The same role has also been played by Katie Manning, the archaeozoologist, who came to the stock-keeping project at a difficult moment and stayed for EUROEVOL. Here they were joined by Sean Downey, Kevin Edinborough and Tim Kerig, and then Enrico Crema and Adrian Timpson when Sean and Tim moved on to other positions. Enrico and Adrian's outstanding computing and statistical skills were fundamental to producing the project's later papers and final database. The new Leverhulme projects too are very fortunate in their post-docs, Alessio Palmisano, Kevan Edinborough, Peter Schauer and the pollen analyst Jessie Woodbridge of the University of Plymouth. I should also add that EUROEVOL benefitted greatly from the input of our invited 'critical friend' reviewers Sander van der Leeuw, James Conolly and Mike O'Brien during the course of the project.

Needless to say, there are many other debts. It has been an inspiration in the last few years to work with Mark Thomas and to learn from the creativity of his rigorous model-building and testing methods, so much more demanding than the usual archaeological story-telling. He was crucial to the development of some of the EUROEVOL methods and our joint supervision of the recently completed PhD project of Elizabeth Gallagher on modelling farming origins has been a very stimulating experience. I have also been fortunate to learn from him something of the complexity of making inferences from ancient DNA data, as this has completely changed our picture of the origin and spread of farming in the last couple of years and forms one of the foundations of this book. I hasten to add though that any misunderstandings and misinterpretations of the genetics presented here are entirely my own. In this respect I must also absolve Joachim Burger, who has provided patient answers to many genetics questions but is not responsible for what I've done with them. Joachim also tried out drafts of several chapters on his students to my considerable benefit. In addition, I'm grateful to Jamie Jones, Barbara Horejs, Andreas Zimmermann, Tim Kerig, Jutta Lechterbeck, Oreto García Puchol and Mike Parker Pearson for reading and commenting on specific chapters. None are responsible for what I've done with their suggestions. Oreto and her co-editor Domingo Salazar-García were also kind enough to invite me to contribute a concluding chapter to their book *Times of Neolithic Transition along the Western Mediterranean*, from which I learned a great deal.

Over the long period in which the material and ideas for this book have been accumulating I have also been inspired and influenced in various ways by others whom I've talked to and/or worked with. They include Jean-Pierre Bocquet-Appel, Sam Bowles, Rob Boyd, Cyprian Broodbank, Clive Gamble, Ian Hodder, Anne Kandler, Tim Kohler, Kristian Kristiasen, Kevin Laland, Ruth Mace, Ian Morris, Johannes Müller, Eduardo Neves, Mike O'Brien, Colin Renfrew, Pete Richerson, Eric Smith, Alasdair Whittle and my outstanding colleagues at the Institute of Archaeology, UCL, especially, in relation to the topic of this book, Dorian Fuller. The Institute provides the best possible open-minded, stimulating and congenial community for archaeological teaching and research, not to mention the wonderful library with its knowledgeable and helpful librarians. It has been a privilege to work there for the last 21 years.

Producing the book has incurred its own debts. I'd like to thank Norman Yoffee for his encouragement and support for its publication, as well as Beatrice Rehl at Cambridge University Press. Two readers for the press, including Mary Stiner who waived her anonymity, were very encouraging and made many helpful comments. I'm most grateful to Denitsa Nenova for producing the excellent illustrations, in particular for being so tolerant and understanding when I changed my mind about things. Sue Colledge systematically tracked down and obtained the necessary permissions for them. Rachel Tyson was the most meticulous copy-editor that anybody could wish for, and Clare Owen at Out of House Publishing was a pleasure to work with in the final stages of production.

Finally, since these projects began my wife, Lúcia Nagib, has been an endless source of love and support as well as an inspiration for the dynamism, perceptiveness and creativity of her own research and publications in the field of film studies. Without her nothing in life would seem interesting or worthwhile and it is to her that this book is dedicated.

CHAPTER I

INTRODUCTION: POPULATION, RESOURCES AND LIFE HISTORIES

The origin and spread of farming had enormous implications for human history, and for this reason has long been established as one of two or three 'big questions' about the human past. Farming has been the foundation for the development of cities and civilisations and at the time of writing supports a world population of 7.5 billion people. It has changed human biology as well as human society. It has therefore attracted an enormous amount of archaeological attention. In recent years, as archaeological research on the prehistory of the human exploitation of plants and animals has expanded on a global scale, it has become increasingly clear that there were not just three or four loci of agricultural origins but a much larger number in different parts of the world, based on different crops and with different evolutionary histories, so we can no longer tell a single story of the origins of agriculture, or even two or three. Nevertheless, south-west Asia remains what we might call the 'locus classicus' of agricultural origins research because the crops and animals that were domesticated there were the subsistence foundations of the early civilisations of the western Old World and their successors and thus form part of the 'grand narrative' of the 'western' societies.

My aim in this book is to take an evolutionary perspective on understanding the interactions between population, subsistence and socio-cultural traditions that resulted in the origin of cereal agriculture in south-west Asia and its subsequent spread westwards into Europe. The book's central argument can be summarised in two claims. Farming originated because broadening their diet breadth led people to increasing sedentism through growing dependence on plant resources that were dense and sustainable; as a result they had more children and more of them survived. Farming spread because it enabled people to be reproductively successful by colonising new territories that had low-density forager populations, so long as they kept passing on the knowledge, practices, and the crops and animals themselves, to their children. The object of this introductory chapter is to present the theoretical foundations for this argument. It is based on ideas from the rapidly developing fields of evolutionary demography, human behavioural ecology and cultural evolution, but has its origin in the debates started by Malthus over 200 years ago on the relation between population, resources and technology. Accordingly, the chapter begins with a review of these debates and then outlines the basic ideas of evolutionary demography and their implications, together with some of the ethnographic and historical evidence for their significance. It goes on to examine the relevance of these ideas to understanding the processes involved in becoming a farmer, first as presented in the concept of the 'Neolithic Demographic Transition' proposed by the French demographer Jean-Pierre Bocquet-Appel, then by looking at some recent historical and ethnographic studies which have thrown light on the demographic dimension of being or becoming a farmer. After a brief initial consideration of the role of cultural transmission, the chapter closes with an outline of the structure of the book.

MALTHUS AND BOSERUP

Since the 1960s debates in anthropology about the role of population have mainly been framed as a conflict between Malthus's view, that increasing population would always come up against limits imposed by technology, and that of the agricultural economist Ester Boserup (1965, 1981), who emphasised what she saw as the positive role of population growth in leading to economic change, though the conflict between the two has been greatly exaggerated (Lee, 1986; Wood, 1998). Central to Malthus's theory, and of course fundamental for Darwin, who took up his idea as the basis for his theory of evolution by natural selection, was that populations have the potential to grow much more rapidly than the food supply and are subject to density-dependent limits based on food availability. Bringing new individuals into the world increases the future labour supply but also increases the demand for food. Other things being equal, the law of diminishing returns will eventually set in and the average amount of food per person will decrease, until the food produced by an additional individual is no more than the amount they need for survival. Thus, population increase starts to slow down and eventually population levels out, or can even go down, for example if over-exploitation of the soil or of the animals available for hunting sets in, as the Malthusian checks of decreasing fertility and increasing mortality begin to operate. If technical or economic innovation to improve outputs per capita or per unit area of land has some sort of costs, then members of a population that has reached a demographic equilibrium may be more prepared to pay them than people who are not in this situation; hence 'population pressure', as in Boserup's model, can be a stimulus to innovation. Nevertheless, it is important to point out that such conditions do not automatically call into being the innovations that could overcome them. Their incidence will be determined among other things by chance and by patterns of contact, not to mention the possibility of technological 'lock-in' making it very difficult to switch from one subsistence strategy to another (Wood, 1998: 109).

As Wood shows mathematically, whatever the subsistence system, at least in pre-industrial societies, population will increase past the point of maximum well-being, where the gap between surplus production and population is at its greatest, and come to an equilibrium (or oscillate around an equilibrium) at the point where births balance deaths, or 'a state in which the average individual is in just good enough condition to replace himself or herself demographically' (Wood, 1998: 110). In most hunter-gatherer societies the population density at that equilibrium point will be much lower than in a complex agrarian civilisation based on intensive agriculture, but the situation will be the same, though in the latter case it may well be impacted by elite 'surplus' extraction. The speed at which populations grow when the potential exists for them to do so is easily underestimated (cf. Richerson et al., 2001); for example a population of 100 would reach more than 2,000,000 after 1000 years at the modest growth rate of 1% per year. Thus, it is clear that for most of the time over the long run, unless there are frequent crashes arising from external factors (cf. Boone and Kessler, 1999), populations will be at the equilibrium limit, or fluctuating around it, so that further increases will only occur when some shift in technology, economy or a relevant external force like climate makes it possible (Richerson et al., 2009). When such changes do occur they will have a 'pull' effect on population until it reaches a new equilibrium.

Thus, Wiessner and colleagues (1998) showed that after the introduction of the sweet potato to the Enga of Highland New Guinea around 1700 AD population increased from an estimated 10–20,000 to 100,000 within around 220 years, an annual growth rate of 0.7%. Population shifts and migrations set off by the new opportunities resulting from the sweet potato were the most prominent catalyst for change mentioned in local historical traditions. By the time of European contact population pressure on land was beginning to act as a constraint. Similarly, a recent global-scale historical analysis (Ashraf and Galor, 2011) found that, 'technological superiority and higher land productivity had significant positive effects on population density but insignificant effects on the standard of living'. Essentially, the fruits of economic growth, at least until modern times, were always turned into people if not confiscated by elites, so the population growth rate associated with a given economic strategy at a specific point in time is a measure of its success.

LIFE HISTORY THEORY

Of course, the Malthus–Boserup models represent large-scale abstractions, while the processes from which they are built go on at a local level in the day-to-day lives of individuals, in particular women, and households. Over the last 30 years, studies of the cost-benefit factors influencing local reproductive decision-making have been revolutionised by the emerging discipline of evolutionary demography, based on the framework of life history theory, in parallel with, and influenced by, the economic work of Becker and others on human capital (see J.H. Jones, 2015; Sear et al., 2016 for recent reviews). Life history theory is a set of ideas from evolutionary biology concerned with the effect of natural selection on how organisms allocate their limited resources through the course of their lifetime. It is concerned with such questions as: how much effort should be allocated to growth at a particular stage of the life cycle? How much to reproduction? As far as reproduction is concerned, to be successful is it best to devote most effort to mating or to parenting at a particular stage in life? Will it be more successful to produce a large number of offspring without caring for them much, or a smaller number in whose care a great deal is invested? Those individuals that come up with the optimal allocations in the light of the specific constraints they face will be most successful in natural selection terms, so, over time, selection should lead to evolved life histories that produce higher fitness. The point of life history theory is to explain how and why life history allocations within and between species vary over the lifespan. This theory provides micro-scale foundations for understanding population processes that are entirely consistent with the more abstract Malthus–Boserup view outlined above. Evolutionary demography is less familiar to archaeologists than another domain of human behavioural ecology: optimal foraging theory, a set of evolutionary principles concerning the costs and benefits of resource choices on a day-to-day and year-to-year basis that will figure prominently in later chapters, but it is arguably even more important, and the processes and outcomes at the two scales are obviously interrelated.

The starting point for its application to humans, of course, is that they are the same as the rest of the living world, in the sense that, as the outcome of millions of years of natural selection, they should have a propensity to maximise their reproductive success and a sensitivity to environmental factors that affect this; strategies that lead to higher reproductive success in a given set of conditions are likely to spread at the expense of less successful ones. It is important to be clear that this does not necessarily involve conscious motivation, although elements of it might do – in general, for example, people consciously want to take care of their children – but some of the mechanisms related to the goal of achieving reproductive success are entirely physiological.

Thus, at any given age humans, like other animals, face the optimisation problem of allocating their lifetime 'income' in terms of energy among investments in survival, improving the possibilities for future 'income', and in reproduction (including parental investment), to give the solution that maximises the energy for reproduction at that age (Kaplan, 1996: 95). Female nutritional status, for example, has a considerable impact on fertility (e.g. Ellison et al., 1993). The closing down of the female reproductive system under conditions of nutritional stress is often seen as a pathological phenomenon, but from the life history perspective it is better seen as an adaptation. It makes much more sense under these circumstances to devote current resources to survival rather than to reproduction, which will probably fail anyway, and to wait for the possibility that resources will improve in the future and make successful reproduction more likely. Similarly, it is no good producing children every year if they die in infancy because it is impossible to provide care and other resources for several of them at the same time. That is to say, there are quantity-quality trade-offs; one must not only produce children but also invest in their upbringing, so that they do not die in childhood but instead become successful reproducing adults themselves. Accordingly, the processes of fertility regulation observed ethnographically and historically should be seen as responses in the individual's interests to the current prospects for reproductive success, which may require, for example, much longer inter-birth intervals than those that are theoretically feasible. Indeed, it has been shown that the most important life history factor affecting fitness is the survival of children, especially over the first four years of life, which makes a massively bigger difference than allocating the same quantity of effort to increased fertility (J.H. Jones, 2009; Jones and Tuljapurkar, 2015). In keeping with this, there is clear evidence of diminishing returns to recruitment (successfully bringing the children to adulthood) with increasing numbers of births (Jones and Bliege Bird, 2014): as women get older it makes more sense to look after the children they already have.

An example that illustrates some of these points well is Gibson's (2014) study of the consequences of a 1990s development project in Ethiopia that involved installing clean water taps in a number of villages. Prior to this development, women in the region had had to walk for hours daily, carrying water on their backs. After the taps had been installed time spent carrying water was dramatically reduced, by over ten times on average in the dry season. This was rapidly reflected in a three-fold increase in the probability of giving birth on the part of women who had access to the taps over those who did not, an outcome that had not been anticipated by those who designed the project. There were also major reductions in child mortality, with a decrease in the relative risk of death of 50% per month of life. In fact, the importance of women's energy levels for their fertility (among many other factors (Vitzthum, 2009)) means that it should have been no surprise that the introduction of local water taps led to an immediate increase in the number of births in the absence of education or incentives for birth control, a pattern also seen in other similar studies (Kramer and McMillan, 2006). However, studies some years after the taps had been installed revealed that children from villages with taps were more likely to be under-nourished than those from villages without them, while the mothers' bodily condition had also deteriorated as a result of the shorter birth intervals. The result has been 'increases in family sizes in a population close to environmental limits under current technology' (Gibson, 2014: 75), so the outcome over the medium to long term remains unclear at this point. Evolution is nothing if not opportunistic and short-sighted.

But it is important to emphasise that a given situation will not necessarily affect everyone in the same way, since the availability of resources obviously has a major impact on any trade-offs required. Thus, Gillespie et al.'s (2008) analysis of historical demographic data from 18th-century Finland demonstrated that there were diminishing returns in maternal fitness with increasing maternal fecundity for women from landless but not from landowning families because the limited resources of the landless women resulted in severe quantity-quality trade-offs. Similarly, Voland (1995), in his study of the 18th-century agricultural community of Krummhörn in Friesland, Germany, found that rich landowner male farmers had much greater reproductive success than the general male population, especially over the long term.

In summary, life history theory provides us with a framework that enables us to understand the processes going on at the individual level that affect population patterns at the larger scale. People have been selected by their evolutionary history to maximise their reproductive success. External conditions have a bearing on the best way of doing this and individuals are sensitive, including physiologically, to these conditions. Birth rate is only one of the requirements and has to be traded off against a whole series of other considerations which are relevant to the production of grandchildren. It is impossible to have both maximum birth rate and maximum offspring fitness, and it is the successful raising and social placement of offspring that decides lifetime reproductive success. Changes in external conditions can shift the costs and benefits of an existing set of trade-offs making it advantageous to have more or less children and fertility can respond on a very rapid timescale even if this has deleterious consequences not very far down the road.

THE EVOLUTIONARY DEMOGRAPHY OF BECOMING A FARMER

In keeping with these ideas from evolutionary demography, since 2000 the French demographer Jean-Pierre Bocquet-Appel (2002, 2008, 2011) has developed the hypothesis that the beginning of farming marked a 'Neolithic Demographic Transition'. The modern 'demographic transition' in developed countries marked a shift from a long-standing high-fertility and high-mortality life history pattern to one of low fertility and low mortality. In Western Europe, in particular England and France, death rates began to fall in the late 18th century. After a period of time fertility rates also began to decrease but not nearly as fast as mortality rates, so the result was massive population increase. In England the process of transition lasted over 150 years, until the mid-20th century, before birth rates and death rates came more or less into balance, and in the interim population underwent a seven to eight-fold increase (Dyson, 2010: 88–89, 217).

But the population increases were not merely local. One huge consequence was the mass migration of European populations, to the New World in particular, where the existing low intensity of exploitation and corresponding low density of indigenous populations made it possible for them to expand still further, disastrously aided by the diseases they introduced (Crosby, 1986). Bocquet-Appel proposed that the high-fertility high-mortality pattern characteristic of agrarian societies had begun with the transition from foraging to farming.

Just as the modern demographic transition was started by a fall in mortality, the argument runs, so the agricultural demographic transition began with a rise in fertility, detectable in the high proportion of young individuals in Neolithic cemeteries, an indicator of population growth (Sattenspiel and Harpending, 1983). In this case it was mortality that subsequently caught up, not least because of the increased incidence of infectious disease; again there was major population increase in the interim. The basis of the fertility increase, Bocquet-Appel proposed, was a major positive shift in female energy balances, resulting from the increased availability of calories from cultivated crops, on the one hand, and decreased mobility on the other, that also fed through into child care.

In fact, we can throw more light on these processes because people in different parts of the world have continued to become sedentary and become farmers up to the present. Consequently, ethnographic and recent historical studies have provided direct evidence of the demographic implications of adopting sedentism and farming. These studies provide strong support for the relevance of life history theory in this context and thus for making the inferences from the archaeological record with its evidential shortcomings that we will see later in this book.

The earliest such study was published by Binford and Chasko (1976). They collected data on the birth and death rates of an Inuit group, the Nunamiut, in Alaska, from the 1930s to the 1960s and found that the crude birth rate doubled during the 1950s, when they were changing from a mobile to a sedentary way of life, levelling out when they became fully sedentary and then decreasing after contraceptives were introduced. Their analysis of the factors leading to the increased birth rate concluded that it was overwhelmingly the result of a reduction in the seasonal variation in food intake and a higher proportion of carbohydrates in the diet because they were able to acquire store-bought non-native foods, especially cereals. Indeed, in their conclusion to the study they anticipated the Neolithic Demographic Transition hypothesis, speculating that

> The first major demographic 'transition' occurring near the close of the Pleistocene was caused by changes in fertility, rather than by the 'normal' condition of changes in mortality that has led to transition in modern times. Dramatic demographic changes can be related in a provocative manner to changes in fertility as conditioned by shifts in labour organisation and diet. (Binford and Chasko, 1976: 142–143)

Other studies have emphasised the effect of sedentism on child mortality, which decreased by 75% among sedentary !Kung in southern Africa, for example, probably because settling at Herero cattle posts gave them access to milk and other weaning foods (Pennington, 1996). Kramer and Greaves's (2007) ethnographic study of demographic parameters of separate groups of Pumé foragers and horticulturalists in Venezuela found both effects at work: women in the horticultural group had an average completed fertility of 7.27 surviving children, compared with 4.25 for the hunting and gathering group; the increase resulted from both higher infant survival rates (contributing 79% of the increase) and higher birth rates (21%). Both are the result of higher food availability among the horticulturalists: young children are very susceptible to food shortfalls, which also affect female reproductive function. As in Gibson's Ethiopian study, the increased energy availability is turned into increased fertility, which compounds with the increased child survival to produce a very rapidly growing population.

The outstanding historical demographic data from local parish records in Finland has provided the basis for a similar study (Helle et al., 2014), in which vital rates from Saami hunting-fishing-gathering groups were compared with those of Finnish farmers who had moved into northern Finland and lived alongside them; these were sedentary agriculturalists who raised cattle and sheep and grew some barley and potatoes in what were marginal conditions for crop growing. After their initial arrival there was very little further immigration during the 19th century so the population growth that occurred was almost entirely the result of local increase. Both populations were growing during the period studied but analysis of life history parameters constructed from the historical records showed that the growth rate for the Finnish farmers was 6.2% higher than that of the Saami hunter-gatherers. Projected over 100 years this would lead to a farmer population nearly double that of the foragers. Importantly, the study was able to show that the differential was due to fertility not mortality differences, and in particular to a higher birth rate for women between the ages of 21 and 30, while the percentage of children brought to adulthood was essentially the same for both foragers and farmers (c.80%).

Another recent ethnographic study (Page et al., 2016) tested the hypothesis that the transition to farming involved a shift in the nature of parental investment trade-offs from a strategy based on investing large amounts of resources in a small number of offspring to investing less in a larger number, a change that is postulated to have resulted in greater reproductive success for those that adopted it, despite the deleterious effects that were also incurred. The study was based on a group of Agta foragers in the Philippines who varied in the extent to which they were mobile and practised foraging, thus providing a basis for relevant comparisons. Settled mothers had an estimated successful completed fertility of 7.7 compared with 6.6 for mobile mothers. The argument we have seen already that the difference is related to nutrition was supported by the fact that there was a positive correlation between fertility and maternal body mass index (BMI) and a negative one between BMI and greater mobility. In addition to sedentism, increased involvement in cultivating as opposed to foraging also positively affected fertility. On the other hand, evidence indicated that individuals in sedentary settlements suffered worse health conditions resulting from a variety of infections; for example, they had a far higher incidence of lymphocytosis, a response to viral infection, and higher rates of helminth infestation in the gut. The poorer health conditions in sedentarised camps were also reflected in increased child mortality, with an increase of over 60% for the children of settled mothers in sedentary camps compared with those of mobile mothers in temporary camps. Nevertheless, despite this, the number of children surviving to age 16 was greater for sedentary than nomadic women because their high fertility more than compensated for the increased mortality. The result was an increase in reproductive fitness of over 15% compared with the nomadic women. The effect of sedentism was compounded by the effect of involvement in cultivation, which resulted in increased fertility compared with foraging but did not have an effect on child mortality.

In this case then the results support the hypothesis that a new trade-off of offspring quality in favour of offspring quantity could account for the combination of increased ill health with more successful recruitment. In fact, the trade-off is in keeping with other studies that point to decreasing parental effort in the face of increased extrinsic mortality, that is to say mortality that is not affected by parental care; for example, Quinlan's (2007) cross-cultural analysis found that maternal care increased with increasing pathogen stress then declined. Since pathogen stress is a factor in child survival that care can do little to mitigate beyond a certain point, it is safer to spread a given amount of care across more children. This may be particularly relevant in the tropical environment of the Agta.

SYNTHESIS

The examples described above show that different combinations of static/increasing fertility and increasing/decreasing child survival can result in increased reproductive success and population growth for sedentary ways of life, including cultivation, compared with mobile foraging, because of reduced metabolic loads and/or decreased risk and improved weaning possibilities. Moreover, improved infant survival and greater reproductive success can still be consistent with poorer health and lower life expectancies for the population as a whole (Pennington 1996). It is important to note though that population growth depends on the sedentary adaptations and cultivation having a higher sustainable carrying capacity – supporting more people per unit area – than mobile alternatives, which is not the case everywhere. Even then, however, high fertility will eventually be matched by high mortality, sooner rather than later given the implications of even low rates of increase, as we have seen. This situation can be mitigated if promising dispersal opportunities are available, as with the European colonisation of North America: growth can continue but it is now spatially expansive rather than locally intensive. Moreover, promising dispersal opportunities also introduce a further consideration, not immediately obvious, that tends to favour life histories that increase fertility: demographic competition for expansion. In terms of the competition for reproductive success, a strategy that postpones reproduction when an expansion opportunity exists will be less fit than one that takes immediate advantage (Voland, 1998).

Finally, the 'variance compensation hypothesis' proposed by Winterhalder and Leslie (2002) is also likely to be relevant to the transition (Bandy and Fox, 2010), in that the costs of having extra children may be higher for non-sedentary hunter-gatherers given the requirement for mobility, so they may err towards the low side of a notional ideal number of children in the face of environmental unpredictability. Agriculturalists on the other hand, may tend to err on the high side, not just because of the increased unpredictability of child survival as a result of increased disease risk but also because children become useful in farming at a young age (Kramer and Boone, 2002). Kaplan et al. (2000) showed that males in hunter-gatherer societies do not start producing more than they consume until the age of 20. In agricultural societies older children actually subsidise the investment in younger ones.

As we will see, traditional archaeological accounts of the link between the origin and spread of farming and population emphasised the idea of population pressure and were puzzled by the evidence that adopting farming seemed to be associated with a decline in human health, as well as increasing amounts of labour: it was seen effectively as expulsion from the Garden of Eden of the 'original affluent society' (Sahlins, 1972). It should be clear now from what has been said that to think in terms of human well-being as a *goal* in this context is mistaken. While levels of well-being at population equilibrium may vary in different populations depending on local circumstances, what matters is the short-sighted evolutionary process of achieving reproductive success in the circumstances prevailing. This is reflected in the long-term global analysis by Ashraf and Gaylor (2011) described above, which showed that technology and land productivity had a positive impact on population density but not standard of living. The ethnographic and historical evidence indicates that the large-scale adoption of sedentism and farming created a Malthusian population *pull* as a result of the increased reproductive success associated with the increased energy availability and improved recruitment that ensued, while high population growth is by no means incompatible with poor nutrition and health (see also Lambert, 2009).

As Page et al. (2016) point out, however, while ethnographic studies like theirs make possible an analysis of variation within the population studied and allow us to distinguish the demographic mechanisms in action in the uptake of farming as a result, they do not allow the exploration of long-term trends or the reasons for them. Why did some Agta become sedentary and start farming given that the reproductive advantages only appear after the changes have occurred? Even studies based on the evidence of historical demography only take us so far in this respect, important though they are. Bocquet-Appel's proposed Neolithic Demographic Transition, on the other hand, gives us a very broad-brush picture of the long term, but again, given that the change is a *consequence* of farming, does not address how it began, and others would place more emphasis on infant survival than increased female energy availability. The chapters that follow will provide a much more detailed long-term picture both of the demographic patterns associated with the origins of agriculture in south-west Asia and its spread westwards, and their causes as well as their consequences. In order to understand these we need to take into account not just the relationships between population, subsistence and environment that have long been the object of discussion but the cultural evolution of subsistence practices.

As we saw with Gibson's Ethiopia example, the circumstances favouring increased reproduction can rapidly dissipate. The long-term consequences of farming depended on the long-term transmission of farming practices from generation to generation and on this continuing to provide a survival and reproductive advantage compared with alternatives. Under standard natural selection, specific versions of genes that provide a selective advantage over others will be passed on from generation to generation and will spread through a population because they improve survival and reproductive success in some way. On the basis of the ethnographic and historical evidence we have seen we can suggest that agriculture represented a cultural strategy that was under natural selection. It was transmitted from generation to generation and spread because it improved survival and reproductive success in comparison with other possibilities, but it depended on the continued transmission of agricultural knowledge and domesticated plant and animal resources. That knowledge could be transmitted from farmers to non-farmers but it could only continue to provide a selective advantage if it was passed on by parents to their children. On average, the grandchildren of anyone who failed to pass on the knowledge and resources would be fewer in number than those of individuals who did. It follows from this that, as well as providing a measure of economic growth at a given point, the population growth rate associated with farming as a culturally transmitted subsistence strategy is also a measure of its fitness, and one that we can get from the archaeological record.

The domestic crops and animals themselves can be regarded as part of a transmitted environment that maintained the selective conditions favouring the farming way of life in a process of 'niche construction' (Odling-Smee et al., 2003), not only by altering physical environments but also by changing the

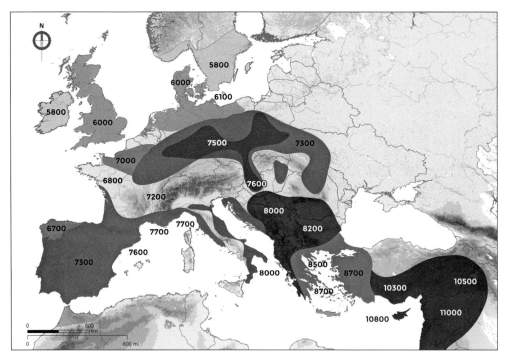

Fig 1.1. Map of the spread of farming from south-west Asia to Europe. Dates shown in years BP. Updated from a map created by Professor J. Burger, with permission.

nature of social institutions such as property rights that would have affected the payoffs of different economic and social strategies (Bowles and Choi, 2013; Gallagher et al., 2015; Shennan, 2011).

On the other hand, if farmers found themselves in a situation where conditions for farming were less favourable, perhaps as a result of climate change, then the selective advantage might disappear, with various possible consequences. People might return to foraging, though this would almost certainly result in a drop in local population and, in many cases, an increase in mobility. However, if the social norms associated with farming practices were very powerful this might not happen and migration to seek more favourable conditions could take place. It certainly cannot be assumed that a technical innovation overcoming the problems created by the new conditions would automatically occur.

STRUCTURE OF THE BOOK

In the light of the theoretical foundations established in this chapter the book provides an account of the processes at work in the origins of agriculture in south-west Asia and the spread of the form of agriculture that developed there westwards into Europe (Fig 1.1). In doing so it makes use of the rapidly growing body of evidence available on population patterns, especially that from the increasing number of analyses of ancient DNA, which give us for the first time direct information on population relationships. Chapter 2 begins by giving an account of the different ideas that have been put forward to account for the origins of agriculture in the region and how these have changed over recent years in the light of new ideas and new discoveries, with a particular focus on the indications of increasing subsistence intensification from the Last Glacial Maximum c.24,000 before present (BP)[1] to the end of the last Ice Age c.11,700 BP and associated demographic patterns. It goes on to describe current evidence and ideas on the emergence of cereal agriculture, accepting the view that this was not something that took place very quickly or in a single location but, on the contrary, that it was a drawn-out process taking 2000–3000 years and going on in many different locations in the so-called Fertile Crescent, from the southern Levant, through south-east Anatolia to the Zagros mountains on the Iran–Iraq border. In a similar vein the evidence for animal domestication is reviewed and it is shown that there is a great deal of variation in the regional trajectories towards increased control and consequent domestication of animals but that it was ongoing across a broad region of the northern Fertile Crescent from south-east Anatolia to the Zagros. Regional population patterns are then discussed before turning to one of the major developments in understandings of the origins of agriculture over the last 20 years, the recognition that it did not just involve subsistence, population and ecology but also major social changes, including new social institutions and property rights, that can usefully be seen from the cultural evolutionary perspective of 'niche construction'.

Chapter 3 looks at the initial expansion of farming in a westerly direction from the broad core zone where it developed, but it begins with an account of the influential model that has framed most accounts of the spread of agriculture as a demographic process, Ammerman and Cavalli-Sforza's (1973) 'wave of advance' model, which raises many of the issues that are considered in this and later chapters. The earliest evidence for the expansion of subsistence practices involving animal and plant management comes from the island of Cyprus, long before a reasonably consistent set of farming practices was developed, and its early date seems surprising given that it involved a presumably risky maritime colonisation. The expansion across Anatolia to western Turkey and across the Aegean Sea to mainland Greece, on the other hand, took place later, when a fairly consistent farming 'package', including dairying, had already been established. This dispersal was extremely fast, but it stopped at the northern edge of the Aegean for 300–400 years before spreading equally rapidly northwards into the Balkans, as far as the river Danube and beyond. New ancient DNA evidence has shown that the Anatolian–Aegean farmers were the starting point for the population expansion that brought farming to the rest of Europe.

Chapters 4 and 5 describe the spread of farming westwards through Central Europe and the Mediterranean respectively. In both cases the ancient DNA evidence now tells us that the mechanism of spread was the population expansion just mentioned and that absorption of local hunter-gatherer populations played a very minor role, at least partly because there were probably very few hunter-gatherers in the areas where farming pioneers settled. Both expansions were rapid: farming communities reached the English Channel by the Central European route and Portugal via the north coast of the Mediterranean within 500 years, but the population growth was not maintained. New data shows that in most places the demographic boom associated with the arrival of farming communities was followed by a crash. In much of Central Europe this seems to have been associated with extensive warfare.

Further expansion into Britain and southern Scandinavia did not occur for another 1000 years. The question is why. Unlike most of the other chapters, which focus on the initial arrival of farming and its consequences, Chapter 6 examines the 7th millennium BP, the period when farming societies were present in most of continental western and Central Europe but the farming frontier in the north and north-west was static. The account given rejects the long-standing view that this was because of ongoing resistance from indigenous hunter-gatherer groups whose societies were only gradually undermined. On the contrary, in much of this broad area farmer populations were declining or static and their distribution restricted to the small areas initially colonised by the first farmers. It was only in the latter part of the 7th millennium that internal expansion out of these small enclaves occurred, so that farmers now occupied much broader areas of the landscape. This led to greater interaction with the local foragers, reflected in the increased forager component in the DNA of the farming groups. However, developments at the western end of the farming zone were distinctive because here communities descended from the Mediterranean expansion met those with a Central European cultural ancestry, a meeting now directly detectable in ancient DNA. The result was new patterns of contact and striking *sui generis* social developments in areas such as Brittany.

Chapters 7 and 8 describe the expansion of farming into southern Scandinavia and Britain and Ireland. Like all the other expansions described it was extremely rapid in both cases. Again the emerging ancient DNA evidence suggests that we are dealing with a population expansion rather than local adoption of farming, effectively a continuation of the expansion that had begun in west-central Europe a couple of hundred years earlier, though there seems to be a greater continuity in subsistence strategies in Scandinavia. In Britain and Ireland and Scandinavia too there was a pattern of population boom and bust, though the timing was rather different. At the height of the boom in both cases large numbers of ditched and banked enclosures of considerable size were constructed, most probably as a result of social competition, and in Britain at least this time also shows evidence of warfare and violence. Following the population crash distinctive new social and cultural patterns emerged in both the British Isles and southern Scandinavia, although the reasons were different in the two cases.

Finally, Chapter 9 draws together the common threads that have emerged and looks at their implications for the ideas developed in the first chapter, focussing on the action of a number of evolutionary processes operating at different timescales.

CHAPTER 2

THE ORIGINS OF AGRICULTURE IN SOUTH-WEST ASIA

EXPLAINING ORIGINS

Ever since Childe (1928), following Raphael Pumpelly, published his 'oasis theory', the idea that farming began as a result of people, plants and animals being forced together by a drying climate, it has been accepted that the origin of agriculture in south-west Asia is in some way connected to climatic changes at the end of the last Ice Age. These changes have now been reconstructed in considerable detail, both globally, through the Greenland ice cores, and locally, for example via east Mediterranean marine sediment cores and terrestrial lake sediments (e.g. Robinson et al., 2006). The cold dry conditions of the Last Glacial Maximum that had begun around 27,000 years ago began to change c.18,000 years ago as temperatures rose and precipitation increased, reaching a peak, the so-called Bølling-Allerød interstadial, a short-term warmer interval c.15,000 years ago, a time when conditions were similar to those of the Holocene. But c.13,500 years ago markedly colder and dryer conditions began to return, leading to the Younger Dryas stadial phase, c.12,900–11,700 years ago, which ended in a very rapid warming period that marks the beginning of the Holocene (see Fig 2.1 for climate chronology). Apart from the general increase in global temperatures, another important feature of the Holocene has been a much greater stability in climate conditions, in contrast to the Late Pleistocene, which the ice core record has shown to be a time of very rapid climate fluctuations of considerable amplitude (Feynman and Ruzmaikin, 2007).

In Lewis Binford's famous paper 'Post-Pleistocene Adaptations' (1968) the argument is that a climatic trigger led to population pressure as sea levels rose at the end of the last Ice Age and large areas of land were lost, resulting in a greater dependence on aquatic resources. This in turn led to sedentism and increasing fertility following a reduced need for birth control measures that regulated population when people were mobile. The resulting population growth led to an overspill into neighbouring areas, and plants and animals were

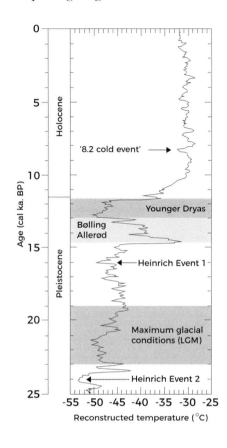

Fig 2.1. Reconstructed air temperatures from the GISP 2 ice core in Greenland. Reprinted from fig 2 in *Quaternary Science Reviews* 25, Robinson, S.A. et al., A review of palaeoclimates and palaeoenvironments in the Levant and Eastern Mediterranean from 25,000 to 5000 years BP: setting the environmental background for the evolution of human civilisation, pp. 1517–1541, copyright 2006, with permission from Elsevier.

domesticated as people were forced to emigrate from the regions where the wild ancestors occurred naturally. In a similar vein, a year later, Kent Flannery (1969) proposed the idea of the 'Broad Spectrum Revolution': that population pressure on groups in marginal habitats led them to widen the range of resources they exploited and in doing so to increase the carrying capacities of their local environments; continuing pressure led eventually to the beginnings of agriculture. The argument was developed more generally, indeed for the world as a whole, by Mark Cohen in his influential book, *The Food Crisis in Prehistory* (1977), in which it was claimed that people were forced into farming by population increase. This claim had two foundations: first, the evidence that the health of agriculturalists was generally worse than that of hunter-gatherers, as we have seen; why would people have voluntarily adopted a way of life that gave them worse health conditions? Second, that gaining a living from farming involved much more work than hunting and gathering; why would people give up a leisured life for one that gave them more work? The second foundation followed on from the ideas of Ester Boserup that we have seen already: population pressure encouraged agricultural innovations in which the amount produced on a given area of land increased, at the expense of a decrease in labour productivity. It also

Table 2.1 Cultural chronology of the southern Levant
(dates based on Zeder (2011) and Borrell et al. (2015))

Start date BP	Cultural division
24,000	Kebaran
18,000	Geometric Kebaran
15,000	Early Natufian
12,500	Late Natufian
11,600	Pre-Pottery Neolithic A (PPNA)
10,500	Early Pre-Pottery Neolithic B (PPNB)
10,100	Middle PPNB
9,500	Late PPNB
8,750	Final PPNB
8,400	Pottery Neolithic

fitted in well with Marshall Sahlins's proposal that hunter-gatherers were the 'original affluent society' (1972; contrast Kaplan, 2000), needing to work only a few hours a week to successfully gain a living. In the case of south-west Asia the belief that people were forced into farming was supported by the growing archaeological evidence in the southern Levant for the Late Epipalaeolithic Natufian Culture (Bar-Yosef, 1998) (see Table 2.1 for cultural chronology) in the final millennia of the last Ice Age; its settlements contained considerable numbers of grindstones, indicative of seed processing (Wright, 1994), and pointed to the existence of relatively sedentary hunter-gatherers. These provided the prelude to farming that the population pressure arguments predicted.

It will be apparent from the last chapter that population remains a key dimension and, as we will see, the Broad Spectrum Revolution is fundamental, but the original population pressure arguments have to be revised. The main reason is that mentioned in the last chapter and already made by Malthus in 1798: the compound growth processes entailed even in very low rates of population increase lead very rapidly to very large numbers of people at timescales that are extremely short by archaeological standards. Effectively population pressure would always have been present throughout human evolutionary history, so why did farming not start much earlier if Cohen and others were right? In the light of the evidence that had emerged from the Greenland ice cores and other sources for extremely rapid climate fluctuations in the Late Pleistocene, Richerson et al. (2001) proposed that there would have been corresponding fluctuations in the distribution and composition of local vegetation communities, which as a result would not have been stable enough to provide a reliable food source to which people could establish a successful adaptation. The point was further developed by Feynman and Razumaikin (2007), who carried out a spectral decomposition of the climate signal in the ice core record, showing that there were large-scale climate fluctuations at a variety of different timescales, from less than 100 to 1500 years, in the Late Pleistocene. It was only with the onset of stable Holocene climates that agriculture became viable and once it did so it provided a 'pull' not a 'push' for population expansion for the reasons described in Chapter 1, thus agriculture was 'impossible during the Pleistocene but mandatory during the Holocene' (Richerson et al., 2001).

The results of excavations at the site of Ohalo II (see Fig 2.2 for all sites mentioned in this chapter) in the Jordan valley also raised questions about the population pressure model. They revealed that 23,000 years ago, at the time of the Last Glacial Maximum, people were apparently settled for a large part of the year, exploiting the seeds of a variety of wild grasses, including cereals, and grinding them to make flour (Piperno et al., 2004). The intensity of plant exploitation here has been much discussed. While Dubreuil and Nadel (2015) have played it down, Piperno et al. saw evidence for a broad spectrum exploitation indicating a wide diet breadth of relatively low foraging efficiency. Snir et al. (2015) go much further, claiming evidence for early cultivation. In any case, the discovery was a surprise, as previously it had been assumed that a more intensive use of resources began c.15,000 years ago with the beginning of the early phase of the Natufian Culture in the southern Levant (Bar-Yosef, 1998), roughly contemporary with the Bølling-Allerød interstadial phase of warmer and wetter climate (Fig 2.1). It was one thing to have a 3000-year prelude to farming, with the Natufian at the very end of the Ice Age, but with the discovery of Ohalo the gap was widened to at least 10,000 years before the beginning of agriculture. How could this be accounted for?

DIET BREADTH AND THE BROAD SPECTRUM REVOLUTION

To understand the subsistence changes going on in the final millennia of the Pleistocene and the Early Holocene we need to return to the Broad Spectrum Revolution and its link between the density of the sustainable human population of a region and its diet breadth. At the same time as Flannery was formulating his idea, concepts and methods were being developed in the field of optimal foraging theory (e.g. MacArthur and Pianka, 1966), like life history theory an aspect of behavioural ecology. In Chapter 1 we saw how life history theory worked at the generational timescale, but any successful adaptation obviously also has to work at the day-to-day level, and optimal foraging theory makes predictions about what is required (Bird and O'Connell, 2006). It postulates that available resources are ranked in terms of their productivity, usually evaluated in calories per hour, taking into account pursuit and handling costs, subject to the requirement that enough resources must be taken to ensure day-to-day survival, support of dependent children, etc. So long as this requirement is met by the current set of resources, other resources, *even if*

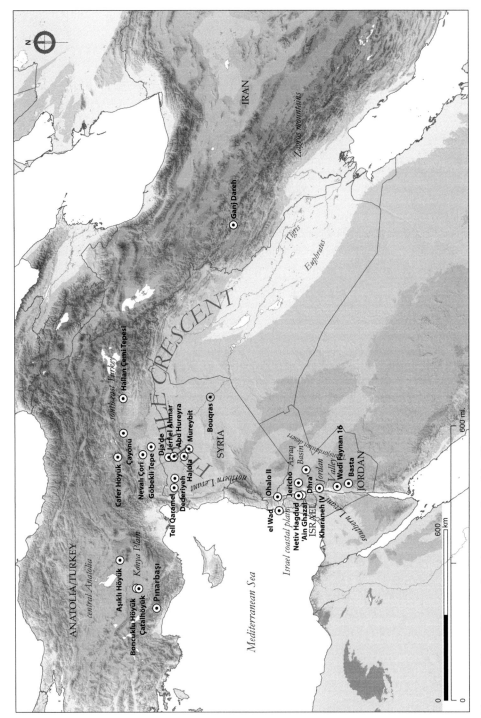

Fig 2.2. Map of sites and regions mentioned in Chapter 2.

they are widely available, will not be exploited if returns per hour are poor. On the other hand, if a high-ranked resource becomes scarce and search times for it increase, for example because of over-exploitation or local environmental change, then the diet breadth will be extended to include resources that give lower rates of return but have lower search times. In an archaeological context, if we find evidence of a broadening diet breadth over time in a region, it is likely to be evidence of resource depletion whether as a result of environmental change or over-exploitation. What happens subsequently depends on the nature of the lower ranked resources available. If there are very few, or they too are vulnerable to over-exploitation, then the regional human population will decline, as a result of either emigration or increased mortality. However, as Winterhalder and Goland (1993) showed, using computer simulation, an alternative possibility is that the new resource that enters the diet because it now gives worthwhile payoffs is sufficiently dense, and recovers sufficiently rapidly, that it can support a larger population that is sustainable over the medium to long term (cf. Bettinger, 2006). In other words, it is potentially possible for populations to grow even when the diet breadth widens and foraging efficiency decreases. Whether they grow or decline depends entirely on the density and sustainability of the yield of the new resource.

The characteristics of the newly included resources will also have a major impact on the nature of subsistence-settlement systems. Thus, for any given group, if resources in a given place grow and recover rapidly, for example annually, they can potentially avoid paying the high costs of mobility outlined by Hamilton et al. (2016). But this will be true for all the groups in a region, so all the good resource patches will become more or less permanently occupied and there will now be neither the need, *nor the opportunity*, to be mobile, though mobility will still be a way of exploiting inferior patches. As a result regional population will increase, based on the exploitation of locally available rather than mobile resources (Gallagher, n.d.), and with it territoriality, as it becomes both more feasible and more necessary to exclude others (Dyson-Hudson and Smith, 1978). Moreover, the move to a more sedentary way of life will *in itself* encourage population increase, as we saw in Chapter 1; how long it continues will depend on the ultimate sustainable carrying capacity of the resource and the speed at which birth–death equilibrium is reached. In other words, pressure on resources at the day-to-day scale, whether it is simply a result of over-exploitation or of externally forced environmental change, can lead to new adaptations that have a population 'pull' effect at the generational life history scale. This is also an implication of Hamilton et al.'s general model of hunter-gatherer mobility: its density-dependence is a function of the area needed for subsistence, and sedentism results from increased effectiveness in using the energy available in a given area; population increase follows, it does not lead (Hamilton et al., 2016). Of course, an important proviso here is that if the high-sustainability resources are only available seasonally they need to be stored.

In the light of the evidence for climate fluctuations, we can now suggest that in some periods in some regions sustainable resources might have become available, so that if people over-exploited those of high-rank and their search times increased, they could have ended up in a low-mobility, high-population equilibrium, which would have had its own Malthusian limit, with few escape options. Equally, that equilibrium would always have been open to disturbance by the next climate change that led to the decline or disappearance of such resources. In other words, there would be no long-term teleological trend to a goal of farming but simply a series of opportunistic subsistence-settlement fluctuations.

INCREASED SEDENTISM AND THE EXPLOITATION OF LOW RETURN-RATE RESOURCES IN THE EPIPALAEOLITHIC

Extensive evidence for the increased use of sustainable resources in the Late Pleistocene has built up over the years. It has already been suggested that the evidence from Ohalo II at 23,000 BP can be seen in this light, as corresponding to a phase when the possibility of a low-mobility subsistence existed, based among other things on the exploitation of grass seeds with high handling costs.

Another such episode seems to be visible in the Azraq Basin of eastern Jordan in the southern Levant at the Early Epipalaeolithic site of Kharaneh IV (Maher et al., 2012). Here there is repeated and very intense occupation by large numbers of people between c. 19,900 and 18,600 BP, without indications of any breaks in stratigraphy, and including evidence of hut structures like those at Ohalo II. There is also evidence for multi-seasonal occupation from the age profiles of the teeth of the gazelle which make up the overwhelming majority of the faunal remains, though at the moment it is unclear whether the site was occupied year-round (J.R. Jones, 2012). The very large numbers of gazelle and the fact that there is no evidence of the selective transport of high meat-yielding parts of the animal to the site indicates that they were locally abundant and predictable, while the continuity of exploitation indicates that they were sustainable (Maher et al., 2016). At the time of occupation the area seems to have been a well-watered grassland and occupation came to an end with climate change and locally increased aridification (Richter et al., 2013). There may have been a similar episode at this time in the north-east Levant (Kadowaki and Nishiaki, 2016).

Quite a good proxy for the productivity of hunting is the size of the animal taken (though see Bird et al., 2009 for reservations). Stutz et al. (2009) show that the proportion of very large game taken, such as aurochs, is very low

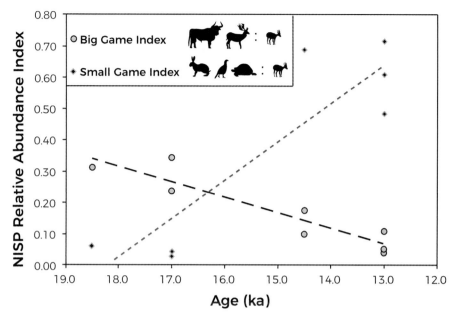

Fig 2.3. Long-term trends in the abundance of large and small game in the southern Levant. Reprinted from fig 4 in *Journal of Human Evolution* 56(3), Stutz, A.J. et al., Increasing the resolution of the Broad Spectrum Revolution in the Southern Levantine Epipaleolithic (19–12 ka), pp. 294–306, copyright 2009, with permission from Elsevier.

throughout the Epipalaeolithic in the southern Levant and the proportion of medium-sized game, such as fallow deer, decreases steadily. In contrast, the small game – gazelle, hare, partridge etc. – increase very markedly, especially in the Late Epipalaeolithic, c.15,000–12,000 years ago (Fig 2.3). The significance of this is three-fold. First, like annual cereals, these species grow and reproduce rapidly and can sustain heavy exploitation pressure without decreasing in numbers. Second, they are fast-moving, so exploiting them successfully would have required the use of the bow and the snare, which, if not new, must certainly have become more common. Third, Stiner and Munro (2002: 197) point out that small game have small territories and that, given their limited size, they would not have merited long-distance hunting expeditions. Thus, their growing importance tells us about increased local hunting intensity and, by extension, about the increased intensity of site use and decreasing mobility at this time.

Yeshurun and colleagues (2014) argue that in the Israeli coastal plain a move towards increased intensity of occupation began in the Early Natufian phase, c.14,500 years ago, when the site of el Wad shows much greater use of small ungulates and other small animals than earlier periods, a situation they see, following Munro et al. (2004), as resulting from restricted mobility and population packing. The high density and diversity of finds, the large size of the site and the existence of stone architecture are also considered to be evidence in favour of sedentism. They see this same pattern of sedentism and intensive exploitation of local resources as continuing into the Late Natufian, albeit in the context of a more dispersed settlement pattern, an argument supported by pollen evidence for a change from a more forested to a more steppic environment with increasing local availability of wild grasses that could have supported intensive exploitation (Robinson et al., 2006). Wright (1994) had already shown that from the Early Natufian an increasing percentage of sites were characterised by the presence of groundstone artefacts, including mortars and grinding stones consistent with an increased importance for seed and nut processing.

In summary, there is consistent evidence from the southern Levant for episodes of intensification and increased sedentism from the Last Glacial Maximum onwards, but particularly from the Early Natufian, during the Bølling-Allerød interstadial, when the intensity of occupation was high, base camps were large and occupation was more sedentary, though year-round occupation has still not been proven. The intensity is also reflected in the higher percentage of sites with grinding slabs that indicate a greater investment in technology for seed/nut processing, though the proportion is still low compared with the following Pre-Pottery Neolithic. Increased sedentism combined with a greater dependence on major calorie sources that were only available seasonally implies a shift from an immediate-return to a delayed-return system (Woodburn, 1982) that would have necessitated some kind of storage.

For the northern Levant/upper Mesopotamia area the picture is less clear cut. At the beginning of the Holocene the site of Hallan Çemi Tepesi on the upper Tigris river has evidence of sedentary occupation based on the intensive exploitation of plant resources, including large quantities of groundstone artefacts, but there is no evidence of depletion of the animal resources: on the contrary, the faunal remains show a massive predominance of highly ranked prey, including caprines and red deer (Starkovich and Stiner, 2009), so this does not easily fit the model outlined above of the route from mobility to sedentism. One possible explanation is that, rather than day-to-day subsistence, the faunal remains reflect feasting activities, for which there is a variety of evidence (Starkovich and Stiner, 2009: 58; Zeder and Spitzer, 2016); a similar pattern is also found at the nearby site of Körtik Tepe (Coşkun et al., 2012). However, another possibility is the operation of a version of 'source-sink' dynamics, a process that has probably not been emphasised sufficiently in the past (Bliege Bird, 2015). In this case it means that as prey herbivores are increasingly exploited around a site (the sink), others from further away (the source) will move in to take advantage of the empty niche.

In any case, it is important to insist again on not reading the evidence in the light of the subsequent cultivation and domestication of the founder cereals and legumes that were the basis for crop agriculture. Savard et al. (2006) pointed out that in the Final Epipalaeolithic of the northern Levant, immediately before the earliest evidence for cultivation, large-seeded grasses like wild wheat and barley made up only a minor element of the archaeobotanical assemblages at the majority of sites. Hallan Çemi Tepesi, just mentioned, shows that year-round occupation could be sustained even though grasses occurred in very low proportions and valley-bottom plants such as sea club-rush were among the staples. Willcox and colleagues (2009) found a similar situation not far away at sites in the upper Euphrates region, northern Syria, where rye, low frequencies of two-grain einkorn, and valley-bottom plants in the Younger Dryas cool period give way to cultivated (but not yet domesticated) barley, emmer and single-grain einkorn during the Early Holocene Pre-Pottery Neolithic A. On the other hand, the Natufian site of Dederiyeh in north-west Syria did have significant quantities of founder cereals (Tanno et al., 2013). Savard et al. conclude that sedentism was not dependent on wild cereals as such but on the availability of reliable and sustainable resources, in keeping with what we have argued above; what those were would have varied according to local environments (cf. Asouti and Fuller, 2012: 157).

In fact, assessing the role of plant exploitation in the Late Pleistocene of south-west Asia is hampered by the generally poor preservation of plant remains from the archaeological sites, with one or two notable exceptions such as Ohalo. However, similar conclusions to those of Savard et al. were reached by Rosen (2013) in her analysis of phytoliths, preserved silica structures in plant tissue, from Natufian sites in the southern Levant. As we have seen, the Early Natufian is roughly contemporary with the Bølling-Allerød interstadial climate phase, the short-lived shift to warmer and wetter conditions c. 15,000 years ago after the Last Glacial Maximum, while the Late Natufian corresponds, again approximately, to the succeeding Younger Dryas cooler and drier phase that immediately preceded the beginning of the Holocene (for discussion see Maher et al., 2011). It is likely that the Bølling-Allerød phase resulted in an expansion of wooded areas, while the conditions of the Younger Dryas led to their contraction. In particular, Rosen suggests, there would have been an impact on the nut yields available. While one option would have been to follow the retreating woodland, the other would have been to shift the goals of plant foraging to more reliance on the grass seeds that were now becoming increasingly available. This suggestion is borne out by the distribution of phytoliths, with grass-husk phytoliths appearing in much greater numbers in Late Natufian sites (Rosen, 2013; Rosen and Rivera-Collazo, 2012). However, an equally important inference from the phytolith data is that there is no evidence for increased dependence on the large-seeded wild cereals, as small-seeded grasses were in the majority.

POPULATION PATTERNS

Recent work (Roberts et al., 2017) has created a high-resolution population proxy for south-west Asia for the period from 16,000 to 9000 cal BP, using summed calibrated radiocarbon probabilities (Figs 2.4, 2.5), thus making it possible to address arguments about the role of population for the first time. It is worth describing the method in some detail here because it is used throughout the rest of this book. The basic idea is that in broad terms the number of sites found and dated by archaeologists is a reflection of the intensity of past activity and occupation, themselves dependent on the size and density of the population (Rick, 1987). Clearly there may be biases affecting the resulting picture but these can be addressed (Shennan et al., 2013; Timpson et al., 2014; Tallavaara et al., 2014). For example, the bias that is potentially introduced by the fact that some sites have far more dates than others can be resolved by down-weighting them so that a site with many dates only has the same weight as a site with one. The probability distributions of the individual dates are then summed across all the sites from the period being considered. This admittedly does not take into account site size and we will return to this below. A further potential complication is that changes in mobility might affect the patterns, with more mobile settlement systems producing more sites. However, as the patterns discussed below show, in fact the numbers of dated sites increase through the Late Epipalaeolithic when sedentism was increasing.

Some of the fluctuations in the summed probability distribution of the dates will be a result not of changing population patterns but of variations in the radiocarbon calibration curve and of sampling effects (Shennan et al., 2013), so it is important to have a method of distinguishing those that are 'real'. Looking at the overall pattern in Fig 2.4b suggests at first sight that it is well summarised by an exponential curve, which is the pattern we would expect for long-term population increase over the period if the pattern after the beginning of the Holocene c.11,700 BP simply continued trends already established in the Epipalaeolithic. We can find out whether departures from the trend are 'real' by simulating the dates expected from an exponential curve a large number of times to establish the variation we expect around the trend. Places where our observed curve falls outside that expected range of variation potentially indicate departures from the exponential pattern, implying periods of population growth higher than the long-term trend, or of population decline, and we can find out whether or not they are statistically significant.

Fig 2.4b shows that for the data from south-west Asia as a whole there are significant departures from the exponential model. The first of these occurs at 13,600–12,700 BP, when inferred population levels fall below the envelope of 'expected' values. The second occurs at c.11,700–11,100 BP, when

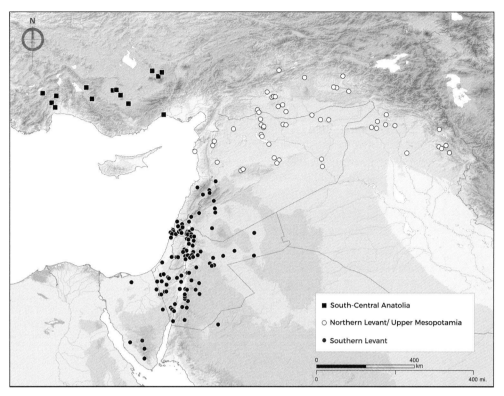

Fig 2.4. a) Map of archaeological sites in the Levant and central Anatolia with radiocarbon dates falling in the time frame 16,000–9000 BP, split by sub-region. Egyptian (except Sinai) and Cypriot dates have been excluded. Reprinted from fig 6 in *Quaternary Science Reviews*, Roberts, N. et al., Human responses and non-responses to climatic variations during the Last Glacial-Interglacial transition in the eastern Mediterranean, copyright 2017, with permission from Elsevier.

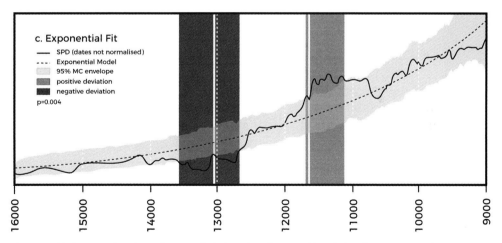

Fig 2.4. b) Summed radiocarbon probability distribution (SPD) for the Levant and central Anatolia for the period 16,000–9000 BP, showing the confidence interval for a fitted exponential model and indicating periods when the observed SPD departs from the exponential model. Reprinted from fig 7c in *Quaternary Science Reviews*, Roberts, N. et al., Human responses and non-responses to climatic variations during the Last Glacial-Interglacial transition in the eastern Mediterranean, copyright 2017, with permission from Elsevier.

inferred population is higher than predicted by the exponential model. In other words, the demographic trend from c.12,700 to c.11,600 BP indicates a continuous period of population growth greater than the long-term exponential rate, through the Younger Dryas and into the beginning of the Holocene, resulting in a five-fold population increase over 1100 years.

Fig 2.5 shows the results subdivided into three regions, the southern Levant, the northern Levant and upper Mesopotamia, and south-central Anatolia. In the same way that the patterns could be compared to those of a model, we can also compare the extent to which each sub-region departs from the pan-regional trend of Fig 2.4b (see Crema et al., 2016). All regions show significant departures (p-value ≤ 0.004) from the pan-regional pattern despite the reduced sample sizes. For the southern Levant (Fig 2.5a) the main departure is in the period c.14,500–13,500 BP, roughly corresponding to the onset of the Bølling-Allerød interstadial and the Early Natufian when population is significantly higher than the overall pattern, in keeping with the other evidence for more intensive occupation at this time. After this the level drops but from c.13,300 BP to the beginning of the Holocene at 11,700 BP there is a six-fold population increase that continued until 11,300 BP, when a limit seems to have been reached (assuming that site sizes did not increase, see below).

The population proxy for the northern Levant/upper Mesopotamia region (Fig 2.5b) is significantly below the pan-regional pattern throughout the period 16,000–13,400 BP, at which point it starts a consistent upward trend that continues throughout the Younger Dryas to reach values that significantly exceed the global pattern from 11,700 until c.10,700 BP, after which it declines. In fact, between 13,400 and the beginning of the Holocene at 11,700 BP population in the northern Levant grows roughly ten-fold, while in the following 200 years it virtually doubles again. In fact, it is worth pointing out that even the last of these only corresponds to a modest annual growth rate of 0.35% per year; in contrast, at the time when they were still living by hunting and gathering the Aché population in Paraguay had a growth rate of 2.0% (Hill and Hurtado, 1996), though of course it is unknown how long that would have continued.

South-central Anatolia (Fig 2.5c) also differs significantly from the overall south-west Asia pattern but contrasts markedly with the other two regions. There is a period of c.500 years from c.15,200 BP when the overall population pattern is significantly exceeded but more noteworthy is the period from c.12,700 to 11,200 BP, most of the Younger Dryas and the first 500 years of the Holocene, when population is flat and lies below the pan-regional confidence interval.

Finally, it should be emphasised that these major differences in regional trajectories are in themselves an indication that they reflect population and cannot easily be accounted for by differential biases.

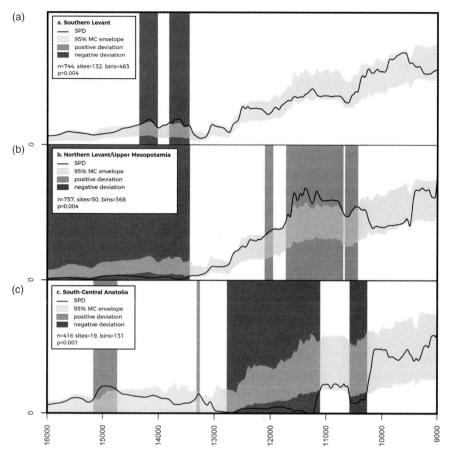

Fig 2.5. Summed radiocarbon probability distributions for the three sub-regions shown in Fig 2.4a and the period 16,000–9000 BP. The observed SPD is compared to random SPDs conditioned on the pan-regional fitted model. a) Southern Levant; b) Northern Levant/Upper Mesopotamia; c) South-central Anatolia. Reprinted from fig 8 in *Quaternary Science Reviews,* Roberts, N. et al., Human responses and non-responses to climatic variations during the Last Glacial-Interglacial transition in the eastern Mediterranean, copyright 2017, with permission from Elsevier.

CLIMATE PATTERNS

How does the behaviour of the population proxy from 16,000 BP to the beginning of the Holocene at 11,700 BP fit in with the proposal that climate fluctuations resulted in relatively short-lived episodes of increased sedentism and subsistence intensification on sustainable resources? We have just seen that in both the southern and northern Levant population increased massively between c. 13,500 BP and the beginning of the Holocene. This period includes the whole of the Younger Dryas cold phase, which has been regarded by many as unfavourable to human settlement in the region. However, recent work (Roberts et al., 2017) indicates a more complex picture. Fig 2.6 presents a series of modelled spatial scenarios based on changes in mean monthly precipitation and mean winter temperature from proxy evidence, from the Late Glacial to the Early Holocene. They show the changing modelled distribution of areas with a reconstructed mean winter temperature of at least -2°C and 20 mm mean monthly precipitation, corresponding to the modern limit for cultivating crops without irrigation. These suggest that reasonably favourable climatic conditions could have existed in the Fertile Crescent at least from the Bølling-Allerød interstadial through the Younger Dryas and into the Early Holocene, allowing continuity of settlement, in contrast to south-central Anatolia, where Younger Dryas conditions were severe.

In summary, such conditions could have provided the basis for the 1500 years of more or less continuous population growth up to the beginning of the Holocene at c. 11,700 BP seen in both the southern Levant and the northern Levant/upper Mesopotamia area, supported by the exploitation of a variety of locally available sustainable resources that enabled an increasingly sedentary way of life. By 11,700 BP, at the start of the Holocene, populations in both regions had reached levels that were completely unprecedented. However, this was not the case in south-central Anatolia, where the severe Younger Dryas conditions are reflected in the lack of any evidence for population increase. In other words, there is strong evidence, both positive and negative, for the *climate episode → sedentism → population pull* model for the successive phases of the Late Glacial period in south-west Asia.

We can speculate that if climate had deteriorated again the low-mobility high-population adaptation would have ceased to be viable and there would have been a reversion to the high-mobility low-population pattern. Of course, that is not what happened. Instead we see the beginning of a long transition to agriculture.

CEREAL AGRICULTURE

The end of the Younger Dryas and the beginning of the Holocene c. 11,700 BP saw an extremely rapid change to warmer and wetter conditions in south-west Asia (Robinson et al., 2006; Roberts et al., 2017), resulting in an increase in plant biomass and primary productivity. As we have seen, warming also had an impact on the plant species exploited (Willcox et al., 2009). At the sites of Abu Hureyra and Mureybit on the Euphrates in Syria rye was being exploited on a small scale during the Younger Dryas together with small-seeded grasses from the floodplain (cf. Colledge and Conolly, 2010). As the Early Holocene warming took hold and plant distributions responded with the expansion of more warmth tolerant species, wild emmer and barley

Modelled climatic limits on cereal growth
Areas with ≥ 20mm monthly precipitation and mean winter temperature ≥ -2°C in light grey

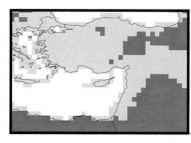

Holocene

Mean winter temperature: Modern (1901–1950)
Mean monthly precipitation 1901–1950

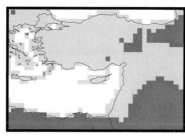

Early Holocene

Mean winter temperature: Modern +1°C
Mean monthly precipitation: 130% modern

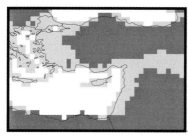

Younger Dryas stadial

Mean winter temperature: Modern −4°C
Mean monthly precipitation: 75% modern

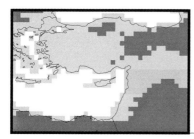

Late Glacial interstadial

Mean winter temperature: Modern –1°C
Mean monthly precipitation: 120% modern

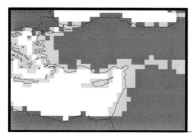

Glacial (H1)

Mean winter temperature: Modern –7°C
Mean monthly precipitation: 120% modern

Fig 2.6. Mapped bio-climatic scenarios for cereal growth during different time periods during the Pleistocene–Holocene transition. Reprinted from fig 9 in *Quaternary Science Reviews*, Roberts, N. et al., 2017, Human responses and non-responses to climatic variations during the Last Glacial-Interglacial transition in the eastern Mediterranean, copyright 2017, with permission from Elsevier.

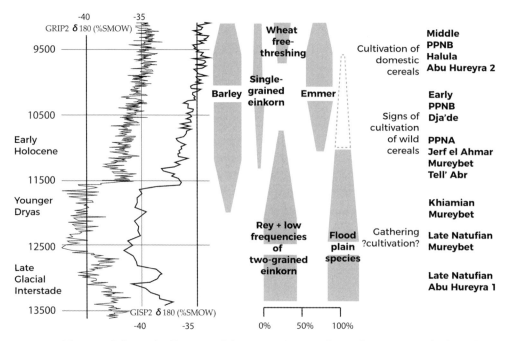

Fig 2.7. Schematic diagram of the approximate relative frequencies of selected grains from the Euphrates sites at the end of the Pleistocene and Early Holocene. Changes in frequencies are shown in relation to the oxygen isotope curve. The two breaks in the bars indicate that the archaeobotanical sequence is not continuous. Reproduced from fig 3 in *The Holocene* 19, Willcox, G. et al., Late Pleistocene and early Holocene climate and the beginnings of cultivation in northern Syria, pp. 151–158, 2009.

began to be exploited and rye gradually disappeared. The use of small-seeded grasses also gradually tailed-off (see Fig 2.7). In other words, what is striking about the archaeobotanical assemblages is that they represent a marked *narrowing* of the diet breadth compared with the broad spectrum assemblages of earlier periods, with a much more focussed concentration on the large-seeded ancestors of the first domestic cereals and pulses, now viable in the new warmer, wetter, more stable conditions. Narrowing the diet breadth is normally associated with increased rates of return. However, the results of experiments led Preece et al. (2015) to question whether the wild ancestors of the domestic crops were more productive than other, smaller-seeded grasses: they had larger seeds but three times fewer seeds per plant. Whether there would have been a difference in processing time remains unclear. The new emphasis on the wild progenitors may simply be a question of changing local availability as plant distributions changed with the climate.

We can get a snapshot of current knowledge of the beginnings of cereal agriculture by focussing on the well-preserved site of Jerf el Ahmar, on the left bank of the Euphrates in northern Syria, one of several similar sites that have been excavated in the region (Willcox and Stordeur, 2012). The site was first occupied c.11,500 years ago, the very beginning of the Holocene, at the start of the Pre-Pottery Neolithic A (PPNA) phase. Occupation at the site lasted for 500 years and analyses of the charred plant remains have revealed the initial stages of development of cereal agriculture. Food plants were dominated by morphologically wild cereals, with ears that disarticulate spontaneously when ripe, unlike domestic cereals that have tough rachises that break only when the plants are threshed. The most common cereals at the site were wild barley and wild rye; wild einkorn appears later in the sequence. On the basis of the co-occurrence in the samples of wild cereals and wild species that are classified as weeds of cultivation it is concluded that, despite their wild morphology, the cereals were cultivated, and not simply gathered (Colledge, 1998; Willcox, 2012). In the later levels of the site the cereals increase in frequency while gathered food plants like small-seeded grasses decrease, pointing to an increased commitment to cereals.

That commitment is confirmed by the presence at the site, particularly in the later layers, of large numbers of quernstones used for grinding grain; small food-processing rooms contain installations of several querns, some set in prepared bases, as well as other features such as stone basins. A large oval semi-subterranean communal building dating to the later levels of the site had a central space surrounded by a series of cells that may have been used for storage (Fig 2.8); the densities of cereal remains found in these cells were greater than the site average. The importance of cereal storage and the permanent sedentism it implies is further confirmed by the presence of the bones of house mice and their droppings. Most archaeobotanical samples were mixed and derived from midden deposits, but the samples with higher than average densities of charred remains, which are more likely to have come from storage contexts, were predominantly either barley or rye, indicating that the two crops were grown/harvested/stored separately. Harvesting was carried out using sickles with inset blades showing the gloss characteristic of cutting reed or grass stems; the blades underwent technical improvement in the course of the site's occupation.

All the evidence then points to an increasing emphasis on the cultivation of cereals, which nevertheless remained morphologically wild through all 500 years of occupation, and on the numerous activities that this would have required at all the various stages from sowing to storage. Other changes also occurred, including a transition in building styles from roughly circular to rectangular houses, and an increase in site size. The presence of apparently communal buildings suggests developments in social institutions. There is, however, no evidence for the keeping of animals during the period the site was occupied. Meat was obtained by hunting gazelle, aurochs and equids.

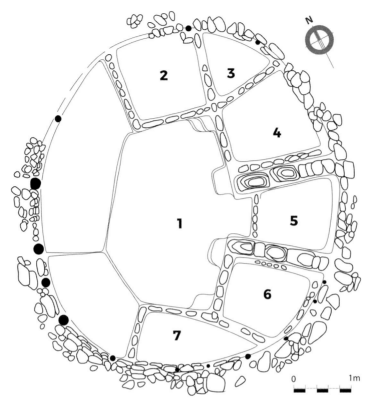

Fig 2.8. Communal storage building at the PPNA site of Jerf el Ahmar.
Reproduced, with permission, from fig 8 in *Antiquity* 86, Willcox, G. and Stordeur,
D., Large-scale cereal processing before domestication during the tenth millennium
cal BC in northern Syria, pp. 99–114, 2012.

The social developments implied by the evidence from Jerf el Ahmar and
other contemporary sites will be considered later but now it is important to
broaden out the consideration of how crop agriculture developed. Twenty
years ago, based largely on work by Hillman and colleagues in the late
1980s/early 1990s (e.g. Hillman and Davies, 1990a, 1990b), the general
view was that the domestication of cereals was a rapid process, beginning
already in the Younger Dryas cold period. The idea that it could be rapid
was encouraged by experiments demonstrating the speed at which selection could occur in favour of the domestication traits of increased size and
a tough rachis (Hillman and Davies, 1990b). Recent work has rejected these
earlier proposals. The botanical evidence from the Younger Dryas phases
of Abu Hureyra, mentioned above, at one time regarded as indicating the
beginning of cultivation, is now seen simply as an expansion of the plant diet
in response to the loss of preferred species with the onset of environmental
change (Colledge and Conolly, 2010). As we have seen at Jerf el Ahmah,
the evidence from a number of sites shows that cereals could be cultivated

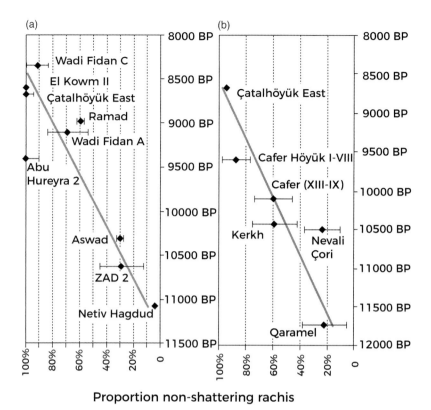

Fig 2.9. Increase through time in the proportion of the non-shattering ear trait in south-west Asia. a) Barley; b) Einkorn wheat. Based on botanical assemblages from each site, mean and standard deviation estimates of the percentage count values of non-shattering rachises are plotted against a time axis, in which a modal or median age estimate has been defined for each site. Reproduced from fig 4 in *Current Anthropology* 54, Asouti, E. and Fuller, D.Q., A Contextual Approach to the Emergence of Agriculture in Southwest Asia: Reconstructing Early Neolithic Plant-Food Production, pp. 299–345, University of Chicago Press, with permission. ©_ 2013 by The Wenner-Gren Foundation for Anthropological Research. All rights reserved.

for hundreds of years without showing domestication traits. A wide-ranging comparative examination of rates of evolution in south-west Asian cereal assemblages has now shown that it possibly took c.3000 years for the non-shattering tough rachis trait in einkorn wheat to go from 22% of the chaff at c.11,700 BP at PPNA Tell Qaramel in northern Syria to c.95% at Çatalhöyük in central Anatolia, c.8700 BP at the end of the Pre-Pottery Neolithic B (PPNB) phase, while barley was slightly faster, going from c.4% at Netiv Hagdud in Israel c.11,100 BP to >90% at c.8350 BP at various sites in different parts of the Fertile Crescent (Asouti and Fuller, 2013) (Fig 2.9). A further indicator of domestication is an increase in grain size (Colledge, 2001; Willcox, 2004). The rate of evolution in this was also slow, similar to the rate of increasing frequency of the tough rachis trait (Purugganan and Fuller, 2011; Araus et al., 2014). Recent experiments comparing traditional landraces of domestic cereals and pulses with their wild ancestors showed that yields were 50% higher on average, for a variety of reasons including the larger seed size (Preece et al., 2017).

Earlier proposals that there were 'core areas' for plant domestication in the northern or southern Levant have also been rejected. Fuller et al.'s study (2011) showed that trends towards the increased frequency of domestication traits in the different cereal and legume species, in different local combinations (Colledge et al., 2004), were occurring simultaneously during the PPNA and Early PPNB all over the Fertile Crescent and were not restricted to a single core area. In keeping with this new picture of widely distributed parallel developments, what had initially been interpreted as genetic evidence for a single origin for some crops has also now been rejected (Allaby et al., 2008). It is not until the Middle–Late PPNB, c.9500 cal BP, that a reasonably consistent domesticated crop complex of cereals and legumes – the so-called founder crops: the hulled wheats[1] einkorn (*Triticum monococcum*) and emmer (*Triticum dicoccum*), hulled barley (*Hordeum vulgare*), lentil (*Lens culinaris*), pea (*Pisum sativum*), chickpea (*Cicer arietinum*), bitter vetch (*Vicia ervilia*) and flax (*Linum usitatissimum*) (see e.g. Weiss and Zohary, 2011) – emerges, and only after c.8000 BP that domestic crops become overwhelmingly predominant (Asouti and Fuller, 2012). In the southern Levant at least this consistent crop package seems to be associated with the appearance of a group of 'mega-sites' (see below) resulting from population aggregation, which arguably depended on a commitment to farming high-yielding domesticated crops for their existence (Asouti and Fuller, 2012, and see below).

There are two points worth emphasising here. First, while there had to be conscious decisions to re-seed wild crops and to re-locate 'fields' in subsequent years, plant domestication was not a goal-directed process aimed at some future outcome but was a process of natural selection acting on the species concerned, of which people were the unconscious agents: features such as non-shattering rachises or increased grain size should be seen as the unintended consequences of different aspects of the cultivation process; the plant rachis, for example, is barely visible to the naked eye so could hardly have been a target of conscious selection (Hillman and Davies, 1990a; Fuller et al., 2011: 625). Harvesting the crop by cutting the stems with a sickle, as opposed to beating the plants and collecting the seeds in a basket as the ears shattered, should have meant that there was selection in favour of those plants that naturally had the tough rachis genetic variant because these would be more likely to be harvested and thus to form the seed stock for the following year. However, the fact that 500 years of sickle harvesting at Jerf el Ahmar and elsewhere did not increase the frequency of this variant suggests that the growing crops were not spatially isolated but were constantly subject to gene flow from wild populations, while harvesting probably took place before the cereals were completely ripe, to avoid the loss from shattering, so that this source of selection in favour of the tough rachis was rather weak (Hillman and Davies, 1990a). This has been confirmed by a recent large-scale regional analysis that looked at the relationship between the incidence of sickles, frequency of cereals and the prevalence of the tough rachis (Maeda et al., 2016). This found that there was a strong correlation between increased sickle use and increased reliance on cereals in the Levant but the sickle was not the driver for the rise in frequency of the tough rachis; rather, it was a cultural response to the growing dependence on cereals that were still changing their morphology.

There would also have been unconscious selection in favour of a variety of other characters, including increasing seed size, arising because larger seeds do better than smaller ones in the deeper burial conditions of human cultivation (Zohary, 2004; Purugganan and Fuller, 2011). The process corresponds to the model proposed by Rindos (1984) for the origins of cereal agriculture, in which certain food plants and people establish a mutualistic relationship. The plants become dependent on people for their dispersal but people increasingly depend on these particular plants as they become the most abundant ones locally available and, increasingly, more productive (G. Jones et al., 2013). Such mutualistic relationships are not uncommon in evolution and in fact, Purugganan and Fuller show, the rates of evolution seen in the increasing frequency of the non-shattering trait and increasing seed size in cereals under domestication are no faster than known cases of natural selection where humans were not involved. Simulation studies by Allaby et al. (2016) have shown that weak selection across many genetic loci is likely to produce a more successful adaptive outcome in more complex and severe environments than strong selection on a single locus.

Second, these new findings concerning the slow pace of domestication give new force to Richerson et al.'s (2001) proposal that rapid climate fluctuations made farming impossible in the Pleistocene. At the time it was published the consensus was still that plant domestication was a rapid process. Now that the evidence suggests it took at least 2–3,000 years for domestication traits to become fully established it is much easier to see that significant commitments to the founder crops at times prior to the Holocene when the opportunity arose would have been open to frequent disruption and, conversely, to agree that if the Holocene had not been stable agriculture would not have taken hold and become a highly successful adaptation. However, although they were much more stable, conditions for crop growing in the Early Holocene were not unchanging. It has recently been suggested, for example, that an apparent hiatus in occupation in the northern Levant c.10,000 BP that was followed by a shift in site locations, was the result of an episode of climate instability at this time (Borrell et al., 2015). Another recent study, of carbon and nitrogen isotopes in cereal grains from sites in the same region, suggests that

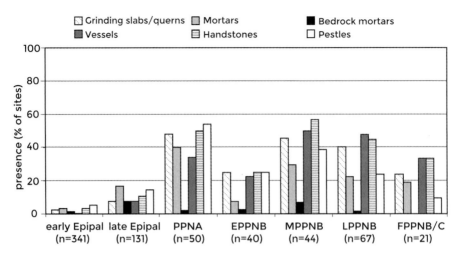

Fig 2.10. Proportions of groundstone tools on Epipalaeolithic to PPNB/C sites in south-west Asia. Unpublished data provided by Dr F. Coward.

conditions for crop agriculture were extremely favourable at the beginning of the Holocene, because soils were naturally highly fertile, but that their fertility gradually declined over the following millennia; however, this was more than compensated by the increased cereal yields resulting from the increased grain size described above (Araus et al., 2014). Manuring could not account for the initial high-fertility values because there were no domestic animals but may have become both possible and necessary later on.

Finally here, it is important to note the significant investment in cereal-processing technology apart from sickles seen, for example, in the grinding installations at Jerf el Ahmar and apparent at many other contemporary sites throughout the Fertile Crescent. In the PPNA 75% of sites have groundstone artefacts compared with 50% in the Late Epipalaeolithic (Wright, 1994), while more differentiated figures for different types of groundstone show that the percentage of sites containing grinding slabs/querns goes from less than 10% in the Late Epipalaeolithic to nearly 50% in the PPNA. Interestingly, however, this is not exceeded in the subsequent PPNB phases and it drops to c.25% in the Final PPNB (Fig 2.10).

ANIMAL DOMESTICATION

As we have seen, at the site of Jerf el Ahmar there were 500 years of cereal cultivation without any indication of a shift from hunting to herding, so the two domestication processes are not automatically connected; however, the issues relating to the archaeological identification of domestication are by no means dissimilar. Just as it was believed that the presence of morphologically domesticated cereals was the key indicator of cultivation, so changes in animal morphology, especially size reduction, were taken to indicate the presence of herding, and, in the same way, recent work has undermined that assumption (Zeder, 2006) and led to the identification of other potentially diagnostic criteria. In some cases at least, these have led to the conclusion that herding began earlier than previously assumed. To illustrate the current state of work on animal domestication and its archaeological identification it is again useful to focus on a site that has been the object of recent work as an example. The site in question is Aşıklı Höyük, a multi-period settlement in central Anatolia, on the western edge of the broad zone where farming started, and which was occupied from the beginning of the PPN in the region, before 11,000 BP, through to the Late PPN, c.9500 BP (Stiner et al., 2014). As at Jerf el Ahmar and many other contemporary sites, there is an architectural sequence from round buildings in the lower layers to rectangular ones in the later PPN. The basal level (5) has not yet been excavated but Stiner et al. have carried out a detailed analysis of the faunal remains from the upper part of level 4, dating to c.10,400–10,100 BP, to the end of the PPN sequence.

Archaeobotanical analyses show that already in the earliest of these phases there is compelling evidence of a commitment to the exploitation of cereals and legumes, and Stiner et al. suggest that the location of the site in a river flood plain indicates an emphasis on plant cultivation. Initially, the faunal evidence shows a broad spectrum exploitation that included larger animals such as aurochs, red deer, caprines and wild boar as well as small game such as hare, and river fish. Though there was an emphasis on caprines (mainly sheep) they made up less than 40% of the total number of bone fragments. Over the course of the occupation this proportion gradually increases so that by the end of the sequence it reaches 90%, still made up largely of sheep, with only small numbers of goats. The age-sex distribution of the caprines shows that by 10,200 BP the site's occupants were disproportionately culling young males, an indication of human management of at least some of the caprine population even if many continued to be obtained by hunting. Moreover, this inference is strengthened by the presence at the site of large dung concentrations deriving almost certainly from sheep, which must have been penned up within the settlement. However, the sheep do not show any signs of an ongoing domestication process. The killing of young males at an early age points to an emphasis on meat production ('meat-focussed type A' culling) (Vigne and Helmer, 2007), while Stiner et al. suggest, on the basis of the pattern of foetal-neonate losses, that this early management was rather experimental in nature and that these early stock-keepers still had a lot to learn. All this suggests that what we see at Aşıklı is a local uptake of caprine keeping, though it may well be the case that the idea came from other groups who were starting to manage herds at the same time. In fact, given that the site was near one of the main sources of the obsidian that was widely exchanged during this period, this seems more than likely.

As the continuity of occupation at Aşıklı and other sites shows, groups focussing on cereal cultivation would almost certainly have been also committing themselves to permanent settlement in a single location. As a result of this, Stiner et al. propose, local prey populations would soon have been depressed by hunting pressure. Longer distance hunting expeditions could have been one response to local scarcity, but a potentially expensive one in terms of time and effort. Another, given the social characteristics of caprines, as opposed to gazelle for example, would have been to keep animals on site as a meat source and gradually learn what this involved if it was to be a reliable option. As Stiner et al. point out, this solution to the 'tragedy of the commons' represented by the suggested over-exploitation of common pool hunted resources would itself have produced new social situations that needed to be negotiated by group members, a topic to which we will return below.

Similar patterns of early kill-off of male caprines indicative of the beginning of husbandry are also to be seen elsewhere (Zeder, 2011), for example at the site of Ganj Dareh in the Zagros mountains of Iran at c.9900 BP (where the emphasis was on goats), and at Cafer Höyük in south-east Anatolia, where the site of Nevalı Çori and others show a steady increase in the proportion of caprines (Peters et al., 2013). In other words, as with the cereals, there was no single core area for sheep/goat domestication, but a broad zone in the northern Fertile Crescent, stretching from central Anatolia to south-western Iran, where experiments with animal keeping were beginning. By c.9500 BP, when morphological changes associated with domestication were becoming increasingly apparent (Arbuckle and Atici, 2013), there is strong evidence from the age-sex distribution at some sites in this northern Levant region (e.g. Cafer Höyük) that goats were being kept at least partly for milk, and not just meat (Vigne and Helmer, 2007).

Evidence for cattle domestication remains less clear. On the basis of changes in average size and the age-sex profile seen in the bone assemblage, Hongo et al. (2009) suggested that cattle may have begun to be domesticated at the site of Çayönü in eastern Anatolia around 10,000 BP; over time the age structure changes, so that by 8500 BP only 35–45% of the cattle at the site survived to adulthood. Not far away, in the Euphrates valley, at sites such as Halula and Dja'de, domestication has been inferred by Helmer on the basis of reduced sexual dimorphism in cattle at c.10,500–10,000 BP (Helmer et al., 2005). Moreover, a mtDNA[2] sample from wild cattle at Dja'de dating to c.10,650–10,250 BP belongs to the T haplogroup, the group to which virtually all domestic cattle belong (Edwards et al., 2007).

It is interesting to compare the difference between the archaeological evidence for widespread caprine domestication and the relatively slight current evidence for cattle, with genetically based inferences of the initial size of the domestic populations of the different species. Bollongino et al. (2012), confirmed by Scheu et al. (2015), inferred an effective population size of 80

for the founding population of female cattle. While effective and census population size can differ significantly, particularly in inbred domestic livestock
populations, the numbers inferred by Bollongino and Scheu are surprisingly
low and point to a geographically restricted and maybe single origin of the
first bovine herds that later became domestic cattle, perhaps because wild cattle
were difficult to manage and breed; in this context it is worth noting that the
sites mentioned above are all in the same relatively small area. In contrast, there
is some evidence that the population size of early sheep domestication was
much larger than in cattle, consistent with a more widespread domestication
process (Meadows et al., 2007; Demirci et al., 2013), and in keeping with the
archaeological evidence noted above for widespread early sheep/goat-keeping
practices.

Early evidence of pig domestication also comes from the site of Çayönü
(Ervynck et al., 2001), where a long-term decrease in molar size has been taken
as an indicator of an ongoing domestication process leading to morphologically domestic pigs by 8800 BP, while other claims have been made for Cafer
Höyük and Nevalı Çori, in the same part of south-east Anatolia; at the latter,
it has been argued, the size of the animals decreased markedly by c.10,500
BP, reflecting breeding pressure (Vigne et al., 2009). However, in contrast to
cattle and sheep/goat, it has been suggested that domestication in pigs started
because, like dogs, they were 'commensals' rather than prey animals and were
attracted to human presence by the possibility this offered for scavenging food
(Zeder, 2011: S228). Recent genetic evidence tends to fit with the archaeological indications that pigs were initially domesticated in south-east Anatolia
and spread westwards from there (Ottoni et al., 2012).

Unlike the case of crops, all the initial animal husbandry and domestication
contexts described are in or around the northern part of the Fertile Crescent,
albeit spread across a broad east–west range. In the southern Levant the earliest
domestic sheep do not appear before 10,000–9500 BP, a lag of up to a thousand years to cover only 500–600 km (Martin and Edwards, 2013), but there
is considerable diversity within the region. It seems that east of the Jordan
valley sheep and goats were introduced and became the main food animals;
thus, at Middle PPNB 'Ain Ghazal caprines made up 70% of the ungulate
bone assemblage. To the west gazelle hunting continued to dominate, sheep
are not found at all and the goats exploited/managed were wild and thereafter possibly locally domesticated, no doubt, if true, after people observed
domesticated sheep elsewhere. Martin and Edwards note that it is the large so-
called 'mega-sites' of the southern Levant that have early evidence of imported
domestic sheep and goat and suggest that this may be connected with the fact
that these sites have other evidence of extensive trade connections with areas
to the north.

Looking again at south-west Asia as a whole, the enormous diversity in
regional trajectories in terms of changing proportions of domestic animals

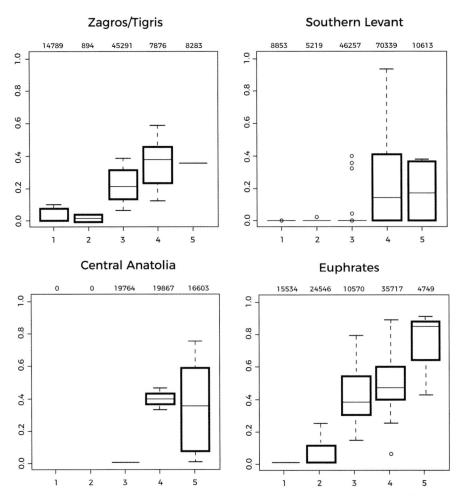

Fig 2.11. Proportions of domestic animals (all domestic species grouped together) from faunal assemblages in different regions of south-west Asia through time. 1 PPNA, 2 Early PPNB, 3 Middle PPNB, 4 Late/Final PPNB/C, 5 Early Pottery Neolithic. Reprinted from fig 3 in *Journal of Archaeological Science* 38, Conolly, J. et al., Meta-analysis of zooarchaeological data from SW Asia and SE Europe provides insight into the origins and spread of animal husbandry, pp. 538–545, copyright 2011, with permission from Elsevier.

over the period 11,000–8000 BP is very clearly demonstrated in the review by Conolly et al. (2011: fig 3) (see Fig 2.11). While some of this variation may arise from local domestication events, a major factor in accounting for the differences is likely to be the great variation in temperature, vegetation and rainfall across the broad area of south-west Asia where domestication processes were taking place, from the mountains of the Iranian Zagros to steppe and desert regions in parts of the southern Levant. For example, it has been shown that variation in temperature and rainfall accounts for over 40% of the variation in the proportion of cattle bone fragments in Early Neolithic

assemblages (Conolly et al., 2012). There are signs, however, that within specific regions faunal assemblages became more consistent. Thus, in south-east
Anatolia the average similarity between faunal assemblages in the date range
11,000–10,000 BP is c.40%, while for assemblages in the range 9500–8500 it is
over 70% (Peters et al., 2013). We will return to this topic in the next chapter
when we begin to examine the spread of the south-west Asia complex outside
its area of origin.

To conclude this section we need to comment on the nature of the animal
domestication process itself. The tendency has been to see this as arising from
an intentional process of directed breeding on the part of the people concerned,
a tendency that has arguably been all the stronger in archaeology because of
the need to establish criteria to distinguish herded from hunted animals on
the basis of the morphology of animal bones. Marshall et al. (2014) question
this emphasis in the light of the growing evidence for early stock-keeping in
south-west Asia. Just as conscious selection models for plant domestication
have been rejected, so can those for animals. There must have been conscious
decisions, for example to pen animals within settlements, just as there were to
re-seed wild crops. Nevertheless, if we take Stiner et al.'s (2014) proposal that
early caprine control at Aşıklı was a response to the decline of local common
pool hunted resources as communities became more sedentary, then their
likely goal in the first instance would simply have been to work out means
of maintaining a reliable meat supply on site. The emergence of domesticated
traits was most probably simply a side-effect of the measures people took over
the generations to ensure that supply, and then take advantage of the possibility
of milking, in the light of their growing body of transmitted knowledge about
what worked and what did not.

From the enormous diversity of plant and animal exploitation patterns
that existed in the earlier PPN, by c.9500–9000 BP a more consistent pattern
was emerging, involving a range of domesticated crops and animals, especially
sheep/goat, and including the practice of milking; however, it is important
to emphasise that even in the later PPNB domesticated resources still do
not make up more than 50% or so of the plant and animal remains recorded
from archaeological sites. It was the integration of these resources into a productive and also portable subsistence system – a new ecological niche – that
formed the basis of subsequent expansion (Bogaard and Isaakidou, 2010)
and current ideas about the nature of this will be examined in the following
chapters.

POPULATION PATTERNS IN THE PRE-POTTERY NEOLITHIC

How do these subsistence developments relate to the evidence for population patterns during the Pre-Pottery Neolithic c.11,700–9000 BP? We have
seen that in the final c.1500 years of the Epipalaeolithic there was massive

population increase in both the southern and northern Levant (Fig 2.5). In the southern Levant the growth episode that begins c.12,000 BP continues until c.11,300 BP, resulting in a near doubling of the population, about half of which had already occurred by 11,700 BP. Over the following several hundred years, population seems to be static or to decline slightly, suggesting that some sort of limit had been reached, assuming no increase in site size. Growth appears to re-start c.10,600 BP, leading to a further doubling by 9500 BP, after which there is a decline. In fact, the radiocarbon population proxy is likely to represent a considerable underestimate of the population increase at this time, the beginning of the Middle PPNB, as it marks the start of a massive increase in the size of the largest sites in the region during this period. More specifically, while the largest settlement size does little more than double over the c.1500 years from the PPNA to the Middle PPNB, over the following 500–1000 years it grows by a factor of nearly five times (Kuijt, 2000, 2008). In the southern Levant, in other words, there is a two-step pattern of population increase, the first associated with the sedentism of the Late Epipalaeolithic, which then continues to be supported by the beginning of cereal cultivation in the Early PPNA up to c.11,300 BP. The second was made possible by the increasing importance of domesticated crops with higher yields (though on average the proportion of domestic as opposed to wild plants was still no more than 50%), but also by developments in storage and, if not a re-organisation of settlement, then at least the emergence of new institutions that provided solutions to the problem of large numbers of people living together that agriculture had now made possible (Kuijt, 2008, and see below).

As we have seen, the pattern differs in the northern Levant/upper Mesopotamia region. After a roughly ten-fold rise from c.13,400 BP to the beginning of the Holocene at 11,700 BP, population virtually doubles again in the following 200 years, coinciding with the first clear archaeobotanical evidence of cereal cultivation and presumably reflecting the increased production possible from cultivation of the progenitors of the founder crops in addition to what increased sedentism had already made possible. It is obviously not coincidental that this is also the context for the appearance of the remarkable monuments at such sites in the region as Göbekli Tepe (see below). From c.10,300 BP, it appears that a short period of rapid decline led to a period of flat population lasting until 9500 BP when growth returned. Although this falls within the pan-regional confidence interval of a slowly increasing trend during this period, it is in keeping with Borrell et al.'s (2015) claims for a settlement hiatus in the region 10,200–9800 BP (cf. Atakuman, 2014) and contrasts with the indications of rapid growth in the southern Levant at this time. Indeed, in the period down to 9000 BP the PPNA peak in the radiocarbon population proxy is never exceeded, though it is likely that increased site size compensates to some degree, with the appearance of large sites like Halula or Bouqras c.9800–9700 BP.

In south-central Anatolia, as we have seen, for most of the Younger Dryas and the first 500 years of the Holocene the population pattern is flat and lies below the pan-regional confidence interval, a pattern that recurs briefly from c.10,600 to 10,300 BP. By contrast, from 10,300 to 10,100 BP very rapid increase to a higher population level appears to occur in south-central Anatolia, contrasting with the apparent demographic decline already noted in the northern Levant during the same period and possibly suggesting out-migration from one region to the other. Given that most of this variation falls within the confidence interval for the combined regions, these suggestions should be treated with caution, and recent genetic work indicates that the population of the region at this time was very low (Kılınç et al., 2016). Nevertheless, it is important to note that the rise in population at c.10,300 BP in the south-central Anatolian region corresponds to the earliest occurrence of sedentism, domestic structures, crop cultivation and initial animal keeping at sites such as Boncuklu (Baird et al., 2012) and Aşıklı Höyük (Stiner et al., 2014). Conversely, the long period of low and flat population over the period 12,700–10,300 BP in south-central Anatolia provides little evidence to see it as part of the core area where crop cultivation first began. Indeed, there is enormous diversity in this region. For example, there is no evidence of the exploitation of wild crop ancestors at the 11th-millennium BP site of Pınarbaşı, where the plant element of subsistence seems to have been based on nut-gathering, while the domestic emmer wheat found at nearby Boncuklu was probably adopted from areas to the south and east. It was adopted by a local group rather than introduced by an immigrant community on the basis of the continuity from local Epipalaeolithic traditions seen in the chipped stone assemblage (Baird et al., 2012); here the main hunting prey seem to have been wild boar and red deer. On the other hand, the hunting of caprines was common at Pınarbaşı, which might be a basis for regarding the herding at nearby Aşıklı as a local development (Baird, 2014).

Boncuklu was succeeded in the Konya Plain by the well-known site of Çatalhöyük, which may have involved the amalgamation of several existing communities. The detailed analysis by Larsen and colleagues (2015) of its population history shows in microcosm the demographic processes that were going on during the later part of the PPN. The site was first occupied c.9100 BP (Bayliss et al., 2015) and abandoned a thousand years later. At its foundation Çatalhöyük was small but grew to a population in the low thousands at its height, before declining in size. This seems to be the result of high local fertility as there is no indication that the population expansion was a result of immigration from elsewhere (Larsen et al., 2015: 37). The juvenility index calculated by Larsen et al. as a measure of fertility increases from 29% in the early period to 46% in the middle period before dropping back to 29%, a pattern matching that inferred from the changing number of houses in the settlement. Surprisingly, given the large population size and the crowded living conditions, there is no evidence that growth and development during childhood and adolescence were compromised in any way. On the other hand, the incidence of dental caries was high, reflecting the high intake of carbohydrates from cereals in the diet, and, in addition, there are significant time trends in the occurrence of osteoperiostitis, an inflammation of the bone that results from localised infection. The incidence of this condition was at its highest in the middle period, corresponding to the time when population size and density were also at their highest, and thus consistent with the idea that these two factors have a strong influence on infection rates, a conclusion confirmed by the late period pattern. This shows a major decline in osteoperiostitis, in keeping with the smaller population indicated by both the reduced settlement size and the decreased juvenility index. At the same time, evidence from isotopes and from indicators of biomechanical stresses on the bones suggests that the population was more mobile than in the previous period. The disease patterns are very much in keeping with those seen in the Agta ethnographic case-study described above (Page et al., 2016), with lower infection rates among the more mobile individuals. On the other hand, the indications that the population increase at Çatalhöyük was a result of local fertility not in-migration show that it was not the kind of insanitary population 'sink' that later towns and cities were, their population maintained by migration from the countryside in the face of high urban mortality rates.

In summary, there is strong evidence that the major population increase that had taken place over the course of the Late Epipalaeolithic continued into the Pre-Pottery Neolithic, supported by the cultivation and then domestication of the founder cereal and pulse crops, with year-round settlement and crop storage. As we have seen in Chapter 1, the increase would have been based on some combination of better female energy balances leading to higher birth rates, and better infant survival rates, both stemming from increased sedentism and the increased availability of carbohydrates, and despite the increased incidence of disease. The viability of an increased commitment to cereals and the increased carrying capacity they afforded in the new warmer, wetter, more stable conditions of the Early Holocene provided a Malthusian pull, enabling people who adopted it to increase their reproductive success. Moreover, we now know that this was going on in genetically distinct populations right across the Fertile Crescent, from the southern Levant, through Anatolia to the Zagros mountains in the southeast (Broushaki et al., 2016; Lazaridis et al., 2016). In this context it is worth recalling a characteristically perceptive remark by Binford that has not attracted as much attention as it should:

> Contrary to earlier arguments, it appears unlikely that agriculture occasioned a major change in carbohydrate intake; it represents instead a new means of production for already important plant materials. The demographic changes

arising from fertility variability in response to increasing carbohydrates and labor-changes in a density-dependent context near the close of the Pleistocene were the driving forces making new productive means of positive adaptive advantage. (Binford and Chasko, 1976: 140)

However, the power of compound growth is overwhelming. As we saw in Chapter 1, a population of 100 would reach more than 2,000,000 after 1000 years at the modest growth rate of 1% per year, thus high rates of population growth are unsustainable even in the not very long term. Births and deaths must come into equilibrium at some point, quite possibly after overshooting what is viable; even out-migration only postpones this problem. In the southern Levant there are indications of a population downturn c.9000 BP, all the greater when it is borne in mind that the largest sites disappeared and settlement became more dispersed. In the northern Levant there already appears to have been a downturn from c.10,200 to 9500 BP before growth restarted. In central Anatolia everything is later and evidence for dispersal, if not overall decline, at Çatalhöyük occurs after 8500 BP (see below).

THE SOCIAL CONTEXT

We have focussed so far on the subsistence, population, climate and evolutionary ecology aspects of explaining the origins of farming. In fact, until relatively recently the origins of agriculture were seen as almost entirely relating to changing subsistence patterns and their population consequences, despite the views of a small number of authors such as Barbara Bender (1978) and Brian Hayden (1990), who argued that pressure to increase production came from the social demands for activities such as feasts created by social competition between would-be group leaders. A different kind of social explanation was proposed by Ian Hodder, in his book *The Domestication of Europe* (1990), which argued that the emergence of a set of concepts based around the symbolic importance of the house was a key driver for the appearance of farming and settled life, in contrast to the standard population pressure arguments of the time. Four years later, Jacques Cauvin's *Naissance des Divinités, Naissance de l'Agriculture* (1994) developed a similar theme, arguing that the origins of agriculture should not be seen in environmental and ecological terms, but as resulting from a 'restructuring of the human mentality' involving the emergence of new religious ideas. It was this, in Cauvin's view, that made possible the development of a farming way of life. In the intervening period the discovery of extraordinary sites like Göbekli Tepe, dating to a time when the cultivation of cereals and the control of prey animals was just beginning, has only added force to such arguments.

Activity at this site in south-east Anatolia, with its remarkable stone enclosures and monoliths with animal carvings, began in the Early PPNA, c.11,500 BP (Dietrich et al., 2012) and continued into the Middle PPNB, c.9500 BP. It is the earlier phase that is more striking, with at least 20 roughly oval megalithic enclosures, which were apparently intentionally backfilled after a period of use. Gazelle represent by far the most common animal remains and their exploitation seems to be seasonal, focussed on mid-summer to autumn, which may have been a period when large numbers of people congregated there (Lang et al., 2013). As at Jerf el Ahmar, however, there are large quantities of grindstones and evidence of morphologically wild cereals, including einkorn, rye and barley, as well as glossed sickle blades.

The interpretation of this site remains controversial. The excavators take it to be a regional temple complex with evidence for large-scale feasting, including alcohol consumption, which they associate with the collective work events that would have been required to build the various enclosures at the site and erect the monoliths standing within them (Dietrich et al., 2012). Banning et al. (2011), on the other hand, while not denying its symbolic content, reject the idea that it was a regional ritual centre for hunter-gatherers essentially without domestic occupation, suggesting that such a view makes an anachronistic distinction between sacred and secular space, between 'temples' and 'houses'. In fact, they propose, spaces with striking sculpture, painting and other evidence of symbolism were very likely both ritual and domestic, while the large amounts of what appears to be domestic debris at the site are best accounted for if we assume that the site was fairly permanently occupied by a relatively large population.

Even if Göbekli Tepe is the most striking example of a novel form of architecture and activity, whatever its character, it is increasingly clear that there were contemporary sites with similar features across the Fertile Crescent. For example, as we have seen, at the settlement of Jerf el Ahmar a large oval subterranean communal building dating to the PPNA included a central space surrounded by a series of radially segmented compartments interpreted as storage structures, that make up the outer part of the building (Fig 2.8). A house from an earlier phase, while it had no obvious storage structures, contained a high density of charred rye as well as four aurochs bucrania that might have been attached to the wall. A different kind of subterranean communal building was found in the following phase, roughly circular with a bench including decorated stone slabs running around the entire inside wall (Stordeur et al., 2000). As the authors point out, it is very reminiscent of the kiva ritual structures of the early farmers of the North American Southwest. Recently, the excavation of the site of Wadi Faynan 16 has shown that such large communal structures also occur in the settlements of the southern Levant in the PPNA period (Mithen et al., 2011) (see Fig 2.12). The site included a roughly oval building made of pisé, much larger than the communal buildings at Jerf el Ahmar, measuring 22 × 19 m and with large posts built into the wall that probably supported a roof. Benches ran around a large part of the inside wall, part of them decorated with a wave

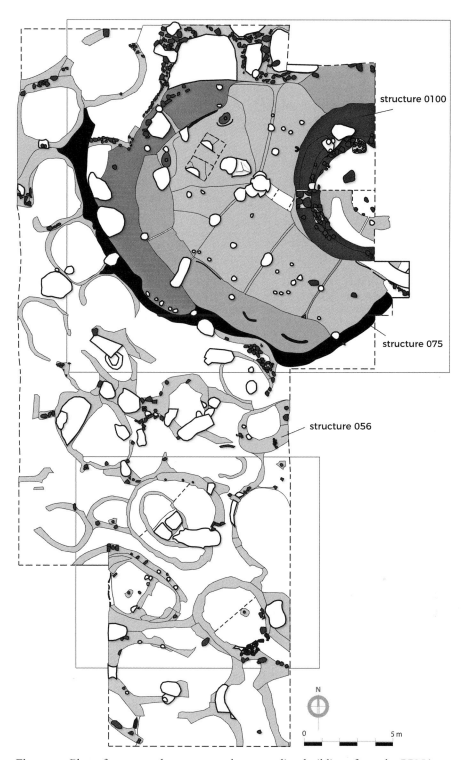

Fig 2.12. Plan of communal structure and surrounding buildings from the PPNA settlement of Wadi Faynan. Reproduced, with permission, from fig 3 in *Antiquity* 85, Mithen, S.J. et al., An 11 600 year-old communal structure from the Neolithic of southern Jordan, pp. 350–364, 2011.

pattern in the mud plaster on the vertical face of the bench. A pair of goat or ibex horn cores was set into a hearth in the middle of the central space. Deposits sealing the floor have dates between c.11,500 and 10,500 BP.

These dramatic recent discoveries and others demonstrate that, far from the origins of agriculture being a matter of subsistence changes alone, they were associated with dramatic changes in the Early Holocene societies of south-west Asia, including their ritual and symbolic practices.

When ideas about the symbolic dimension of these developments were first put forward they were seen as the antithesis of the original ecological thesis of farming origins, an argument for the reversal of the causal arrows. However, the demographic patterns described above show that they appear when regional populations were reaching a peak after a millennium or more of massive growth associated with increased sedentism and then the beginning of cultivation.

In this light they appear as a response to the social challenges that these would have raised, not least the maintenance of social cohesion in the face of increased social scale and differentiation, growing territoriality and the need for new means of managing the changing nature of risk. The new types of site, structures and art are the evidence of the institutions and practices that were developed to deal with those challenges in a set of complex feedback relationships that can be described as a process of mutual niche construction (Sterelny and Watkins, 2015). In fact, working things out socially may well have been just as problematical as arriving at successful animal keeping practices or crop combinations; probably more so, because successful social practices depend on the people you live with, not just yourself, and it may be much more difficult to establish what strategies work (Richerson and Boyd, 2001).

In keeping with these ideas, Hodder and Meskell (2011) have proposed that, despite the inter-regional variation, a broad symbolic *koiné* is detectable across the Fertile Crescent covering the whole 3000-year range of the PPN, from Göbekli Tepe to Çatalhöyük. These common features are unsurprising, the authors suggest, in the light of the evidence for widespread interaction such as the extensive distribution of eastern Anatolian obsidian (Ibáñez et al., 2015), though they become more striking in the light of the new evidence that the populations in Anatolia, the southern Levant and the eastern Fertile Crescent were all genetically distinct from one another (see below). The themes of this *koiné* included 'skulls and birds of prey, wild cattle, and other dangerous animals and masculinity' (2011: 250), as well as the piercing of human flesh, and its development was linked to the social complexities of long-term village life.

While we can see these striking patterns and acknowledge that in broad terms these symbols, ideas and ritual practices had some role in shaping seden-tary community life and addressing the challenges it posed, it is much harder to specify how they might have worked. However, one concrete challenge that has been widely acknowledged is that posed by the potential link between agriculture and the privatisation of property. How is it possible to get from the sharing rights generally prevalent among mobile hunter-gatherers to the private property rights over land, herds and produce that are seen extensively among farmers and herders? Such new conventions have to be agreed by a whole community and for a customary practice as deep-rooted and important as sharing, agreement on a change may be difficult to achieve. Thus Bowles and Choi (2013; cf. North, 1981) argued that farming could not have developed in the context of generalised sharing rights, because there would have been no incentive to undertake the work required for cultivation. This required a way of ensuring that people had a valid claim to the results of their work. Simulations of their model of the process showed that farming could only take off if private property rights co-evolved with it, and that this depended on the resources of farmers being excludable and defensible; conversely, such rights were not viable where subsistence depended on mobile or thinly distributed wild resources whose day-to-day exploitation was subject to high levels of uncertainty. Further exploration of their model by Gallagher et al. (2015) showed that the emergence of farming was more probable in a population structured into separate groups, with small (but not too small) group sizes, a very low level of behavioural experimentation, and the presence of 'farming-friendly' property rights. However, we should not assume that the transition was a sudden one. Studies of Martu hunter-gatherers in Australia show that in larger, long-term camps resulting from decreased mobility and dependent on renewable resources such as small game, the average amount of food that people give to their dependents, rather than to others, is greater (Bird et al., 2016: 113). This is associated with reduced inter-individual variability in returns because the quantity of small game obtained depends much less on chance and much more on the effort expended. In other words, there is a much closer link between effort and return. Of course, the same is also true of plant resources. Thus, the broad spectrum economies of the Late Epipalaeolithic with their increasing populations and lower mobility had probably already created conditions favourable to private property rights associated with farming.

One real archaeological context in which the issue of property rights can be seen is in the development of storage, which becomes increasingly apparent from the PPNA, as we have already seen at Jerf el Ahmar. The site of Dhra', in the Jordan valley in the southern Levant, has revealed what the excavators have interpreted as purpose-built communal granaries in the PPNA phase (Kuijt and Finlayson, 2009), the earliest dating to c. 11,300 BP, a time when cereals were beginning to be cultivated. These roughly round structures had a suspended floor to enable air to circulate and to protect the contents from rodents and they were located in spaces between other buildings that contain evidence for plant processing and were presumably residential. Kuijt (2008) proposes that from 10,500 BP (the beginning of the PPNB) storage patterns began to change, with a move to storage within houses, followed by evidence for dedicated storage rooms within houses a thousand years later. These developments are taken to indicate changing property institutions and a move to household-based ownership. Bogaard et al. (2009) have also argued that at Çatalhöyük the storage of crops was privatised, with storage bins within individual houses.

The theoretical arguments made above about the conflict inherent in changing property rights and the evidence for the importance of storage and some degree of privatisation of property at the household level (at least of the product of farming if not of the land on which crops were grown for which we have no evidence one way or the other), lead us to expect evidence of conflict, on the one hand, and growing inequality on the other. In fact, evidence for conflict is striking in terms of its lack so far (Ferguson, 2013). Evidence of social inequality is more equivocal. There are no indications of marked social stratification in terms of vast differences in the wealth and monumentality of burials or the size and elaboration of houses but there are signs of more limited social differentiation. A number of authors have argued that the well-known plastered skulls placed under house floors, and more generally the evidence for secondary burial rites accorded to limited numbers of individuals, as well as the existence of formal cemeteries, point to an emphasis on ancestry which is often associated with resource control by corporate groups (Price and Bar-Yosef, 2010; cf. Freeman and Anderies, 2015). Items obtained by long-distance exchange, such as obsidian, are also found more frequently at some sites, for example Jericho in the PPNA of the southern Levant, than others. At the site of Çayönü in the northern Levant, during the PPNB Plaza phase there is a major size difference between houses close to the Plaza and a group further away to the west; the latter were also less elaborate in their internal structure. Close to the larger group, at the eastern edge of the Plaza, there was a large cult building, the Terrazzo building with stelae running up to it across the Plaza. However, Atakuman's (2014) analysis of this and other northern Levant sites emphasises the lack of directional trends in organisation and symbolism. Moreover, while it has often been suggested that the construction of the monuments at Göbekli Tepe must have required centralised leadership, the circular/oval plans of the kiva-type communal structures at Jerf el Ahmar and elsewhere point towards the importance of meetings of small numbers of men (most probably), perhaps representing different corporate groups.

The existence of the well-known Late/Final PPNB 'mega-sites' that have been referred to several times already in the course of this chapter is also relevant to this discussion. Sites such as Basta and 'Ain Ghazal in the southern Levant, Abu Hureyra in the north and Çatalhöyük in central Anatolia grew to have populations in the low thousands at their height and they lasted for hundreds of years. Since the work of Johnson (1982) and later Dunbar (1993) it has been clear that communities tend to fission at numbers in the low hundreds unless measures to maintain or increase cohesion are introduced (Alberti, 2014), but the 'mega-sites' had populations an order of magnitude greater than this, so there must have been social means of countering centrifugal tendencies. The needs of defence are often proposed as a stimulus for settlement nucleation but, as we have seen, there is little if any evidence of conflict and Çatalhöyük, at least for much of its life, seems to have been the only settlement in the Konya Plain. Neither can collective subsistence security be the answer. All the sedentary inhabitants of a given place are vulnerable to the same pests or environmentally induced crop failures (Halstead and O'Shea, 1989), not to mention poor sanitary conditions. Moreover, it is hard to reconcile the sizes of these sites with independent household level agricultural decision-making even if we have evidence of household level storage. Winterhalder et al. (2015), for example, draw attention to calculations that the size of the storage bins at Çatalhöyük provided enough for the needs of a family for a year (Bogaard et al., 2009) but not enough for variance compensation, covering possible shortfalls in the harvest the following year, which raises the question of who decided how much should be stored. Finally, from the point of view of the logistics of the day-to-day activities of crop agriculture and stock-keeping, the size of the sites and their population would have been extremely inefficient (Kuijt, 2009; Bogaard and Isaakidou, 2010). The latter authors suggest that these PPNB sites saw the beginning of a successful integration of crop production and animal keeping, with the use of sheep for manuring farming plots and regular community redistribution of the best plots for crop growing, but, as they point out, such intensification would almost certainly have been more easily achieved at the household level. Since relatively small settlements were the original state of affairs, and indeed continued in many places, we again return to the question of how the mega-sites came to emerge and it is hard to see how the answer can be in the sphere of cost–benefit considerations.

This takes us back to the remarkable symbolic elaboration that is visible from the beginning of the Pre-Pottery Neolithic in south-west Asia and what its role might have been in ensuring the astonishing long-term success of sites like Çatalhöyük. There must have been a broadly common set of beliefs and institutions, even if we cannot specify the role they played. Students of technological evolution have come up with the idea of 'breadth first search' when a new technological space first opens up and a wide range of different possibilities are explored, to be subsequently narrowed down as less effective ones are winnowed out (e.g. Lake and Venti, 2009). One such possibility that crop agriculture had enabled was bringing together large numbers of people on a more or less permanent basis, not just seasonally as in the past (though Asouti and Fuller (2012) would put the causal arrow the other way round). As we have seen with plant cultivation and stock-keeping themselves, there was no doubt plenty of trial and error as communities confronted with new situations experimented with equally new ways of doing things socially, the benefits and drawbacks of which were not necessarily obvious. But also, almost certainly, there was ongoing adoption of what were perceived to be successful practices from other places, linked, for example, by obsidian exchange, in a range of different fields, from harvesting techniques to dispute-solving mechanisms and fertility rituals.

The reasons for the demise of the mega-sites and the widespread shift to more dispersed settlement patterns at the end of the PPN have been much discussed and, perhaps needless to say, remain highly disputed. They include the effects of reduced rainfall and ecological degradation resulting from the effects of a large population on its local environment (Kuijt, 2009), the impact of insanitary crowded conditions on the incidence of disease (Goring-Morris and Belfer-Cohen, 2010), as well as more general social stresses of living in these conditions that might have gradually undermined communal values and perceived ritual effectiveness (Kuijt, 2000), so that existing institutions, the social glue, came to be seen as having failed; of course none of these are mutually exclusive.

In any case, it seems that the impact of such factors led to growing pressure for independent household economic decision-making, resulting in a widespread pattern of dispersal. In other words, households that started to make their own production, storage and distribution decisions, and perhaps claimed household landownership, did better and were emulated as a result. This seems to be well seen in the increasingly dispersed late phase at Çatalhöyük (cf. Düring and Marciniak, 2005) and reflected in the changed activity patterns there identified by Larsen and colleagues (2015). The next chapter looks at the beginnings of spatial dispersal.

CHAPTER 3

THE FIRST WESTWARD EXPANSION OF FARMING

So far we have focussed entirely on developments in the broad zone of the Fertile Crescent and central Anatolia where farming began and have traced them up to the beginning of the pottery Neolithic. It is now time to turn to the first westward expansion of farming. In fact, as we will see, this involved two distinct developments: the spread of the fully developed new economy across western Anatolia and the Aegean after 9000 BP, and the colonisation of Cyprus. Both of them are surprising, in different ways: the latter because it was both unique in character and unexpectedly precocious, the former because it was unexpectedly delayed. However, before examining these cases we need to look at the theoretical framework for explaining expansion in the light of the arguments that the success of farming was essentially demographic.

The basic framework for understanding spatial dispersal in the context of population expansion was established many years ago and is relevant not just to people but to other animal populations as well. It corresponds to what archaeologists know as the 'wave of advance' model for the spread of farming from south-west Asia to Europe (Ammerman and Cavalli-Sforza, 1973). It has generally received a bad press from archaeologists, sceptical as they tend to be of general processes and more inclined to be concerned with identifying local patterns in data, but it has continued to be explored extensively by mathematicians and quantitatively inclined archaeologists interested in explaining population dispersals in prehistory, not just the spread of farming. The literature is reviewed in detail by Steele (2009), which provides the basis for the account that follows.

The model consists of an equation which predicts the changing population size over time at a given place on the basis of two elements: local population growth and the speed of spread across space. The population growth rate depends on two factors: the maximum growth rate when it is unrestricted, and the local carrying capacity, the population density when births and deaths are in balance. As this is approached the growth rate slows to zero;

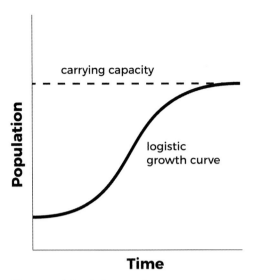

Fig 3.1. a) Logistic growth curve.

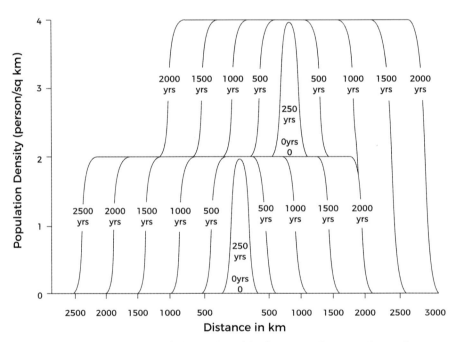

Fig 3.1. b) The classic 'wave of advance' model of an expanding population from a point of origin. The outcome of an initial low-density expansion may be overlaid by a subsequent one of higher density. Reproduced, with permission. from fig 17 in *Genes, Memes and Human History*, Shennan, S., 2002, Thames and Hudson.

the resulting pattern corresponds to a logistic curve (Fig 3.1a). The speed of spread, the diffusion rate, depends on the distances moved by individuals in the time between birth and reproduction; the direction of movement is assumed to be random. The result is a circular wave front of increasing population (Fig 3.1b) expanding at a speed dependent on the population growth rate and the diffusion rate. In principle, archaeological data can be used to estimate some of these quantities. The speed of the wave front can be obtained from the arrival dates of, for example, the first farmers in different locations. Population growth rates in a given region can be estimated from measures of the changing numbers of sites through time, such as the summed radiocarbon probabilities used in the previous chapter. Estimates of movement distances between birth and reproduction are generally taken from ethnographic information on marriage distances.

The original study of the spread of farming with this model (Ammerman and Cavalli-Sforza, 1973) used ethnographic data for all the quantities described above and found a speed of advance of the wave front of c.1 km/year, consistent with that estimated from a regression analysis of radiocarbon dates of the earliest Neolithic sites in relation to their distance from a putative origin of agriculture in Jericho. There have been many subsequent studies. Recently, Fort et al. (2012) again used ethnographic estimates of the various quantities described above but introduced both mountain barriers and faster rates of spread where sea travel was involved; they also took as their origin date, not the very earliest farming, but the date by which it was well established, the late Pre-Pottery Neolithic, c.9000 BP, as we saw in the last chapter. They found that all these features improved the fit of the model but there was still a mean error of over 500 years between the actual arrival time of farming at a given location and that predicted by the model.

In fact, as Steele emphasises, there are many ways in which the basic model can be modified and the danger is that you can simply add new factors until you get a good model fit. Nevertheless, there are some factors that have a good theoretical and/or empirical basis for being considered as potentially relevant to any dispersal situation. So-called *Allee effects* are one (named after the biologist who first described the principle), situations where small populations do worse in natural selection terms than larger ones. Thus, isolated populations, particularly those at an expanding wave front, may have a high extinction risk as a result of a lack of mates or of social support; such effects will tend to slow the speed of expansion. Another general factor is *density-dependent dispersal*, a tendency to move preferentially into areas where the population density is furthest from carrying capacity. However, as Steele (2009: 128) shows, this by no means always results in increasing the speed of the wave, as might be expected, and in some cases can lead to its slowing down. The existence of a *delay between birth and dispersal*, effectively the length of a generation, also slows things down; with the standard estimates of human generation length the front speed is only three-quarters of what it would otherwise be. In the case of the spread of farming into Europe this seems highly relevant and has been included in a number of models (e.g. Fort et al., 2012). A further consideration is that the basic model assumes that the environment is the same in all directions, when in fact there is likely to be preferential movement in the direction of areas with

superior resources, known as *advection* in the literature, at least until occupation starts approaching carrying capacity (see Davison et al. (2006) for its
inclusion in a model for the spread of farming into Europe, based on preferential spread along the Danube river network). The final relevant factor
to be considered here is the form of the distribution of movement or dispersal distances. The basic model assumes that this is roughly bell-shaped or
normal, but in many empirical studies examining the distribution of animal
and human movement this turns out not to be the case: there are more
short-distance movements than the normal distribution predicts, but also
more long-distance ones; the distributions are 'fat-tailed'. Such distributions
result in greater front speeds; in some circumstances, in fact, the speed of
expansion will accelerate, though isolated groups a long way from the main
population front are still vulnerable to Allee effects. Archaeologists studying
the spread of farming into Europe have recognised the significance of this
factor and the importance of long-distance movements by coining the term
'leapfrog colonisation' (van Andel and Runnels, 1995), initially to describe
the Neolithic expansion in the Aegean but subsequently used much more
widely (see later chapters).

One type of relevant 'fat-tailed' distribution is that resulting from *Lévy walks*
or *Lévy flights*; these produce 'power-law' distributions where most of the move
distances are short but very long jumps can also occur. It has been shown
that random walks whose steps follow a Lévy flight distribution provide an
optimal means of searching for targets that are rare and patchily distributed
and where prior knowledge of their distribution is lacking. Such patterns are
found widely in ecological studies of animal foraging patterns and have also
been identified in a study of the daily activities of Hadza foragers in Tanzania
(Raichlen et al., 2014). Thus, Lévy flights may provide a suitable model for
the dispersal distances of colonising farmers seeking suitable new patches to
occupy.

Steele (2009) goes on to review situations where the expanding population
meets and interacts with a pre-existing population, which obviously generates
further complexities, and again such models have been applied to the spread
of farming into Europe (Ackland et al., 2007). However, for reasons that will
become apparent I do not think that these are as relevant as many people have
assumed. Even so, it is clear that there is some justification for the archaeologists'
scepticism about the 'wave of advance', because in the past the values of the
parameters that produce the best-fit models have themselves been used to
infer whether farming spread by means of cultural diffusion, the transmission
of domesticates and farming practices from one local population to the next,
or population expansion (so-called demic diffusion). Genetic information is
now available to distinguish these two from one another (see below) and in the
chapters that follow I will argue that the model remains both conceptually and
practically important in understanding the spread of farming, albeit in a more

limited way than its more ardent proponents have assumed. With these points in mind we can now turn to the earliest evidence of the population expansion that ensued from the beginnings of farming.

THE EARLIEST NEOLITHIC IN CYPRUS

It is debatable whether the Final Pleistocene and Early Holocene human occupation of Cyprus should be included here or in the previous chapter. The discoveries of the last 20 years have produced some of the earliest evidence for the human manipulation of animal populations and at the same time have shown that this was associated with human colonisation of a previously uninhabited island rather than an *in situ* development such as those we have seen in the Fertile Crescent. Indeed, it is precisely because Cyprus was the object of colonisation that the manipulation of the animal populations is detectable, while the fact that human groups were deliberately seeking out new territories at a very early date fits in with the evidence presented in the previous chapter for major population increase through the Younger Dryas and earliest Holocene in the northern Levant, the most likely starting point for voyages to Cyprus. Several studies have shown that even in the Late Glacial period Cyprus was a considerable distance from the mainland and its occupation could not possibly have happened as a result of chance events (Simmons, 2012).

Colonisation episodes to relatively remote and difficult to access places are inherently risky to the groups concerned and are potentially subject to the 'Allee effects' just mentioned, the risks of failure when the number of individuals in a group on the colonising frontier is too small. The first colonists must have weighed up what they thought were the costs and benefits of going into the unknown and concluded that it was worthwhile. Of course, we don't know how many attempts there may have been to colonise Cyprus, or how many failed. The earliest evidence comes from the rock-shelter site of Akrotiri-*Aetokremnos* (Simmons, 2011) (see Fig 3.2 for map of sites), c. 12,500 BP, still in the Younger Dryas period, where the upper layer contains shell and fish bone, but also a small number of bones of wild boar, of a much smaller size than contemporary specimens on the mainland, and in fact smaller than the first domestic pigs on the mainland (Vigne et al., 2009). Since there is no trace of wild boar at any of the earlier natural palaeontological sites on the island, Vigne and colleagues concluded that they must have been taken there by people at an earlier date and been subject to the natural process of dwarfism characteristic of populations of large animals on islands.

It is possible that occupation at this time consisted solely of occasional visits but there can be no doubt that the next occupation for which there is evidence, starting in the 11th millennium BP, the PPNA, represents permanent settlement. There is evidence of cereals, most probably grown locally rather than imported, though the nature of the evidence, in the form of impressions

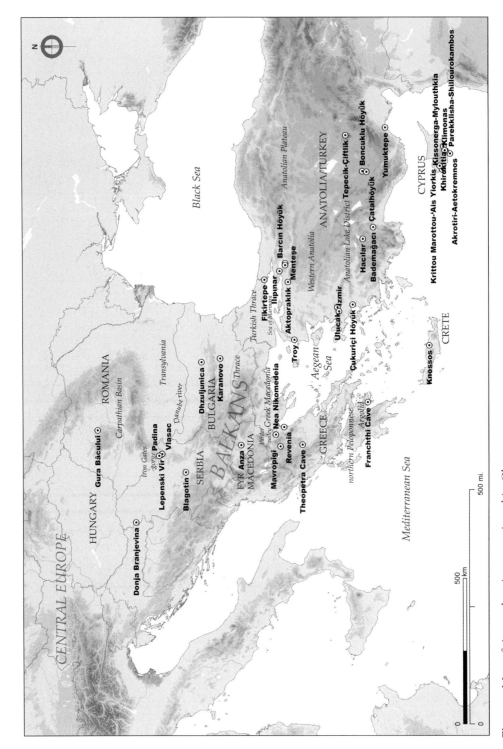

Fig 3.2. Map of sites and regions mentioned in Chapter 3.

in burnt daub, means that it is impossible to say whether they were wild or domestic. There was no trace of sheep, goat or cattle and the majority of the faunal remains consisted of the same small pig found earlier at *Aetokremnos*, which continued to be hunted rather than herded on the basis of the age distribution of the remains (Vigne et al., 2009). Interestingly, however, domestic dog and cat were both present, the latter probably to protect stored cereals against rodents. Most importantly, the site of *Klimonas* (Vigne et al., 2012), dated to c.11,000–10,600 BP, includes a large circular communal building, containing ritual deposits of stone artefacts, of the type we have already seen in the mainland PPNA at sites like Jerf el Ahmar and Wadi Faynan 16. In other words, it was not just a subsistence economy that was introduced but also a way of life, with its symbols, rituals and social institutions, derived from the adjacent Levant, within only a few hundred years of its origin on the mainland (Peltenburg et al., 2001).

The large Cypro-PPNB settlement site of Parekklisha-*Shillourokambos*, which dates in its early phase to c.10,500–10,100 BP, reveals the next phase in the sequence, with the addition of domestic cattle and goat, in addition to the dwarf wild boar and domestic dog and cat already present, while evidence from the contemporary site of Kissonerga-*Mylouthkia* shows that the commensal house mouse had also been introduced (Cucchi et al., 2002). The scale of the networks of which Cyprus was now a part is also shown by the presence of Anatolian obsidian (Peltenburg et al., 2001). Around 10,000 BP the site sees the introduction of three more species: domestic sheep, together with fallow deer and fox. From this time too it is clear that pig exploitation was mainly through stock-keeping, though whether this involved a local domestication or the introduction of pigs from elsewhere is not clear. As Vigne (2014: 131) points out, the presence of the fallow deer confirms that people somewhere on the mainland must still have been experimenting with the control of wild animals, though in Cyprus they always seem to have been hunted. The fact that the domestic sheep arrived 500 years later than the goat, on the other hand, presumably indicates that the latter had arrived from a region where domestic sheep were still unknown. The complex range of different relationships between people and prey animals seen in Cyprus is further emphasised by the results of analyses carried out by Vigne and colleagues (2011) on the size and sex ratios of the remains of the goats introduced to the island. They suggest that although they must have been through a domestication process on the mainland, in Cyprus they were initially hunted and then underwent a local domestication a thousand years later, at which point they began to be used for milk. The imported domestic sheep, however, were not hunted and were managed for both meat and milk, but this population went through a major size decrease c.9500 BP, with signs of stress, and may have died out completely, at a time when the role of stock-keeping in general, compared with hunting, seems to have declined, and when there are also indications of over-hunting of the fallow deer population (Vigne et al., 2011: S263, S266). However, it was followed by the introduction of a more robust sheep variety from the mainland, whose mortality profile suggests exploitation for meat and perhaps for wool (Vigne, 2014: 133). A new variety of cattle may also have arrived at this time but, for whatever reason, they decline to very low frequencies and later largely disappear from the faunal spectrum. Nevertheless, it is only during this time, in the final centuries of the 9th millennium BP that the proportion of meat produced from stock-keeping as opposed to hunting reaches 60–75% and therefore implies a relatively stable animal production system, with sophisticated differential exploitation of sheep, goat and pig, in contrast to the two millennia of experimentation that had preceded it. The significance of these changes is indicated by the fact that the density of animal bone refuse in relation to volume of excavated earth increases 25 times in this period compared with the previous phases (Vigne et al., 2011).

The evidence for domestic crops broadly parallels this pattern. As we have seen, it is unclear from the evidence of impressions at Late PPNA *Klimonas* whether the barley and emmer wheat were wild or domestic in form but they were almost certainly cultivated locally. Slightly later, in the Early PPNB phase at *Mylouthkia*, domestic barley, emmer and einkorn all occur, associated with high proportions of weed taxa, leading to the conclusion that the samples probably represent fine-sieving residues from crop processing (Peltenburg et al., 2001; Colledge and Conolly, 2007: 56). Lentils and flax were also found. A thousand years later in the Final or Late PPNB, at the time of the intensification of the stock-keeping economy seen at *Shillourokambos*, the crop spectrum in the later phase at *Mylouthkia* remains the same; free-threshing wheat appears during the 9th millennium BP at the site of Khirokitia, as well as additional species of pulses.

As we noted at the beginning of this chapter, the interesting thing about Cyprus is that it lies outside the broad mainland region where the wild progenitors of the domestic plant and animal species occurred, but the people who colonised it were involved in manipulating many of the wild species concerned. The complex history of animal movement and manipulation has already been outlined, but the island's situation also has implications for early crop domestication. The previous chapter explained that current evidence points to a long period of cultivation before morphologically domestic species evolved, at least partly because there would have been continued backcrossing of the cultivated plants with wild plants from the surrounding area. However, in the case of Cyprus the early cultivated plants had been removed from their natural surroundings so one might expect them to evolve more quickly under the selection pressure of cultivation, while there might also have been a bottleneck effect if only a relatively small sample of seeds was brought over and formed the founding population. A recent study of the archaeobotanical assemblage from the site of Krittou Marottou-'*Ais Yiorkis*, dated to c.9500 BP (Cypro-Middle/ Late PPNB) showed exactly this pattern (Lucas et al., 2012), by comparing the size of grains of two-grain einkorn at the site with contemporary sites on the mainland. It is clear that the thickness and breadth measurements were well above the average for their date. There are currently no known earlier occurrences of two-grain einkorn on Cyprus and Lucas et al. suggest that the new combination of cereals found at the site may represent a second wave of introductions, possibly from the Syrian Middle Euphrates area, where the same combination is found, and where the first indications of a grain size increase in two-grained einkorn occur at around the same time. Once in Cyprus grain size increased between three and six times faster than the rate of size increase on the mainland. The distinctiveness of the cereal 'package' suggests a one-off introduction, or at least only very limited further imports, otherwise it would have been persistently diluted, eventually producing a mix of crops similar to that found at many sites on the mainland. Whether this was true for the other imported cultivated species remains to be seen but it makes a marked contrast with the evidence for several animal introductions described above. The evidence for the introduction of the commensal house mouse, mentioned above, is particularly interesting because the mainland and Cypriot lineages never diverged. The high rate of gene flow this indicates apparently implies that there must have been voyages leading to the unintentional introduction of groups of mainland mice to the island several times a year (Vigne et al., 2014). This is a remarkable result, in terms of both the high level of maritime skill and technology implied by a practice of regular crossings, and also the intensity of the links maintained with the homeland.

There are then a number of different lines of evidence suggesting that contacts between Cyprus and the mainland were intensive, complex and differentiated. All the more surprising then is the fact that in the subsequent period, from about 8500 BP, equivalent to the Khirokitia culture, Cyprus became gradually more isolated from the mainland, although never losing contact completely, and developed its own very distinctive and long-lasting architectural and material culture traditions. Even more surprisingly, this was just at the time when farming was expanding into western Anatolia and the Aegean.

ANATOLIA AND THE AEGEAN

With the exception of Cyprus, expansion westwards from the core area seems to have begun around 9000 years ago or shortly thereafter, equivalent to the Late and Final PPNB period, and this in itself may be seen as something of a puzzle. If people were prepared to go by boat to Cyprus, taking animals with them, why did they not move westwards from central Anatolia sooner than they did? Conversely, why did the delay not last longer? While new evidence may come to light, and work on the Early Neolithic of western Anatolia is still relatively recent, the evidence for the delay currently seems clear and is well demonstrated by examination of the radiocarbon dates for the region (Brami, 2015; Schoop, 2005), which indicate a delay of at least 1500 years between the first central Anatolian sites with evidence for crop cultivation and/or animal keeping and the earliest sites in western Anatolia and the Aegean with domesticates. It is at this point that we come across for the first time the key question of what it was that spread: people bringing a whole way of life based on domestic crops and animals and a set of social practices and institutions that had developed over the preceding two millennia, the spread of a way of life that was adopted wholesale by existing local forager groups, or something more limited – domestic plants and animals and some key agricultural sub-sistence practices, or even just the latter? These questions have been contro-versial for at least 50 years and will keep recurring throughout the rest of this book, but, as we will see, answers are beginning to emerge. In what follows we will look first at the archaeological and bioarchaeological evidence for the expansion of farming in the region, then at the results of new whole-genome ancient DNA analyses of human bone, before considering possible explanations, a topic that will take us back to some of the issues raised at the end of the last chapter.

While the evidence for the Aegean has remained fairly static in recent years this is not the case with western Anatolia and Turkish Thrace, on the nor-thern side of the Sea of Marmara (see map, Fig 3.2). Fieldwork here over the last 20 years has completely changed the previous picture, filling a long-existing gap between the sites of Çatalhöyük in central Anatolia and Hacılar in the Anatolian Lake District, known since the 1960s, and those of the Early Neolithic of south-east Europe, which had become known through major excavation programmes in the 1960s and 70s, as Özdoğan (M. Özdoğan, 2011) describes. There was also an academic gap, as Özdoğan likewise points out, between different sets of specialists, one set with expertise in the Balkan Neolithic and the other with knowledge of the Near East. Western Anatolia really only figured on the agenda of Bronze Age specialists, because of the presence of Troy. This has now all changed, with the excavation of over 25 sites in four main geographical groups: the Anatolian Lake District, where Hacılar was already known, the Aegean coast, the Marmara region and Turkish Thrace.

The archaeological evidence for Neolithic farming occupation west of cen-tral Anatolia has recently been extensively reviewed (Düring, 2013; E. Özdoğan, 2015) and goes back to the earlier 9th millennium BP at Hacılar and Bademağacı in the Anatolian Lake District and the earliest phases at Ulucak and Çukuriçi Höyük, on the Aegean coast of Anatolia near İzmir, at all of which pottery was rare but not non-existent. M. Özdoğan (2011) sees them as relating to an initial exploratory spread of farmers from central Anatolia, by land or by sea along the southern coast of Anatolia, or possibly both, that lasted until c.8500 BP. The earliest occupation of Knossos on Crete shortly after 9000 BP (Douka et al., 2017) also relates to this early phase and, despite the evidence now for Mesolithic occupation on Crete, undoubtedly represents a colonisation by agropastoralists; the Initial Neolithic phase, c.8700 BP, at Franchthi Cave on the Aegean coast of the Argolid, mainland Greece, also falls into this period. In other words, the west Anatolian and Aegean expansions were part of the same simultaneous process.

Expansion on a greater scale then follows, between c.8600–8500 BP, with many more sites known in the Anatolian Lake District, Aegean western Anatolia, and the Sea of Marmara region in the north-west, as well as in the Aegean, including mainland Greece as far north as Macedonia, as recent work has revealed (Karamitrou-Mentessidi et al., 2013). Despite the contemporaneity of the expansion across this broad region, a striking feature of its material culture, architecture and settlement layouts is its diversity and distinctiveness from one region to another, and also from what must be, at least in general terms, the ancestral area of these developments, which was the broad area of central Anatolia and its coastal zone to the south (Düring, 2013; Horejs et al., 2015; E. Özdoğan, 2015). Analyses of the formal and stylistic elements of the pottery from this Early Neolithic phase in Anatolia and the Aegean shows that there is no relation between how far apart sites are and the similarity of their ceramic inventories (de Groot, 2016).

One of the most distinctive regional assemblages is that represented by the Fikirtepe Culture of north-west Anatolia, around the Sea of Marmara, where the earliest site so far known is Barcın Höyük, which dates from c.8600 BP and has a fully Neolithic subsistence with pottery and rectangular architecture, and this is followed slightly later by sites such as Aktopraklık and Menteşe, beginning c.8400 BP (Gerritsen et al., 2013). The inland sites of this culture are characterised by a farming economy, rectangular architecture and separate cemeteries while coastal sites have evidence of a mixed economy, including the exploitation of marine resources, circular/oval houses and underfloor burials. This is often cited as evidence that the Fikirtepe Culture represents an integration between incoming farmers and existing forager groups exploiting the coastal resources of the region (e.g. M. Özdoğan, 2016), but this is by no means uncontested (see below).

The broad chronological pattern is clearly seen by examining the relevant radiocarbon dates (Brami, 2015) (see Fig 3.3). There are indications in the radiocarbon record that expansion out of central Anatolia to western Anatolia, Greece and the Aegean began around 9000 BP but that there is a major expansion from c.8500 BP. For the Balkans north of the Aegean coastal zone, on the other hand, the earliest indications are around c.8200 with a major expansion slightly later (see below).

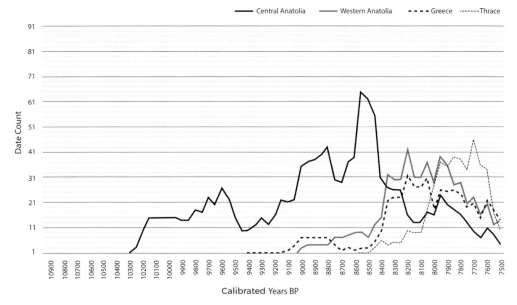

Fig 3.3. Summed calibrated radiocarbon dates for the Aegean–Anatolian region. Reproduced from fig 5 in *Archaeological and Anthropological Sciences* 7, Brami, M.N., A graphical simulation of the 2,000-year lag in Neolithic occupation between Central Anatolia and the Aegean, pp. 319–327, 2015, with permission from Springer.

Subsistence Patterns

The overall pattern seen in the spread of domestic animals broadly fits with those described above for the material culture. The importance of domestic sheep and goat was a common factor throughout. Beyond south-eastern Turkey the earliest occurrence of the combination of all four domestic animals: sheep, goat, cattle and pig, is not in central Anatolia but in the earliest occupation layer at Ulucak, dating to the earlier 9th millennium as we have seen, on the south-west Aegean coast (Arbuckle et al., 2014). Domestic cattle are not found in central Anatolia until the mid–late 9th millennium, when they are introduced from elsewhere, while the earliest morphologically domestic pigs do not occur until the mid-7th millennium (Arbuckle, 2013). In other words, it cannot be automatically assumed that inland central Anatolia was the source of all developments further west. Other early occurrences of the full combination of domestic animals are found on the south coast at Yumuktepe and at Bademağacı in the Lake District, both fitting in with the idea of a broadly southern and coastal spread to the west. The Fikirtepe tradition of the Marmara region, which we have already seen is distinctive in terms of its material culture, is also different in its faunal assemblage, from which domestic pig is absent until c.7800 BP, when it was adopted from neighbours to the south. This would fit in with suggestions that there is a link between the Marmara region and central Anatolia, across the Anatolian plateau, in the mid–late 9th millennium BP.

However, not everyone agrees with the suggestion, noted above, by Özdoğan and others, that the Marmara group may represent a mingling of indigenous foraging and incoming farming traditions, a claim made on the basis that there is evidence for exploitation of shellfish and other marine resources at coastal Fikirtepe sites and that houses at these sites are round/oval rather than rectangular. As Çakırlar (2013) points out, there are farming sites with round houses in Anatolia, and on Cyprus, and there are no known definitely Mesolithic sites with houses with which the Fikirtepe sites can be compared. In addition, the exploitation of aquatic resources was a feature of the subsistence economy of a number of coastal sites of later periods in the general Marmara region, including Early Bronze Age Troy, so cannot simply be taken as an index of hybridisation or a forager–farmer transition. Finally, animal husbandry was fundamental at all the sites, both inland and coastal, including dairy exploitation, indicated by the results of analyses of residues in pottery vessels that have demonstrated their use in the processing of milk products by the end of the 9th millennium BP (Evershed et al., 2008). At Ulucak, 300 km to the south of the Fikirtepe sites, the age-sex distribution of the animal bones in Phase VI, the earliest phase, dating to the first half of the 9th millennium, points to a risk-buffering strategy concerned with the maintenance of sheep, goat and cattle herds, with more of an emphasis on domestic pig during Phase V, c.8500–8000 BP. In the following phase, at the beginning of the 8th millennium BP, there is an increase in cattle at the expense of pig, and culling patterns change in sheep/goat, most probably associated with systematic milk production.

Recent studies of the mtDNA in pig bones from Ulucak, Bademağacı and Menteşe (Ottoni et al., 2012) have shown that both wild and domestic pig populations possessed the Y1 mtDNA haplotype, which is specific to western Anatolia, and not the Arm1T haplotype that characterises early domestic pig populations further east, and it is the west Anatolian haplotype that characterises the Early Neolithic pigs of south-east and Central Europe. Given all the other evidence for eastward connections, the likely inference is that it was domestic pigs of east Anatolian origin that moved westwards with the early farming communities out of the core zone but there was admixture with the female wild boar of western Anatolia, whose Y1 lineage then replaced them, probably simply as a result of genetic drift in small domestic populations at these early settlements.

Unfortunately, far less work has been carried out in recent years on evidence for the archaeobotanical side of the spread of farming outside the core area and there are as yet no up-to-date reports from the sites described above for which the latest faunal analyses have done so much to change our picture. However, the correspondence analysis carried out by Colledge et al. (2004) on crop and weed taxa at early sites across the east Mediterranean showed a clear distinction between the archaeobotanical assemblages in the core zone, which include wild ancestor species, and those immediately outside it to the west, as well as between different regions in this latter group. The assemblages from sites in central Anatolia, such as Çatalhöyük, are clearly different from those of sites in Cyprus, Crete and mainland Greece, which all share among other features a prevalence of glume wheats and hulled barley, together with a reduced range of weed species. While ecological conditions in new fields outside the core area are likely to be part of the explanation for this, another possible factor is the transport of the domestic crops by human agency to new locations on islands such as Crete, but also probably *via* islands in the case of the sites included in the study from mainland Greece. Moreover, it seems that there was a strong preference for the domestic cereals over the wild ancestors of hulled barley and einkorn, which were widely available in Anatolia and the Aegean outside the core area but were little used. The botanical evidence from the apparently aceramic phase at Knossos, dating to the beginning of the 9th millennium BP, fits in with the faunal and other evidence we have seen above for the importance of an Anatolian coastal route for the expansion of farming out of the core area. The fact that Knossos has the full range of domestic animals at such an early date (Isaakidou, 2008) also fits in with this picture since this occurs earliest on the coast, as we have seen at Ulucak and Yumuktepe.

The other important very early site in the Aegean is Franchthi Cave, on the Aegean coast in the northern Peloponnese. Recent results (Perlès et al., 2013) have confirmed a date in the early 9th millennium BP for the Initial Neolithic at this site, which follows on from the Final Mesolithic after a gap of perhaps 200 years. The dates were on seeds of morphologically domesticated crops; those present included emmer wheat, barley and lentils, which appear for the first time in this phase (Hansen, 1991). The Initial Neolithic layer also shows a complete change in the faunal spectrum at the site, from a broad range of hunted wild species to an overwhelming predominance of caprines, mainly sheep, which are not native to the Aegean; at the same time there is a major decline in evidence for fishing (Munro and Stiner, 2015). The age distribution of the animals indicates that they were mainly exploited for meat, with perhaps some milking, while their very small size in comparison to earlier managed sheep populations in the Fertile Crescent shows that they had already undergone intensive selection. Interestingly, the size of the sheep from the west Anatolian sites of Ulucak and Ilıpınar is almost identical to Franchthi.

Despite the radical change in subsistence to an economy based on introduced domesticated resources, the strong similarity between the Final Mesolithic and the Initial Neolithic in terms of stone tool assemblages and ornaments suggests to Perlès and colleagues (2013) that the Initial Neolithic actually represents the adoption of agriculture by local hunter-gatherers. This is indeed one of the very few known cases where there seems to be an indigenous adoption of domestic crops and animals and farming practices outside the core area, though increasing numbers of Mesolithic sites are becoming known in the Aegean,

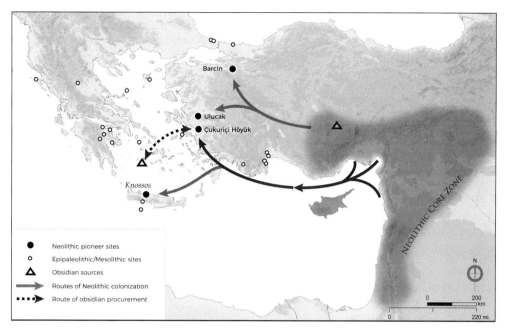

Fig 3.4. Neolithisation of western Anatolia with suggested routes of colonisation. Reproduced from fig 15 in *Journal of World Prehistory* 28, Horejs, B. et al., The Aegean in the Early 7th Millennium BC: Maritime Networks and Colonization, pp. 289–330, 2015. Creative Commons license.

including Crete (e.g. Carter, 2016), so more sites with evidence of local forager traditions adopting agriculture with imported crops and animals may be found. However, in the case of Franchthi we should not simply assume that it was local descendants of the Final Mesolithic population that re-occupied it 200 years later. As Munro and Stiner point out (see also Reingruber, 2011), the Initial Neolithic occupants were part of a maritime network and thus could have been colonists from elsewhere in the Aegean where similar Mesolithic traditions to those of Franchthi prevailed (Çilingiroğlu, 2017); the extensive evidence for the exploitation and distribution of obsidian from the Cycladic island of Melos already in the Mesolithic, even as far as Crete (Carter, 2016), is testimony to the interaction that was occurring. What is certain is that there must have been direct contact between groups with Mesolithic traditions in material culture and others with a wholly agricultural subsistence of long standing, based on crops and animals domesticated generations earlier and imported from central Anatolia or areas further south and east (cf. Horejs et al., 2015) (see Fig 3.4).

Regardless of the role of local forager populations, an issue to which we will return below, the transition to a way of life based on domestic crops and animals in the Aegean and mainland Greece generally seems to have been rapid rather than piecemeal. In terms of the faunal data from the earliest farming sites, there is negligible evidence for hunting, and sheep predominate (Manning et al., 2013a). Halstead and Isaakidou (2013: 136) conclude from a variety of lines of evidence that numbers of domestic animals would have been small and that their movements were controlled, restricting them to cultivated land, where they would have had a role in manuring; they appear to have been exploited largely for meat on the basis of the mortality patterns, and overall they were subordinate to the crop element of the economy.

GENETIC EVIDENCE FOR THE NATURE OF THE AEGEAN EXPANSION

New light has now been thrown on the relations between Anatolia and the Aegean, and their role in the spread of farming to the rest of Europe, by whole-genome ancient DNA analyses (Hofmanová et al., 2016; Kılınç et al., 2016; Lazaridis et al., 2016; Lipson et al., 2017; Mathieson et al., 2017). The significance of whole-genome studies, i.e. studies of the genes in the cell nucleus that are inherited from both the mother and the father, is that they represent a sample of the genes from many of the ancestors of the individual concerned, along many different lines of descent, and therefore even a single individual can provide a good representation of a population, in contrast to mtDNA or the Y chromosome. These analyses have now conclusively shown that the farming groups of this region represent well the ancestral population of the groups that introduced farming to west Mediterranean and Central Europe, and thus that farming spread through migration. The implications of this will be explored below for the Balkans and in subsequent chapters but here the focus is on the Aegean and Anatolia.

The Anatolian Neolithic samples came from the site of Barcın in the Marmara area that we have already seen; the Aegean Neolithic samples came from several sites in northern Greece. The earliest samples, from Barcın and Revenia, date to the third quarter of the 9th millennium BP. The genomes from Anatolia and Greece are very similar but it is currently impossible to identify a directional dispersal from one to the other. However, there are apparently small amounts of admixture in the Early Neolithic Greek genomes with the 'Western Hunter Gatherer' (WHG) group (Hofmanová et al., 2016). This WHG genome group is characteristic of Mesolithic populations in western and Mediterranean Europe, from Iberia to the Balkan peninsula, probably reflecting a range expansion from south-east Europe at the end of the last Ice Age (Mathieson et al., 2017). One of the interesting things about the genetic similarity between Barcın and the northern Greek sites is that it is in some respects surprising. Barcın belongs to the culturally distinctive Marmara group discussed above and Milić's (2014) study shows that virtually all its obsidian comes from central Anatolia and not from the Melos source, which is overwhelmingly predominant in Aegean-facing western Anatolia and in mainland

Greece. Moreover, it now appears that southern Greece may be genetically different from the north. Analyses of four individuals from the Peloponnese, including one from Franchthi Cave, show a pattern indicating ancestry in a population that had split off from that characteristic of north-west Anatolia and the northern Aegean and may indicate an independent migration via the coast of south-west Anatolia (Mathieson et al., 2017). This would fit in with some of the archaeological evidence discussed above for early trans-Aegean contacts, though it is worth noting that none of the DNA samples seem to date to the earliest Neolithic.

Recent work has now established that the genetic pattern found in north-west Anatolia and the northern Aegean derives from populations in south-central Anatolia (Kılınç et al., 2016). Individuals were analysed from the site of Boncuklu in the Konya Plain discussed in the last chapter, where local hunter-gatherers seem to have taken up crop cultivation by c.10,300 BP and occupation continued until c.9500 BP; and from the nearby site of Tepecik-Çiftlik in Cappadocia, close to important obsidian sources, where occupation began c.9500 BP and continued until c.7800 BP. The genomes grouped with those of Barcın and the European Early Neolithic, thus suggesting that the hunter-gatherer population represented by Boncuklu was ancestral to Barcın though we still do not know its full geographic range. As noted in the last chapter, the Boncuklu data indicated a small ancestral population size, comparable with European Mesolithic hunter-gatherers, but the later Çiftlik and Barcın populations were much more diverse, indicative of wide-scale interactions in the intervening period.

In summary, current evidence indicates that pioneer farming groups started moving westwards from a broad core region including central Anatolia and the coastal zone to the south, already linked together by the southward exchange of Anatolian obsidian. They followed an overland route on the one hand, leading to the foundation of sites like Barcın in the Marmara region, and a coastal and island route on the other, along which people were already interacting, represented by Ulucak and Çukuriçi Höyük in Aegean Anatolia, Knossos on Crete and other early island and mainland sites in Greece (Horejs et al., 2015) (see Fig 3.4). The Franchthi Initial Neolithic evidence suggests that these interactions also led to the adoption of an already developed farming economy by groups with a forager cultural ancestry in some cases.

THE BALKANS

In terms of material culture patterns it appears that the expansion of farmers into the Balkans took place via northern Greece and not via the Fikirtepe Culture of the eastern Marmara region into eastern Bulgaria (M Özdoğan, 2016). One reason may be that the Sub-Mediterranean-Aegean climatic conditions in northern Greece and in the valleys of rivers such as the Vardar flowing from the north into the northern Aegean were more favourable than in Turkish Thrace, with less severe winters, and thus opened a way to the north (Krauss et al., 2017). It is in any case now apparent that this expansion was significantly later than in Anatolia and the Aegean. Dates for the earliest farming sites north of the Aegean coastal plain are virtually identical from the site of Anza in the Vardar valley of FYR Macedonia in the south to the southern edge of the Carpathian Basin in the north, including sites like Donja Branjevina in northern Serbia and Gura Bâcului in Transylvania, covering the last two centuries of the 9th millennium BP and the first century of the 8th millennium. In other words, the expansion from the northern borders of the Aegean several hundred miles to the north seems to have taken less than 200 years (Biagi et al., 2005), borne out by strong material culture similarities across the area.

The place that has attracted by far the most attention in connection with the expansion of farming through the Balkans is the site of Lepenski Vir, located in the Iron Gates gorge of the river Danube that marks the boundary between Serbia and Romania at this point. It has been the focus of interest for several reasons: the extraordinary stone sculptures and trapezoid houses that it has produced; the evidence it provides of Mesolithic occupation; and the fact that it provides some of the best evidence of contacts between farmers and foragers. In fact, it is one of a number of sites in the Iron Gates that were occupied from the Late Palaeolithic through the Mesolithic (Borić, 2011). The reason for their location is the outstanding possibilities offered by the gorge for successful fishing for large sturgeon and other river fish, including carp and catfish. As the landscapes of Europe became increasingly forested following the end of the last Ice Age, the density of game and other resources accessible to forager communities to see them through the year, including the winter, decreased dramatically, meaning that when only terrestrial wild resources were available population densities were low (cf. Binford, 2001; Discamps, 2014; Gurova and Bonsall, 2014). It was only places where aquatic resources were available that could sustain higher population densities, and do so on a long-term basis, and the archaeological evidence reflects this. In the Early–Middle Mesolithic of the Iron Gates, 11,500–9400 BP, there is no evidence that these fishing communities had any other than local connections, but in the Late Mesolithic, c.9400–8200 BP, there are indications of long-distance contacts in the form of marine shell beads that must have come from coastal regions. Genome studies of over 30 individuals have now shown that these Mesolithic populations are characterised by over 85% WHG ancestry, with the great majority of the remainder coming from the Eastern Hunter Gatherer (EHG) group, both very widespread in the Mesolithic of western and eastern Europe respectively (Mathieson et al., 2017).

After a period of abandonment, and an apparent decrease in the use of the Iron Gates river bank sites that may have been the result of increased flooding during the so-called 8.2 ka BP cold period (Bonsall et al., 2015), the site of

Lepenski Vir itself was re-occupied shortly after c.8200 BP, marking the beginning of the so-called Transitional Phase, which is also represented at some
other Iron Gates sites; on the basis of the numerous radiocarbon dates available
the phase probably lasted c.160 years (Borić, 2011). Occupation was at least
semi-sedentary; subsistence continued to be heavily based on fishing, and no
domestic animals were found, but the site provides evidence of a remarkably
creative 'cultural hybridity' (Borić and Price, 2013). Pottery characteristic of
the Balkan early farmers occurs as well as polished stone axes, flint characteristic of farmer exchange networks coming from 200 km away in Bulgaria,
and new Neolithic bone tool forms. At the same time this was the period of
construction of the famous trapezoid houses and of the extraordinary stone
sculptures. Moreover, recent strontium isotope studies (Borić and Price, 2013)
have shown that, in contrast to the previous phases, some individuals in burials
from the Transitional Phase, virtually all of whom are females, have evidence
of non-local isotope signatures. It has now been established that one of these
females with a non-local signature was of entirely Anatolian farmer ancestry
and had a mixed terrestrial and aquatic diet, while a boy of about eight years
old had a diet largely based on aquatic resources but an ancestry that was
predominantly Anatolian with some WHG and EHG admixture (Mathieson
et al., 2017). As Porčić and Nikolić (2016) point out, the evidence for population growth that they find in this phase must be at least partly linked to this
in-migration. That Lepenski Vir was not unique in this respect is indicated by
two individuals from the corresponding phase at the nearby site of Padina,
one of whom was of entirely WHG ancestry, while the ancestry of the other
was c.50% Anatolian farmer (Mathieson et al., 2017). In the following phase,
beginning c.7930 BP, the evidence from Lepenski Vir becomes fully Neolithic.
The trapezoid houses are abandoned; the burials change from the traditional
extended form to the crouched burials characteristic of farming communities;
the full range of domestic animals occurs and the dietary isotope signatures
point to a shift to a more terrestrial diet; while the strontium isotopes continue to indicate that some women were non-local. This phase continues until
c.7500 BP, when the site was abandoned.

However, there is no reason to believe that Lepenski Vir and the Iron Gates
were typical of what happened with the introduction of farming to forager
groups in the Balkans. Their relatively high local population densities and
at least semi-sedentary way of life depended on their aquatically based subsistence. Terrestrial foragers would have been both more mobile and more
dispersed, with lower population densities. Analysis of Early Holocene site
distributions in the interior Balkans shows a major population reduction
from the Upper Palaeolithic to the Late Mesolithic as forests spread, reducing
the terrestrial animal and plant resources available for human consumption
(Gurova and Bonsall, 2014). It seems likely that as farming expanded they
would either have retreated, perhaps to areas like the now submerged Black

Sea coast where aquatic resources would have been available, or been absorbed on a piecemeal basis into the incoming farming communities that brought farming to the region. The genomic picture for the Balkan Neolithic overall indicates an average of 98% Anatolian ancestry (Mathieson et al., 2017) but there is variation. Studies of early 8th-millennium BP individuals from the Starčevo and Kőrös cultures at the northern end of the Balkan farming expansion in Hungary (Lipson et al., 2017) showed that five out of six individuals were essentially no different from Neolithic Anatolians but one had c.8% WHG genetic ancestry, resulting from an admixture event in the previous three to five generations. Another study (Gamba et al., 2014) of a man from a Kőrös site found that he was of mainly WHG forager ancestry and indicated that the population from which he came must have been small in size.

In summary, the genomic and material evidence from the Balkans indicates a rapid range expansion by farmers of Anatolian ancestry but shows interactions with local forager groups in places like the Iron Gates with denser populations. Those interactions produced some extraordinary but short-lived cultural developments.

SUBSISTENCE AND CULTURE OF THE BALKAN EARLY NEOLITHIC

In terms of the animal economy the picture is very clear. While in Greece the faunal spectra are largely dominated by sheep/goat, in the Balkans to the north they are much more diverse (Manning et al., 2013a; Orton, 2012 for the central Balkans). Ovicaprines are far less dominant and there is a stronger emphasis in many places on cattle, a pattern explicable at least in part by lower temperatures and higher rainfall (Conolly et al., 2012); there is also a greater terrestrial wild component. Strikingly, domestic pigs play an extremely minor role in the central Balkans compared with areas further to the south – less than 2% compared with c.10% of the number of identified specimens (NISP) in Greece and Bulgaria – even though the wetter environmental conditions here would lead one to expect the opposite; while even though ovicaprines are less dominant than in the south they are still surprisingly frequent given the local environmental context.

Recent ancient DNA work (Scheu et al., 2015) has thrown new light on the domestic cattle in particular, confirming that they are the result of a population expansion of cattle domesticated in south-west Asia as farming spread, as opposed to local domestication. Local wild cattle are characterised by different mtDNA lineages and there is no evidence of any significant inter-breeding, indicating that the domestic herds must have been under reasonably careful control. It is also clear that the farming expansion from the Aegean and western Anatolia did not lead to a bottleneck in the cattle population of the Balkans; the majority of the genetic variation in the ancestral populations is still found in the south-east European Early Neolithic (EN) cattle populations, which group with western Anatolian cattle in terms of genetic distance. Some gene flow between Anatolia and south-east Europe seems to have continued for c.1000 years before ceasing (Scheu et al., 2015). As we will see in later chapters, the situation in Europe west of the Balkans is very different.

The domesticated crops show essentially the same picture. The founder cereals einkorn, emmer and hulled barley are present in the majority of sites in south-east Europe, as in south-west Asia, while free-threshing wheat and naked barley are also present in at least 50% of the sites in the two regions, based on the data analysed by Colledge et al. (2005). South-east Europe also has the full set of founder crop domestic pulses that are found in south-west Asia: pea, lentil, bitter vetch, chickpea and grass pea (an early addition to the founder crops). Where there is a difference between south-west Asia and south-east Europe is in the number of weed species represented, with 92 from 44 sites in the former compared with 58 from 40 sites in the latter. In this respect south-east and Central Europe are more similar. This reflects the fact that many of the plants that grow in cereal fields originated in south-west Asia, while the process of transporting crops out of their original environment into new areas would have led to the loss of these weeds through successive founder effects generated by crop cleaning after the harvest and the lack of possibility of re-invasion (Kreuz et al., 2005). However, the nature of ground preparation could also have been relevant; continuous annual cropping, for example, is likely to lead to more of a decrease in perennial weeds than slash-and-burn farming (Bogaard, 2004a).

Traditionally, the main feature characterising the first farming communities of the Balkans and linking them to their Aegean and Anatolian ancestors has been their pottery, which has long provided the basis for defining the material culture patterns of the EN: the Starčevo Culture in Serbia and adjacent areas, the Kőrös Culture in Hungary, the Criş in Romania and the pre-Karanovo and Karanovo I in Bulgaria. Despite the local variations, for example in the frequency of painted pottery and the style of the painting, the pottery shows strong patterns of stylistic similarity linking the region from the southern Carpathian Basin in the north to Macedonia and Thrace in the south. As noted above, this is unsurprising given the rapidity of the initial spread, a maximum of eight human generations of 25 years, as we have seen, but there is some evidence for continuing interaction in the existence of some common stylistic trends across the broad region. There is also evidence of long-lasting common technical traditions in the choice of clays and the use of organic temper including cereal chaff, while similarities occur across the broad region in other elements; for example bone spoons, as well as symbolic items like female figurines and so-called altars (Spataro, 2010), also point to continuing interaction. Despite local variation in construction methods and size, houses are similar across the whole Anatolian, Aegean and Balkan area, all the way up to the Carpathian Basin (Brami, 2015), in that they are mainly square to rectangular structures based on a single central multi-purpose room, with evidence for cooking and storage. Many of the Balkan EN sites belonging to the regional pottery cultures are also linked together by the occurrence of high-quality 'Balkan flint' from a source probably in northern Bulgaria (Gurova and Bonsall, 2014).

In summary, just as there was a rapid spread of farming from central Anatolia and adjacent areas to western Anatolia and the northern Aegean, in less than 500 years, by 8500 BP, c.300–400 years later there was an equally rapid spread from the northern Aegean zone to north of the Danube in the period c.8200/8100–7900 BP (e.g. Weninger et al., 2014). This Balkan EN shows a set of common features in material culture, domestic plant and animal subsistence and domestic animal genetics that links it closely to the Aegean–Anatolian region and demonstrates continuing links well into the 8th millennium BP.

EXPLAINING THE EXPANSION

In the light of the Aegean–Anatolian and Balkan whole-genome ancient DNA results that we have seen, and all the other evidence, we can be confident that the expansion into the Balkans involved a dispersal of early farmers, with very limited admixture with local foragers except in one or two very specific places, unsurprising in view of their generally low population density. This followed the initial population expansion from south-central Anatolia into western Anatolia and the Aegean. Thus, Özdoğan was correct in seeing the expansion process as essentially a demographic one, but of a particular kind, 'an unorganized movement, more like an infiltration' (M. Özdoğan, 2010: 890), with small groups moving autonomously from different parts of the core area to different locations to the west, coming into contact with one another and exchanging cultural elements, thus accounting for the fact that 'the composition of Neolithic elements are [sic] a mishmash of diverse origins'. On the basis of the ceramic and faunal evidence there may have been two relatively distinct expansions from a broad core zone: one across continental Anatolia, and the other along the southern coast of Anatolia and through the Aegean islands to southern Greece. Expansion took place very quickly, with farming settlements at the western end of Anatolia and in northern Greece within at most 300–400 years.

The speed of expansion is not consistent with the gradual spread of farming population implied in the original version of the 'wave of advance' model for the spread of farming, but with the mechanism proposed by van Andel and Runnels (1995) for the Neolithic expansion in the Aegean, 'leapfrog colonisation', the founding of successive daughter settlements in one 'island' of suitable farming conditions after another. The results of leapfrog colonisation look much more like the patterns produced by the *Lévy walks* or *Lévy flights* discussed above, which seem to represent an optimal search method when knowledge of resource distributions is lacking. Advection, preferential movement in certain directions, may also have played a role, for example along the coast given the established maritime traditions.

Where colonising communities came into contact with indigenous groups they could have merged with them, though this would have been rare on the western Anatolian plateau, where hunter-gatherer populations were seemingly very sparse. In the Aegean they may have been denser, based on marine resources such as tuna fishing, and the occurrence of domestic crops and animals in the Initial Neolithic layer at Franchthi may be evidence of the adoption of farming by local forager groups. The new communities that were founded, in some cases no doubt with mixed origins, then became the basis for further expansion through 'leapfrog colonisation' or 'chain migration' (Anthony, 1997; M. Özdoğan, 2010).

There is no need to see these communities as refugees from climate change catastrophes, or from the collapse of Near Eastern/Anatolian mega-sites like Çatalhöyük. Even if a period of rapid climate change began in Anatolia c.8600 BP (Weninger et al., 2014) there is no evidence that it had a major disruptive effect at Çatalhöyük. On the contrary, as we saw in the previous chapter, the middle period at the site (defined as c.8560–8200 BP) was the period of maximum population growth (Larsen et al., 2015). In the following phase (c.8360–8100 BP) the site becomes smaller and the nature of the site organisation gradually changes to a more dispersed pattern, perhaps linked to increasing household autonomy (Marciniak et al., 2015), before the east mound is abandoned c.8000 BP, but by this time there are other sites in the Konya Plain and the occupation of Çatalhöyük West begins.

Of course, the Konya Plain was not the only source for the initial farming expansion to the west, but in the light of the evidence for population growth at Çatalhöyük in the first half of the 9th millennium BP, just when expansion was beginning, and also of the general theoretical considerations reviewed in Chapter 1, it seems most probable that we are seeing an expansion based on population increase, not on the movement of refugees from one region to another. This is reflected in the massive rise in the population of the northern half of Greece during the course of the Early Neolithic (Perlès, 2001). It resulted from the emergence by 9000 BP of an integrated farming system of crop agriculture and domestic animals, including dairying, that led to increased reproductive success. The increased household autonomy and dispersal we see in the later phases at Çatalhöyük may have been both a cause and effect of the spatial expansion since the new settlements do not match Çatalhöyük in size. For Bogaard and others (Bogaard, 2005; Bogaard and Isaakidou, 2010) this integrated farming system had specific features to which increased household autonomy was very relevant. It involved intensive small-scale cultivation with high labour inputs, on small permanent plots maintainable by individual households, made possible by the use of domestic animal dung as manure by grazing them on stubble areas. This implies fairly close control of animal movement, for which there is also other evidence, for example the collection of dung for fuel and the lack of introgression from wild populations in the cattle DNA (Scheu et al., 2015). In cultural evolutionary terms, this is a tightly bound package of subsistence, and no doubt other, practices that was under strong positive selection. With this agriculturally based population expansion went the spread not just of a few cultural elements but a village way of life that had originated in the core area, albeit with the loss of some of the more elaborate elements (M. Özdoğan, 2010, tables 1 and 2).

In other words, this demographic expansion was associated with a process of cultural descent with modification, as people carried their new beliefs, practices and environments with them and passed them on to their children. Some items and practices were lost as a result of cultural drift and successive founder effects in these small communities. The fact that they were small may again have been both cause and effect of the loss of these more elaborate elements. Perlès (2012) points out, for example, that, in contrast to the core area, in the Greek Early Neolithic there is no evidence of large cult buildings that might have been associated with central authority, and that this might have been one of the reasons why settlements outside the core were small, fissioning once they got to a certain size, with daughter settlements moving on to new opportunities. But, to reiterate a point made in the previous chapter, it is also possible to see this pattern in a more positive light than simply as an example of cultural loss. As we saw in the last chapter, it seems highly unlikely that the so-called mega-sites of the core area and central Anatolia, with their populations in the low thousands, were optimal from the point of the efficiency of farming; the reasons for their existence must have been social/cultural/religious rather than economic. The small settlement units that were characteristic of the spread westwards would have been better suited to farming efficiency. Equally, while loss of elaboration is one part of the story, no doubt the major one, innovation is also occurring, perhaps most visibly in the growing complexity and sophistication of the decorated ceramics.

However, as we have seen, the expansion was not a continuous one. After arriving in northern Greece and western Anatolia it was another 300–400 years before farming spread into the Balkans north of the Aegean, and again it was a rapid spread once it started, to the Danube and the southern side of the Carpathian Basin within a couple of hundred years; a corresponding massive population increase is visible in the central Balkans from c.8000 BP (Pilaar Birch and Vander Linden, 2017). This expansion northwards begins to take the domestic cereals to colder and wetter areas outside the environmental conditions to which their wild ancestors were naturally adapted and in this case it may well have been the colder and wetter conditions associated with the well-known 8.2 ka BP Rapid Climate Change event that created a barrier to the spread of farming beyond the Aegean zone until conditions changed (see e.g. Krauss et al., 2014), because farming and farmers spread north immediately thereafter.

CHAPTER 4

THE SPREAD OF FARMING INTO
CENTRAL EUROPE

As we saw in the previous chapter, after a pause of around 300–400 years at the northern edge of the Aegean farming spread rapidly through the Balkans from about 8200 BP, reaching the southern edge of the Carpathian Basin and southern Transylvania within 200 years. There the farming frontier stopped again. It was 400–500 years later that the expansion resumed, with the beginning of what is generally referred to by its German name as the *Linearbandkeramik* (LBK) Culture, after the characteristic bands of incised decoration on the pottery (Fig 4.1). It provides what has become the paradigmatic example of the archaeology of the first farmers in Europe, and has been the focus of many debates about the processes that led to the spread of farming. The main reason for this is its extensive and striking settlement record of large post-built longhouses (see Fig 4.2), which have been revealed in their thousands across Central Europe, from Hungary to the Paris Basin, in the post-war period as a result of large-scale open area rescue excavations in advance of open-cast mining, road-building and industrial developments. The Early Neolithic settlements of the southern Balkans, and later of south-east Europe as a whole, were characterised by the build-up of settlement layers derived from collapsed mud-brick and wattle-and-daub built houses. In contrast, in the environmental conditions of Central Europe there was no such accumulation of sediment as the result of settlement activity. On the contrary, in most places there has been significant erosion, so that all that have survived are the lower parts of pits and post-holes; houses with their floors intact, commonplace in the Balkans, are still virtually unknown despite the thousands that have been excavated. The lack of stratigraphy has led to the devotion of an enormous amount of effort to constructing chronologies of the sites by other means, especially through seriation of the ceramic assemblages preserved in the pits, so that many sites and regions have finer grained relative typo-chronologies than virtually any other period in prehistory. Absolute chronologies, on the other hand, have remained problematic, except in the broadest terms, because the resolution of radiocarbon dates over the period concerned is relatively

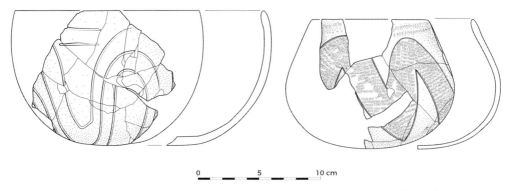

0   5   10 cm

Fig 4.1. Examples of earlier and later LBK pottery. Reproduced from plates 6.3 and 29.7 in *Die Bandkeramik im Merzbachtal auf der Aldenhovener Platte*, Boelicke et al., 1994, Habelt, Bonn, with permission from the publisher.

poor and archaeologists in some regions have been correspondingly reluctant to pay for them.

Recent work (see below) has shown that the LBK originated in Transdanubia, in present-day western Hungary, and adjacent parts of Austria, from the local late Starčevo Culture, which had developed as part of the north Balkan expansion that we saw in the last chapter. Beginning c.7600–7500 BP, by c.7300 BP it had spread westwards as far as the river Rhine, over 1000 km away, and northwards into north-central Poland, on the edge of the North European Plain. Less than 300 years later it had reached Normandy in the west, and the Ukraine, nearing the coast of the Black Sea, in the east (see Fig 4.3a for the LBK distribution, and Fig 4.3b for sites mentioned in this chapter). Across the whole area its archaeological record is remarkably uniform, not just in the architecture of the houses but also in the pottery, the crop-based agriculture and in soil preferences and settlement locations. The speed of its initial spread across such a large area of continental Europe has always seemed surprising, and this, combined with the distinctiveness of the LBK Culture and its marked difference from the Early Neolithic cultures of the Balkans, has provided the main basis for a long-standing debate on whether the expansion was the result of the rapid adoption of crops, animals and a farming way of life by local hunter-gatherers or the dispersal of immigrant farmers spreading from the south-east.

THE GENETIC EVIDENCE FOR THE MECHANISM OF LBK EXPANSION

As we saw in the last chapter, this debate is now being resolved in favour of the dispersal view as a result of the growing number of analyses of ancient DNA from human skeletons, initially from mtDNA but now increasingly using the huge amounts of information available in whole-genome data. In effect, over a remarkably short time, the ancient DNA evidence has become strong enough to provide the framework for the archaeology of the spread

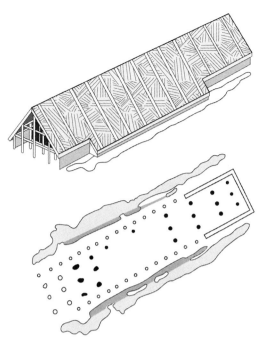

Fig 4.2. a) Plan and reconstruction of an LBK house. Reproduced with permission, from fig 46 in *Jahrbuch Römisch-Germanischen Zentralmuseums Mainz* 35, Lüning, J., Frühe Bauern in Mitteleuropa im 6. und 5. Jahrt. v. Chr., pp. 27–93, 1988.

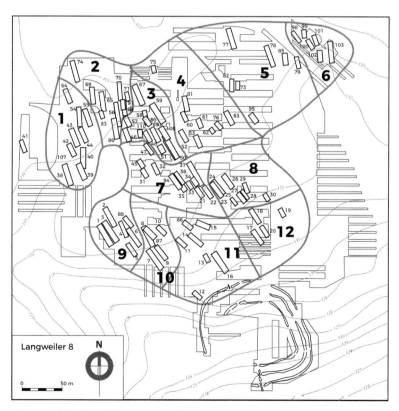

Fig 4.2. b) Plan of the Langweiler 8 LBK settlement in the Merzbach valley. Reproduced from *Die Bandkeramik im Merzbachtal auf der Aldenhovener Platte*, Boelicke et al., 1994, Habelt, Bonn, with permission from the publisher.

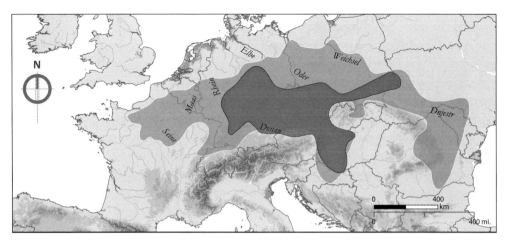

Fig 4.3. a) The distribution of the LBK. Reproduced, with permission, from fig 4 of *Jahrbuch Römisch-Germanischen Zentralmuseums Mainz* 35, Lüning, J., Frühe Bauern in Mitteleuropa im 6. und 5. Jahrt. v. Chr., pp. 27–93, 1988.

of farming in general, and the LBK in particular, rather than vice versa, so it is here that we need to start. In 2009 a comparison of ancient mtDNA samples from European Mesolithic human skeletons with samples from LBK bones (Bramanti et al., 2009) found that the two populations were strongly differentiated; there was a vanishingly small probability that the LBK farmers could be descended from the Mesolithic foragers. Subsequent analyses have only confirmed this.

We saw in the last chapter that the first farmers in the northern Balkans were overwhelmingly of Aegean–Anatolian ancestry. The LBK farmer genome data now available (Haak et al., 2015; Lipson et al., 2017) show the same pattern. In the LBK origin area of Transdanubia the average hunter-gatherer ancestry is only around 1%. Further west, in Germany, the corresponding figure is around 4%, with the additional hunter-gatherer admixture being acquired from individuals with genomes of the 'Western Hunter Gatherer' (WHG) group in Central Europe after c.7500 BP as the farming population expanded rapidly westwards.

In other words, the expansion of farming into the Carpathian Basin and then across Central Europe with the LBK was the result of a demographic expansion from the south-east and ultimately from the Aegean and Anatolia.

THE ARCHAEOLOGICAL RECORD OF FARMER–FORAGER INTERACTION

The recent genetics results have obvious implications for what we should expect archaeologically of the farming expansion into Central Europe. If the evidence points to very low levels of hunter–gatherer admixture then we

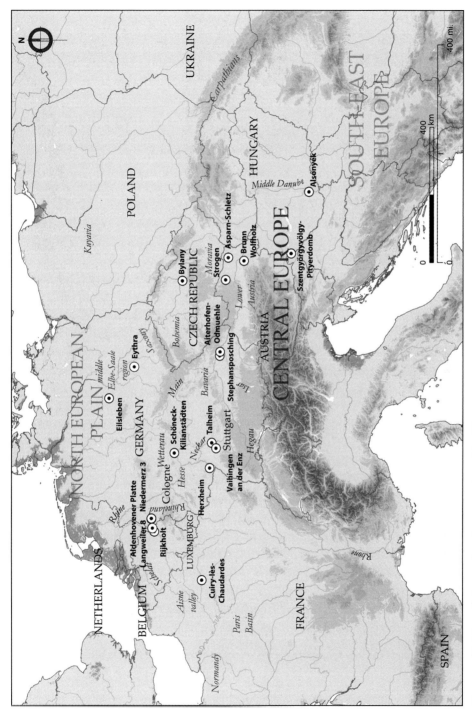

Fig 4.3. b) Map of sites and regions mentioned in Chapter 4.

should expect very little archaeological evidence of farmer–forager inter-action, whether because there were very few foragers present to interact with or because they kept separate from one another, or some combination of the two.

Just as in the case of the Balkans discussed in the last chapter, on eco-logical grounds we would expect Mesolithic population levels to have been very low away from riverine areas with rich aquatic resources because the oak-lime forest cover that had developed in lowland Central Europe in the course of the Early Holocene would only have supported low dens-ities of prey animals (e.g. Discamps, 2014). For the more easterly part of the LBK region a recent review of the evidence (Kaczanowska and Kozłowski, 2014) makes clear that there was very little Mesolithic settlement in the LBK origin area of western Hungary and the same is true of adjacent Lower Austria, where only three putatively Late Mesolithic sites are known. Importantly, the sites around the west Hungarian source of radiolarite, a high-quality lithic raw material widely exchanged among early LBK sites, are not Mesolithic, as has been claimed, thus the proposal that early farmer groups were interacting with local foragers to obtain the material must be rejected, an argument confirmed by the fact that there is no evidence of radiolarite use at the Late Mesolithic sites in Lower Austria. North of the Carpathians, in contrast, traces of Late Mesolithic occupation are exten-sive but they occur in areas of sandy soils, avoiding the loess, the fertile wind-blown sediments laid down during the Ice Age, preferred by the LBK. Despite the fact that these areas were intermixed, so that settlement was 'mosaic' in character, there are no indications of Mesolithic impacts on LBK lithics, but isolated finds of LBK polished tools such as adzes do occur in Mesolithic areas, though not in actual Mesolithic assemblages. A similar situation is found in the Saxony region of Germany: farmers and foragers co-existed in different soil/ecological zones but with little initial contact, which only developed later (Stäuble and Wolfram, 2013 and see below).

At the western end of the LBK distribution, a study of trends in Mesolithic occupation in the Low Countries, on the basis of the chronological and spa-tial distribution of microliths, found that those areas of the Low Countries that subsequently became LBK early farming nuclei had long been devoid of Mesolithic occupation (Vanmontfort, 2008). It appears that the loess areas settled by the incoming LBK farmers were marginal to already low-density Mesolithic populations. In general, the evidence for farmer–forager interaction during the LBK in the west is slight. In the Netherlands and Belgium, for example, there are no definite occurrences of Mesolithic artefacts on LBK sites, while at least the great majority of the LBK artefacts found outside the loess settlement areas do not have Mesolithic associ-ations, suggesting that they represent special-purpose LBK sites (Amkreutz and Vanmontfort, 2008); recent finds of LBK-associated Limburg pottery at sites in the marshland of the river Scheldt are equivocal in their significance though at least one site has produced definite evidence of farmer–forager contact (Crombé et al., 2015). The earliest LBK settlements in Germany east of the Rhine and then in the Rhineland itself obtained much of their flint from the Rijkholt source in the Netherlands, outside the LBK settlement area at this time, so it is assumed that this implies contact with local hunter-gatherers, but the evidence in terms of finds in LBK settlements is slight. As in the eastern part of the LBK area, it is not until much later that there is stronger evidence of contact. Whether the lithic technologies of the western LBK were influenced by the local Mesolithic population remains a matter of debate, with strong arguments made both for and against (e.g. Löhr, 1994; Robinson et al., 2013).

The strongest evidence for interaction of some sort comes from the presence of a specific, distinctive type of pottery, the La Hoguette type, found both on early (but not the earliest) LBK sites in south-west Germany and also by itself on a number of sites in the Rhône valley and further west, as far as Normandy. From a detailed analysis of the technology and decoration of a find of La Hoguette pottery that indicates a very high level of skill and from a consideration of its regional context, Pétrequin and colleagues (2009) conclude that it represents the expansion of a group from the south that had acquired pottery, crops and farming skills from the early colonising farmers who first settled on the coast of southern France early in the 8th millennium BP (see Chapter 5). The occurrence of sherds on LBK sites presumably indicates exchange and there are parallels between the distribution of La Hoguette pottery and of *Columbella* shells that were arriving in the Upper Rhine area during the Mesolithic. The other very distinctive pottery tradition found on LBK sites in the north-west part of the LBK distribution, which has also been regarded as indicative of non-LBK pottery traditions and forager–farmer interaction, is Limburg pottery. However, a recent detailed technical study sees it as probably a special-purpose variety of LBK ware (Gomart, 2014), and it has no closed associations with Mesolithic flint (Amkreutz et al., 2010).

In summary, hunter-gatherer populations in the loess areas of Central Europe favoured by the LBK farmers existed at very low densities and had little to do with the expanding farming groups. In fact, as we will see, the distribution of the first farmers was restricted to certain extremely specific environments that were very limited in extent. Outside these areas hunter-gatherers must have continued to exist but are largely archaeologically invisible. It was only when farming and farmers expanded their distribution in the late 7th millennium BP that interaction on a larger scale occurred (see Chapter 6).

LBK ORIGINS

While the Neolithic across the Balkans and the Aegean is generally agreed to have considerable similarities in terms of material culture, the LBK is different and represents much more of a break from the material culture of its south-east European ancestors. In the past that could be ascribed to the impact of local Mesolithic groups. Now that the genetic evidence has made this argument untenable it needs to be seen in a different light.

As noted already, the LBK seems to have originated in Transdanubia, western Hungary, and adjacent areas of Austria. Work in recent years has shown that Starčevo occupation reached here, the north-west limit of its distribution, c.7800 BP (Bánffy et al., 2016) and on its northern fringes the sites of Brunn/Wolfholz on the outskirts of Vienna (Stadler, 2005) and Szentgyörgyvölgy-Pityerdomb (Bánffy, 2004) in the Lake Balaton area seem to represent formative sites of the LBK, overlapping with the local late Starčevo, c.7500 BP. However, recent formal modelling suggests that the rapid LBK expansion did not begin until the 74th century BP (Bánffy et al., 2016; Jakucs et al., 2016), implying that it was even faster than previously thought. The site of Alsónyék in southern Transdanubia, just outside the formative area, has a Starčevo occupation beginning just after 7800 BP and continuing until c.7500 BP. It is then abandoned and a new settlement lasting over 300 years is founded on the same site c.7300 BP by people using early (but not formative) LBK pottery and building LBK longhouses.

As with the other standstills in farming expansion, the reasons in the Starčevo-LBK case remain unclear. One reason might be a need for cereal crops to adapt genetically to more northerly temperate environments but the only work carried out so far, on barley, suggests that the spread of a variety with a mutation that switched off the sensitivity of the plant to increasing day length was later than the initial spread of farming (Jones et al., 2013). Work on emmer and einkorn wheat, much the most important LBK crops, remains to be carried out, but it may be that the standstill is connected to the major cultural reformulation that the LBK represents, for example the development of the characteristic LBK longhouse, which may have been associated with new patterns of kinship and residence.

It is proposed here that the origin of the LBK should be seen as an example of the cultural equivalent of 'peripatric speciation' (Mayr, 1954; Rosenberg, 1994). This occurs when a small population on the edge of a larger one becomes isolated from it. The formation of new cultural patterns such as that which characterises the LBK is more likely to occur in small groups physically separated to some degree from their parent population, for a variety of reasons; the sanctions that help to maintain the existing pattern may be weaker, for example, allowing social innovations. Moreover, the new pattern that emerges is likely to have a considerable chance element to it, especially founder effects, in that a small peripheral sub-population will not contain all the elements of the parent population, or even necessarily a representative sample, while innovations may be idiosyncratic. These founder effects will be further enhanced by the chance vicissitudes arising from transmission in small populations. Such patterns may be particularly prevalent in the context of migration. If we think of this in terms of the tempo and mode of evolution, the tempo on such occasions is fast, corresponding to punctuated rather than gradual change, while the mode is the creation of a new branch of the evolutionary tree, 'phylogenesis' in the jargon, or evolutionary diversification. This represents a very significant difference from the spread of farming into the Balkans; the latter does not represent a cultural 'speciation' but a gradual development ('anagenesis'), through innovation, adaptation and no doubt some drift, from its Aegean and Anatolian ancestors.

What evidence do we have for such a mechanism in this case? If founder effects and drift are occurring then they should also be visible in the genetics of the human population. Comparison of the Aegean and Anatolian Early Neolithic genomes described in the last chapter with those from Central Europe indeed produced evidence of founder effects in samples from Hungary and Germany (Hofmanová et al., 2016). Similar evidence of founder effects is seen in a marked reduction in the mtDNA genetic diversity of cattle associated with the LBK, especially the more westerly samples, compared with south-east Europe, and in high levels of genetic distance from regions to the south-east closer to the location of initial cattle domestication (Scheu et al., 2015).

A loss of diversity is also seen in the crops found in the archaeobotanical assemblages from LBK sites compared with south-east Europe. The suggestion that this might arise as a result of drift and founder effect was explored by Conolly et al. (2008, following Colledge et al., 2005). They first of all excluded crops that might have been deliberately dropped through selection owing to the changing climatic and growing conditions as farming expanded to the north, such as lentil and chickpea. In fact, even when sensitive crops and a number of rare species were excluded, there was still a statistically significant loss of diversity in the LBK compared with the Balkans, which might be accounted for by drift and founder effect. In the event the actual reduction in diversity with the LBK was much greater than that produced by the drift models constructed by Conolly et al. so they rejected the hypothesis, suggesting instead that, in addition to the selective factors leading to the dropping of environmentally sensitive crops like chickpea, there was a cultural preference for the glume wheats, emmer and einkorn, the only two cereals present in a majority of LBK sites. However, Pérez-Losada and Fort (2011) were able to show that if you introduce a spatial dimension to the simulation and consider only the small number of pioneering settlements at the expansion front, then the observed reduction in diversity is indeed achieved, so it may be that no further process is needed to account for it after all.

The basis for this is the phenomenon known as 'surfing on the wave of advance', a process, like the wave of advance itself, first described for the genetics of species range expansions (Edmonds et al., 2004; Excoffier and Ray, 2008). It results in a loss of genetic diversity in spatially expanding populations because the few individuals at the front of the wave are likely to be the most successful; the same will be true of their offspring. As a result, 'the pioneer genotypes are continually transmitted forward and surf along with the wave' (Lehe et al., 2012: 1). The more likely it is that a mutation close to the wave front becomes fixed, i.e. becomes the only one present, the more likely it is that it will then dominate the gene pool when the expansion finishes, and the greater the loss of genetic diversity. The argument is that the same applies to cultural innovations: those that occur at the front of the wave are likely to become predominant and, because the numbers at the wave front are small, chance will play an important role in determining which ones prevail. This is relevant to the loss of LBK diversity not just in subsistence and the genetics of the human population but in other domains as well. The pottery is extremely uniform across the broad area of the earliest LBK (Cladders, 2001), and far less diverse than its Balkan ancestors, and it is only in the middle and late LBK that this changes. But there is more going on here than just drift. The lack of innovation in the LBK has often been pointed out (e.g. Sommer, 2001) and is at least as apparent in the longevity of the striking architecture of the longhouses (Coudart, 1998) and in the choice of site locations (see below) as in the crops and pottery already mentioned. The close connection now demonstrated between the genetic and cultural patterns suggests why, because it indicates a pattern of strongly vertical cultural transmission from parents to children. This is inherently conservative because it leaves little scope for the adoption of innovations from outside the local group that challenge existing practices. The result is strong path dependence: once a set of knowledge and practices has become established it defines the range of options that can be envisaged in the future.

The picture we have then is of a group of communities with a common origin that as a result of initial innovation and drift, on the borders of the Balkan Early *Neolithic koiné,* developed a novel way of life which turned out to be extremely successful as an adaptation and then became fixed in an extremely conservative formula for their economic and cultural activities. This combined with a strongly expansionist ethos that led them in many cases to make the risky decision to move long distances in search of somewhere suitable to settle. Promising dispersal opportunities are chances for increased successful fertility and if others are already taking advantage of them it makes no sense to postpone reproduction.

THE SPEED OF THE LBK SPREAD

Although the speed of the LBK expansion has always attracted attention, it should be clear from what we have seen of the spread of farming into western

Anatolia, the Aegean and the Balkans that it is not so exceptional. In all these cases when expansion occurred it was rapid, following the 'leapfrog' or Lévy flight pattern, but was then followed by a pause of several hundred years. The LBK is one more example. Studies have clearly shown that the earliest LBK was thinly distributed over a zone from Hungary to western Germany (see e.g. Lenneis, 2008: fig 1), including areas that were much more densely settled later in the LBK, and the same is true of the LBK expansion further west, in northern France (Dubouloz, 2012). In other words, here, as in the Aegean and the Balkans, people were moving on from one area to the next long before those areas had reached the occupation density that the LBK agricultural system was later capable of supporting; in all these cases there was an initial phase of long-distance dispersal, followed by short-distance infilling. This may have had negative consequences in some cases through 'Allee effects', as discussed in the previous chapter. In fact, this may be the reason that relatively few of the very earliest LBK sites continue into later phases and that there was to some degree a 'recolonisation' later in the LBK at much greater densities (Cladders and Stäuble, 2003); the earliest settlements, especially those far away from the founding zone, were often failures.

In the case of the LBK the speed of the spread would have been increased by advection – preferential movement in the direction that gave colonisers the best returns – in this case given by its focus on a spatially rather narrow band of suitable micro-environments, the loess soil areas already mentioned, together with a narrow range of temperature and precipitation conditions. The soils that form on loess are extremely fertile because their high proportion of silt particles provides both good water availability and aeration as well as easy plant root penetration and cultivation; they are also rich in potassium and nitrogen. Field experiments have demonstrated that there is a much smaller yield difference between unfertilised and well-fertilised fields on deep loess soils than on soils on other surface geologies, especially in drier conditions (Catt, 2001).

Zimmermann's (2009b) detailed spatial analysis of the LBK in the Lower Rhine Basin shows that sites were concentrated in small patches that were relatively densely occupied at the time of the LBK population peak. Thus, in this area where soils classified as suitable for early farming made up 11.6% of the land area, settlement was largely concentrated in 3.8%, only a third of the suitable area. Most of the difference can be accounted for by the fact that LBK settlement seems to have been further restricted to areas with annual precipitation of less than 800 mm, but even so it is clear that there were suitable areas west of the Rhine where, at the height of LBK occupation, settlement does not occur. Further east, the same environmental restrictions on the LBK distribution, in terms of loess soils, annual rainfall between 500–800 mm and annual mean temperature no lower than 7 8°C, have also been demonstrated for Austria by Lenneis (e.g. 2008), though here too there seem to have been suitable areas that were never occupied. It is clear then that LBK pioneer farmers were extremely particular about where they settled. This is illustrated

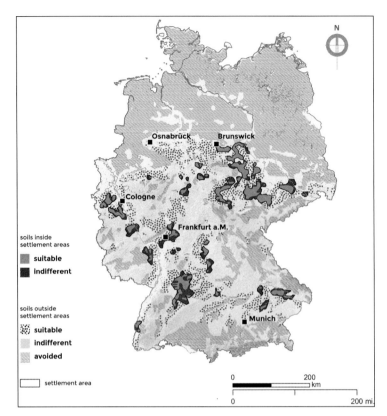

Fig 4.4. Map of the distribution of LBK settlement in Germany. Reproduced from fig 4 in *Proceedings of the Prehistoric Society* 75, Zimmermann, A. et al., Landscape Archaeology in Central Europe, pp. 1–53, 2009, Cambridge University Press.

clearly by Fig 4.4, which shows the spatially limited nature of LBK occupation at the scale of Germany as a whole. Moreover, those preferences seem to have changed little over the course of the LBK, again pointing to the conservatism of the agricultural system. The one exception to this pattern are the LBK communities found on the non-loess soils of the North European Plain along the lower Vistula and lower Oder in Poland, which might be argued to have 'overshot' the best areas in the long-distance search for new areas to colonise, rather than filling in the prime habitats to the south (Bogucki et al., 2012).

The rich archaeological record of the LBK and its long history of research make it possible to explore the processes involved in the expansion in more detail than the regions examined in Chapter 3. Extensive data is now available on LBK demography, both at broader and more local scales, and they confirm one another. On the basis of studies of the number, size, and density of settlements across a number of different regions, Petrasch (2001, 2010) calculated extremely high population growth rates, between 0.9% and 2.7% per year, for the LBK. Zimmermann et al. (2004: fig 15, table 6) estimate that there would have been about 15,000 LBK households in western Central Europe in the 71st century BP, a population of 100,000 or more on the basis of the usual estimates of the number of people per house. This implies an annual growth rate of c.2.4% given that the LBK had started expanding 300 years earlier. Regional population patterns inferred from summed radiocarbon probabilities (Shennan et al., 2013; Timpson et al., 2014) (see Fig 4.5) also show significant increases. In all cases the population grows rapidly before reaching a peak and then declining at the end of the LBK in three of the four regions shown (see below).

In the LBK case these broad regional patterns are repeated at the micro-scale where detailed work has been carried out. In the Lower Rhine Basin, an area to the west of Cologne in Germany where there has been large-scale excavation in advance of strip-mining for brown coal, we see population grow to a peak after 200 years, followed by a dip and then a rise to a slightly higher peak followed by decline and abandonment 100 years later (Zimmermann et al., 2009a: fig 6) (see Fig 4.6). A detailed study of all the site records from a small region of Moravia in the eastern Czech Republic, albeit with less temporal resolution, shows a very similar picture (Kolář et al., 2016), while Dubouloz (2012, 2008) comes to the same conclusions about demographic patterns in the western LBK.

LBK ECONOMIC AND SOCIAL ORGANISATION

In terms of domestic animals the LBK does not differ markedly from its north Balkan ancestors though cattle and pig tend to be more frequent and caprines less so, but there are time trends within the LBK variation (Manning et al., 2013a), for example, a tendency for there to be higher proportions of domestic pig at the end of the LBK while cattle dominate in the preceding phase. More striking is the trend in the exploitation of terrestrial wild animals, which is highest in the earliest LBK and then declines. In the past this would have been seen in terms of 'Mesolithic influence' but in the light of the genetics this is no longer tenable. In fact, the early sites with high proportions of wild species are all in southern Germany, where uplands with wild animals are closer to agricultural areas, and this pattern continues there through the next phases, so it is probably linked to source-sink ecological dynamics: there was a reservoir of game populations that continued to fill the vacancies created by hunting. In contrast, the evidence for the exploitation of terrestrial wild species in the Polish LBK is negligible (Marciniak, 2013). There is relatively little information on the age-at-death distribution of the faunal assemblages and its relation to different strategies for animal keeping, though what there is does not support a specialised dairying pattern (Fraser et al., 2013); however, the occurrence of specialised ceramic sieve vessels with residues confirming that they were used for cheese-making is indicative that milking was important, most probably of cattle (Salque et al., 2013). Moreover, there is every reason to believe from what we know ethnographically that cattle were slaughtered for community events

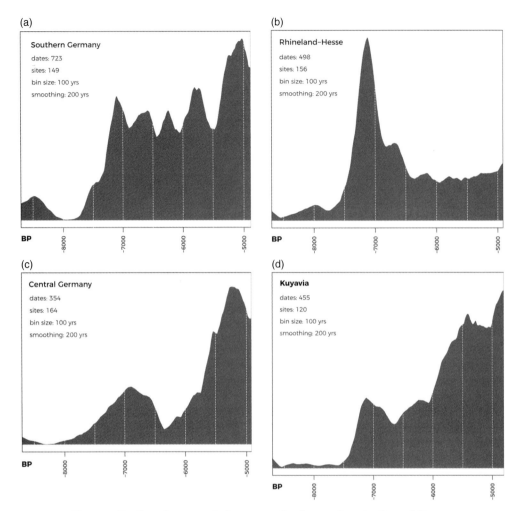

Fig 4.5. Radiocarbon population proxy for four regions in Central Europe:
a) Southern Germany; b) Rhineland and Hesse; c) Central Germany; d) Kuyavia.
a), c) and d) Data from EUROEVOL project; b) Data from EUROEVOL project
updated by Professor A. Bevan.

such as feasts rather than to provide a daily meat ration, for which milk is likely
to have been much more important. Both cattle and pigs seem to have been
carefully controlled; no doubt the same is true of sheep and goats. In the case
of cattle and pigs this is indicated by the lack of mitochondrial evidence for
introgression of local aurochs genes into the domestic cattle and the evidence
that the domestic pigs from the LBK site of Eilsleben in Germany continued
to be of the Anatolian/Near Eastern mtDNA haplotype, which is not present in pre-Neolithic wild pigs in Central Europe (Larson et al., 2007; Ottoni
et al., 2012). However, new still unpublished genomic data, which contains
much more information than mtDNA, is now suggesting that some introgression with local aurochs, even if minimal, did occur and that, despite the

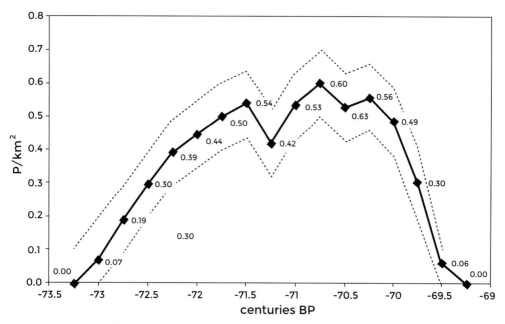

Fig 4.6. LBK population density in the Lower Rhine Basin. Reproduced from fig 6 in *Human Biology: The International Journal of Population Genetics and Anthropology* 81(2–3), Zimmermann, A. et al., Estimations of Population Density for Selected Periods Between the Neolithic and AD 1800, pp. 357–380. Copyright © 2009 Wayne State University Press. With permission from Wayne State University Press.

Eilsleben finding, Anatolian pig lineages were already beginning to be replaced by European ones during the Balkan earlier Neolithic (Burger, pers. comm.). In any case, subsequently Near Eastern pig lineages died out completely and were replaced by European ones.

We have already seen that the LBK crop agriculture system represented a significant decrease in diversity in comparison with the Balkans, with the majority of sites including only two cereals: emmer and einkorn. Peas are also widely found, as well as flax, while opium poppy occurs on later LBK sites, though whether as a local domestication in the north-western LBK or as an import from the west Mediterranean is currently unclear (Salavert, 2011). Now, however, we need to look more closely at how the agricultural system functioned. Early LBK studies, such as those of Soudsky at the famous Czech site of Bylany, postulated that its subsistence was based on slash-and-burn farming, with frequent movement of the settlements, one way to account for the rapid spread. However, on the basis of a functional ecological analysis of the weed species found in the archaeobotanical assemblages at LBK sites, indicating a lack of the perennial weeds that would be expected in newly cleared ground and a dominance of annual species, Bogaard (2004b) argued that they indicated long-term cultivation of the same sites, resembling small-scale 'garden' agriculture, a continuation of the system that we have already seen postulated for Anatolia, the Aegean and the Balkans. This argument was later further supported by stable isotope analyses of carbonised seed remains from LBK settlements, which showed increased nitrogen isotope values, indicative of an enhancement of soil nitrogen, implying the addition of manure to maintain fertility (Bogaard et al., 2013); this would be in keeping with the evidence just mentioned that cattle and pigs were closely controlled. At the site of Vaihingen, south-west Germany, for example, the $\delta^{15}N$ nitrogen values were higher than those inferred for herbivore forage and imply an application of 10–15 tons/hectare of manure on the basis of comparison with experimental cereal-growing plots. Manuring at this rate would have been intensive in terms of labour requirements but also in its land use, in its high inputs to a small area. In any case, as we have seen, loess soils are capable of maintaining moderate cereal yields even without the addition of fertiliser (Catt, 2001). The argument that the cultivated areas were small is strengthened by the remarkably low impact of the archaeologically highly visible LBK in local pollen diagrams, where indicators of forest clearance and crop cultivation are generally slight (see e.g. Bogucki et al., 2012; Lechterbeck et al., 2014), though see Kreuz (2012: 70) for evidence of clearance in pollen spectra). This does not mean that the rest of the landscape was unused, however. Isotope studies have shown that least in some cases cattle were moved seasonally to non-loess areas, even if those were not very far away (Knipper, 2011).

On the basis of assumptions about daily calorific needs and the yield of a hectare of land, Kreuz (2012: 124) calculates that for the daily nutrition of a community of 20 people for a year it would only have been necessary to use c.10 ha, 3% of the available land within a kilometre radius of the settlement, for growing crops, so it is clear that even if her yield estimates are considerably exaggerated large numbers of people could easily be supported. On the basis of figures calculated by Russell (1988) for the time taken to produce a kilo of cereal per person per day, from preparing the field by hand to grinding the grain, it would have taken about 25% of the available annual labour time.

At least as important as the basic framework of subsistence, however, is how it was organised, both in economic and social terms. The most sustained attempts to address such topics have been focussed on the site of Vaihingen just mentioned (Bogaard et al., 2011). This was founded during the earliest LBK and its occupation continued for c.450 years, through to the late LBK, during which several phases can be distinguished. It is believed that at its height, in the earlier LBK Flomborn phase, there were 40–50 longhouses, corresponding to 300–400 people on the most widely used estimate of the average number of people who would have occupied a house, dropping to 15–18 houses at the transition to the middle LBK. From an analysis of the characteristics of the archaeobotanical assemblages and their distribution in relation to the different houses it has been claimed that in the earlier periods of occupation different house groups had differential access to specific cultivated areas over generations, and that one group in particular had access to the best plots, those on loess-based soils nearest to the village. This would certainly fit with the practice of intensive garden cultivation and the labour investment in plots of land that this implies, but the specific claims depend on the disputed identification of different parts of the village as associated with different 'clans', while an attempt to find a similar pattern at Langweiler 8, the dominant settlement in the Merzbachtal cluster in the Lower Rhine area was unsuccessful (Zimmermann, pers. comm.).

Nevertheless, claims of inequality fit in with inferences that can be made from strontium isotope studies of teeth from human skeletons to identify patterns of mobility. They point to a widely occurring pattern of greater variability among females than males, resulting from the fact that many more females were non-local, i.e. they did not pass their early lives in the place where they were buried (Bentley et al., 2012). The authors see this as pointing to patri-local residence patterns, where women moved on marriage to the residence of their husband's family. The pattern often occurs where there are kin group property rights, such as land rights, that are inherited through the paternal line. Males buried with distinctive stone adzes, made of material obtained by long-distance exchange, also had more uniform isotope signatures than those without from the same site, with values corresponding to those for loess soils, pointing to inequality among males.

POPULATION ECOLOGY OF THE LBK EXPANSION

To gain more insight into the processes that produced these patterns we need to return to the broader scale of the LBK expansion. As we have seen, it was an overwhelmingly demic one similar in its pattern to that which brought farming to the northern Aegean and then to the Middle Danube; long-distance movements took place leading to the colonisation of new places long before existing settlement areas reached densities anywhere near the carrying capacity of the Early Neolithic farming system. Generic reasons have been suggested for the pattern, for example that Lévy flights represent an efficient search procedure in situations of uncertainty, but the detailed data on the history of LBK settlements makes it possible to look at relevant considerations in more detail.

As outlined by Shennan (2008), the basis for understanding the characteristics of the LBK expansion is provided by principles derived from natural selection thinking as they relate to decision-making concerning spatial behaviour (Sutherland, 1996; Winterhalder and Kennett, 2006: 16). These principles predict the distribution of individuals in relation to resources on the basis of the 'ideal-free distribution'. When individuals (of any species) seeking to maximise their probability of survival and reproductive success move into a new area they will occupy the resource patch which gives them the best returns. As more individuals occupy the patch the returns to each individual decline, to the point that the returns to an individual from the best patch are no better

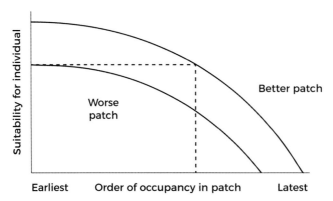

Fig 4.7. The ideal despotic distribution. Reproduced from fig 1.5 in Sutherland, W.J., *From Individual Behaviour to Population Ecology*, 1996, Oxford University Press, with permission from the publisher.

than those from the next best patch, which at this point has no occupants. Now the returns from both patches are equal and they will be occupied indiscriminately until such time as the population grows to the point at which there is an equal benefit to be gained by occupying a still worse patch, and the process is repeated, with the relative quality of the patches being reflected in their different population densities.

When there is territoriality, however, the situation is different. Here the so-called 'ideal despotic distribution' applies (Fig 4.7). The first individual occupying an area is able to select the best territory in the best patch. Subsequent individuals settling there do not affect the first arrival, but have to take the next best territory, and so on, until there comes a point where the next settler will do just as well by taking the best territory in the next best patch. Subsequent individuals will then take territories in either patch where the territories are equally suitable. In contrast to the ideal-free distribution, where interference competition from new settlers decreases the mean return for everybody, including those who arrived first, in the case of the ideal despotic distribution the returns depend on the order of settlement, so that the initial settlers of the best territory in the patch will do best, so long as they can defend the territory against anyone who might seek to take it from them.

In the case of the spread of farming into Europe, the new households being formed as population expanded would have been evaluating the costs and benefits of staying near their parents' household or finding somewhere else, following the principles of the ideal despotic distribution. In principle, all that would have been required for further spatial expansion is a shift in the balance of costs and benefits between accepting the next best local territory available and taking the risk of finding and settling a new top quality patch some distance away, allowing for the fact that to be the very first occupant of a more distant patch might have disadvantages, as we have already seen. In fact, we need to qualify this somewhat. While there are settlements in which the earliest phase consists of a single house (e.g. Strogen, Lenneis, 2008), in the case where it was the first settlement in a local region it generally consisted of several houses; for example, at Langweiler 8 in the Rhineland there were four (Zimmermann, 2002), at Stephansposching in Bavaria it was between two and six (Pechtl, 2012). This would have mitigated the risks of isolation.

In the light of these population ecology principles, it seems likely that in the case of the LBK there was a massive advantage in being the founding settlement in a high-quality area, so that the groups breaking away as settlements grew and fissioned were always competing for this role. Thus, Kerig (2008) was able to demonstrate that LBK settlement in Hesse in western Germany followed the principles of the ideal despotic distribution, with the best territories occupied first, while in the Aisne valley in northern France, at the western end of the LBK distribution, long-lasting settlements were located in places with higher proportions of land suitable for cereal agriculture than short-lived ones (Dubouloz, 2012). On this basis we expect the founding settlement in a particular area to be the dominant one and this is generally what we find. Vaihingen, already described, is one example and in fact has no local 'offspring' settlements. Another is Langweiler 8, just mentioned, the first settlement founded in the valley of the Merzbach stream, which was occupied throughout the c.400 years of the local LBK sequence and was always the largest (Boelicke et al., 1994). Even if its location was only one of the best available in the region from the farming point of view, it would have had founder advantage in terms of control of local territory, and its leading position is also suggested by the fact that it seems to have acted as a redistribution centre for lithic resources. These were obtained from the major source of high-quality flint at Rijkholt, some distance away to the west, either as a result of controlling exchange relations with local foragers beyond the agricultural frontier or through direct access to the source (Zimmermann, 2002). Moreover, it was at Langweiler 8 that a ditched enclosure of possible ritual significance was constructed in the latest local phases of LBK occupation, a subject to which we will return.

Bell and Winterhalder (2014) have shown that despotic conditions can slow down rather than increase the rate of migration by increasing the time required for the despotic habitat to reach carrying capacity, the opposite of what is argued here, but their model assumes that it is only subordinates, as opposed to dominants, that would want to move. In the LBK context, with its patrilocal residence system and probable patrilineal inheritance, there is no reason why it should not have been younger sons of successful founding lineages who led fissioning community segments, rather than subordinates whose wealth and reproduction had been restricted, as in the case of European aristocracies whose primogeniture rules led to more risky but potentially lucrative careers for younger sons, often in distant colonies. In studies of known recent settlement fissioning, disputes and conflicts of various kinds have been the motive (Walker and Hill, 2014). However, the small number of houses at the earliest sites in different regions seems to indicate that their populations were well below the 100–200 associated with significantly increased levels of scalar stress (Alberti, 2014), though this certainly changed in the course of the LBK. In the expansionary context described here there may simply have been a socio-cultural expectation of moving on and establishing founder advantage.

Initially then there was rapid settlement fission associated with founding new settlement nuclei in new regions, quite possibly involving 'leapfrog' migration in the sense described by Sahlins (1961), citing Bohannan (1954) for the Tiv in Nigeria, with groups from within the already established LBK area moving out beyond the frontier – this is suggested by the long-distance connections of some early sites (Schade-Lindig and Schade, 2010). Then there was local infilling, with founding settlements increasing in size and small, local daughter settlements being established; this is seen, for example on the Aldenhovener Platte in the western Rhineland (Zimmermann, 2002) but also in the Wetterau region north of Frankfurt (Schade, 2004). Relatively rapidly though, as a result of this infilling, the individual micro-regions began to fill up and reach a ceiling. The empirical existence of these ceilings is visible in the demographic proxy data discussed above but what produced the limits on equilibrium population is unclear. As we have seen earlier, Zimmermann has argued that, even allowing for the very restrictive soil and climate conditions required for LBK agriculture, there would still have been more than enough land available for the small-scale intensive agriculture that was most probably practised, but ensuring the availability of fodder for cattle would have required very large territories. Schmidt et al. (2004) have suggested that fluctuations in the total number of houses once an initial ceiling had been reached, as on the Aldenhovener Platte, were affected by local climatic patterns, with slight rises indicating more favourable conditions and declines pointing to downturns. Such sensitivity would suggest that local populations did indeed near the carrying capacity sustainable by the LBK subsistence system during the later LBK when long-distance expansion had ceased.

It is likely that the local growth in population would have led to increased inequality between different communities if the 'ideal despotic' principle prevailed. Potentially too it would have increased competition between those communities, although founder settlements would have retained an advantage in any such competition; in the Rhineland, for example, Langweiler 8 was always the largest settlement in its area. The evidence for increasing inequality comes from settlements as well as cemeteries. For the settlement evidence the case was made by van der Velde (1990), on the basis of sites in the south-eastern Netherlands and the Aldenhovener Platte discussed above. LBK houses seem to be made up of three modules: a north-west, central and south-eastern part, each with different functions. Some houses only have the central part, presumed to be the main living area, some a central and north-west element, and others have all three parts; the south-eastern part, believed to be the front, is generally argued to have included a granary. Van der Velde proposed that the distinctions between houses with larger and smaller numbers of elements relate to the wealth and status of their associated households and cannot be explained by changing household composition arising from family life-cycles. At the Dutch sites the houses with all three elements had more room than the others (the individual house elements were larger) and more stone adzes were associated with them. At the site of Langweiler 8 cereal-processing waste was preferentially associated with the large houses (Bogaard, 2004b). On the basis of a spatial analysis of the settlements he studied, van der Velde also showed that the units of which the settlements were made up suggest the existence of long-term social patterns: particular households and groups of households seem to have persisted through time, with continuing inheritance of status witnessed by the rebuilding of houses of the same type in the same places. Coudart's (1998) analysis of LBK houses led her to conclude that major rank or wealth differentiation did not exist but she too points to some indications of status differences. She notes, for example, that granaries were never associated with small houses and that some buildings were more spacious than others. Interestingly, she also suggests that perhaps the largest houses were associated with the groups that had first established the settlement.

A recent analysis of the late LBK (c.7050–6900 BP) site of Cuiry-lès-Chaudardes in the Aisne valley of northern France (Gomart et al., 2015) identifies two groups of houses that existed throughout the duration of the occupation. One group was characterised by large houses, which showed a dominance of stock-keeping and cereal-grinding evidence and homogeneous and conservative pottery-making traditions. The other group was made up of small houses, with more evidence of hunting and craft activities and a greater diversity of pottery-making techniques. The first is argued to represent houses showing 'continuity and strong produc-tion capacity with possible surplus' that were occupied by long-established fam-ilies and the second a 'process of integration and economic maturation' (Gomart et al., 2015: 244 and fig 9), houses occupied by small newly established families, including some belonging to newcomers. On the basis of what we have seen for the LBK more generally, it seems probable that the pattern represents a contrast between founding families with superior wealth and status and late comers with diminished wealth and property rights.

As far as burials are concerned, it is clear that there were complex patterns of spatial differentiation involving both burial within settlements and also the exist-ence of separate cemeteries, mainly of individual inhumations, which are very rare in the earliest LBK phases. Jeunesse (1997) concludes that the earliest ones present a picture of relatively egalitarian societies, with indications of achieved status for older men, while the later ones tend to have a small group of graves, including child burials, clearly distinguished from the rest by the presence of markedly richer grave goods and possible symbols of power. This is the case, for example, with the cemetery of Niedermerz 3 that belonged to the settlements of the Merzbachtal on the Aldenhovener Platte and was established in the 72nd century BP. Cemeteries would have come into existence for precisely the reasons proposed in the long-standing Saxe-Goldstein model (Saxe, 1970; Goldstein, 1981; Morris, 1991): to represent an ancestral claim to territory in the face of increasing competition as local carrying capacities began to be reached.

Similar processes to those seen in the western LBK can also be seen in Lower Bavaria, along the Danube, where it is joined by the river Isar and other tributaries (Pechtl, 2012). The major site of Stephansposching rapidly grew eight-fold from the founding two to six houses. Here too there are persistent rebuildings of houses on the same sites showing the importance of maintaining the continuity of the household and its rights, Pechtl suggests. Given that the lives of the houses seem to have been much shorter than would have been necessary from the structural point of view, new houses may have been built with each new generation, as a new household head replaced his predecessor. What is particularly interesting in this region though is the evidence for the settlement pattern (see Fig 4.8). On the edge of the plain here

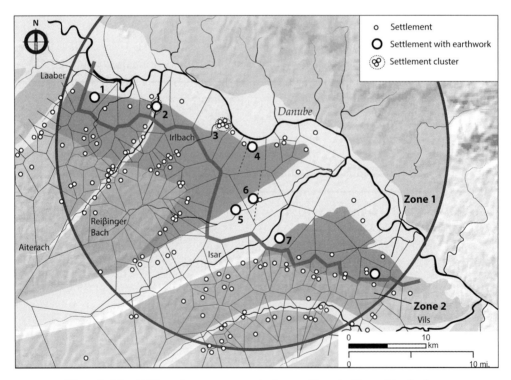

Fig 4.8. The LBK settlement pattern in Lower Bavaria. Site 2 Aiterhofen; 4 Stephansposching. Reproduced from fig 5 in Pechtl, J., Stephansposching, Lkr. Deggendorf, und die Linienbandkeramik des Isarmündungsgebietes. In Wolfram, S. and Stäuble, H. (Eds.), *Siedlungsstruktur und Kulturwandel in der Bandkeramik*, pp. 130–140, 2012, with permission from the author.

and in the hillier land behind it there are numerous LBK sites scattered along small streams at intervals of no greater than 2 km. Most of these are small, with few houses, an average of six from the excavations that have taken place, and little evidence of rebuilding, suggesting that they were only occupied for short periods. On the lower river terraces closer to the main river valleys, however, the situation is very different. There are fewer sites, at greater distances from one another, and they are different in character, the majority including earth-work enclosures. Thus, the site of Stephansposching and its two neighbours all have enclosures, indicative of prestige competition Pechtl argues. One of these sites, Aiterhofen-Odmuehle, also has a cemetery with burials containing rich grave goods. These sites are mainly large, densely occupied settlements lasting hundreds of years, which deserve the title of villages. While the average number of houses known from excavation areas at these sites is 44, the number in a given settlement as a whole was certainly much larger than this.

As local micro-regions became more fully occupied, competition between lineages would have become increasingly important and members of the senior line would increasingly have had to assert their position in order to maintain it. The deposition of rich grave goods as a form of costly signalling (Neiman, 1997; Bliege Bird and Smith, 2005) might have had a role here. In this case, the number of rich burials would not simply be a reflection of the size or power of the senior lineage but of the competitive pressure it was under in par-ticular places and times. Pechtl (2009) sees the construction of exceptionally large longhouses in a similar light, as associated with inter-lineage competition. Most of them date to the late LBK when population was at its highest.

THE DECLINE AND DISAPPEARANCE OF THE LBK

The development of local inequality based on priority of access during the colonisation process is not the only widespread institutional trend to be observed in the course of the LBK. The appearance of ditched and/ or palisaded enclosures (see Fig 4.2b for the enclosure at Langweiler 8) in growing numbers in later occupation phases seems to characterise many if not most LBK settlement micro-regions; the overall picture is well brought out in Fig 4.9a, which shows a rapid rise to a peak in the number of enclosures at c.7000 BP, followed by a fall. There has been considerable discussion of the function of these late enclosures, but some are certainly associated with violence. The site of Herxheim, for example, has extensive evidence of can-nibalism in the human remains buried in the ditches (Boulestin et al., 2009), while the idea that defence was often among their roles has been supported in recent years by the finding of three massacre sites dated to local late LBK phases in three different regions.

Kerig (2003) has suggested that the enclosures represent the emergence of a new type of social institution integrating larger numbers of people into a

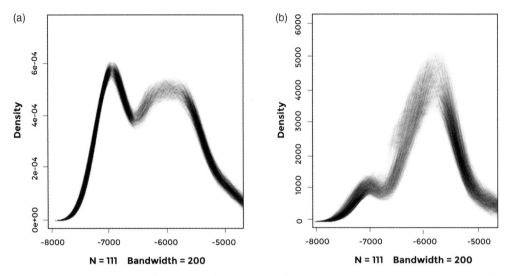

Fig 4.9. Chronological distribution of enclosures in Central Europe. a) Number of enclosures; b) Number of enclosures weighted by their size. Distributions created by using an aoristic method and repeated sampling from known enclosure date ranges.

single social unit, which would presumably have incorporated the patrilineal land-holding lineage system that has been postulated above. The existence of institutions capable of bringing large numbers of men together for warfare, at least on a temporary basis, is suggested by the scale of all three known massacres. At Talheim in south-west Germany the remains of 34 individuals were recovered (Wahl et al., 1987); at Asparn-Schletz in eastern Austria at least 67, even though the enclosure ditch into which they had been dumped was only partially excavated (Teschler-Nicola et al., 1996); at Schöneck-Kilianstädten in Hesse, western Germany, there were 26 individuals, with evidence of torture and/or mutilation (Meyer et al., 2015). These figures imply very large numbers of attackers. A possible analogy comes from Fredrik Barth's description of the Faiwolmin group in New Guinea (Barth, 1971, cited in Soltis et al. (1995). Barth pointed out that the western Faiwolmin communities lived in nucleated villages centred on cult houses whereas populations in the east were more dispersed. The centralised communities thus had a military advantage and, as a result, were able to expand towards the east, where the social system could not organise as many people for defence.

Whether the LBK enclosures were themselves always defensive constructions then is not really the point if one accepts that they represent a new kind of social institution involving larger scale integration and mitigating scalar stress. In a similar vein Zimmermann (2012) sees them as corresponding to the size of the largest cooperating social unit at the time, and, on the basis of his spatial method for population estimation (e.g. Zimmermann et al., 2004), estimates this to be in the low hundreds. We have already seen it postulated that enclosures appeared in Lower Bavaria as a result of prestige competition between long-lasting major settlements. In the light of the evidence for massacres it can be suggested that once institutions emerged that integrated larger numbers of people into a cooperating unit that was competitively successful, other groups had little option but to copy them if they wished to avoid potentially disastrous consequences. The general context in which to see this is the reaching of local carrying capacities in many of the areas where LBK farmers had settled; by this time one group's gain was another's loss.

Important further light can be thrown on the whole LBK settlement and social sequence just described by considering the 'self-centered decision model for reproductive decisions' developed by Read and LeBlanc (2003) and its implications for understanding the consequences population processes can have on social behaviour and institutions. Their key point is that, while an individual/family-centred cost–benefit model of the kind presented earlier in this book is always central to reproductive decision-making, the institutional consequences of the aggregated local reproductive decisions vary, depending on three factors: resource density, resource patchiness and the extent to which the reproductive decisions of families are decoupled from the fate of the larger group of which they are a part (see Fig 4.10). The LBK situation was one in which resource density was high and the degree of patchiness low at the level of individual settlement catchments, though high at the larger scale. In the early phases of settlement expansion it seems that small groups of households were relatively autonomous and settlements could fission at will. As population grew, intra-group inequality increased, as we have seen. Moreover, since all the local settlement regions were becoming full at the same time, it would increasingly have been the case, in Read and LeBlanc's words (2003: 62), that, 'The demographic dynamics of one group [would] impact the population dynamics of neighbouring groups', thus the fortunes of individual families and their corporate groups would have been increasingly closely bound together. The prediction of the model in these circumstances is inter-group conflict. Thus, the role of the social institutions associated with the enclosures in mitigating scalar stress, and helping corporate groups act more effectively as entities, as described above, would have become more important as the dominant social dynamic shifted from a position on the lower left of the space in Fig 4.10 to the upper right.

The widespread occurrence of enclosures is not the only indicator of change in the later LBK. Long-distance lithic exchange also declined. Throughout most of the LBK period supplies of high-quality flint were obtained from special sources and exchanged very widely (e.g. Zimmermann, 1995). In the latest phase, exchanged lithic raw materials declined in frequency at settlement sites and increasing proportions of the lithic assemblages were made up of material from local sources of poorer quality. Relations between adjacent groups may have broken down so completely that long-distance exchanges, with material passing through many hands, became impossible.

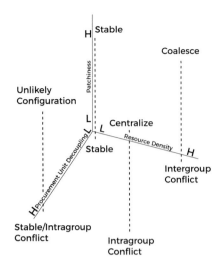

Fig 4.10. The three dimensions identified as affecting the outcomes of Read and LeBlanc's decision-making model and the outcomes predicted for the eight configurations defined by extreme values on each dimension. H, high; L, low. Reproduced from fig 1 in *Current Anthropology* 44, Read, D. and LeBlanc, S., Population growth, carrying capacity and conflict, pp. 59–85, University of Chicago Press. Reproduced with permission. ©_ 2003 by The Wenner-Gren Foundation for Anthropological Research. All rights reserved.

This process may have been one of the factors that led to a population crash in many LBK areas just after 7000 BP, including all those with evidence of massacres. If you look at the aggregate radiocarbon pattern for the four LBK regions shown in Fig 4.5 you find clear evidence of population decline at the end of the LBK in southern Germany, the Rhineland and Kuyavia. However, this is not universal. The exception is central Germany, one of the largest settlement areas, which does not show a marked decline until the later 7th millennium BP (Müller, 2001: 424 and fig 261) and where there is also a continuous cultural development from the LBK to its successor *Stichbandkeramik* (SBK or Stroke-Ornamented Pottery), for example at the site of Eythra (Cladders et al., 2012). Bohemia, another large LBK settlement area to its south-east, shows a similar pattern of cultural and demographic continuity into the mid-7th millennium BP, with a population peak c.6800 BP (Demján and Dreslerová, 2016).

These large-scale patterns are confirmed by evidence from specific local regions. They are seen, for example, in the abandonment of the Aldenhovener Platte region of western Germany (Zimmermann, 2002) and of the LBK areas of the Netherlands (Crombé and Vanmontfort, 2007), as well as in pollen and settlement evidence from Hesse (Eisenhauer, 1994; Schweizer, 2003) showing a marked decrease in occupation intensity at the end of the LBK. The Hegau region of south-west Germany shows a similar picture, as does the Upper Rhine area, with a gap between the end of the LBK and the beginning of the subsequent Hinkelstein phase (Denaire et al., 2017). Climatic factors may have been relevant to these collapses though the evidence so far is equivocal (Schmidt et al., 2004; Gronenborn et al., 2014). Simulations of climatic impacts on the LBK settlement system (Bocquet-Appel et al., 2015) show that adverse conditions could have an impact on the size of the population but it is short-lived: population 'bounces back' very quickly. Accounting for the longer-term population decreases or regional abandonments that occurred remains problematical, and the same is true of other features of the LBK. What was it about the LBK farming system that meant that it did not expand beyond the narrow band of loess soils, which would obviously have solved local pressure problems? Given the apparent availability in some regions of suitable settlement areas that were never occupied, as we saw above, were there other limitations that contributed to the crisis in many regions? These are questions that remain to be addressed.

CULTURAL TRANSMISSION, NICHE CONSTRUCTION AND THE LBK

We have seen that the LBK was overwhelmingly a demographic expansion, into which small numbers of hunter-gatherers were absorbed. In such a context, as we would expect, we see the wholesale transmission of a way of life from one generation to the next and from one place to the next. Because of its dependence on annual cereals and mobile domestic animals it was a very portable way of life that was extremely successful, though only within a limited range of environmental conditions. That way of life had developed in the western Carpathian Basin in the mid-8th millennium BP, in the context of the innovations and drift associated with the cultural equivalent of peripatric speciation. It included the material resources represented by crops and animals as well as traditions of social, cultural and economic knowledge and practice. Some of those practices were the basis for the expansion, for example in the area of subsistence and perhaps the social relations reflected in the longhouses. Others, like the pottery decoration for example, would have been simply the 'cultural baggage' associated with the expanding population and largely governed by fashion and drift. Because people and practices had a recent common origin, communities in Poland and the Paris Basin, for example, were similar in many respects to one another, no doubt they had a common language, though regional differences would gradually have developed. The vertical transmission implied by the strong correlation between genetic and cultural patterns would have been inherently conservative. In other words, once the initial successful formula had been established it would have been hard to imagine alternatives.

In the next chapter we will see that many of the patterns and processes characteristic of the LBK can be found in the spread of farming along the north coast of the Mediterranean.

CHAPTER 5

MARITIME EXPANSION IN THE CENTRAL AND WEST MEDITERRANEAN

It has long been recognised that the spread of farming from south-west Asia across Europe involved two different routes: one through Central Europe, described in the last chapter, and one along the north coast of the Mediterranean. Until recently, however, much less was known about the Mediterranean expansion west of the Aegean. Far less work had been carried out and the chronological details, especially those concerning the relationship between the Mesolithic and the Neolithic, were very unclear, not least because the vast majority of radiocarbon dates came from cave and rock-shelter sites with complex and often disturbed stratigraphies. In particular, the fact that both Mesolithic and Neolithic material were apparently found in the same layers led to the conclusion that the mechanism of the transition in the Mediterranean must have involved the gradual and piecemeal adoption of elements of a farming way of life, especially stock-keeping, by local foragers. In the last 20 years our knowledge has been transformed. There has been a revolution in the understanding of the spread of farming in the west Mediterranean, especially in Iberia, thanks to the work of a new generation of archaeologists trained in modern scientific methods.

Key to the new understanding was the recognition in the late 1990s of the importance of 'chronometric hygiene' in the evaluation of radiocarbon dates and their contexts. Once bulk samples of charcoal potentially subject to old wood effects and from uncertain contexts were excluded and only short-lived samples from reliable contexts considered, it became apparent that the initial spread of farming in the central and west Mediterranean was rapid, in fact even more rapid than the one through Central Europe, with farming reaching the Atlantic coast of Portugal by c.7300 BP if not earlier. Moreover, it involved the full Neolithic 'package' of domestic crops and animals, as well as pottery, not just domestic animals used in a pastoralist version of previous mobile Mesolithic ways of life. On the basis of this reassessment it was proposed that farming spread as a result of a maritime expansion of pioneer farmers from the east Mediterranean (Zilhão, 2001).

This view has come to be widely accepted, though not completely (e.g. Berrocal, 2012), and has been confirmed by the recent whole-genome aDNA studies (Haak et al., 2015; Hofmanová et al., 2016; Lipson et al., 2017; Mathieson et al., 2017). The genome of the Mesolithic forager from La Braña in north-west Spain represents a local variant of the 'Western Hunter Gatherer' (WHG) group of Haak et al., which, as we have seen, also includes individuals from right across the southern half of Europe as far as the Balkans. The genomes of the seven Early Neolithic (EN) farmer individuals, five females and two males, dating to the late 8th millennium BP and with Cardial Ware associations, from the sites of Cova Bonica, El Prado de Pancorbo and Els Trocs in north-east Spain, on the other hand, have the same Aegean–Anatolian origin as the Balkan Early Neolithic and LBK individuals from Central Europe (Hofmanová et al., 2016; Olalde et al., 2015), demonstrating that early farmers on both the northern and Mediterranean branches of the agricultural expansion into Europe were descended from a common ancestor in the Aegean–Anatolian region. The percentages of WHG hunter-gatherer admixture are higher than in Central Europe, c.8–10% (Lipson et al., 2017) but it is important to note that the samples do not represent the very earliest farmers in the west Mediterranean, associated with the Impressa pottery of the first half of the 8th millennium; Cardial Ware, with which the samples were associated, seems to represent a secondary farming expansion of descendants of the very earliest farmers (see below). Interestingly, the small hunter-gatherer component in the genome of the EN individual from Cova Bonica in Catalonia, with Cardial Ware cultural associations, has closer affinities with a hunter-gatherer individual from Hungary than with the Mesolithic sample from La Braña, suggesting that it was not a result of interaction with local hunter-gatherers in Iberia but had occurred some time before (Olalde et al., 2015). This ties in with estimates of the date of the admixture by Lipson et al. (2017) and is in keeping with other evidence for the Cardial (see below). Admixture from hunter-gatherers later increases. Individuals from the site of La Mina, dating to the early 6th millennium BP, at least 1500 years after the arrival of the first farmers, have a hunter-gatherer admixture of over 20%. However, estimates suggest that the majority of this took place not long after farmers had arrived. Ancient genome evidence is not yet available from regions of early farmer occupation in southern France and Italy or from the earliest sites in Iberia, but three individuals from Impressa contexts at the site of Zemunica Cave in Dalmatia on the eastern side of the Adriatic all had Anatolian farmer genomes with negligible WHG admixture (Mathieson et al., 2017). In this light and given the evidence presented below for a lack of contact between farmers and foragers, the prediction must be that the very earliest Impressa farmers in the central and west Mediterranean will also turn out to have markedly lower levels of Western Hunter Gatherer admixture than the individuals from Cardial contexts.

In short, the processes of farming expansion along the northern and southern branches must have been very similar, with groups moving to new enclaves favourable for the farming system they knew, then growing and rapidly fissioning, with descendant groups moving on to find new places to settle. Modelling of the spread in the western Mediterranean by Isern et al. (2017) indicates that a process of coastal maritime 'leapfrog' expansion with jumps of 350–450 km and a population growth rate of c.2.3–2.4% per year produces results that most closely match the dates of arrival in France and Iberia. The growth rate is extremely high and virtually identical to that calculated for the LBK in the previous chapter. As we have seen already, the evolutionary logic is clear. In principle, if others are taking advantage of new dispersal opportunities then those who do not take advantage of them will fail to benefit; on the other hand, as we have also seen, this needs to be balanced against all the potential risks arising from isolation on the dispersal frontier, all the greater when the newly fissioned communities were moving on in small boats. We do not know how many failures there were but, as in other phases of the farming expansion, some people at least clearly decided that the risks were worth taking. This would have created considerable opportunities for the loss of cultural features through drift and founder effects and the generation of new ones, by chance transmission errors as well as trial-and-error learning in the new environments, just as with the LBK.

THE HISTORY OF CENTRAL AND WEST MEDITERRANEAN EXPANSION

We saw in Chapter 3 that even though farming communities had reached northern Greece and north-west Anatolia well before 8500 BP it was the best part of 400 years later before their sudden rapid spread further north to the Danube and beyond. The same is true of the spread west into Adriatic Italy and beyond. In this case, the delay is arguably more puzzling. It was suggested earlier that the delay in the northward spread might have been accounted for by the colder and wetter conditions created by the rapid cooling climate event that occurred around 8200 BP and that expansion restarted once it was over, but the expansion westwards through the Mediterranean involved the same climatic conditions as the Aegean, so it seems unlikely that this could account for the delay in this case.

   The best evidence so far for its starting point comes from the site of Sidari, on Corfu in north-west Greece (see map Fig 5.1 for all sites in this chapter). This site has been known since the 1960s but it is only recently that a new study has elucidated its stratigraphy. Berger et al. (2014) show that Mesolithic contexts on the site are dubious or mixed and that its earliest Neolithic occupation dates to c.8400–8200 BP, characterised by Monochrome style pottery like that found

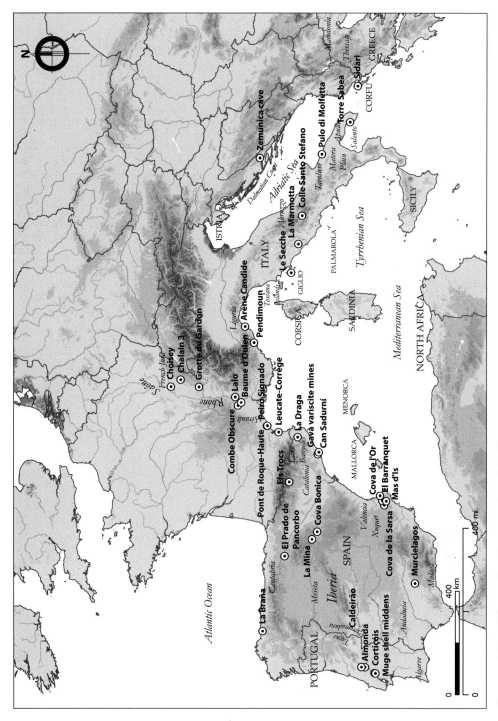

Fig 5.1. Map of sites and regions mentioned in Chapter 5.

elsewhere in Greece in the EN. The authors suggest there is then a hiatus, with indications of erosion associated with the 8.2 ka event, followed by two more EN layers with Impressa pottery dated c.8062–7960 BP, slightly earlier than the earliest dates across the Adriatic in south-east Italy. Western Greece is usually seen as the origin of the Impressed Ware, but Çilingiroğlu (2010) has pointed to the appearance of distinctive impressed pottery on both sides of the Aegean as well as the Levantine-Syria area at the end of the 9th millennium BP. She notes that its appearance in Thessaly does not correspond to any break in local cultural sequences but that in the northern Aegean, Macedonia and Bulgaria, where it appears at the start of new settlements, it may be connected with the appearance of new groups using sea routes. Whether or not she is right, it seems to me to make more sense to see the initial expansion of Impressed Ware into the Adriatic as related in some way to this broader phenomenon, not least because of the maritime connection.

THE ADRIATIC AND ITALY

From the coast of western Greece farming spreads west to Italy and northwards, on the eastern side of the Adriatic, along the Dalmatian coast, reflected there in the rise in population indicated by the radiocarbon population proxy in the early centuries of the 8th millennium BP (Pilaar Birch and Vander Linden, 2017). The earliest farming dates in southern Dalmatia are a little before 8000 BP and by c.7900–7800 BP there is Neolithic evidence as far north as the southern side of the Istrian peninsula; all these occupations are associated with Impressed Ware (Forenbaher and Miracle, 2014). Further north than this the earliest farming dates are c.7600 BP and by this time the style of the pottery had changed to that recognised as the Danilo Culture, the local successor to the Impressed Ware. This relatively slow coastal spread to the head of the Adriatic contrasts with the speed of the spread from northern Greece along the Balkan river valleys to the Danube, which had already occurred by c.8000 BP (Biagi et al., 2005), and also with the spread west. The earliest sites with pottery and domestic animals, overwhelmingly caprines, and with very little hunting, are caves, and there is generally a time gap between Mesolithic and Neolithic layers, reflected in a very abrupt change from layers with wild fauna to domestic assemblages. So far, the earliest open farming settlements, with evidence of cereals and the same faunal assemblages as the cave sites (Orton et al., 2016), date to c.7900–7800 BP. In the light of this evidence and given that the karst limestone terrain of much of coastal Dalmatia is more suitable for herding than cereal agriculture, it has been suggested that the first farming colonists were indeed mobile herders. Comparisons of carbon and nitrogen isotope values between Mesolithic and Neolithic skeletons show that there is a much lower marine component in Neolithic diets (Lightfoot et al., 2011), while the genome data confirm that the farmers were of Anatolian origin.

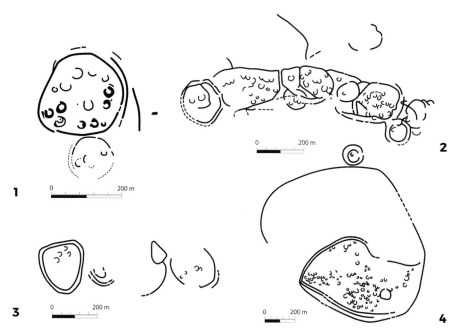

Fig 5.2. Early Neolithic enclosures in the Tavoliere plain, south-east Italy. Reproduced from fig 8 in *Journal of World Prehistory* 17, Malone, C., The Italian Neolithic: A Synthesis of Research, pp. 235–312, 2003, with permission from Springer.

The initial expansion of farmers westwards across the Adriatic to south-east Italy takes place around the end of the 9th millennium BP and current evidence points to a hiatus or at most a short overlap between this and the preceding Mesolithic (Grifoni Cremonesi and Radi, 2014; Perrin and Binder, 2014) in all those areas of peninsula Italy that were occupied by early farmers, with the possible exception of the far north of the Adriatic, but even here there seems to be a gap (Bonsall et al., 2013). As we will see, this lack of archaeological evidence for hunter-gatherer occupation immediately prior to the arrival of farmers is characteristic of many parts of the central and west Mediterranean.

Early Impressed Ware is found at a number of sites in south-east Italy but Neolithic occupation is most strikingly documented in the Tavoliere plain of Apulia, where it is characterised by the presence of a large number of ditched settlements, over 500 in total, initially recognised by aerial photography just after World War II (see e.g. Malone, 2003: fig 8) (Fig 5.2); this settlement pattern lasts around 1000 years and is also found in the Matera plain immediately to the south in Italy's instep. Robb (2007) notes that much of the area inside the enclosures was not occupied by houses and suggests that the smaller ones may have contained no more than a dozen households. He argues that these communities were egalitarian, with little evidence for either prestige or large-scale ritual and sees at least one function of the ditches as defensive, linking this

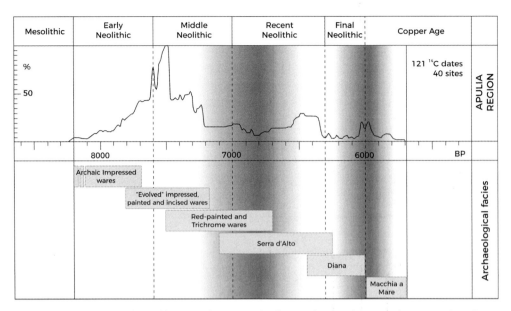

Fig 5.3. Radiocarbon population proxy for Apulia, south-east Italy. Reproduced from fig 3 in *The Holocene* 23, Fiorentino, G. et al., Climate changes and human–environment interactions in the Apulia region of south-eastern Italy during the Neolithic period, pp. 1297–1316, 2013. Grey bands indicate drier periods.

with the remains of two possible massacres (2007: 61) to suggest that warfare between communities was common.

A recent review of the radiocarbon evidence in the Tavoliere and adjacent areas of south-east Italy (Fiorentino et al., 2013) shows a common pattern, with the number of settlements rising to a peak c.7600–7500 BP and then gradually declining, and the Tavoliere apparently being abandoned by 7000 BP (Fig 5.3). The population pattern seems to reflect climatic factors: the region experienced relatively wet conditions for the first half of the 8th millennium BP but after that drier conditions became increasingly marked in the second half, continuing until c.6600 BP. After the later 8th-millennium BP decline, settlement in the region seems to increase slightly in a wetter phase 6600–6300 BP but never reaches levels similar to the peak of the mid-8th millennium.

In material culture terms, the Impressed Ware that begins the sequence develops more complex forms of geometric impressed and incised decoration, associated with the emergence of a coarse ware/fine ware distinction; these varieties are joined in the mid-8th millennium by the introduction of painted wares from the Balkans, which continue with increasing elaboration into the late 7th millennium BP, when the Serra d'Alto and other styles are widespread across southern Italy (Malone, 2003).

The crop pattern is dominated by emmer, einkorn, barley and legume species, which vary slightly in their frequency over time (Fiorentino et al., 2013; Reed, 2015). There are not many well-documented faunal assemblages but the Impressed Ware site of Torre Sabea on the coast of the Salento hills area of south-east Italy has produced data of good quality, indicating an overwhelming emphasis on domestic animals, which make up 94% of the mammal fauna. The majority are caprines (62%), with 23% cattle and 6% pig. The age distribution suggests that both caprines and cattle were used for milk production (Rowley-Conwy et al., 2013: 162) and this suggestion has been confirmed by the finding of dairy fat residues in vessels from the site of Pulo di Molfetta in Apulia at the very beginning of the Impressed Ware sequence c.8050–7930 BP (Spiteri et al., 2017). Stable carbon and nitrogen isotope studies of human skeletons from south-east Italy have produced evidence of a minor marine component in the diet of individuals buried near the coast but otherwise diets were based overwhelmingly on terrestrial, it is safe to say agricultural, resources (Lelli et al., 2012).

In Italy north of Apulia and adjacent regions in the far south, the earliest Impressed Ware occupation dates to c.7800–7700 BP. The Impressed Ware site of Colle Santo Stefano in the Abruzzo region of central Italy, with radiocarbon dates between 7790 and 7410 BP, has produced a faunal assemblage dominated by domestic animals, largely sheep/goat. Ceramic residue analyses showed that the majority of vessels tested contained ruminant adipose fats, from meat, while pork fats were also found, but dairy fats were detected as well in a number of vessels, confirming that here too dairying and milk processing were part of the subsistence practices of the earliest Impressed Ware farmers (Salque et al., 2012).

The waterlogged Impressed Ware site of La Marmotta, near Rome, with tree-ring dates between c.7640 and 7180 BP has provided evidence of the technology that made the west Mediterranean farming expansion possible: a dugout canoe more than 10 m in length and a metre wide, made from a large oak, which would have been capable of carrying animals as well as people. As Robb (2007: 255) points out, the fact that it does not have a keel would have made it unstable in open sea conditions, but seagoing versions with outriggers could have existed and an experimental replica successfully made the voyage along the coast from central Italy to Portugal. In any event, it is now clear that the initial expansion of farming and farmers into the west Mediterranean basin was based on maritime movement.

Until some years ago it was believed that the earliest farming occupation in northern Italy was associated with the cockleshell-edge impressed pottery known as Cardial Ware and dated to the mid-8th millennium BP. However, as noted above, we now know that there was a significantly earlier phase associated with so-called Impressa pottery. Bernabeu Aubán et al.'s (2017) analysis of radiocarbon dates on short-lived samples from Impressa sites in the west Mediterranean suggests that the earliest Neolithic in Liguria and Provence goes back to c.7700 BP; in Languedoc to the west it is at least as early, and farmers had already reached the Valencia region of eastern Spain by 7500 BP, though the distribution was not a continuous one from east to west but involved scattered enclaves along the coast.

The seaborne nature of the expansion is confirmed by the presence of Impressa sites on some of the Toscana islands in the Tyrrhenian Sea, and the earliest Neolithic occupation of Sardinia and Corsica also probably occurs c.7700 BP, though possibly slightly later because the earliest ceramics so far found are Cardial in style rather than Impressa; sheep, goat and pig all occur but the earliest evidence for the presence of cattle dates to the beginning of the 7th millennium BP. There is evidence of Mesolithic occupation on Corsica and Sardinia c.10,000–8600 BP but nothing after that date for nearly a millennium until the first Neolithic settlement, and no indication of cultural continuity (Rowley-Conwy et al., 2013: 174).

The cave of Arene Candide in Liguria, not far from the French border, with a 95% probability date range on a short-lived sample of 7740–7590 BP, is one of the key sites for our knowledge of the earliest Neolithic in the west Mediterranean basin, especially because of the light it throws on the earliest domestic animal assemblages. Once again, there is no Late Mesolithic evidence from the region and the chipped stone assemblage does not have any Mesolithic affinities. The EN faunal assemblage is dominated by caprines, mainly sheep, though domestic cattle also occur, but the pigs that are present are most probably wild; the domestic species does not appear until the Late Neolithic. The age distribution of the sheep falls between the typical meat and milk patterns suggesting an element of dairying (Rowley-Conwy et al., 2013: 173). Wheat, barley and lentils also occur (Nisbet, 2008), as well as quernstones and sickle blades, confirming the presence of cereal agriculture, though it seems to have had little impact in terms of woodland clearance (Branch et al., 2014). There are also indications of wide-ranging contacts, including the presence of so-called Bedoulian flint from up to 200 km away in southern France, Scaglia Rossa flint from 150–300 km distant in central Italy and obsidian from the islands of Sardinia and Palmarola, confirming the significance of maritime movement.

SOUTHERN FRANCE

To the west of Liguria, evidence of Mesolithic occupation is found in the middle Rhône valley as late as 7500 BP but there are no indications of interactions with the first farmers, who almost certainly arrived by sea, occupying discontinuous sections of the coast where there was no Mesolithic occupation from c.7700 BP; they are found, for example, at the Pendimoun rock shelter in Provence, in association with Impressa pottery (Rowley-Conwy et al., 2013: 175). The Pendimoun faunal assemblage is overwhelmingly dominated by domestic caprines, and emmer wheat and barley were cultivated. Further west again, on the other side of the Rhône in Languedoc there is the same hiatus and lack of continuity, perhaps attributable to the effect of the climatic deterioration event at 8200 BP on local forager populations (Berger and

Guilaine, 2009). Like Pendimoun, the adjacent sites of Pont de Roque-Haute and Peiro Signado, the earliest known Neolithic sites, date to c.7700 BP and are associated with Impressa material culture. Of particular significance at Pont de Roque-Haute is the occurrence of obsidian from the island of Palmarola off the western Italian coast, albeit only in small quantities, which ties in with the strong similarity in material culture identified with the site of Le Secche on the island of Giglio a bit further to the north, providing strong evidence that the first inhabitants of Pont de Roque-Haute were maritime immigrants from this region. Peiro Signado also has obsidian, from both Palmarola and Sardinia, but its pottery has stronger affinities with the Ligurian Impressa. In subsistence terms both sites have a classic EN profile, with domestic sheep dominating the faunal assemblage and evidence for the cultivation of emmer, einkorn and bread wheat (Rowley-Conwy et al., 2013: 180).

The maritime connection is further confirmed by Vigne's morphometric studies of sheep bones from EN sites in the west Mediterranean (Vigne, 2007). He distinguished two separate lineages with different limb proportions: one found in central Italy and Corsica, but also at Pont de Roque-Haute, strongly suggesting that the animals were imported by sea. The other lineage was characteristic of the subsequent Cardial phase and is found from Liguria to Languedoc, including in the earlier Impressa phase at Arene Candide (Vigne, 2007: fig 125) (Fig 5.4). It appears that the newly founded sites and their successors on the French coast had a range of different Italian origins.

In contrast to the maritime dispersal of the Impressa, the Cardial phase in southern France marks the beginning of a period of local land-based demographic expansion and consequent regional cultural and economic differentiation, as well as probable interaction with hunter-gatherer groups that continued to exist inland. Expansion may have started in north-east Italy (Ibáñez-Estévez et al., 2017). As one indicator, Ibañez-Estévez et al. draw attention to the distribution of the distinctive La Draga-type sickles, which are found in north-east Italy in the mid-8th millennium BP and then spread westwards through the coastal regions of southern France as far as Catalonia, where they are found at the site of La Draga itself (see below), and in the interior of Iberia. This spread led, they suggest, to the gradual substitution of the La Marmotta sickle type by the La Draga type among the pre-existing Impressa farming communities. By the end of the 8th millennium this process had led to a stable pattern in sickle distribution, with the La Draga type found from northern Italy to northern Iberia and the La Marmotta type in southern Iberia, which was never reached by the second expansion, and peninsula Italy. This may seem an elaborate edifice to build on the basis of sickle types, but in support of the dual expansion process proposed, the authors point to Vigne's analysis of the characteristics of the Early Neolithic domestic sheep of the west Mediterranean summarised above. The Cardial sheep were similar to those from Liguria and could have had an origin in continental northern Italy, and

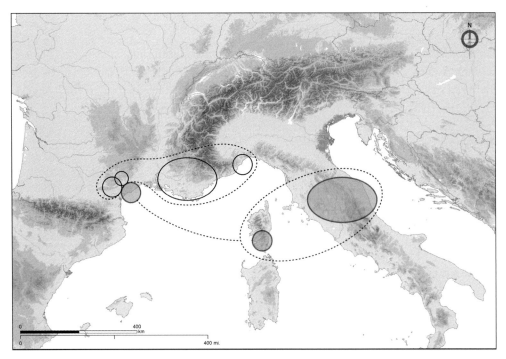

Fig 5.4. The geographical pattern of similarity in sheep morphology in the Early Neolithic of the western Mediterranean, suggesting two different interaction patterns. Reproduced from fig 125 in Vigne, J.-D., Exploitation des animaux et néolithisation en Mediterranée nord-occidentale. In Guilaine, J., Manen, C., Vigne J.-D. (Eds.), *Pont de Roque-Haute. Nouveaux regards sur la néolithisation de la France méditerranéenne.* Toulouse: Archives d'Écologie Préhistorique, pp. 221–301, 2007, with permission from the author.

ultimately the northern Adriatic (Vigne, 2007: fig 127). Further support for these separate waves of expansion, the authors suggest, is given by the difference in cattle mtDNA haplotypes between La Draga (T1) in Catalonia and Cova de l'Or in Valencia (T3, Colominas et al., 2015). It would also fit with the Cardial genome evidence from Cova Bonica, north-east Spain, with its evidence of hunter-gatherer admixture from further east.

Cardial exchange links reflect this terrestrial pattern. The obsidian originating from Palmarola and Sardinia found at the early pioneer maritime Impressa sites from Liguria to Languedoc disappears, only reappearing in the context not of migration but of expanding exchange networks in the Middle Neolithic (Manen, 2014; Manen and Convertini, 2012), hundreds of years later. Moreover, ceramic decoration becomes increasingly differentiated. While the Impressa pottery of Peiro Signado and Pont de Roque-Haute is very similar to that of their respective putative Italian ancestors, this is not the case with the Cardial. For example, the Tyrrhenian Italian sites use a variety of different shells for ceramic decoration, but the French-Iberian Cardial uses the only the *Cardium* shell, even though the other shells were available on the south

French coast and were sometimes used to make ornaments. Differences also develop in vessel-forming techniques and in the vessel forms. On the other hand, there is evidence of *intra*-regional connections between c.7300 and 7000 BP in the Languedoc region. A ceramic characterisation study found that all sites contained some non-local pottery, including a number of vessels made of clay from the west bank of the river Hérault, which were found at eight different sites, including one over 100 km to the west. In contrast, no such vessels are found to the east of the Hérault, which may therefore have been a territorial boundary. A contrasting pattern is found with the distribution of lithic raw materials. At this time, only the areas to the east seem to have been part of the networks that circulated Bedoulian flint and Alpine jadeite.

Cardial faunal assemblages are diverse, with caprines most frequent when proportions of hunted animals are low. Rowley-Conwy et al. (2013: 184) point out that the faunal patterns tend to be local, so that particular sites tend to have specific patterns that are found in successive layers. The proportion of hunted animals increases with distance inland from the coast and one reason for this may be that inland areas tend to be more mountainous, and probably forested. However, the difference is also apparently reflected in the pottery, which is Cardial near the coast and tends to be 'Pericardial' inland, so the pattern may be indicative of a gradual adoption of elements of farming culture by descendants of indigenous foraging communities. Domestic pigs are absent initially in the Cardial faunal assemblages but appear by c.7300 BP. The limited age-distribution data available suggest the sheep were exploited for both meat and milk whereas goats were specialist milk producers, but it is important to note that the sites of Combe Obscure and Baume d'Oulen, whose assemblages were studied, were cave sites.

Indeed, as elsewhere in the EN of the central and western Mediterranean, the majority of known Cardial sites in southern France continue to be caves and rock shelters, which would have been largely activity-specific herding or hunting sites, as their faunal assemblages indicate. Geomorphological work by Berger and colleagues in the middle Rhône valley (Berger, 2005) has revealed the biases introduced into this picture by successive waves of erosion and deposition that would have destroyed or hidden open-air sites in river valleys and basins, not to mention the effects of coastal inundation revealed by the discovery of the submerged site of Leucate-Corrège (Guilaine et al., 1984); moreover, the suitability of the soils for farming would also have been affected (Berger, 2005: 169–170).

The exceptional sedimentation conditions at Lalo in the middle Rhône valley reveal some of the details. Here, radiocarbon dates in the range c.7650/7600–7400 BP associated with early Cardial material came from pits in a period of quiet river conditions suitable for settlement close to the river Citelle. However, this was followed by a period of river braiding and strong erosion of the higher areas of the river basin lasting from c.7350 to c.7100 BP and probably linked to a period of cooling and increased rainfall (Berger, 2005). Subsequently, a new, late Cardial, occupation occurred at c.7100 BP. In fact, both here and elsewhere there are numbers of late Cardial sites on river terraces following the renewed stabilisation of the rivers and the development of new soils.

Berger's soil studies have shown that conditions in the Rhône valley at the beginning of the Neolithic were very different from those of today, which are the result of a long series of erosion and deposition episodes since that time. In fact, at the beginning of the Cardial EN the majority of Rhône valley soils would not have been particularly favourable for farming, he argues, because they would have had low fertility and would have required either the use of manure or cultivation under a bush or forest fallow system to be exploited successfully. However, the erosion of these ancient Holocene soils from c.7400 to 7200/7100 BP rejuvenated the soil cover, exposing lower horizons rich in nutrients. The result was that when the phase of erosion was over conditions for occupation became favourable again because the soils had been naturally improved. This, Berger suggests, accounts for the agricultural expansion that ensued from c.7200–6900 BP. Studies in the Rhône delta have shown the existence of a similar pattern of hydrological episodes there as well, confirming their large-scale impact, but also revealing another episode of Rhône floods, c.6800–6500 BP, at the early–middle Neolithic boundary.

Fieldwork in connection with the construction of the Mediterranean high-speed train line led to the discovery of 38 EN sites in the alluvial plains, 17 of which were buried. On the basis of a predictive model that took into account knowledge of the distribution of sediments and of the conditions associated with the buried sites, it was estimated that there would have been a density of 0.15 *contemporary* sites per sq.km, or one for every 6 sq.km (Berger, 2005: 195), but this calculation assumes an even spread of sites across the entire 800 years from the beginning to end of the Cardial, whereas in fact the great majority are late Cardial. Berger suggests that this expansion could have led to problems of territorial competition. It certainly resulted in the northward expansion of the Cardial to the upper Rhône and Saône valleys (see below). There is little overlap in the radiocarbon dates of the Early and Middle Neolithic and the latter begins c.6800/6500 BP (Manen and Sabatier, 2003), with a further expansion.

The overall demographic impact of the arrival of farming in Mediterranean southern France and the Rhône valley is shown in Fig 5.5, with a significant rise in population after its arrival, followed by indications of a slight drop, before a higher peak is reached c.6000 BP, in the Chasséen cultural phase. The inland expansion seems to have involved interaction or at least overlap with local Mesolithic groups at the end of the 8th millennium BP. Perrin's (2003) analysis of the stratigraphic sequence at the Grotte du Gardon in the upper Rhône/south-west Jura area showed that, while layer 58 had a typical EN lithic assemblage, the four layers overlying it contained arrowheads characteristic of

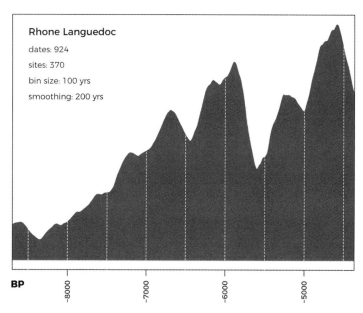

Rhone Languedoc

dates: 924

sites: 370

bin size: 100 yrs

smoothing: 200 yrs

BP -8000 -7000 -6000 -5000

Fig 5.5. Radiocarbon population proxy for Mediterranean France and the Rhône valley. Data from the EUROEVOL project.

the local Late Mesolithic, and all the layers concerned were *in situ*. In the following layers Neolithic techniques of using indirect percussion to produce blades were used to produce arrowheads that were much more Mesolithic in form, pointing to an assimilation process in Perrin's view.

At the site of Chalain 3 in the French Jura, at the border between the west Mediterranean and the Central European expansions, there is evidence of agricultural clearance c.7500–7200 BP (Pétrequin et al., 2009), but without any cultural material that would point to the ancestry of these farmers. However, as mentioned in Chapter 4, the nearby site of Choisey has produced a find of early La Hoguette pottery of local clay, showing a very high level of technical expertise. The very early appearance of farming and its material attributes in this region, rather remote from the main axes of expansion, may be best explained at present as a result of its adoption by Mesolithic groups who had links with the early Cardial to the south. As noted already, La Hoguette pottery spreads very rapidly to the north, where it is found in early LBK contexts in south-west Germany and beyond, by routes that had been used earlier for the exchange of *Columbella* shells from the Mediterranean. In the authors' view the high level of technical expertise seen in the pottery must imply a movement of potters, if not whole communities, throughout the area where the early La Hoguette style is found.

To the west, the impact of the Mediterranean Cardial tradition can be traced all the way across south-west France to the Atlantic, albeit that, in the words of Marchand (2007: 231), 'The traces are extremely diffuse', the main indicator being the presence of Montclus-type arrowheads, a type believed to have Cardial associations, in Mesolithic contexts in the late 8th millennium. It is only later, in the earlier 7th millennium BP, that clear evidence of Neolithic settlement becomes apparent in the Atlantic zone. However, despite the current lack of evidence, it is becoming increasingly obvious that the north-westward expansion from the Mediterranean was of enormous importance (see Chapter 6).

IBERIA

It is now apparent that the introduction of farming to Iberia took place through the same mechanism as Italy and France: pioneer maritime colonisation. Although this had been proposed earlier it was by no means clearly apparent in the late 20th century, when, just as in southern France, a combination of mixed stratigraphies from cave sites and bulk radiocarbon samples from uncertain contexts led to the belief that farming, and animal husbandry in particular, must have spread through contact between local hunter-gatherer groups if it did not have a local origin. Continuing 'chronometric hygiene' studies (Zilhão, 2001; García-Puchol et al., 2017; Juan-Cabanilles and Oliver, 2017) have removed the foundations of these arguments and led to the now generally accepted inference of maritime colonisation. There was an early arrival in eastern Spain and shortly thereafter in Portugal, which ongoing work continues to confirm and elaborate. Its specifically maritime nature fits with the results of the simulation studies of Isern et al. (2017) described above, showing that a model with a sea travel range of at least 300 km per generation and leapfrog coastal movement gives the best prediction of the arrival times of farming in southern France and Iberia from an assumed starting point in north-west Italy. Early farming dates and likely starting points for expansion into inland Mediterranean Spain are found not just in Catalonia but in Valencia and further south in Andalusia (Bernabeu Aubán et al., 2015). In fact, this might suggest a connection via Sicily and North Africa (Sánchez et al., 2012). Modelling of the dispersal of farming within Iberia on the basis of radiocarbon dates found that the best fit was given by assuming two starting points, one in Catalonia, the other in North Africa (Isern et al., 2014). Given that the earliest sites, such as El Barranquet and Mas d'Is in Valencia have Impressa rather than Cardial pottery (Bernabeu Aubán et al., 2009), this would appear to confirm their connection with the first farmers in southern France and western Italy. However, it does not exclude the possibility of movements of farmers from southern Italy with Impressa styles arriving via the southern route. Much more work is needed in North Africa before this issue can be resolved, and especially more radiocarbon dates, though archaeobotanical evidence from recent excavations in Morocco confirms the presence of crops that point to connections with the north shore of the Mediterranean, with dates between 7500 and 7000 BP (Morales et al., 2016). We can be reasonably confident in excluding a direct sea crossing from Italy to Spain on the basis of what we know about the available maritime technology and the fact that the Balearic Islands of Mallorca and Menorca, in the middle of the west Mediterranean, were not colonised until the later 5th millennium BP, the last significant islands to be occupied in the entire Mediterranean (Broodbank, 2013: 330–331).

In a recent study Bernabeu Aubán et al. (2014) carried out a further analysis of radiocarbon dates on short-lived samples from good contexts at Mesolithic and Neolithic sites in Iberia. The earliest Neolithic dates are c.7650–7600 BP and a rapid expansion in the number of dated sites follows, both in coastal regions and inland. At the same time there are developments in the pottery styles, with a classic Cardial phase emerging c.7500/7450 BP and continuing until c.7100. An Epicardial style emerges c.7350 BP, and initially is found only in inland Iberia while the Cardial continues in the coastal zone; after c.7100 BP, however, Epicardial styles take over everywhere. Further to the west, in Portugal the earliest evidence is dated to c.7500/7400 BP and is found in the Algarve and Estremadura regions (Carvalho, 2010), slightly earlier in the former; in the latter area radiocarbon dates from short-lived samples associated with Neolithic occupation at the cave sites of Almonda and Caldeirão have produced dates of 7500/7300 BP. The rapid nature of the spread is clearly demonstrated by Isern et al.'s spatial analysis of early farming dates (Isern et al., 2014: fig 1), which shows that by far the greater part of Iberia was occupied by 7000 BP. The well-known exception, clearly visible in their map, is the Cantabrian region of north-west Iberia, a very different climatic and biogeographical region, where agriculture does not begin until c.6800 BP and where more substantial forager populations may have persisted (Cubas et al., 2016).

Elsewhere, the Neolithic expansion goes hand in hand with an extremely rapid decline in the number of dates from Mesolithic contexts and little overlap, with the exception of central Portugal, where there seems to be an overlap of c.400 years between the occupation of local Neolithic sites and the continuing occupation of the famous Mesolithic Muge shell middens at the mouth of the Tagus, though there is no evidence for contact between the two. In several parts of Iberia, such as the Mediterranean coastal zone of Valencia and Malaga, Catalonia and the central Meseta, hardly any Final Mesolithic material has been found at all, despite extensive fieldwork (Bernabeu Aubán et al., 2014; Juan-Cabanilles and Oliver, 2017; though see Salazar-García et al., 2014, for an exception), a situation that corresponds to what we have already seen in much of southern France. Like their LBK counterparts, the Neolithic colonisers of the western Mediterranean occupied areas that were at most very thinly occupied by Mesolithic foragers at the time of their arrival. In southern Iberia Sánchez et al. (2012) suggest that sea level rise between c.8000 and 7000 BP would have flooded major river estuaries and therefore inundated

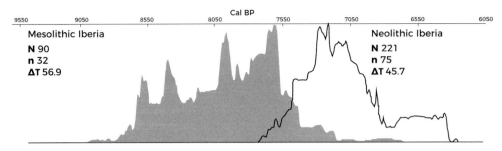

Fig 5.6. a) Iberian Mesolithic and Neolithic summed radiocarbon probabilities. Reprinted from fig 5 in *Environmental Archaeology* 19, Bernabeu Aubán, J. et al., Socioecological dynamics at the time of Neolithic transition in Iberia, pp. 214–225, 2014. Taylor & Francis Ltd. www.informaworld.com. With permission.

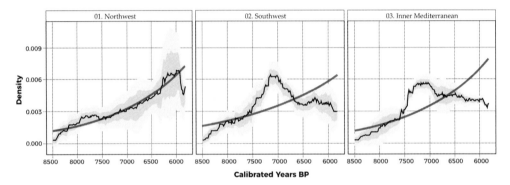

Fig 5.6. b) Summed radiocarbon date range population proxy for Mediterranean and south-west Iberia. Reproduced from fig 2 in *Journal of Archaeological Method and Theory* 24, Drake, B.L. et al., Regional Demographic Dynamics in the Neolithic Transition in Iberia: Results from Summed Calibrated Date Analysis, pp. 796–812, 2017, with permission from Springer.

the resources that local forager populations would have depended on, while contemporary changes in west Mediterranean sea circulation would probably also have negatively affected local marine food webs and may thus have created opportunities for incoming farming communities.

The summed radiocarbon probability distribution of dated EN sites from Iberia (Bernabeu Aubán et al., 2014: fig 5) (see Fig 5.6a) shows that the arrival of farming led to a rapid rise following the preceding Late Mesolithic decline, to a peak at c.7200 BP, reflecting the population increase resulting from the new economy. But here, as in most other areas of Europe, the high population levels were not sustained. Following the 7200 BP peak there is subsequently a fall in the summed probability which Bernabeu et al. suggest may represent some sort of collapse in Neolithic settlement. This coincides with increased regionalisation in pottery styles, perhaps indicating that the initial contact networks that existed when farmers first arrived were breaking down.

Moreover, the large-scale pattern in the summed probabilities is mirrored at a local scale by those obtained from the Xuquer-Segura region in Valencia, one of the areas of earliest Neolithic settlement, where a programme of detailed work has been carried out, which shows an occupation decline unrelated to any climatic factor. Another recent, regionally based analysis of summed dates from Iberia, based on a slightly different methodology and not differentiating dates with Mesolithic and Neolithic associations (Drake et al., 2017), shows the same pattern in the regions of Mediterranean Iberia that were analysed. First, there is a statistically significant increase in this population proxy following the arrival of farming, and then from c.7000 BP (according to their data) there is a collapse back to the pre-existing long-term exponential growth pattern (Fig 5.6b). Their proposal that farming increased the carrying capacity of these regions makes sense but, as in the other cases we have seen, the reasons for the subsequent fall are not so obvious, especially if climate change is excluded. It may be significant that this is roughly the date estimated for the increased proportion of forager admixture visible in the Middle Neolithic individuals from the site of La Mina discussed earlier in this chapter (Lipson et al., 2017).

Settlement and Subsistence

The presence of open-air sites indicating sedentary settlement, with structures, hearths, storage pits and walls or palisades, as well as evidence of cereal agriculture and stock-keeping is now well-established in Catalonia and areas to the south, from c.7500 BP (Oms et al., 2016), actually a bit earlier to the south, as we have seen. They are found not just on the coastal plains but also in the valleys of the interior and are one element of a larger subsistence-settlement system that also includes caves used for collective burial and others used as sheepfolds. In Valencia the site of Mas d'Is (Bernabeu Aubán et al., 2003) is an open-air site with an initial phase of occupation c.7550–7450 BP, represented by a single house. At the beginning of the subsequent phase, however, c.7450 BP, a small ditched enclosure is constructed, followed by a second larger one c.7150 BP, and another a short distance away c.6900 BP. These would have involved a major labour investment at a time when the regional population was relatively low (Bernabeu Aubán et al., 2006), suggesting that the site acted as a centre for settlements in the whole valley. At the same time striking assemblages are found in two caves on the edge of the settlement basin: the Cova de l'Or and the Cova de la Sarsa, including bracelets made of slate that must have been imported from southern Spain, ochre, pottery decorated in unusual styles and large quantities of cereals, as well as burials.

However, the most important EN open-air settlement in Iberia, because of the quality of the evidence it has provided, is the partially underwater site of La Draga (Palomo et al., 2014; Tarrús, 2008; Terradas et al., 2017), on what was then a peninsula on the shore of Lake Banyoles, in Catalonia. The dates for the two apparently continuous occupation phases at the site range from c.7300 to 6800 BP but it is likely that the actual length of the occupation within that period is much shorter. In material terms the site has a classic Cardial ceramic assemblage, most similar to that at the south-east French coastal site of Leucate-Corrège rather than other coastal sites in Catalonia or further south. There were two rows of structures, one at the shore and one slightly further away, each of eight to ten structures measuring c.10–12 × 3–4 m; the total area of the site is estimated at c.0.8 ha. Of particular significance among the large number of wooden artefacts that have been found are the sickles that have been discussed above, and a number of digging sticks, 24 in all, whose use as such has been confirmed by experimental reproduction and comparison of the use-wear traces. Large quantities of stored cereals have also been found at the site, with naked wheat making up the great majority, as well as broad beans, peas and opium poppy. The faunal assemblage has relatively high proportions of cattle and pig bones, not unusual at lowland open-air sites across the Mediterranean, as we have seen. The impact of the site is clearly visible in the local pollen sequence (Revelles et al., 2015), with an increase in grassland and a decrease in deciduous oak, unsurprising in the light of the thousands of oaks that must have been cut down to build and maintain the site structures over the course of its life. However, there is apparently no evidence of an increase in charcoal associated with the decline in woodland cover, which would argue against the establishment of farming here by slash-and-burn methods.

Evidence for Iberian EN subsistence patterns is not as extensive as in France but the same overall picture is confirmed in Saña's review of Iberian faunal evidence (Saña, 2013). Correspondence analysis of the faunal assemblages from EN sites (7700–6500 BP) shows considerable variety. The majority of sites are characterised by the full domestic faunal assemblage of sheep/goat, cattle and pig, with domestic proportions of over 90% at some sites; caprines generally dominate (42–76%) although there are also sites with high percentages of cattle, up to 63% in one case. At some sites, however, the majority of the faunal remains represent hunted animals and some of the assemblages of wild fauna show an emphasis on rabbit, also seen in south-east France (Manning et al., 2013b). There is regional variation in these patterns and also a certain amount of variation between the assemblages at different types of site, with cattle better represented at open-air sites than caves and rock shelters, as we would expect from what we have already seen in southern France. Overall though, there is as great a variety of different types of assemblages, from mainly domestic to mainly wild, including those with a significant rabbit component, at both caves and open-air sites. In the following Middle Neolithic (MN) phase (c.6500–5300 BP) the assemblages are less diverse and much more dominated by the domestic animals than the EN (Saña, 2013: fig 10.9). For Portugal the picture is similar, with domestic caprines and cattle present from the EN onwards, but also exploitation of wild boar and red deer; however, the evidence is extremely poor and lacks detail. As in southern and central Italy, analyses of ceramic residues from Cardial ceramics at the site of Can Sadurní (5475–5305 cal BC) in Catalonia have provided evidence of dairying and milk processing, confirming that the production and consumption of dairy products was a key part of the west Mediterranean farmer expansion (Spiteri et al., 2016, 2017).

As regards crop agriculture, there is evidence of directly dated cereals from Can Sadurní at c.7470–7300 BP and even earlier from further south, in Valencia, where the open-air site of Mas d'Is has produced a cereal date of 7620–7480 BP, while further south again, at the site of Murcielagos, the earliest cereal dates are slightly later (Zapata et al., 2004). A wide variety of crops are known from the Iberian EN, comparable to the crop packages in southern France and Italy that arrived there as part of the same movement. The hulled wheats, einkorn and emmer, both occur as well as free-threshing wheats and barley, and pulses are also recorded, including pea, lentil, broad bean, bitter vetch and grass pea, the latter two mainly animal fodder crops. Other crops include flax and poppy; the latter may have been domesticated in the west Mediterranean. Its earliest occurrence is in Italy at c.7800 BP (Rottoli and Pessina, 2007), while it is known in Andalucia, south-east Spain at c.7250 BP (Jordà et al., 2011). Zapata et al. suggest that it was initially used for its oily seeds but apparently there is evidence of opium compounds in Late Neolithic skeletons from the Gavà variscite mines in north-east Iberia. In Portugal the evidence for EN agriculture is sparse. The site of Cortiçóis in central Portugal has produced blades with sickle gloss indicating that they were similar in their hafting technique to those found at EN sites in Valencia and Andalusia but there is as yet little or no EN archaeobotanical evidence from here (Carvalho et al., 2013).

In comparison with the LBK, crop diversity is much greater, but there is considerable regional variation in the use of the different crops, even taking into account the likelihood that preservation and recovery factors are affecting the patterns of variation observed (Stika, 2005; Antolín et al., 2015). The reasons for this may be partly environmental but may also be linked with the presence of different cultural traditions and a contrast between the initial Impressa in Valencia, the south French coast and Liguria, apparently more associated with hulled wheats, and the later Cardial ceramic tradition where free-threshing wheats are more prevalent (Pérez-Jordà et al., 2017). In fact, even within the single region of Catalonia there seems to be a genuine difference between a north-eastern area where free-threshing wheat was overwhelmingly predominant and a central area where hulled wheats and barley are more prevalent (Antolín et al., 2015: fig 9) (Fig 5.7), which may again relate to different traditions. There was apparently a reduction in cereal diversity over time, with the hulled wheats, emmer and einkorn, decreasing in frequency, and free-threshing wheat and barley becoming the dominant types.

What of the nature of the agricultural system? As we have seen, Halstead (e.g. 2006) proposed that in the Aegean it was based on the continued cultivation

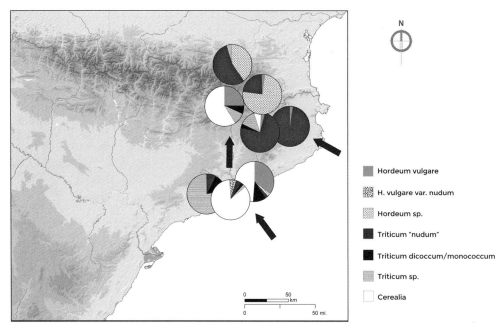

Fig 5.7. Early Neolithic regional crop variation in Catalonia. Reprinted from fig 9 in *Journal of Archaeological Science* 61, Antolín, F. et al., The hard knock life. Archaeobotanical data on farming practices during the Neolithic (5400–2300 cal BC) in the NE of the Iberian Peninsula, pp. 90–104, copyright 2015, with permission from Elsevier.

of small garden plots whose fertility was ensured by systematic manuring, and Bogaard has argued that this was the farming system that characterised the farming expansion into Europe more generally. Although the evidence is much more limited, this seems to be the case in the west Mediterranean as well (Antolín et al., 2015; Pérez-Jordà et al., 2017). Weed assemblages, for example at the site of La Draga, are largely made up of annuals, and woodland types are almost absent, while the pollen evidence from near the site, as we have seen, shows a strong clearance signature but no traces of charcoal that would indicate slash-and-burn.

SUMMARY AND CONCLUSION

We have seen overwhelming genetic and archaeological evidence that farming and the material culture associated with it were introduced to the west Mediterranean by pioneer farmers whose ancestors originated in the Aegean. The areas in which the first Impressa farmers initially settled were very thinly occupied, if at all, by pre-existing Mesolithic populations. The genome evidence for the following Cardial phase provides evidence of a degree of admixture but there is at least some evidence that this occurred prior to arrival in Spain. Unfortunately, we know very little about the social and spatial organisation of the earliest farmers, with the exception of the Tavoliere. They brought with them a farming system based on a broad range of cereals and pulses and also on domestic animals, especially caprines and cattle, that were used for milk as well as meat; indeed, dairying now appears as a fundamental aspect of the first farming in the central and western Mediterranean (Spiteri et al., 2016). Marine resources formed at most a small proportion of the diet of coastal groups. There is some evidence that the farming system was based on the type of small-scale intensive cultivation proposed by Halstead and Bogaard. As in the other cases of farmer colonisation, movement was not delayed until currently settled regions were fully occupied; for example, the dates show there were already settlements in eastern Spain at a time when occupation in Italy was only half way to its peak (García-Puchol et al., 2017: fig 3).

Given the nature of the dispersal process and the crucial role played by sea-borne movement (Isern et al., 2017), it is hard to imagine that the colonisation was anything other than extremely risky for the pioneer farming communities that undertook it. Of course, we do not know how many attempted colonisations failed but the fact that they took place shows that some people at least thought the prospective payoffs were worthwhile. The Cardial expansion, if indeed this too was based on population movement, seems to have involved shorter distances and been largely terrestrial so would not have entailed the same degree of risk.

The process of group fission and movement, especially by sea, would potentially also result in random drift and founder effects, depending on both the specific knowledge and practices of the fissioning part of the community and the particular seed stock and animals they took with them. The fact that crop diversity was maintained in the west Mediterranean, and also that both milking and milk-processing practices were consistently transmitted points to strong cultural selection in their favour. Where the predicted effects of drift are seen very clearly, however, is in the mitochondrial diversity of Early Neolithic cattle, which shows reductions to very low levels in the west Mediterranean (Scheu et al., 2015), reflecting successive founder effects. Innovations would similarly have been subject to chance effects, both in their initial occurrence and their subsequent transmission.

Are the material culture patterns seen in the west Mediterranean pioneer farmer expansion consistent with this sort of process? Bernabeu Aubán et al. (2017) have proposed and tested a 'cultural hitchhiking' model (Ackland et al., 2007), to account for the distribution of the different Early Neolithic ceramic decoration techniques in the west Mediterranean. Cultural traits without any intrinsic benefits of their own can spread if they are linked with traits that do have such an advantage. The demic expansion of pioneer farming communities provides precisely such a context, as we suggested for the LBK. The farming economy provides the advantageous trait because it leads to demographic expansion. Pottery as a technology is part of that advantageous complex, for example for milk processing, as we have seen. However, on the cultural hitchhiking hypothesis the particular decorative attributes that spread are simply the 'cultural baggage' that happens to be associated with the groups that are fissioning and founding new settlements; they are transmitted with them, together with other attributes that are invisible to us, such as their language. If cultural hitchhiking is the mechanism responsible for the spread of the decorative techniques we should expect drift and innovation to be operating, and probably quite powerfully given the small size of the communities concerned. As a result, assemblages further from the origin in time and space should become increasingly different from those at the origin, and also from one another as the length of their histories increases, unless there is interaction between them. Bernabeu Aubán et al.'s analysis of the relationship between the distance of the sites from a south Italian origin and the between-site assemblage similarity does show the expected correlation between increasing distance and decreasing inter-assemblage similarity but the results are by no means conclusive, as they explain, and further work is required to explore this.

The fact that regional populations increased as a result of farming and that it spread rapidly inland from the places where it was introduced confirms its success as a subsistence strategy that would have paid off in terms of the reproductive success of the colonists and their descendants. However, as we have seen with many areas of the LBK, that success was not lasting. The boom was followed by a bust that saw major reductions in population from the initial peak in many areas, for reasons that remain unclear.

CHAPTER 6

CONTINENTAL TEMPERATE EUROPE
7000–5500 BP: INTERNAL EXPANSION AND
ADAPTATION

In tracing the spread of farming in Europe we now need to return to what was happening in temperate Europe after the end of the LBK around 7000 years ago. We have seen already that the expansion was always a process of stops and starts, Guilaine's *arrhythmic spread* (2003), but the delay of over 1000 years before farming spread to Britain and Scandinavia c.6000 BP is the most striking of all, since LBK settlements existed only 100 km south of the Baltic coast and southern Scandinavia well before 7000 BP and close to the English Channel coast in Normandy by 7000 (Billard et al., 2014). Since the mid-1980s the standard model of the spread of farming in temperate continental Europe beyond the loess zone has been the following: an initial period when know-ledge of agricultural resources and other aspects of farming material culture were available to local foragers; a substitution phase when foragers interacted increasingly with farmers and their existing lifeways were disrupted, because of such processes as a loss of hunting territories and increasing preferences of women in forager communities to marry farmers; and, finally, the full-scale adoption of farming (Zvelebil and Rowley-Conwy, 1984). As we will see, it is increasingly clear that this model of steadily growing pressure of farming populations on surviving hunter-gatherer groups does not fit the evidence that is becoming available; it is only late in the 7th millennium that this begins to occur, and then not in the form originally envisaged.

In order to explain this delay, we need to understand the demographic, subsistence and social developments that took place in western and Central Europe during the 7th millennium (see Fig 6.1 for all places mentioned in this chapter). In contrast to all the previous chapters, which described the first appearance of farming and farmers in entirely new regions previously occu-pied only by hunters and gatherers, this one is mainly concerned with more localised 'internal colonisation' and the post-LBK history of those regions where farming was already established; consequently, the issues that arise are rather different. In what follows we will begin by looking at the first half of the

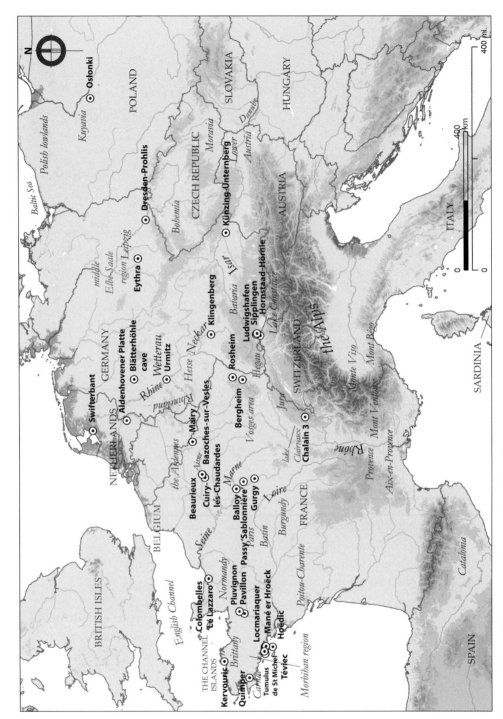

Fig 6.1. Map of sites and regions mentioned in Chapter 6.

7th millennium BP, first in Central Europe, then in western France, where spatial expansion continued, but also, more importantly, where the Mediterranean and Central European branches of the farming expansion came together after more than a millennium of separation. The next part of the chapter focuses on the last half of the 7th millennium BP and the early 6th, when a new phase of expansion began that was to provide the basis for the spread of farming into southern Scandinavia and the British Isles. After describing the pattern of expansion and the social and cultural developments associated with it, discussion turns to the nature of the subsistence-settlement system that made it possible, which has been a subject of heated debate.

POST-LBK DEMOGRAPHIC AND CULTURAL PATTERNS IN CENTRAL EUROPE

As we saw in Chapter 4, on the basis of the summed radiocarbon probabilities the regional population patterns for the main agricultural regions where farming arrived with the LBK, all show that the LBK represented a local population peak that in many cases was never exceeded, at least not until much later. In many regions the end of the LBK seems to be characterised by a population 'bust'; the evidence for unrest in several of these regions at this time has already been discussed in Chapter 4. As we have seen, the human reproductive potential for rapid population growth when the right conditions exist is effectively limitless and is reflected in the rapid rise in population when farming first arrived in these regions, so the fact that these populations remained effectively stuck at, or even below, LBK levels seems to indicate that some sort of limit had been reached. This inference is confirmed by a comparison of the spatial extent and distribution of the main LBK regions in Germany (Fig 4.4) with those of the following Middle Neolithic (Fig 6.2), down to c.6600/6500 BP. They show no expansion beyond the LBK's limits and in some cases, for example the Rhine area, there is a decrease.

In western Germany all the main settlement regions show evidence of a population decline and/or a cultural hiatus. One such example is the Upper Rhine region, with a hiatus of c.150 years now established between the end of the LBK and the beginning of the Hinkelstein phase (Denaire et al., 2017). The latter is the first in a series of cultural phases defined in terms of pottery styles, successively the Hinkelstein, Grossgartach and Rössen, that together make up the Middle Neolithic of the region and represent a continuation with modification of the LBK tradition, not just in terms of pottery but also house forms (Friederich, 2012). The details of settlement history vary from region to region though the basic pattern of constraint within LBK limits is a constant. In the Lower Rhine area there is no settlement continuity with the LBK and it is only in the Rössen phase (c.4750–4600) that a similar population density to the LBK is reached again (Nowak,

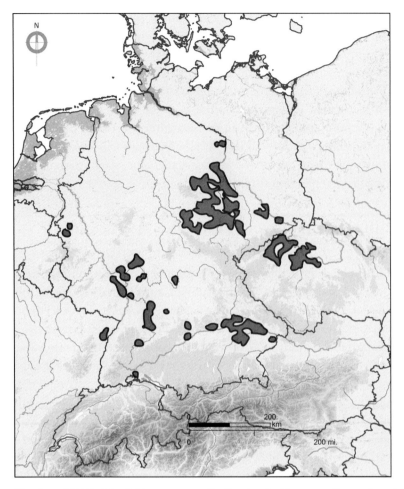

Fig 6.2. Middle Neolithic core area distribution in Germany. Reproduced from fig 12 in *Proceedings of the Prehistoric Society* 75, Zimmermann, A. et al., Landscape Archaeology in Central Europe., pp. 1–53, 2009, Cambridge University Press.

2012). By contrast, in the Upper Rhine the population reaches LBK levels again in the Grossgartach phase, when all the previous LBK settlement areas except one are re-occupied, while the subsequent Rössen has only half as many sites and they have a lower density of structures, without any evidence of house remains. The settlement history of the Neckar region of south-west Germany is not dissimilar. It shows the same basic continuity of settlement area from the LBK in areas with rainfall lower than 750 mm per year and similar settlement density to the LBK, though there is little continuity at individual sites (Friederich, 2012).

In the northern half of Poland the LBK is succeeded by the Late Band Pottery Culture (LBPC) in the period c.6900/6800–6500/6400 BP and sees settlement dispersal and shorter occupation. There is also evidence of contact with hunter-gatherers, which had not existed during the LBK (Czerniak, 2012), increased use of local flint as opposed to the previously imported flint from south-east

Poland, and more hunting. Pyzel's analysis of the settlement history of Kuyavia (2012) shows that the LBPC represents a major population decline compared with the LBK; Bogucki et al. (2012) note a general hiatus in settlement of the Polish lowlands in the first two centuries of the 7th millennium BP. The LBPC is succeeded by the Brześć Kujawski Culture (BKC) c.6500/6400 BP, which occupied the same areas as the LBK, with very similar site location preferences and settlement forms, specifically groups of longhouses. But the houses are now trapezoidal and differ quite considerably from those of the LBK. It seems likely that the BKC in Kuyavia represents a recolonisation of the region, taking advantage of the LBPC population decline, by agricultural communities of Lengyel Culture origin from the Middle Danube area, who were themselves LBK descendants. However, in addition to the Danubian tradition the material culture now shows hunter-gatherer elements, especially in terms of ornaments, such as animal teeth necklaces (Czerniak, 2012; cf. Rigaud et al., 2015). At the site of Osłonki BKC settlement lasted for several hundred years, with possible short interruptions, and had a much greater local environmental impact than the earlier short-lived LBK settlement in the same area (Bogucki et al., 2012).

The end date of the BKC is unclear, but it seems to have been a relatively slow transformation extending over the period 6000–5650 BP and the dates arguably overlap with the earliest dates of the subsequent Funnel Beaker Culture (generally referred to as the TRB Culture on the basis of the German word for Funnel Beaker (*Trichterbecher*)) in the region. The novelty here, Czerniak (2012) suggests, is that the TRB marked the earliest exploitation of widely available areas of sandy soils and thus a new farming adaptation, associated with a gradual cultural transformation from BKC to TRB. The radiocarbon summed probability curve for Kuyavia shows a significant increase in population in the centuries following 6000 BP, corresponding to the TRB, declining again 600–700 years later (Fig 4.5d).

In the Middle Elbe-Saale region of central Germany, on the other hand, it is very clear that there is a seamless continuity from the latest LBK through to the succeeding *Stichbandkeramik* (SBK), or Stroke-Ornamented Pottery, which represents no more than a stylistic change (Link, 2012). At sites such as Dresden-Prohlis and Eythra, near Leipzig (Cladders et al., 2012), as we saw in Chapter 4, the stylistic transition can be seen during the life of a single settlement. Nevertheless, although there is no break in settlement history, and the great majority of SBK settlements show a continuity from the LBK, there is a tendency towards nucleation during the Middle Neolithic and, as elsewhere, little sign that the settled area expanded (Starling, 1983). Where there is a break is at the end of the 7th millennium BP. The following Middle Elbe-Saale I phase (Müller, 2001) marks the beginning of a new tradition, the central German TRB, which shows a continuous development for the next millennium. The transition coincides with a marked population decrease in the last couple of centuries of the 7th millennium BP visible in the radiocarbon population proxy, and the beginning of a trend of increasing population through the 6th millennium (Fig 4.5c) (Müller, 2001: fig

261, 424; Shennan et al., 2013). Moreover, the downturn at the end of the 7th millennium is found not just in the archaeological record but also in the pollen indicators of settlement during this period (Gleser, 2012: 63–64). It is striking that the Middle Elbe-Saale region was not immune from crisis given that the region has the largest area of loess soils in Central Europe and on Zimmermann et al.'s calculations (2004) would have had the largest LBK population, while from the early 6th millennium BP into the Bronze Age it was one of the major cultural centres in Europe. The drop in population must have led either to a local cultural reformulation and changed subsistence-settlement strategy or to an expansion of other groups from neighbouring areas.

The same immediately post-LBK cultural sequence is found in Bohemia, while along the Danube valley from Bavaria to Slovakia and Hungary we find versions of the *Stichbandkeramik* in the west and Lengyel painted pottery, another LBK descendant, towards the east. In Bohemia, as in central Germany, there is no indication of a population crash at the end of the LBK itself; it is later. A rising population pattern is apparent until c.6800 BP, after which there is a long-term decline and occupation becomes concentrated in the agriculturally more favourable areas of central and north-west Bohemia (Demján and Dreslerová, 2016); in eastern Bohemia the number of sites drops by over 50% (Končelová, 2012). A similar pattern of major decline from around 6500 BP is visible in Kolář et al.'s (2016) recent study of a region in Moravia, based on settlement data, and in the radiocarbon population proxy for the Lower Austria/Moravia region. However, the latter also suggests a drop in population at the end of the LBK before a rapid rise to at least previous levels in the first half of the 7th millennium (Timpson et al., 2014). This is not visible in the Kolář et al. study, which in any case addresses a much smaller area, and it remains to be seen whether or not this is because of the lower chronological resolution of the settlement data used.

In summary, the settlement and population picture for Central Europe for most of the 7th millennium BP is one of stasis or decline.

EXPANSION IN THE WEST AND THE DEVELOPMENT OF NEW SOCIAL PATTERNS

If we turn now to the Paris Basin, the western end of the LBK colonisation wave, we find that here too the LBK marks a limit but there is a difference in that expansion was able to continue further west. The LBK, in the version known locally as the *Rubané Récent du Bassin Parisien* (RRBP) reached here c.7100 BP or slightly before. A series of rescue archaeology projects in the Aisne valley, like those in the Aldenhovener Platte further east, have revealed the characteristic LBK settlement pattern, one made up of small groups of houses and larger hamlets 1–2 km apart along the river valley terraces, with a small number of larger sites with longer periods of occupation, such as the site of Cuiry-lès-Chaudardes, described in Chapter 4.

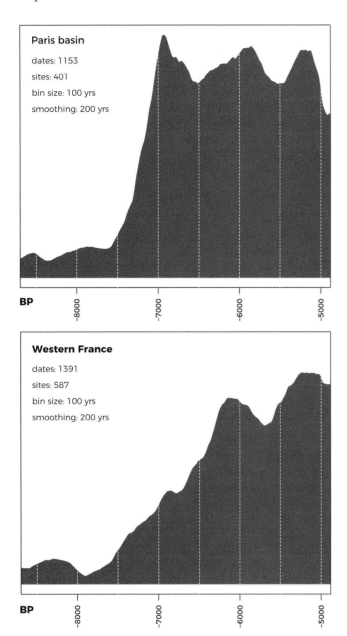

Fig 6.3. Radiocarbon population proxies for: a) Paris Basin; b) Western France. Data from EUROEVOL project updated by Professor A. Bevan.

Fig 6.3a shows a very steep population rise with the arrival of the LBK – in fact it must have been even steeper than it appears because the ends of the date probability distributions make the start look earlier than it was. It peaks at c.6900 BP and then declines, as elsewhere, before rising and falling again twice in the following two millennia. To the west, however, we see considerable expansion of the settlement area, also reflected in the population proxy, which shows population rising until 6200 BP (Fig 6.3b). The settlement of

Colombelles 'Le Lazzaro' in Normandy, dating to c.7000 BP (Billard et al., 2014), shows that the RRBP had already reached the coast of the English Channel. The distribution of the subsequent Villeneuve-St-Germain (VSG) phase, c.6850–6700/6600 BP, indicates that expansion continued well beyond those areas favoured by the RRBP, to the west and to the south. Nevertheless, the VSG inherited the preferences and constraints of the LBK farming system. It is still almost entirely focussed on patches of loess and loess-derived soils, and it simply carried on westwards far into Brittany until these finally ran out, even getting as far as the Channel Islands, which would have required a sea crossing (Scarre, 2011). Occupation sites with longhouses are known from central Brittany, for example at the site of Pluvignon, with dates of c.7000–6700 BP (Pailler et al., 2008; Scarre, 2011: 52). Here the high-quality flint being used was coming from well to the east, showing that colonising communities maintained their ancestral connections. There are also indications of late VSG occupation from the far west of Brittany, including a settlement of several trapezoid houses at the site of Kervouric, at Lannion on the north coast (www.inrap.fr/des-maisons-du-neolithique-ancien-lannion-cotes-d-armor-5359), and a site at Quimper dating to the first quarter of the 7th millennium BP, with evidence of long-distance connections, including to the Loire valley (Tinevez et al., 2015). As we have seen elsewhere, there is no evidence that Mesolithic occupation continued for any length of time after the arrival of the first farming communities (Scarre, 2011: 64), but again it is worth remembering that the areas of farming occupation would initially have been limited.

A further contrast to areas further east, where the Mediterranean and Central European farming expansions were entirely distinct from one another, is that in France they come together after a millennium of separation. The RRBP already has indications of connections with the Cardial tradition. As we saw in Chapter 5, this had arrived centuries earlier in southern France and gradually spread northwards and westwards though its traces are limited. Thus, the site of Chalain 3 in the French Jura, produced evidence of agricultural clearance c.7500–7200 BP (Pétrequin et al., 2009), but without any cultural material that would point to the ancestry of these farmers. In other words, the expansion of farming observed in France is from both north and south but we know far more about the former.

The connection between the northern and southern streams has now been shown incontrovertibly by mtDNA evidence from the site of Gurgy 'Les Noisats', a cemetery of inhumation graves in the Yonne valley, on the south-east side of the Paris Basin (Rivollat et al., 2015, 2017). Radiocarbon dates show that it was used from c.7000 to 6000 BP, most intensively from 6900 to 6500. The results indicated admixture between descendants of farmers of both LBK and Mediterranean origin as well as of Mesolithic hunter-gatherers, though the latter was not necessarily recent and could have occurred much earlier to ancestors of the northern and southern farmers who met there. MtDNA evidence is relatively weak because it does not contain much information compared with whole genomes, but the existence of this southern ancestral connection is further confirmed by recent evidence that the genomes of Early Neolithic farmers in Britain are closer to Middle Neolithic genomes from southern France than to Central European ones (Olalde et al., 2017, and see Chapter 8).

This connection makes many of the cultural developments in the northern half of France during the region's Early and Middle Neolithic distinctly different from areas further east. For example, stone rings of limestone, serpentinite and jadeite from Provence and northern Italy are found in RRBP contexts in the Paris Basin already at the end of the 8th millennium BP (Pétrequin et al., 2015a, 2015b) and Cardial influences are seen in pottery decoration and in bone working (Sidéra, 2010). The material culture of the following VSG phase, like the LBK successors further east, is very much in the LBK tradition but there are indications of strengthening contacts to southern France in the pottery styles, and the architecture of the longhouses changes. In the Aisne valley there are fewer known sites and they are generally smaller than those of the RRBP, with c. two to four houses. Surprisingly however, despite the indication that occupation was sparser than before, sites are now found not just on the Aisne valley terraces but also in the valleys of its tributaries and on the edge of the plateau above (Allard, 2014), suggesting spatial extensification of the subsistence system.

The following Cerny Culture in northern France (Middle Neolithic I), beginning c.6700 BP, continues the LBK tradition (Marcigny et al., 2010), although it is modified still further, and evidence of houses becomes increasingly rare. The characteristic longhouses disappear and there is greater variety in domestic structures, including small rectilinear buildings and also circular forms, which are foreign to the ancestral LBK and may relate to the southern traditions about which so little is known. It also seems that structures become more isolated (Last, 2013), suggesting a more dispersed settlement pattern. In contrast, we see the emergence of a monumental burial tradition not matched in Central Europe, with the appearance in the valleys of the Seine, Yonne and Marne, for example at the site of Passy 'Sablonnière', of the so-called 'Passy' enclosures (Chambon and Thomas, 2010: fig 4; Thomas et al., 2011: fig 2). These are mounds/enclosures of timber and earth ranging in length from 25 to 300 m and c.8 m wide, expanded at one end, which make up cemeteries of successive pairs or triplets of mounds, again mostly containing single burials, though there is debate about whether they reflect social inequality. Here grave goods seem to be largely local items linked to hunting, including beads made of various wild animal teeth but including a mysterious item called an 'Eiffel tower' by French archaeologists, only found in monumental burials; they are made from a deer scapula and were apparently hafted, while the pointed end has use traces; they are found only with males. The fact that these novel monuments occur in the same region as the Gurgy cemetery, mentioned above, with its evidence of mixing between northern and southern populations , must surely be significant.

Probably rather later, c.6400/6300 BP, the first monumental burials in Normandy occur. They are represented by long low banks of earth bounded on each side by shallow ditches and oriented east–west; these may be up to 300 m long though the average is c.80 m. They are out of all proportion with the burial pit for a single individual that they contain, which is located either in the middle or at one end. The burial pits themselves are also large, 3 x 1.5m, and individuals within them are accompanied by grave goods; typically these comprise bone points, boar's tusks, transverse arrowheads probably in a quiver, as well as remains of sheep and goats, both joints of meat and whole animals (Marcigny et al., 2010: 151). The authors see these monumental burials as evidence for significant social inequality, marking a major break with what went before.

Further west, the feature that differentiates the Breton Early Neolithic from other regions is its remarkable concentrations of megalithic monuments, in the Morbihan region of southern Brittany in particular. It remains an open question whether these represent a continuity of tradition from the slab-covered burials of the Final Mesolithic at the famous coastal shell mound sites of Téviec and Hoëdic (see e.g. Scarre, 2011: 57–64). There can be no doubt that they started being built within 200 years or less of the local arrival of farming, and the extensive imports of Alpine axes, mainly from Monte Viso on the border between France and Italy, point strongly to a southern connection. Although the dating of the monuments is by no means straightforward, it seems likely that the earliest were shaped standing stones, probably erected between c.6750 and 6250 BP, and long mounds. The shaping and erection of the largest of the standing stones, notably the 21-metre-long Grand Menhir Brisé at Locmariaquer, part of a line of shaped standing stones erected towards the middle of the 7th millennium BP (Cassen et al., 2012), must have been an enormous undertaking, indicative of both the size of the regional population (see Scarre, 2001), and of the force that drew them together for this mammoth enterprise; its subsequent fall was probably the result of an earthquake. Adjacent to the Grand Menhir and the alignment associated with it, but probably of a later date, is the mound of Er Grah, 140 m long, echoing in shape the VSG trapezoidal houses, dated to c.6300–6200 BP and including a closed chamber covered by a capstone made of a menhir fragment; inside the chamber were some variscite beads imported from north-west Iberia and a miniature axe pendant of Alpine jadeite (Cassen et al., 2012: 964–965), but there were probably more grave goods in the past.

The most striking of the long mounds is the Tumulus de St Michel, at Carnac, 120 m long, 60 m wide and 10 m high, 30,000 m³ in volume, with a closed chamber radiocarbon-dated to the mid-7th millennium BP, which contained 13 remarkable highly polished stone axe blades of jadeite from the Italian Alps, one of them 37 cm in length, as well as variscite beads imported from Iberia. Both Er Grah and the Tumulus de St Michel are examples of so-called 'Carnac mounds', of which seven are known in the Morbihan area, probably dating to the last half or third quarter of the 7th millennium BP. These were mounds of massive size, with large chambers closed to the outside, inside which exotic items were deposited, in particular Alpine axes of extraordinary quality, probably associated with individual inhumation burials. Apart from the Tumulus de St Michel, two others stand out for their rich contents. Beneath the chamber floor at the mound of Mané er Hroëck, was a deposit containing over 100 axes, including 11 of Alpine jadeite, as well as imported variscite beads and pendants, while on the floor of the chamber itself was a jadeite ring and a superb polished axe with the pointed butt resting on the edge of the ring as if penetrating it (Cassen et al., 2012: 947). The other striking example is the huge round mound of Tumiac (Cassen et al., 2012: 940–941), still 15 m high, which contained 18 Alpine axes as well as variscite beads. The other axes at these sites were made of fibrolite, which, like the variscite, may also have come from Iberia. It has been established that the characteristic shape of the imported axes was obtained by regrinding and polishing them to the preferred local form, which is also seen in the axes carved on the walls of the nearby passage grave at Gavrinis. Pétrequin et al. (2012b: 614) have argued that these three burials formed a sequence, with the earliest being Mané er Hroëck, and the Tumulus de St Michel the last. Other mounds also contain exotic goods but nothing to compare in quantity with the three outstanding examples even in cases where the mounds are of comparable size.

Passage graves (tombs with a passage linking the burial chamber to the outside world) are considered to be later than the closed mounds, though the reliable radiocarbon dates that are available still point to c.6250–5900 BP (Scarre, 2011: 76, 145), and finds of exotic objects tend to be less frequent in them. Although there are concentrations of passage graves in southern Brittany, they are found much more widely, on the north coast as well as in Normandy and in the region of Poitou-Charente to the south of the river Loire.

The scale of the monuments and the concentration of exotic polished stone axes and other items in Brittany in roughly the third quarter of the 7th millennium BP is unique. The number of superbly shaped and polished axes of Alpine jadeite is far in excess of what would be expected in a region so far away from the source (Fig 6.4a and b) and there can be no doubt that they had both a social and a ritual significance. Apart from the artistic

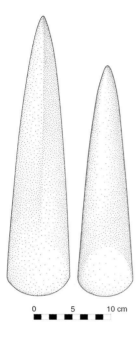

0   5   10 cm

Fig 6.4. a) Examples of jadeite axes from the Carnac mound of Mané er Hroëck, Brittany. Reproduced from fig 18 in Cassen, S. et al., Dépôts bretons, tumulus carnacéens et circulations à longue distance. In Pétrequin, P. et al. (Eds.), *Jade. Grandes haches alpines du Néolithique européen, Ve et IVe millénaires av. J.-C.*, pp. 918–995, 2012, Presses Universitaires de Franche-Comté, with permission from the author.

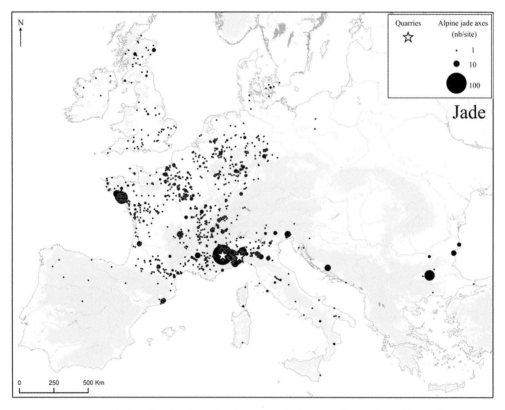

Fig 6.4. b) The distribution of jadeite axes in Europe. Reproduced from fig 2 in Pétrequin, P. et al., 2015b. *Projet JADE 2*. 'Object-signs' and social interpretations of Alpine jade axeheads in the European Neolithic: theory and methodology. In Kerig, T. and Shennan, S. (Eds.), *Connecting Networks*, pp. 83–102, 2015, Archaeopress, with permission from the author.

representations in which they figure, the axes were frequently carefully placed in groups when they were deposited, standing with the butt in the ground and the cutting edge upwards. Moreover, they were not just deposited in tombs but in other clearly ritual contexts in the same region, sometimes in considerable numbers; for example, blades are found at the foot of standing stones (Cassen et al., 2012: 979).

It is equally clear that the concentrations of massive monuments and exotic imports associated with single individuals in burials, especially those in the three pre-eminent Carnac mounds, imply an enormous concentration of wealth, power and authority, with an extraordinary ritual dimension. In western Europe it was only in southern Brittany that large Alpine axes were placed in burials; elsewhere they were ritual depositions in places of special significance, whether natural, for example caves, bogs or rock outcrops, or man-made, such as standing stones (Pétrequin et al., 2015b: 87). As Cassen et al. (2012: 980–982) emphasise, the nature of the concentrations of power implied by the Breton monuments eludes us, though its rituals and artefactual forms seem a long way from the LBK tradition. This may be a result of the impact of indigenous Mesolithic traditions, or, more likely, of the connections to the south and the Mediterranean sphere that are evident in the exchange links and that are likely to reflect at least partly the ancestry of the Breton population given the new genetic evidence for north–south connections. The basis for the concentration of wealth and monumentality in this particular place is also unknown, though the fact that it occurs when the western France population seems to be rising to a peak is worth noting. We know very little about settlements and subsistence in Brittany, although one possibility is that salt production, which was important in later periods in Brittany, played a role in attracting symbolically powerful exotic objects (Cassen et al., 2008). Such a suggestion may be strengthened by the recent discovery of a major salt-producing centre in Bulgaria (Nikolov, 2010) c.50 km from the extraordinary gold and other wealth concentrations of the Varna cemetery, which is similar in date and is also connected to Brittany by the fact that some of the burials contain axes of Alpine origin (Pétrequin et al., 2012a). Regardless of this, it is increasingly clear that it is hard to exaggerate the uniqueness of the Breton centre itself, even though the height of its wealth and power already seems to be over by the beginning of the last quarter of the 7th millennium and its concentration of wealth does not begin to be matched until the Breton early Bronze Age, two thousand years later. However, its cultural influence is demonstrated by the way in which Alpine axes that had been re-shaped into Breton styles subsequently spread very widely and were imitated in local rocks, and also by the occurrence elsewhere of similar 'object-signs' to those engraved on Breton monuments (Pétrequin et al., 2012c).

THE 'YOUNG NEOLITHIC': c.6400–5500 BP IN NORTHERN
FRANCE, GERMANY AND THE LOW COUNTRIES

From c.6400/6300 BP archaeologists recognise further changes in the material
culture of the Paris Basin and northern France in general, especially in pottery
traditions, marking the beginning of Middle Neolithic II, with the development of the northern Chasséen Culture in the more westerly part. It seems to be
reflected in a renewed boom in the Paris Basin radiocarbon proxy from c.6500
BP to a peak at c.5900/5800 before another decline (Fig 6.3a). Immediately
to the east of the Chasséen the Michelsberg Culture develops. In fact, the
Chasséen and the Michelsberg have many similarities in their material culture
and practices, including the extensive construction of enclosures (see below).
It is now widely accepted, following Jeunesse (1998), that the Michelsberg
Culture began in the eastern Paris Basin, in the area of the confluence of
the Seine and the Yonne. However, whereas the northern Chasséen represents
continuity from its predecessors in settlement terms, beyond its likely area
of origin the Michelsberg marks a new phase of agricultural expansion. It is
unclear whether or not this represents a demographic expansion like the LBK
from a single region, though recent mtDNA analysis for a Michelsberg site
in eastern France would support this (Beau et al., 2017), or corresponds to
the spread of new stylistic norms among groups across a wide area that were
beginning to adopt new and expansive settlement strategies and, as a result, also
interacting with the forager groups that continued to exist outside the areas of
agricultural settlement (see below). Regional assemblages, for example pottery,
have broad family resemblances. Where and when the Michelsberg appears,
however, it seems to mark the final break with the preceding Danubian tradition inherited from the LBK, in terms of settlement and house form as well
as material culture and symbols (Jeunesse, 2010). As we will see below, it also
seems to mark a break with the LBK subsistence system.

   If we assume that there was indeed a single origin in the south-east Paris
Basin, the evidence cited earlier from the Gurgy cemetery in the same region
might link it with the development of novel ways of life that emerged among
the mixed groups that developed there. The recent mtDNA results just
mentioned, suggesting western affinities and a difference from the preceding
Rössen, would fit in with this, as the authors point out, but need confirming
with whole-genome results, and even if relevant here do not necessarily apply
to the Michelsberg as a whole.

   However that may be, by c.6300 BP the Michelsberg has spread to Belgium,
the Rhine and the Neckar valley and by 6000 it has reached as far as Bavaria
and central Germany and the borders of Scandinavia in the north. Moreover,
whether or not it involved the expansion of a population with a single origin,
the key process at the heart of the Michelsberg spread is the expansion of human
populations beyond the previously favoured patches of loess, an internal expansion into zones between the old LBK settlement areas and an external one to

the north. At the same time there is also an expansion to the south, with the beginning of occupation on the lake shores of the Alpine foreland. The history of settlement in the area of present-day Belgium provides an excellent example of the process. After the end of the post-LBK Blicquy phase, the local equivalent of the VSG that we have seen further south, the small loess islands occupied by the LBK seem to be abandoned: there is no evidence of renewed occupation until the Michelsberg, c.6400/6300 BP, when large sites, including enclosures, appear. Adjacent sandy areas, previously occupied by hunter-gatherers, also see the first appearance of farming, though the Michelsberg sites here are smaller (Vander Linden, 2011). The contrast between the limited spatial distribution of the LBK and the much more extensive Michelsberg distribution is shown in Fig 6.5. It is also reflected in the population proxy for the region.

To the south, intensive archaeological and pollen analysis work in the Lake Constance region of south-west Germany has also demonstrated major settlement pattern change (Bofinger et al., 2012). Here it was the fertile loess soils of the Hegau region that were occupied in the LBK, an occupation that continued and intensified in the first half of the 7th millennium BP. Around 6300 BP,

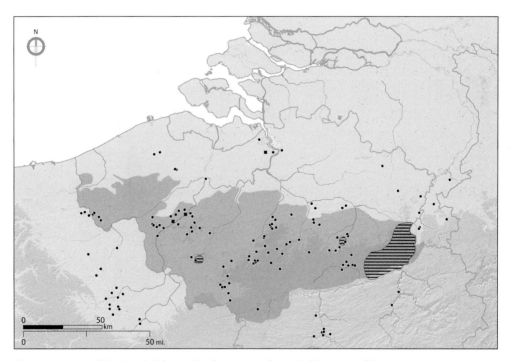

Fig 6.5. Map of the Michelsberg distribution in the Scheldt basin of the Low Countries showing the contrast with the LBK. Horizontal hatching: LBK core areas. Dark grey: the loess area. Squares: Early Neolithic isolated finds. Dots: Michelsberg sites. Reproduced from figs 1 and 4 in Crombé, P. and Vanmontfort, B., The neolithisation of the Scheldt basin in western Belgium. In Whittle, A. and Cummings, V. (Eds.), *Going Over.* Proceedings of the British Academy 144, pp. 263–285. © The British Academy 2007. With permission from the British Academy.

however, intensive occupation began around the shores of Lake Constance itself, reflected in both a major rise in the radiocarbon population proxy for the area and an increase in secondary woodland indicators in the pollen diagrams (Lechterbeck et al., 2014); at the same time settlement intensity in the Hegau was decreasing. In fact, the late 7th millennium marks the beginning of agricultural occupation of the Alpine foreland region of southern Germany and Switzerland more generally, reflected in a rapid population increase which slows at c.6100 BP, reaching a peak at c.5700 BP before declining rapidly (Fig 6.6) (Timpson et al., 2014). Evidence for a growing human impact at this time was also found by Colledge and Conolly (2014) in their analysis of the plant macro-remains preserved by waterlogging at the lake settlements. They were able to show that indications of greater use of wild plant foods from woodland habitats were not a reflection of taphonomic biases but an indication of greater exploitation of these areas linked to expanding clearance for cultivation. One of the most striking features of the Alpine foreland expansion is the short-lived nature of the settlements, which we know from dendrochronology often lasted only 10–20 years; its significance will be discussed further below.

The expansion is visible at a broad scale in Zimmermann et al.'s map of the 'Young Neolithic', c.6400–5500 BP, in Germany and adjacent areas (see Fig 6.7). In contrast to the preceding phases discussed earlier in this chapter (see Fig 4.4, 6.2), the settlement area is greatly extended. However, that does not necessarily mean it was occupied throughout at the same density as the previous core areas; it represents an *extensification* of settlement.

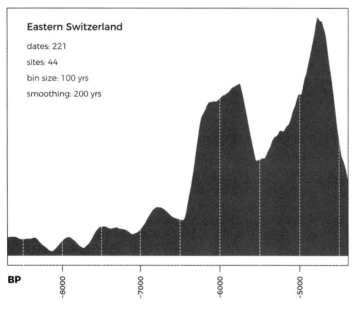

Fig 6.6. Radiocarbon population proxy for eastern Switzerland. Data from EUROEVOL project.

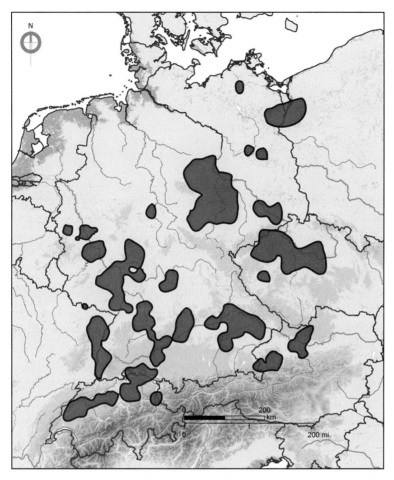

Fig 6.7. 'Young Neolithic' core area distribution in Germany. Reproduced from fig 12 in *Proceedings of the Prehistoric Society* 75, Landscape Archaeology in Central Europe, pp. 1–53, 2009, Cambridge University Press.

Zimmermann et al. (2004) have shown that for the LBK core areas that include the vast majority of occupation, settlement areas can be defined as those where sites are no more than 4 km apart. For the Michelsberg, however, the corresponding figure is 12.5 km, made up of a lower density of sites within settlement nuclei but also greater distances between those nuclei, each made up of open settlements and an enclosure. In other words, the settlement area was much bigger but, at two different levels, the sites were much more widely spaced than in the LBK.

Despite the evidence for expansion, the Michelsberg Culture remains somewhat enigmatic in terms of its archaeological record. Burials are not common, though the presence of a Michelsberg long barrow over 15 m in length containing two burials at the site of Beaurieux, adjacent to the open settlement of Cuiry-lès-Chaudardes, is worth noting (Colas et al., 2007). The best-known sites are the enclosures already mentioned (see below); open sites are not common, though this is likely to reflect at least in part the nature of the evidence, which mainly consists of groups of pits with little evidence of houses; these were presumably of lighter construction than the post-built houses of earlier periods. According to Seidel (2010), the groups represented by the open settlements were small and short-lived, which suggests that Michelsberg extensification was associated with greater settlement mobility, as in the lake village region, where it is much better documented (see below).

Enclosures in 7th-Millennium Western and Central Europe

The striking exception to the pattern of short-lived settlements is the c.20 post-built longhouses, up to 40 m in length at the enclosure site of Mairy in the Ardennes, apparently occupied for 400–700 years, but it is unlikely that this represents a normal settlement.

Enclosures are one of the major legacies of the LBK across most of temperate western and Central Europe during the Neolithic. As we saw in Chapter 4, they appear in large numbers over a broad area in the late LBK, as part of a process involving the creation of larger scale social institutions integrating larger numbers of people. Zimmermann (2012) estimates that the local enclosures of the late LBK would have corresponded to units of c.250 people. Following the LBK, in the earlier part of the Middle Neolithic along the Middle Danube a new very specific type of enclosure appears, the so-called 'rondel' or *Kreisgrabenanlage*, a roughly circular enclosure with concentric ditches and palisades, an interior that seems to have been largely free of features, and four entrances at roughly 90 degrees from one another, sometimes apparently oriented on key celestial events. They often occur with large settlements, for example the site of Künzing-Unternberg (Fig 6.8) in Bavaria, where the rondel was within a settlement of c.9 ha. They are also found in numbers in Bohemia and central Germany in association with *Stichbandkeramik* pottery (Bertemes and Meller, 2012). It appears that they spread rapidly across the whole of this area c.6800–6700 BP and that their period of construction was a century or less (Petrasch, 2015), after which some were left to decay while others were levelled; in some cases they were replaced by systems of concentric palisades only, without the ditches. For the region in Bavaria south of the river Isar near its confluence with the Danube, Petrasch (2012) shows that the rondels were regularly spaced c.5–10 km apart at the centre of small settlement regions, and that the sizes of these regions correlate well with the sizes of the enclosures, thus likely reflecting the size of the local populations that built and used them.

However, these represent a very specific and short-lived phenomenon and in general the first half of the 7th millennium is a period when only small numbers of enclosures were constructed. This changes in the middle of the millennium when a major expansion of enclosure construction begins in the

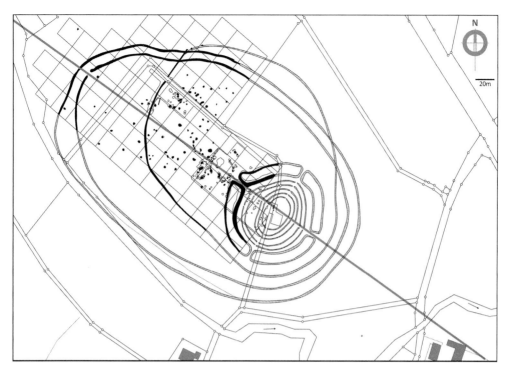

Fig 6.8. Plan of the 'rondel' enclosure at Künzing-Unternberg, Bavaria.
Reproduced from fig 5 in Petrasch, J., Die mittelneolitischen Kreisgrabenanlagen
in Zentraleuropa: Forschungsstand und Interpretationstheorien zu Funktion und
Bedeutung. In Bertemes, F. and Meller, H. (Eds.), *Neolithischen Kreisgrabenanlagen
in Europa*, pp. 41–66. (Tagungen des Landesmuseums für Vorgeschichte Halle,
Band 8, 2012). Landesamt für Denkmalpflege und Archäologie Sachsen-Anhalt-
Landesmuseum für Vorgeschichte Halle (Saale), with permission from the publisher.

northern half of France and western Germany that continues until c.6000 BP
(see Fig 6.9a for an example). The overall chronological pattern is well seen
in Figs 4.9a and b, which shows the resurgence in enclosure building and also
that these new enclosures are much bigger than their LBK predecessors; their
changing spatial distribution is shown in Fig 6.9b. One of the earliest is adjacent to the cemetery of monumental Passy burials at Balloy described above,
in a Cerny context, at the confluence of the Seine and Yonne rivers. It was an
enclosure with interrupted ditches and a palisade with eight entrances; there
was no evidence of house plans but a great deal of refuse indicated domestic
activities, suggesting the possibility that the site was used for gatherings
of people related to activity at the cemetery (Mordant, 2008: 136, fig 24).
Roughly contemporary with Balloy is the site of Rosheim, and others like
it, in eastern France, associated with Bischheim pottery, where an enclosure
with interrupted ditches was constructed on the edge of a group of houses;
however, it has been suggested that at Rosheim only a single ditch segment
was open at any one time so that an 'enclosure' would effectively have never

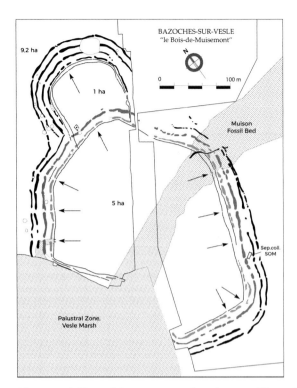

Fig 6.9. a) Plan of the causewayed enclosure of Bazoches-sur-Vesle. Reproduced from fig 26 in Mordant, D., En France du nord. In Tarrête, J. and Le Roux, C.T. (Eds.), *Archéologie de la France. Le Néolithique*, pp. 120–142, 2008, Picard. Publisher's permission requested.

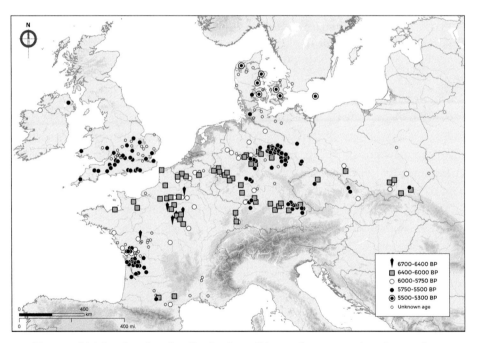

Fig 6.9. b) Map showing the distribution of dates of causewayed enclosures in temperate Europe. Reproduced from fig 123 in Klassen, L., *Along the Road: Aspects of Causewayed Enclosures in South Scandinavia and Beyond*, 2014, Aarhus University Press, with permission from the publisher.

existed (Lefranc and Jeunesse, 2012). There is enormous diversity in these enclosures within the broad template of one or more interrupted ditches with or without an internal palisade. Human remains are frequently found in both pits and ditches, as well as large quantities of animal bones that appear to be feast remains, and carcasses of whole animals that were presumably sacrificed; at some of the sites 'bucrania' have been found, partial cattle skulls with the horns attached, that seem to have been displayed.

About 120 Michelsberg enclosures are known (Jeunesse and Seidel, 2010), most of them no bigger than 40 ha, which is still, nevertheless, a substantial size, but there are four giant ones, including Urmitz in the Rhine valley, which enclose nearly 1 sq.km. Enclosures are found throughout the Michelsberg distribution area, though more densely in some areas than others, and their construction continues from the earliest ones in the Paris Basin c.6400/6300 BP, until c.5700/5600, though they are both more numerous and larger in the period down to c.6000. Like the settlements, they were often relatively short-lived, such as at the Klingenberg in south-west Germany, c.5800 BP, though the site of Mairy shows that this was not always the case.

For the Rhine area, Zimmermann (2012) calculates that each enclosure would have had a settlement catchment area of c.1000 sq.km (Fig 6.10), giving c.6000 people per enclosure area on the basis of his population density estimate for the period, compared with c.250 people for the units corresponding to the local enclosures of the later LBK, and c.1000 for the post-LBK Middle Neolithic; a scale difference reflected in the size of the enclosures concerned (Fig 4.9b), with corresponding labour implications. In keeping with the discussion in Chapter 4 about the nature of the late LBK enclosures, Zimmermann suggests that the enclosure catchments reflect the size of the largest collectively acting group, which might be linked to the scale of group needed for defensive reasons, and some authors see strong indications of violence in Michelsberg contexts. A recent find in a pit, from the Michelsberg site of Bergheim in eastern France, of the simultaneous burial of seven individuals with their left arms amputated and evidence of violent blows to the head in one case, is seen by the authors of the report as evidence of inter-group armed violence and they point to other examples in the bones from enclosure ditches as well as skull finds that have been interpreted as trophies (Chenal et al., 2015). It seems that there were concentrations of enclosures at the Michelsberg colonisation frontier, for example on the northern edge of the German Mittelgebirge (Geschwinde et al., 2009), which might be an indication that, at least on occasion, colonisation movements were undertaken by relatively large and organised groups as opposed to small numbers of households.

Despite these indications of higher order organisation, there is little evidence for social inequality in the Michelsberg Culture, for example in burials or differences in the material culture between enclosures and open settlements, and also little sign of the circulation of valuables, in contrast to the remarkable burials of Brittany.

(a)

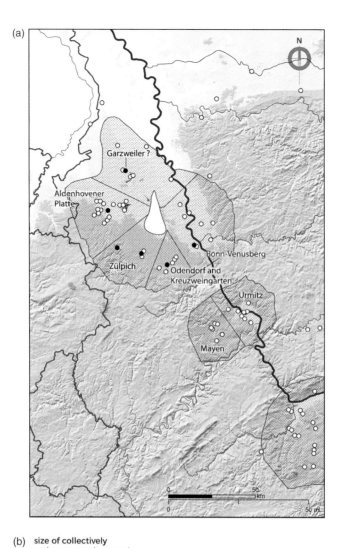

(b) size of collectively
acting groups (persons)

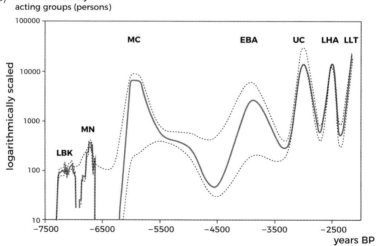

Fig 6.10. a) Map of enclosure catchments in the Rhineland; b) The increasing size
of the largest cooperating group. Reprinted from figs 2 and 3 in *Quaternary
International* 274, Zimmermann, A., Cultural cycles in Central Europe during the
Holocene, pp. 251–258, copyright 2012, with permission from Elsevier.

POST-LBK GENETICS AND THE RE-EMERGENCE OF INDIGENOUS HUNTER-GATHERERS

As we have seen, recent studies have shown that the groups that brought farming into Central Europe and to southern France and Iberia were the descendants of populations from south-east Europe and the Aegean, with evidence of only small amounts of admixture with local populations. In the Central European case the tightly restricted distribution of the LBK, even allowing for pasturing activities outside these core areas, would have left much the greater part of the landscape available to low-density hunter-gatherer groups. The same would have been true of the LBK's immediate descendants in the first half of the 7th millennium BP. As we have seen, the LBK settlement area was not extended during this period and some regions at least underwent decline and abandonment; the only exception was western France, where expansion is associated at least in part with the still little understood spread of farming from the south.

In west-central Europe, however, the late 7th-millennium expansion we have been describing represented the beginning of the major encroachment on hunter-gatherer territories that the Zvelebil–Rowley-Conwy model of the impact of agricultural expansion (1984) long ago postulated, and the hunter-gatherers are now becoming visible to us as a result of their reproductive interactions with farmers, revealed by mitochondrial and whole-genome ancient DNA evidence at both a local and a broader scale. At the broader scale, whole-genome analyses of individuals from farming cultural contexts from the period 6000–5000 BP, from Spain through Germany to Sweden, show evidence of increased admixture from the Western Hunter Gatherer group compared with their Early Neolithic ancestors (Haak et al., 2015; Mathieson et al., 2017). Lipson et al.'s study (2017) of samples from Germany showed an increase from c.4–5% Western Hunter Gatherer admixture in the LBK to c.17% in 6th-millennium BP Neolithic samples.

Most dramatic is the window provided by two stable isotope and ancient DNA studies of burials from the Blätterhöhle cave in north-west Germany (Bollongino et al., 2013; Lipson et al., 2017), the first based on mtDNA, the second using whole-genome analyses. At this site there were two phases of activity: one very early in the Mesolithic c.11,000 BP and another in the Neolithic, with dates covering the range 6000–5000 BP. The Mesolithic individuals all had the U haplogroup characteristic of European Mesolithic hunter-gatherer populations. The Neolithic individuals, on the other hand, had both Mesolithic and Neolithic haplotypes. The stable isotope analysis identified three groups of individuals. The Mesolithic group were characterised by isotope signals indicating a diet of terrestrial resources, while the Neolithic samples showed two distinct patterns: one corresponding to the terrestrial resources, presumably crops and domesticated animals, found at other Neolithic sites, and the other indicating a diet with a large component of dietary protein derived from freshwater fish. These latter individuals all had U-type Mesolithic hunter-gatherer-fisher lineages, while the group with the agricultural diet was made up of members of both mitochondrial groups: some farmers and some foragers. In fact, the whole-genome analysis revealed that some of the mtDNA samples previously analysed had come from the same individual, but the conclusions were the same. The three individuals with the farmer dietary isotope signal were farmer descendants with 40% hunter-gatherer admixture, while the one with the forager-fisher dietary signal was a Western Hunter Gatherer descendant with 25% farmer admixture; the gene flow is estimated to have taken place c.6200–6000 BP. In other words, the results suggest that some individuals, and presumably groups, maintained a foraging way of life for 2000 years after the arrival of farming, albeit interacting with farmers, while others became subsumed into farming groups, and in the time span represented here both were burying their dead in the same cave.

In short, it is after the LBK, and probably after c.6300 BP, that the long-assumed relatively intensive interaction between farmers and foragers in Central Europe occurs, in the context of the secondary farming expansion just described. This is also the period when farming penetrates the wetlands along the coast of the Low Countries. The so-called Swifterbant Culture characteristic of this region begins c.7000 BP with the appearance of point-based pottery similar to that of the contemporary Ertebølle Culture of north Germany and southern Scandinavia (see below), but subsistence continues to be based on hunting, fishing and gathering. From perhaps c.6700 BP small numbers of domestic animals occur in Swifterbant contexts but it is only c.6300–6000 BP that cereal agriculture begins, evidenced not just by finds of emmer wheat and barley from settlements but of spade-cultivated fields on the creek-bank at the site of Swifterbant itself (Huisman and Raemaekers, 2014). Culturally, especially in the pottery, the sites show continuity from the Late Mesolithic, while subsistence evidence and isotope studies of human bone show use of a mixture of wild and domestic and aquatic and terrestrial resources (Cappers et al., 2008; Smits et al., 2009). It would appear that here we finally have evidence of foragers adopting farming, in a drawn-out and piecemeal process, though of course aDNA results are needed to settle the question one way or the other. However, as we will see in the next two chapters, this adoption of farming by local foragers remains the exception not the rule.

SETTLEMENT AND SUBSISTENCE

So what accounts for this major settlement expansion in the late 7th millennium BP? There is currently an apparent conflict here between inferences based on the nature of the farming system from the plant macro-remains at settlement sites and the system inferred from pollen diagrams: the former pointing to a continuation of the intensive LBK system and the latter seemingly to a change in the nature of agricultural production, to a system based on mobile slash-and-burn farming, in which the burning of the cut-down trees provides a short period of soil fertility after which crop yields fall and it is necessary to repeat the process elsewhere (most recently Jacomet et al., 2016; response Rösch et al., 2017).

Those emphasising the continuity of the LBK system have argued that the pollen evidence showing a coincidence of clearance and burning events is not sufficiently fine-grained in its chronological resolution to be decisive on this question (Bogaard, 2004b: 26), and that the detailed and high-resolution archaeobotanical evidence from the lake village sites of the Alpine foreland points to a continuation of the same intensive long-term commitment to fixed plots of land whose fertility was maintained by manuring that began with the LBK. Thus, at Hornstaad-Hörnle IA on the shore of Lake Constance in southern Germany, a settlement dated by dendrochronology that lasted from 5918 to 5902 BP, study of the cereal remains revealed high levels of nitrogen ($\delta 15N$) believed to result from manuring rather than burning, because the weed seeds found associated with the cereal remains did not include perennial and especially woodland species (Styring et al., 2016). Interestingly, the spatial distribution of the stored crops and their isotope values suggests that the households were independent in subsistence terms. Similarly, at the site of Sipplingen, on a different shore of the lake, which was occupied for a number of short periods during the earlier 6th millennium BP and then again on several more occasions, following a gap of over 300 years, there is consistent evidence of high $\delta 15N$ levels in the crop remains. This is taken as evidence of a consistent strategy of maintaining land fertility by manuring.

Schier (2009), on the other hand, sees a change both in social patterns, and in the farming system. In both the north and south of Central Europe expansion was into glacial 'Young Moraine' landscapes with boulder clays that were also cooler and had higher rainfall than the regions previously occupied; they also still most probably contained forager groups, as we have seen. For Schier the key to expansion is a shift from intensive cultivation of the best soils to extensive slash-and-burn that made it possible to exploit soils of lower quality, but only for short periods before fertility fell; it was a form of farming that would have paid off in areas that were otherwise suboptimal. It would have led to lower population densities in the occupied areas than previously but greatly increased their extent, the situation suggested by Zimmermann's maps. The argument is supported by the existence of evidence for clearance, including burning in many cases, in pollen diagrams and soil profiles from northern Germany from the late 7th millennium BP. It could also have become relevant to the long-occupied loess regions, where a millennium of agriculture might have led to a decline in fertility and where there is also evidence of burning in some places (Eckmeier et al., 2008). Once the primary forest had been turned into secondary forest in the first round of clearance, in subsequent years the effort involved to clear plots prior to cultivation would have greatly decreased because virtually all the secondary growth could be burned and thus both suppress weeds and contribute to soil fertility (Schier, 2009: 34).

Experiments with reproducing slash-and-burn farming in the Forchtenberg forest in southern Germany (Ehrmann et al., 2009; Schier et al., 2013) indicate that such a swidden system could have been several times more productive in terms of net yield per hour of work, which raises the question of why it was not adopted much earlier. However, it would have required an area of land 16–20 times larger than the area cultivated in any one year to allow for fallow and forest regeneration, so would only have been viable even for a short period where plenty of land was available. Nevertheless, cultivation for longer periods could have been made possible by grazing animals on planted areas after harvest, or cutting down secondary growth elsewhere and bringing it in for burning on the plots.

The resulting large areas of regenerating forest would have been available for grazing and foddering animals, and it is on the animal husbandry dimension, rather than slash-and-burn cereal agriculture, that the pollen analyst Kalis (2010) places the emphasis in explaining the new developments of the Michelsberg subsistence system. He sees it as involving a new style of cattle keeping, on a larger scale, that made major inroads into the forest for forest pasture, reflected in the late 7th-millennium BP elm decline and other changes (see also Kreuz et al., 2014: 92 for examples); the existence of micro-charcoal in some pollen diagrams could also be related to burning to improve pasture. Apart from the elm decline, the pollen spectra also show an unprecedented frequency of hazel, alder, birch and ash, pioneer species that are quick to colonise areas that have previously been cleared. From c.5800 BP there was a peak in hazel pollen that lasted 300 years, resulting from the destruction of the tree layer over wide areas and the creation of a scrubby landscape.

One would expect a swiddening subsistence system, or one in which animal herding and forest products played a greater role, to show a significant degree of settlement mobility and that is what the Michelsberg seems to show. As mentioned earlier, much better evidence comes from the high-resolution dendrochronologies of the circum-Alpine lake settlements, contemporary with the later part of the Michelsberg, which show that these were generally short-lived. Thus the site of Sipplingen, with its apparent evidence of intensive cultivation of long-term plots, was occupied on four different occasions for between 10 and 50 years over the period 5920–5680 BP, with gaps of between 20 and 50 years (Styring et al., 2016), in contrast to the long-term occupation of LBK founder sites. The same pattern of short periods of repeated occupation is found at the settlements of the contemporary 'Burgundy Middle Neolithic' around the lake of Clairvaux in the French Jura. Pétrequin and colleagues conclude that Middle Neolithic farming at lake Clairvaux was indeed based on shifting cultivation, including occasional longer distance movement by groups from outside the local region (see also Loubier and Burri, 2011 for evidence of extensive mobility). As time went on, evidence of forest degradation suggests that population was growing too fast to allow the forest to regenerate between farming phases (Pétrequin and Pétrequin, 2015: 1403–1405). In keeping with this, the pattern of population growth in the Jura region during the Burgundy Middle Neolithic shows a rapid rise from c.6300 BP to a peak at c.5900 that continues for 300 years before a rapid population collapse after c.5600 BP (Pétrequin et al., 2005: fig 13) (see Fig 6.11), which may be a result of climatic deterioration leading to abandonment.

Rösch and Lechterbeck (2016) have suggested that agriculture in the south German and Swiss lake area 'was forest-based with quite intensively worked small fields', a view that goes some way towards reconciling the

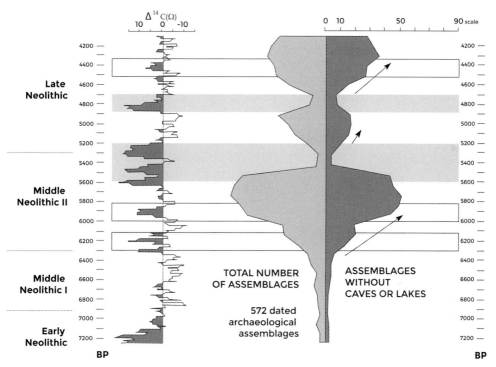

Fig 6.11. Comparison between the changing values of residual ¹⁴C in the atmosphere (an indirect indicator of climate) and archaeological measures of population in Franche-Comté. Population curve on the left based on all sites (572 dated assemblages); on the right excluding cave and lake sites. Reproduced from fig 8 in Pétrequin, P. et al., Habitat lacustre, densité de population et climat – L'exemple du Jura français. In Della Casa Ph. and Trachsel M. (Eds.), *WES'04 – Wetland Economies and Societies. Proceedings of the International Conference in Zurich, 10–13 March 2004*. Collectio Archæologica 3, pp. 143–168, 2005, Zurich: Chronos. With the author's permission.

different positions. They also (Rösch et al., 2017) raise the possibility that slash-and-burn might have been a short-term low-effort strategy contrasting with a more stable long-term high-effort strategy of inputs into permanent fields. This is not out of keeping with the view of Jacomet et al. (2016), who propose that a continuing use of relatively intensively cultivated fields was combined with new kinds of landscape management, including the use of fire, linked to the creation of pasture that led to the formation of extensive areas of secondary forest. However, it is clear that much work needs to be done before the differences in the on-site and off-site positions can be resolved.

In any case, it should not be assumed that because they were relatively short-lived and mobile, settlements were always small or insignificant. The site of Ludwigshafen on Lake Constance has dendrochronological dates in the range 5867–5861 BP but it was a large village and included a building with wall painting and modelled female breasts. At the virtually contemporary village of Sipplingen, close by, during phase B, with dendrochronological dates of 5857–5835 BP and building repairs down to 5817, there were at its height 12 rows of houses, probably 80–100 buildings altogether, and again a building with wall paintings (Schlichtherle, 2010). Of course, we do not know how far the households that formed these short-lived communities were moving or whether they all moved together from the same place – there is certainly evidence at some sites of individual households moving independently – but it is striking that settlements containing hundreds of inhabitants and with evidence of some kind of central institution would come together and be abandoned so quickly, even as it seems improbable that such a large settlement could have been supported by slash-and-burn (cf. Baum, 2014).

In contrast to north Germany and Scandinavia, where growth continued (see Chapter 7), a decline in the Michelsberg subsistence system is seen in the pollen diagrams, with large-scale reafforestation taking place almost everywhere in the Michelsberg distribution area in the mid-6th millennium BP, paralleling that just noted in the Jura (Kalis, 2010). Significant population decline is also implied by Zimmermann's settlement map for the Rhine valley and south-west Germany in the period 5500–4800 BP (Zimmermann et al., 2009b: fig 12c), which shows very few settlement concentrations even though the region was not altogether devoid of occupation. The summed radiocarbon probabilities show that, after a massive rise at the end of the 7th millennium and a peak in the first part of the 6th millennium with the Pfyn Culture, there was a major population decline in the area of Lake Constance and the Swiss lake villages around 5600 BP (Lechterbeck et al., 2014; Timpson et al., 2014; Fig 6.6). Rösch et al. (2017) see the decline in beech pollen over the course of the Pfyn Culture as an indicator that large areas were now under secondary woodland and that the increased population evidenced in the radiocarbon curve had taken the slash-and-burn system they postulate to its limits. Climate change may have tipped the system over the edge (Peters and Zimmermann, 2017).

Finally, it should be pointed out that a similar trajectory of expanding settlement and the importance of stock-keeping can be seen in southern France over the same period, even though the agricultural system was probably distinctly different (Delhon et al., 2009). The importance of cereal agriculture is unclear. Geoarchaeological work has demonstrated the existence of a characteristic soil horizon found over broad areas in the Rhône valley and elsewhere that dates to c.6500–5500 BP and indicates continuous grassland cover, spanning the period of the Chasséen. On the other hand, charcoal evidence indicated that oak woodland cover was at its most extensive at this time. This may point to the existence of a distinctive kind of 'agro-sylvo-pastoral management', analogous to the 'Dehesa' system still found in certain environments in Iberia (see e.g. Olea and San Miguel-Ayanz, 2006). These have a parkland appearance and comprise grazed grassland with areas of cereals interspersed with managed trees, especially oak, exploited for a variety of products including leaf-fodder (Delhon et al., 2009: 56–59). The vegetation beneath the trees would have been maintained as grassland both by the grazing and by regular controlled fire-setting. Bréhard and colleagues propose that in the middle Rhône valley there would have been extensive movements of both sheep and cattle herds and that the large lowland sites present here must have been seasonal gathering places rather than year-round settlements (2010: 186), corresponding to the marked lack of evidence for structures that might be permanent houses.

For Lemercier (2010: 318) the Chasséen Middle Neolithic of this region represents 'the end of the process of neolithisation of [continental] western Europe and the completion of the process of establishing an agro-pastoral system, and at the same time a major territorial expansion of Neolithic societies, that reach their furthest limits. This world was now full and suggestions of social transformation were already very apparent' (my translation). Such a claim is confirmed by the peak in the Rhône valley summed radiocarbon probability curve at just after 6000 BP, after which the curve shows a steep decline to a trough in the middle of the 6th millennium (Shennan et al., 2013) (Fig 5.5). Lemercier suggests that problems may have been exacerbated by a shift to wetter and cooler climate conditions from c.5700 BP and also proposes that a population decrease in the mid-6th millennium would make sense of the scale of the changes and of the scarcity of sites in this period. The 'agro-sylvo-pastoral' system of the Chasséen Middle Neolithic in the Rhône valley comes to an end at this time (Delhon et al., 2009: 62). Wetter conditions lead to the erosion or illuviation of the black soils characteristic of this system, which had lasted for the best part of a thousand years, and result in a change in settlement pattern that involved leaving locations in the lower plains.

SUMMARY AND CONCLUSION

In western France the appearance of farming at the end of the 8th millennium BP initiated a millennium of population growth and spatial expansion, following the spread of farming groups from the south, which had begun earlier and about which we still know very little. The process of increased exchange and social intensification that also ensued, most strikingly visible in the megalithic monuments of Brittany, linked these regions more strongly to the south than to developments in Central Europe. There can be no doubt that the Breton monuments are evidence of a concentration of social, symbolic and ritual hierarchical power, although we have very little idea of its foundations. The apogee of jadeite prestige/ritual (for want of a better word) axe production in the Alps in the second half of the 7th millennium BP is contemporary with this and is reflected in the concentrated deposition of the axes in the Breton tombs. Elsewhere, there is much less evidence for concentrations of power and the deposition of Alpine axes occurs in ritual rather than burial contexts. Nevertheless the symbolic and social significance of long polished stone axes, not just those from the Alps, points to patterns of male hierarchy, ritual and competition that are elusive in terms of the standard social typologies but that Pétrequin and colleagues convincingly relate to those prevalent in highland New Guinea.

To the north and east the post-LBK 7th millennium does not see expansion but a varying pattern of population decline in many regions and a more or less steady state in others, with settlement still restricted to areas with the conditions preferred by the LBK. This changes from c.6400 BP with the appearance of the Michelsberg, corresponding to an expansion of the area occupied by farmers, both internally – beyond the borders of the long-standing LBK regions – and externally, to the north and south, as well as re-occupation of some areas, such as parts of the Low Countries, which had been largely abandoned post-LBK. Why this expansion occurred, into areas whose agricultural potential was generally worse, in terms of temperature, rainfall and soil conditions, than the LBK regions, and why it happened at this time, is not at all clear, but it clearly represented an overcoming of the limits of the LBK system. If the process did indeed start in the Paris Basin it may have involved adoption of models that had already been established in the Cerny of northern France, perhaps derived from forms of subsistence that had already proved successful in the northward expansion of Mediterranean farmers, which seems to have been much less closely tied to the distribution of loess soils. Whether, like the LBK, the Michelsberg was associated with a population expansion or simply represented a novel adaptation that spread very rapidly is unclear.

As we have seen, the nature of the farming system remains a matter of debate, so it is hard to evaluate what the costs and benefits would have been in relation to the previous system. One possibility is that new and more tolerant crop land races had emerged by this time. Changing household labour budgets may also be relevant. The reduced labour inputs of slash-and-burn compared with more intensive cultivation methods have already been mentioned. Kerig (pers. comm.) has suggested that the increased use of naked as opposed to hulled cereals that one finds in the Michelsberg and related cultures would have led to a massive saving in household energy budgets because dehusking was no longer needed, and this would have opened the way to taking up other activities. What does seem clear is that the new system involved the creation of large areas of secondary forest and was more extensive than the LBK system, because settlement was at lower density and more spatially dispersed. In other words, it was a strategy that was successful despite decreased returns per unit area, perhaps because returns per unit time increased. Population increase was not upwards, increasing in density, but outward, with expanding frontiers.

The settlements associated with this new system were generally relatively short-lived and the lake village evidence suggests that their membership was flexible. However, the enclosures found in many regions show that higher levels of organisation did exist, and it may be that these are an indicator of competition between groups in regions where population was high relative to the requirements of the extensified subsistence system, and where competition for expansion was occurring, both linked to inter-group violence.

This expansion had important consequences. While in the southern half of France it is likely that forager–farmer interaction was already going on by 7000 BP if not before, it was not until the Michelsberg, three-quarters of a millennium later, that farmers in the broad region of west-central Europe were brought into more intense contact with foragers, reflected in the increased evidence of genetic admixture into farmer populations as foragers joined farming communities, but also in an apparent symbiosis in which some foragers maintained their way of life but became linked to farming groups, as the Blätterhöhle evidence suggests. It was this new system that provided the basis for the colonisation of southern Scandinavia, by people whose genetic background now included the results of forager–farmer interaction, which will be considered in the next chapter.

CHAPTER 7

FIRST FARMERS IN SOUTHERN SCANDINAVIA

As we have seen, farming and farmers had reached the southern edge of the North European Plain, not far south of the Baltic coast, before 7000 BP (Fig 1.1; see map Fig 7.1 for all places mentioned in this chapter) but a fully developed agricultural economy based on cereals and a range of domestic animals was not established in northern Germany and southern Scandinavia until 1000 years later. Unsurprisingly given this proximity, there is long-standing evidence of contacts with groups of the Late Mesolithic Ertebølle Culture in north Germany, southern Scandinavia and the western Baltic during the 7th millennium BP, in the form of stone axes and other artefacts. Until recently the contacts were believed to include the import of domestic animals and it was generally assumed that the final transition to farming was the result of the increasing adoption of domesticated resources by local foragers in the course of the 'substitution phase' of the model of farming adoption discussed in the previous chapter. This belief was strengthened by the fact that from at least the mid-7th millennium the Ertebølle foragers made and used pottery, long assumed also to derive from the farmers to the south. The prolonged resistance to farming was ascribed to the fact that in the Baltic area the use of marine resources could successfully support relatively high population densities so there was no incentive to adopt new forms of subsistence. One factor that might have tipped the balance was climate change that had a deleterious effect on shellfish resources, specifically oysters (Rowley-Conwy, 1984; Lewis et al., 2016).

In recent years many aspects of this picture have changed. It is now appreciated that the Ertebølle pottery derives from a long tradition of hunter-gatherer pottery manufacture and use that goes back to an origin in eastern Eurasia over 12,000 years ago and gradually spread westwards, probably linked to the processing of aquatic resources (Jordan et al., 2016); it has nothing to do with connections to the early farmers to the south. It had also been suggested on the basis of pollen studies that those same trans-Eurasian connections might have brought crops such as buckwheat to

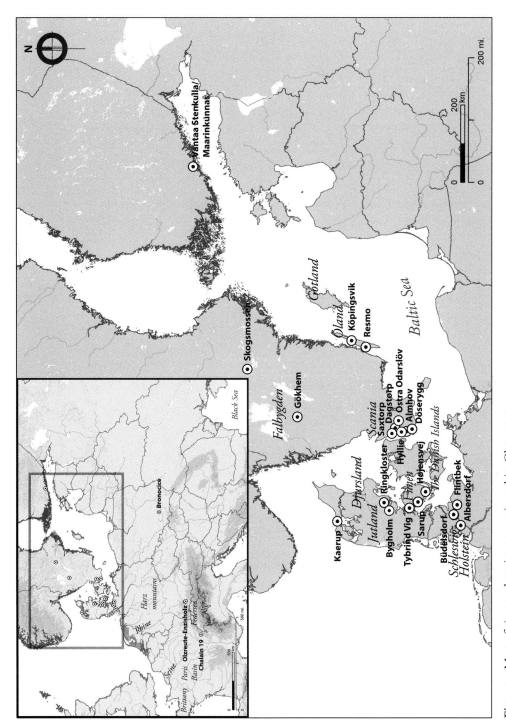

Fig 7.1. Map of sites and regions mentioned in Chapter 7.

the Baltic region at an early date (Alenius et al., 2013), and more generally that there was a long period of 'sub-Neolithic' farming by hunter-gatherers on the eastern side of the Baltic, going back before 6000 BP. However, the buckwheat argument now seems very unlikely (de Klerk et al., 2015) and a 'chronological hygiene' analysis has shown that there is no reliable evidence for farming in the eastern Baltic before 5000 BP (Piličiauskas et al., 2017). Moreover, most of the earlier claims that the links to the south included the import of domestic animals, especially cattle, have been discredited (Rowley-Conwy, 2013), though there is now evidence of the presence of domestic pigs of both Near Eastern and European mtDNA lineages in Ertebølle contexts in Baltic north Germany c.6500 BP (Krause-Kyora et al., 2013), even if its significance is disputed (Sørensen, 2014: 92). The pottery, of the early TRB (or Funnel Beaker) Culture, associated with the appearance of cereal agriculture in north Germany and southern Scandinavia, beginning c.6100 and 6000 BP respectively, is technologically different from the Ertebølle and can be linked to the Michelsberg Culture (Sørensen, 2014: 118–121). This is reflected in finds such as the assemblage from the site of Flintbek LA 48 in Schleswig-Holstein, where early Funnel Beakers are associated with Michelsberg pottery, indicating the presence of Michelsberg settlers according to Mischka et al. (2015).

THE GENETIC EVIDENCE

The key evidence to change our picture though comes once again from whole-genome ancient human DNA studies and, in keeping with the material evidence for Michelsberg connections, strongly indicates that the appearance of farming in southern Scandinavia is largely the result of a population expansion from the south. To recapitulate a point made earlier, the significance of whole-genome studies, as opposed to those of mtDNA or the Y chromosome, is that they represent a sample of the genes from many of the ancestors of the individual concerned, along many different lines of descent, and therefore even a single individual can provide a good representation of a population, in contrast to mtDNA or the Y chromosome, which only provide information on single genetic lineages. Skoglund et al. (2012) carried out a whole-genome analysis of a skeleton found in a TRB megalithic tomb from Gökhem in Sweden dating to c.5000 BP and found that its closest affinities were with present-day Mediterranean populations. Contemporary individuals from burials on the island of Gotland associated with material of the Pitted Ware Culture (PWC), which had a heavily marine hunting and fishing subsistence base, contrasted strongly with the TRB individual and had affinities with present-day north Europeans. Further studies (Haak et al., 2015; Mittnik et al., 2017; Skoglund et al., 2014), based on a larger number of individuals from Sweden and the eastern Baltic, including a number of Mesolithic individuals, have confirmed and expanded this picture. The Mesolithic individuals from Sweden form a distinct group, Haak et al.'s 'Scandinavian Hunter Gatherers' (SHG) a mixture of the Eastern Hunter Gatherer (EHG) group that probably came into Scandinavia from the north, in keeping with the archaeological evidence provided by Sørensen et al. (2013), and the Western Hunter Gatherer (WHG) group that characterised the Mesolithic of the greater part of Europe, as we have seen in previous chapters. In contrast to Sweden, the Mesolithic individuals from the eastern Baltic as far north as Estonia, analysed by Mittnik et al. (2017), were entirely of the WHG group, with no evidence of any other admixture.

The TRB farmers from Sweden, on the other hand, fall squarely in the group of Middle Neolithic individuals from further south that we saw in the previous chapter, of Anatolian farmer ancestry but with a higher level of forager admixture than their Early Neolithic predecessors. As noted above, the first Swedish TRB farmer sample analysed, from Gökhem, comes from a context dated around 5000 BP, a thousand years later than the local arrival of farming, so the question of whether the earliest farmers had Anatolian ancestry remained open. Analysis of the genomes of two Early Neolithic individuals from the site of Saxtorp in Scania at the southern tip of Sweden (Mittnik et al., 2017) has now resolved this question by showing that they too belong to the Central European Middle Neolithic farmer group with its WHG admixture. There is no evidence of mixing with the local (SHG) group but the samples for this are from further north in Sweden so the occurrence of some admixture within southern Scandinavia remains possible. However, it is clear that the main mechanism for the arrival of farming in the region was demographic expansion from further south.

Genomes of Pitted Ware Culture individuals, contemporary with the TRB Middle Neolithic but more dependent on marine resources (see below), show that they were descended from the local Mesolithic population, with a small amount of farmer admixture, suggesting gene flow from the latter, contrasting with the absence of evidence for local gene flow from forager to farmer noted above. A lack of genetic diversity among these PWC individuals indicated that these hunter-gatherer-fisher groups had a history of low population size, perhaps as a result of occasional subsistence crises resulting in population bottlenecks.

On the eastern side of the Baltic things are completely different. Groups of hunter-gatherer-fishers of WHG descent continued here, and there is no evidence of any sort of incursion of Neolithic farmers from the south, while high levels of genetic diversity point to a large population presumably supported by a successful forager economy. There is no major change until c.5000 BP, when genomic analyses indicate the incursion of a population like that of the Central European Corded Ware, with a strong element of steppe ancestry (Mittnik et al., 2017), which also introduces farming.

THE SPREAD OF FARMING INTO SOUTHERN SCANDINAVIA

It follows from the account given above that part of the answer to the question of why it took so long for farming to expand to southern Scandinavia is linked to the broader question examined in the last chapter, of why the distribution of farming and farmers in Central Europe more generally remained so restricted until the second half of the 7th millennium. When the expansion happened, it was a consequence of the late 7th-millennium spatial expansion of the Michelsberg and related groups that involved widespread internal colonisation and expansion in the south, not just the north. Nevertheless, this may not be the whole story. As we saw above, explanations for the expansion to the north have been much discussed and suggestions have included both the failure of the oyster populations that Ertebølle groups exploited, and climatic improvement that would have made farming more successful (e.g. Bonsall et al., 2002). A recent study supporting the second of these suggestions has shown a steady rise in Baltic Sea Surface Temperature (SST), beginning c.6000 BP, the time of farming arrival, and continuing for 500 years. This correlates strongly with a rise in population in the region following the arrival of farming, seen in the summed radiocarbon probability distribution, with the population increase lagging the SST rise by about 60 years (Warden et al., 2017) (see Fig 7.2). Modelling studies indicate that a warming climate in Scandinavia could induce shifts in the northern limit of cereal suitability by 100–150 km per °C (Carter et al., 1996) and it is striking that the northern boundary of the TRB agricultural economy in southern Scandinavia corresponds almost exactly to the boundary of the area that today has more than 175 growing days. This is shown in Fig 7.3a, while Fig 7.3b shows the distribution of point-butted axes, an indicator of Early Neolithic settlement (see Sørensen, 2014: fig II.5, fig V.112). In addition to improving the conditions for agriculture, the temperature rise seems to have increased the prevalence of de-oxygenated conditions (hypoxia) in the Baltic, which can have an adverse effect on marine resources. However, analysis of coastal archaeofaunal assemblages dated to this period shows no evidence of a decrease in the proportion of aquatic fauna (Warden et al., 2017).

The spread into southern Scandinavia was extremely rapid, as Rowley-Conwy (2013: 303) emphasises, probably via maritime movement along the coast. Direct radiocarbon dates on charred cereal grains of wheat and barley show their presence across southern Scandinavia as far north as middle Sweden in the period 4000–3700 BC, with dates essentially indistinguishable between north and south, and the same is true for directly dated domestic animal bones, including sheep/goat and cattle (Sørensen and Karg, 2014).

As with the LBK, and indeed all the other farming expansions that have been examined, this one cannot have involved a gradual filling up of the landscape before onward expansion of farming continued and it seems almost certain

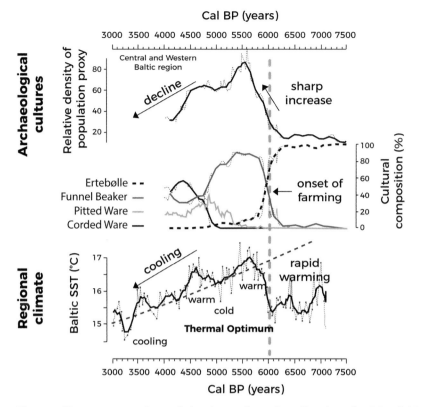

Fig 7.2. Temperature and population in southern Scandinavia at the Mesolithic–Neolithic transition. **Top:** Population proxy using a summed probability distribution (SPD) of archaeological radiocarbon dates from southern Scandinavia. **Middle**: Cultural composition (%) based on the subset of the radiocarbon dates with cultural affiliations. Dotted lines show the complete time series, solid and dashed lines show a 200-year rolling mean. **Bottom**: Summer sea surface temperature (SST) record based on TEX_{86} palaeothermometry. The solid line plots the 5-point rolling mean. June insolation at 60°N (in W m^{-2}) is plotted as a dashed line. The population levels increased synchronously with a period of warming after 6000 cal yr BP. Reproduced under Creative Commons licence from fig 4 in *Scientific Reports* 7(1), Warden, L. et al., Climate induced human demographic and cultural change in northern Europe during the mid-Holocene, 15251, 2017.

that it resulted from a leapfrog colonisation process by pioneering farming groups. Again, as in the other instances we have seen, major population growth was rapid over the c. 300–400 years from 6000 BP, reaching a peak c. 5700–5600 BP, as Fig 7.4 shows for the Jutland peninsula, the Danish islands and Scania, the southern tip of Sweden, before rising to an even higher peak c. 5200 BP in the Danish islands alone (Shennan et al., 2013; cf. Hinz, 2015; Hinz et al., 2012). The increased human impact is also visible in regional pollen diagrams, with the elm decline in northern Germany, for example, apparent from c. 6100 BP and increasing evidence of hazel, indicative of woodland clearance, especially

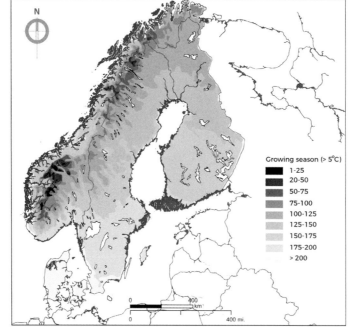

Fig 7.3. a) Map of the mean length of the agricultural growing season in southern Scandinavia. Reproduced from fig 3.4 in Tveito O.E., et al., Nordic Climate Maps. Report No. 06/01. KLIMA. DNMI Report, 2001. Norwegian Meteorological Institute. Creative Commons license.

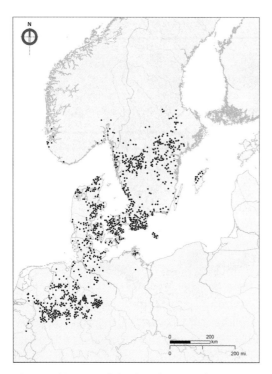

Fig 7.3. b) Map of the distribution of type 1 and 2 point-butted axes. Reproduced from fig v.112 in Sørensen, L., *From Hunter to Farmer in Northern Europe: Migration and Adaptation during the Neolithic and Bronze Age.* Acta Archaeologica 85.1, 2014. © 2014 by Wiley, Oxford, with permission from the publisher.

after 5950 BP (Feeser et al., 2012); a similar picture of increasing clearance is also found in Denmark and Sweden (Sørensen, 2014: chapter 7).

In terms of the subsistence economy, the beginning of the TRB represented the introduction of the full farming package, indicated by the presence of cereal remains and the bones of the full range of domestic animals (Sørensen and Karg, 2014). At the site of Hyllie in Scania, for example, a cereal sample from house 1 is dated to 6240–5970 BP and cattle, pig, sheep/goat, wheat and barley all occur in EN I contexts. The cereals that are found in southern Scandinavia include tetraploid free-threshing wheat, a species characteristic of the Michelsberg and contemporary early lake village cultures to the south (Maier, 1996; Schlumbaum et al., 1998). This is demanding in terms of its ecological conditions and would have been well-suited to the initial clearances on soils developed over centuries of forest cover. It declines in significance after the EN I phase and one reason for this may have been soil depletion (Kirleis and Fischer, 2014).

There is also evidence of complex animal husbandry practices. In the EN I phase at the Scanian site of Almhov (see again below), c.5800–5700 BP, domestic animals dominate the faunal remains but, more importantly, recent isotope analyses of cattle tooth enamel show that the cattle were reared locally and that there was more than one season of birth per year (Gron et al., 2015). The main reason for this intensive practice, which involves providing fodder through the winter, is to extend the cow's lactation period so that it provides milk throughout the year. The existence of this complex and specialised practice in the very Early Neolithic in southern Scandinavia is in keeping with the genomic evidence described above that farming was introduced by immigrants rather than adopted piecemeal by local foragers. The evidence of large-scale flint mining to produce axes, dated to c.6000–5800 BP, from the nearby site of Södra Sallerup also fits in with this picture, part as it is of the general appearance of deep mining for flint in Michelsberg and Chasséen north-west Europe at this time.

However, use of the full suite of domestic crops and animals does not mean that wild resources ceased to be exploited. At Hyllie, for example, seal bones are also found in EN I contexts. When coastal and lakeside sites are distinguished from inland ones they generally show very high proportions of wild fauna, and even at inland sites from the EN I phase the contribution of wild fauna can be significant, although there is a shift towards much higher proportions of domestic livestock in later phases at all sites (Sørensen and Karg, 2014, figs 13 and 14).

A further source of subsistence evidence comes from the extensive stable isotope and lipid analyses that have been carried out in recent years on both human bone and ceramic residues, to examine dietary patterns during the Mesolithic and Neolithic of southern Scandinavia. A stable isotope study of human bone by Richards et al. (2003) indicated a wide-ranging diet for Mesolithic individuals, including in part terrestrially based protein.

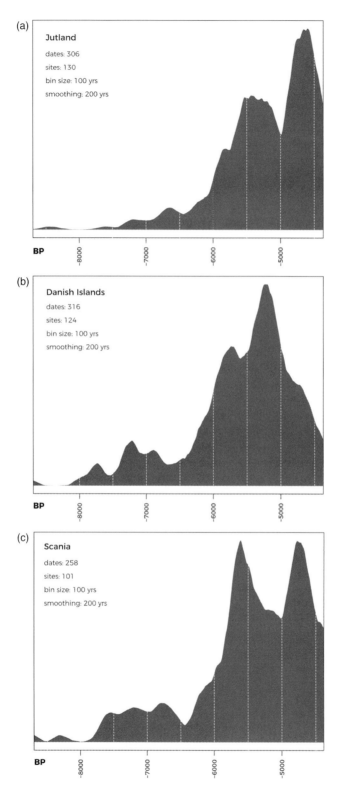

Fig 7.4. Radiocarbon population proxies for three regions in southern Scandinavia. a) Jutland; b) Danish islands; c) Scania. Data from the EUROEVOL project.

Neolithic diets, on the other hand, were much more uniform and based entirely on terrestrial protein, most probably from domesticated resources. Fischer et al.'s (2007) isotope study of human and dog bones from Mesolithic and Neolithic sites found that Mesolithic samples indicated heavy dependence on marine resources, especially high trophic level fish, even at inland sites. With one exception the Neolithic samples indicated a general shift towards a diet based on terrestrial foods with some low trophic level freshwater and marine food. However, Early Neolithic samples from coastal sites have not yet been analysed.

Isotope analyses by Craig et al. (2007) found that ceramic residues from Late Mesolithic Ertebølle pottery from the coastal site of Tybrind Vig in Denmark indicated that the vessels were mainly used 'for processing marine products', and that these were strongly represented even at the inland site of Ringkloster. The results of analyses of residues from TRB Neolithic vessels indicated the processing of freshwater fish as well as terrestrial products including animal fats. A further study by Craig et al. (2011) of a much larger number of ceramic residues from Ertebølle and Early Neolithic TRB vessels in Denmark and the Baltic coastal area of Germany found that EN vessels from coastal sites had been heavily used for marine animals while evidence of freshwater resources was found at inland sites. However, a third of the TRB vessels, including samples from the coastal sites, also had evidence of dairy fats indicating that milking was a common practice. It seems then that there was not a complete switch to domesticated resources with the beginning of farming in southern Scandinavia and that the first farmers initially combined both marine and domestic animal resources. Analyses of TRB EN ceramic residues from the site of Skogsmossen in eastern middle Sweden (Isaksson and Hallgren, 2012) produced similar results to those of Craig et al., including evidence of both dairy fats and marine resources. These conclusions are supported by the analysis of the relative proportions of aquatic and terrestrial fauna in archaeofaunal assemblages from the Mesolithic and Neolithic of southern Scandinavia referred to above, which found no evidence for a decrease in the proportion of aquatic remains. This pattern makes an interesting contrast with Britain (see next chapter), where there is no evidence for continuing exploitation of marine resources after the arrival of farming and farmers. It also raises important questions about cultural transmission and innovation patterns in these early farming groups. Given that the first farmers were Michelsberg immigrants from the south, as the genome and other evidence indicates, with little if any evidence of local forager admixture, how did they acquire the skills to exploit the fish and seals of the western Baltic?

As regards the nature of the farming system, the pollen evidence for clearance has already been mentioned. There is also micro-charcoal evidence of increased burning in northern Germany, though Feeser et al. (2012) are doubtful that this is an indicator of swidden cultivation and suggest that burning may have been carried out to produce secondary woodland and improve woodland pasture. This is followed c.5750 BP by decreased evidence for burning and indications of more extensive cultivation, including permanently open areas, with further intensification occurring c.5500 BP, at the beginning of the local EN II phase. These agricultural developments in the first half of the 6th millennium are also reflected in evidence from north Germany of soil erosion and colluviation (Dreibrodt et al., 2010). The evidence from Denmark and Sweden is similar and raises the same issues concerning the nature of early cultivation. There are certainly charcoal peaks in EN pollen diagrams but, as Sørensen (2014: 104–105) points out, this does not necessarily mean a mobile slash-and-burn system, as opposed to initial forest clearance, since the integrated plant and domestic animal system characteristic of the European Neolithic would always have provided opportunities for manuring, especially by cattle, which seem to have been closely controlled. Recent nitrogen isotope analyses of cereal grains from Danish prehistoric sites have suggested that manuring was already taking place in the EN but that it increased in intensity in the course of later prehistory (Kanstrup et al., 2014). However, the Neolithic examples do not date to the initial appearance of farming but to the EN II period, c.5500–5300 BP, by which time we know that there were permanent fields cultivated with the crook ard, an early form of plough, because we have evidence of plough marks visible in ancient ground surfaces preserved beneath burial mounds.

ANIMAL TRACTION, THE PLOUGH AND THE WHEEL

In fact, one of the most striking features of the TRB EN is that it has the earliest evidence for the use of the plough in Europe, in the form of plough marks preserved in ancient ground surfaces protected under later burial mounds. There is no evidence that the plough was part of the initial farming system described above but it appears quite soon afterwards. This makes a marked contrast with the regions to the south and east, where there is a gap of 2000 years between the arrival of farming and the beginning of plough agriculture.

At the site of Højensvej on the island of Funen in Denmark, plough marks precede a pit cut through them containing hazelnut shells with a radiocarbon date around 5700 BP (Sørensen, 2014: 79), while at Flintbek, in north Germany, Bayesian analysis of a complex stratigraphic sequence of long barrows and dolmens covering old land surfaces has produced a date for plough marks between 5500 and 5400 BP and for wheel tracks c.5400 BP (Mischka, 2011) (Fig 7.5). Both appear as population is reaching its regional peak and can be linked to a process of agricultural intensification, or rather, extensification (see below). That these dates are not simply related to the vagaries of the preservation of ancient ground surfaces under burial mounds is confirmed

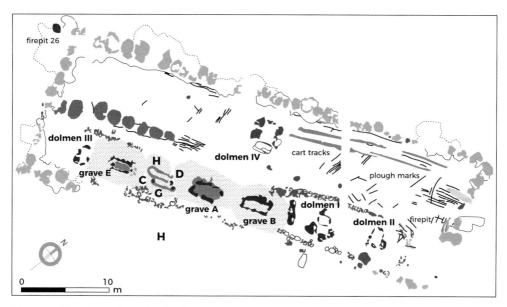

Fig 7.5. Plough marks and wheel tracks preserved under a long barrow at Flintbek LA 3, north Germany. Reproduced, with permission, from fig 2 in *Antiquity* 85(329), Mischka, D., The Neolithic burial sequence at Flintbek LA 3, north Germany, and its cart tracks: a precise chronology, pp. 742–758, 2011.

by an analysis of the incidence of traction-related pathologies on Neolithic cattle bones in Denmark (Johannsen, 2006). A male individual from the site of Kaerup, aged 6–8 years at death and probably sacrificed, showed clear evidence of traction pathologies and was dated to 5650–5360 BP, while the frequency of traction-related pathologies increases from the beginning of the MN, c. 5300 BP.

However, the appearance of paired animal traction together with the plough and the wheel was certainly not an independent development. It was part of a spatially widespread phenomenon described by Sherratt (1981) as the 'Secondary Products Revolution'. While many elements of Sherratt's initial claims for this have now been rejected and it is clear that there is earlier evidence for animal traction (e.g. Isaakidou, 2006), the appearance of a novel and widespread animal traction complex based on paired oxen pulling wheeled carts and ploughs in the mid-6th millennium BP still seems undeniable. The current evidence for the use of the wheel has recently been reviewed by Mischka (2011), who shows that Flintbek is among the very earliest occurrences, together with a picture of a cart on a sherd of pottery from the TRB settlement of Bronocice in south-east Poland probably dating to c. 5500–5350 BP, as well as representations from Uruk period Iraq and wagon graves from the Maikop Culture in the north Caucasus. However, although the place of origin of paired animal traction has been endlessly discussed, this is less important than the fact that it must be considered a single phenomenon, one that spread across much of Europe and adjacent south-west Asia, if not instantaneously, certainly very fast. Effectively, an innovation that in areas to the south and east only appeared thousands of years after the local arrival of farming spread so rapidly that in southern Scandinavia it almost caught up with it, giving the earlier Neolithic here a distinctive character that is associated with later Neolithic phases in these other regions. The broad connections of the region at this time are confirmed by the occurrence of copper items in hoards and graves, beginning c.5700 BP and showing an exponential rise in frequency to a peak at c.5400–5300 BP, followed by total collapse (Fig 7.6). The hoard from Bygholm in eastern Jutland, Denmark, for example, included four flat axes, a dagger and three arm-rings (Klassen, 2000). The copper objects probably came from the east Alpine region, where large quantities were being produced at this time but using metal that most probably came from further east. Although it is always difficult to evaluate the occurrence of valuables in the archaeological record because it depends on deposition practices whose rules we do not understand, it seems probable that, like the jadeite axes in Brittany a thousand years earlier, the concentration of copper items in the Scandinavian TRB region, which does not occur in areas further south, is genuine and reflects an attraction power that these societies had and others did not. However, their disappearance probably reflects the demise of the copper production system that was supplying the eastern Alps rather than social or depositional changes in southern Scandinavia.

That animal traction was ritualised and highly significant to the societies in which it appeared is very clear, though most of the evidence is rather later. A strong case has been made (Johannsen and Laursen, 2010) that the so-called stone heap graves of north-west Jutland c.5100–4800 BP represent individual graves dug in the form of a cart pulled by two cattle, while the cattle burials from TRB and Globular Amphora contexts in Poland and the Elbe-Saale region of Germany date to this same period at the end of the 6th millennium BP, as do those in Baden Culture contexts in Hungary (Jeunesse, 2006). The roughly contemporary representations on the walls of megalithic tombs such as Züschen of the Wartberg Culture in western Germany point in the same direction, as do the representations of ploughing that appear among the rock-engravings of the southern French Alps and northern Italy from c.4900 BP (e.g. Saulieu, 2004; Fedele, 2006). However, that does not mean that ploughs, wagons and animal traction generally were of purely ritual significance, as some have claimed in the past (e.g. Vosteen, 1999). Indeed, the wetland finds of preserved wheels often have indications of extensive use (Burmeister, 2012: 88). However, as Burmeister says, despite the undoubted practical benefits, it is hard to explain the rapid spread of the innovation of wheeled vehicles and the animal traction complex in these terms alone. In the beginning it must have been linked to special social and ritual statuses and have been dependent on wealth; it indicated social distinction and its impact was felt in the imaginary

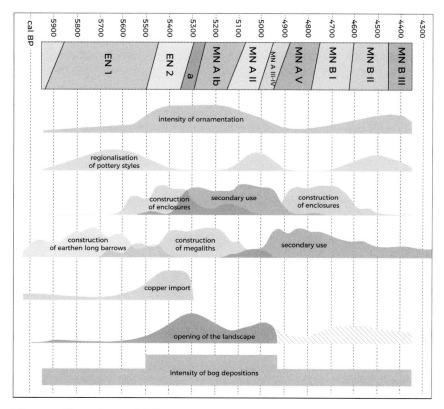

Fig 7.6. Chronology of different site types and activities in Neolithic southern Scandinavia. Reproduced from fig 4 in Klatt, S., Die neolithischen Einhegungen im westlichen Ostseeraum. Forschungsstand und Forschungsperspektiven. In: T. Terberger, T. (Ed.), *Neue Forschungen zum Neolithikum im Ostseeraum. Archäologie und Geschichte im Ostseeraum* 5, pp. 7–134, 2009 Verlag Marie Leidorf GmbH, Rahden/ Westf. With the author's permission.

of these societies and not just in their daily lives, as the scenes in the Alpine rock-engravings, for example, demonstrate.

The costs and benefits of using the plough, as opposed to other forms of cultivation, have been extensively discussed (e.g. Halstead, 1995). The key benefit is that cultivation of a given area of ground is significantly quicker so that it is possible for a household with a two-oxen plough to increase its total production by increasing the area cultivated, though this has the potential problem of creating a labour bottleneck when it comes to harvesting. The ethnographic and historical data gathered by Kerig (2007: 379) show that without draught animals farm sizes range from 2 to 5 ha, while with oxen there is a minimum size of 4 ha and a majority in the range 8–10 ha. There is a minimum area because of the significant costs of keeping a team of oxen. Those costs must be met before gaining any benefits from the higher cultivation rate, which also has to make up for the fact that the yield per unit area tends to be lower than for hand-dug fields because the cultivation is less intense. In turn, the increased area to be cultivated raises the transport costs of both the harvested crops themselves and materials like firewood obtained from beyond the cultivated area (Kerig, 2013: 16). A consequence of this is that using a cart for transport of bulk loads becomes a greater advantage than it would previously have been, so justifying a further investment, which could also be used for other purposes, such as building megalithic tombs, as Flintbek shows. Thus Kerig (pers. comm.) calculates that the transport of firewood for one household for a year from beyond the edge of a minimal garden-like clearing with a diameter of 80 m requires more than 1,400,000 kg★m (kilo metres), while the corresponding figure for a minimal ploughed clearing of 132 m diameter is greater than 2,300,000 kg★m; as a comparison, a small dolmen, an early type of megalithic tomb in southern Scandinavia (see below), may have required 1,573,000 kg★m. Albeit later in date and in a different region, the recent find of several wheels dated to c.2900 BC at a settlement in the Olzreute marsh in south-west Germany, next to the remains of a heap of leaf-fodder that had been brought into the settlement, fits in with this sort of local use (Schlichtherle et al., 2010), as do the heavy use traces on some of the wheels from the same region, including indications of over-loading (Schlichtherle, 2006).

The labour demands associated with harvesting larger quantities of crops might be expected to lead to increased household sizes, or to greater differentiation between households that could support a plough team, a cart and the labour to take advantage of the larger quantities of crops grown, and those which could not. There is certainly evidence for considerable variation in house sizes in the TRB EN of southern Scandinavia, potentially reflecting differences in storage capacity (Sørensen, 2014: 178), a pattern that Kerig (2013: 17) suggests is also visible at settlements in the region of the Federsee in south-west Germany at the end of the 6th millennium BP (cf. Bogucki, 1993, 2011).

In other words, the introduction of paired animal traction with the use of the plough and the cart most probably had much broader implications than merely changing the way in which the soil was cultivated, including increased inter-household inequality and possibly changed gender relations, since it is generally the case that it is males who are responsible for plough agriculture (for further discussion see Bogucki, 1993; Goody, 1976; Sherratt, 1981).

SOCIAL INTENSIFICATION IN THE SOUTHERN SCANDINAVIAN NEOLITHIC

It appears that for most of the 6th millennium BP settlement was dispersed in single farmsteads or small hamlets made up of two-aisled rounded rectangular houses, such as the site of Dagstorp in Scania, southern Sweden (Müller, 2011: 52), that were probably autonomous units from the point of view of subsistence production and consumption. It may be that during the early rapid spatial expansion of farming communities they were also independently choosing settlement locations according to the principles of the ideal-free distribution that we saw in Chapter 4. However, it is not long before we see evidence of collective action. The site of Almhov at the southern tip of Sweden, for example, whose early phase dates to c.6000–5700 BP, shows evidence of a concentration of ceremonial activity, including apparently paired pits with large concentrations of cattle bone, and an individual burial, dated to 5890–5610 BP, in a long barrow burial mound measuring 90 x 8 m, with a façade made of timber posts at the eastern end; it was built on top of earlier activity (Artursson et al., 2016). Andersson et al. (2016) see a distinction between sites like Almhov, corresponding to regional gathering sites, and others such as Östra Odarslöv, with small clusters of burials, including long barrows and façade graves (burials associated with a row of several timber or stone posts) belonging to individual settlements.

The construction of non-megalithic long barrows starts at a similar date to the houses, c.5800/5700 BP (Fig 7.6) (Furholt, 2012; Klatt, 2009) continuing until 5500 BP; their closed chambers contained individual burials and sometimes include imported copper ornaments as grave goods. Clearly, only a small proportion of the population were buried in these monuments and Andersson et al. (2016) see them as local leaders whose monuments represent claims to territory based on ancestry. Long barrows are found across large areas of north and north-west Europe at this time, including Britain. The apparent delay of c.200 years between the arrival of farming communities and the first construction of long barrows is thought to be linked to the time involved in initial forest clearance and establishing claims to the first cleared areas for agriculture; that the long barrows are sometimes placed on top of earlier houses makes this point very clearly (Sørensen, 2014: 215).

About 5600 BP, and coinciding with a decline in the construction of earthen long barrows, the construction of megalithic graves within both long and round mounds begins (Furholt, 2012: 117), peaking c.5400–5200 BP though continuing until c.5100. They are differentiated from the long barrow burials in that access to the burial chamber remained open to the outside; in places such as southern Sweden where soil conditions mean that bones have survived it appears that individuals were placed inside them sitting against the wall (Ahlström, 2009). The great majority of these megalithic burials are so-called 'dolmens', made of groups of unmodified local boulders, and even with the surrounding mounds would not have been beyond the efforts of a small group. The fact that their construction coincides with opening up the landscape for a new kind of agriculture involving the plough, which would have required the removal of the large numbers of boulders left scattered across the landscape by glaciation, can hardly be accidental, though they appear at a time when there are also indications of contacts with Brittany (Müller, 2011: 15). Moreover, the small scale needs to be put into the context of estimates that 40,000 megalithic tombs were built in Denmark alone during this period (Furholt, 2012: 124) (though see Iversen et al. (2013) for a lower estimate of c.25,000), the great majority most probably in the 300 years between c.5500 and 5200 BP, or around 100 tombs per year during a period when enclosures were also being constructed (see below). These numbers are truly remarkable and are plausibly taken as a measure of the intensity of local-scale competition, which seems to have been unparalleled in Neolithic Europe. It was focussed on north Germany, the Danish islands and adjacent parts of Jutland to the west; Scania and the west coast of Sweden to the east and north; and Falbygden, the small island of limestone soils suitable for farming in central southern Sweden (map Fig 7.7). In Denmark, it is clear from the soil map that there is a very strong correlation with the distribution of fertile luvisol soils. At a more local spatial scale, the tombs also seem to be linked to enclosures, as is the case at Sarup on the island of Funen, where c.110 megalithic tombs are situated in the vicinity of the well-known enclosure (Andersen, 2008), or at Döserygg in Scania. Here two palisades and a number of long dolmens were constructed c.5600–5500 BP and a row of standing stones and more dolmens in the following 200 years (Fig 7.8) (Artursson et al., 2016: fig 4); there were many other dolmens in the

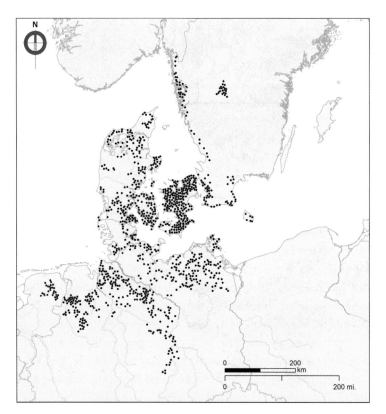

Fig 7.7. The distribution of megalithic tombs in northern Europe. Reproduced from fig 1 in Fritsch, B. et al., *Dichtezentren und lokale Gruppierungen - Eine Karte zu den Großsteingräbern Mittel- und Nordeuropas*, 2010. www.jungsteinsite.de. Version of 20.10.2010. Creative Commons license.

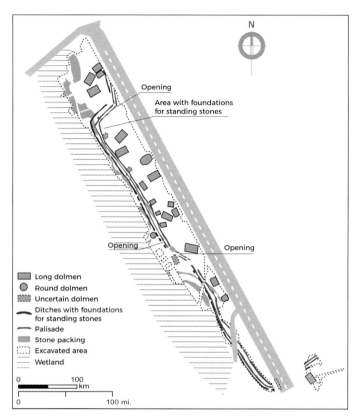

Fig 7.8. Plan of Doserygg enclosure and megaliths. Reproduced from fig 41 in *Journal of Neolithic Archaeology* 18, Andersson, M., Early Neolithic Landscape and Society in South-West Scania – New Results and Perspectives, pp. 23–114, 2016. Creative Commons license.

surrounding region. At Albersdorf and Büdelsdorf in north Germany construction of megalithic tombs began at the same time as the local enclosure. Often, individual tombs underwent quite complex sequences of modification, for example the site of Flintbek in north Germany (Mischka, 2011), and there were extensive offerings over a long period at some tombs, evidenced by large quantities of broken decorated pots; such foci of ritual activity often occur in the centre of regional clusters of megaliths (Müller, 2011: 43).

The first causewayed enclosures in Denmark begin to be constructed in the 57th century BP, continuing until c.5200, with the majority constructed between c.5500 and 5300 BP, though the number whose construction phase is securely dated by radiocarbon is actually small (Klassen, 2014: 199–206). This is also the period of peak copper imports and megalith construction. As we saw in the last chapter, the construction of enclosures of a similar general form and associated with similar sets of activities was part of a long-established tradition of practices, of which the TRB was an inheritor, connected to creating and maintaining collectively acting groups. From 6400 to 6000 BP

they are found in considerable numbers in the distribution area of the early
Michelsberg Culture, from the Paris Basin in the west to the Harz mountains
in the east, as well as in contemporary Chasséen contexts in France. There is
further enclosure building in the period 6000–5750 BP, though less than in
the preceding period, and the distribution expands to both the west and the
north (Klassen, 2014: 210, fig 122) (see Fig 6.9). In the period 5750–5500 BP
the area in which enclosures are constructed expands to include Scandinavia
and the British Isles (see Chapter 8), but this is also a period of extensive construction in various regions of Germany: in west-central Germany, associated
with the late Michelsberg, and immediately to the east, in the Middle Elbe-
Saale region, with the Baalberge group of the TRB. In contrast, the regions
of France, Belgium and Germany where enclosures were previously built saw
little new construction in this period; between the Rhine and the Seine none
are currently known and in north-west Germany not only is there little or no
new construction but existing enclosures fall out of use (Knoche, 2008, cited
in Klassen, 2014: 215).

The recently excavated site of Büdelsdorf in north Germany (Hage, 2016)
provides a good example of one of the more complex and long-lived sequences.
It was begun c. 5750 BP, with three ditch circuits enclosing an area of 5 ha. It was
renewed in the 55th century BP, then, after a gap of about a century in which
there was some regeneration of the local woodland, a 4 ha settlement was built
on the site, with an estimated 40–50 contemporary houses, lasting from late in
the 54th century into the 53rd. This settlement, apparently now demolished,
was succeeded by a new enclosure, estimated to have lasted around 60 years in
the 53rd century BP, at a time when the pollen evidence indicates a farming
regression, and it was renewed for the last time in the 51st century.

It is increasingly clear that enclosure construction in all these regions
increased as populations were increasing and peaked at the same time or slightly
later, in the case of southern Scandinavia c. 5500 BP. As we have seen, this is
also the time when copper imports from the south were rapidly increasing
(Klassen, 2000), as well as ritual deposits of various kinds. As population rose
towards the peak, the landscape became increasingly open and the plough
came into use here; this in itself would have increased the competition for land
since significantly larger areas could now be cultivated (Johannsen, 2006). The
explosion in the number of megalithic burials, including the more elaborate
passage graves, as well as the construction of the causewayed enclosures, should
be seen as a consequence of the growing competition between local groups
that ensued. In the intensively surveyed area of Djursland in eastern Jutland
enclosures seem to be 5–10 km apart, though it is not clear whether they were
in contemporary use, and they are generally under 10 ha in area (Klassen, 2014);
this is far smaller than the ones to the south whose population catchments
were estimated by Zimmermann (2012) and therefore correspond to much
smaller numbers of people.

Not only could enclosures serve as claims to territory but the effort expended on them would have acted as a form of costly signalling conveying the strength of the group concerned. And while high regional populations meant increased competition they also meant that large amounts of labour were available to invest in such activities. As Roscoe (2009) points out, signalling group strength in this way not only has benefits in inter-group competition but in doing so it also increases social cohesion through cooperation in a joint endeavour where participation is visible to all; it thus creates reputational pressure to be involved. At the same time, these efforts to deter conflict are likely to become more conspicuous and elaborate as the risk of warfare grows and maintaining security becomes an ever-greater priority. The fact that enclosures in southern Scandinavia were not at the centre of group territories, but on borders, and may even have been on routes of varying scale and importance (Klassen, 2014), does not contradict this argument. On the contrary, it is precisely in such places that one would expect group strength to be advertised.

However, although the beginning of the monument construction peak c.5500 BP seems to coincide with the population peak, in the following 200 years when construction is at its height, in some regions at least the population seems to have already begun to decline, a decline that correlates with the beginning of a period of decreasing temperatures that may have had an effect on crop-growing conditions (Hinz, 2015; Warden et al., 2017; see below). This could only have increased the intensity of inter-group competition as conditions deteriorated.

After c.5200 BP causewayed enclosure construction in southern Scandinavia fades away but secondary use continues and some at least seem to become more nucleated settlement sites, though a new type of small palisaded enclosure appears in some areas c.4900 BP (Iversen et al., 2013; Müller, 2011: 69; see below). Construction of megalithic tombs ceases c.5100 BP but they continue to be used. Immediately to the south of Denmark, in Schleswig-Holstein, the end of tomb-building at this time is clearly reflected in a decrease in the pollen evidence for open land and indications of forest regeneration (Feeser and Furholt, 2014; see also Kirleis and Fischer, 2014). It may be that the intense competition and high population density were eventually unsustainable for the local farming system and the soil resources on which it depended, especially if conditions for agriculture were becoming worse, but much more regional work is necessary to address these issues

THE DECLINE OF THE TRB

At the end of the 6th millennium BP other important changes also begin to take place in the south Scandinavian region, indicating the decline of the TRB economic and social system. One is the southward expansion of the Pitted Ware Culture from the more northerly part of the Baltic in the final centuries of the 6th millennium BP. People in these northern areas had continued to be totally reliant on wild plant and animal resources. Thus, recent lipid analyses of ceramic residues from the Combed Ware site of Vantaa Stenkulla/ Maarinkunnas in southern Finland c.3900–3300 BC, contemporary with the TRB further south, show that they derive from resources of marine origin, in keeping with the faunal remains from the site (Cramp et al., 2014b). At this time central Sweden is part of the agricultural TRB sphere, but there was a significant change here c.5400/5300 BP with the appearance of sites belonging to the Pitted Ware Culture (Larsson and Broström, 2011). The difference between the TRB and PWC adaptations is well seen at two contemporary sites from the Baltic island of Öland. Isotopic analyses of human bones from the MN TRB site of Resmo, c.3400–2800 BC, showed a mixture of marine and terrestrial resources, while the Pitted Ware Culture site of Köpingsvik showed a heavy reliance on marine mammals, with a possible addition of marine fish, as in the Mesolithic phase at the site (Eriksson et al., 2008). The faunal assemblages from Pitted Ware sites on the island of Gotland (Rowley-Conwy, 2013: 291, table 15.1) support this picture; there are wild boar, and very large numbers of seals and fish, while domestic animals are either completely or virtually absent.

By c.5000 BP, PWC sites are to be found in northern Jutland and the northern parts of the Danish islands and they continue until c.4450 (Iversen, 2010: 9), again with a strong emphasis on the exploitation of marine resources although in places there is some evidence of animal husbandry, for example at Kainsbakke, eastern Jutland, where cereals and quernstones also occur (Iversen, 2016). Moreover, the location and organisation of settlements also differs from TRB contemporaries; they are largely seasonal and in more coastal locations. As we have seen, the long-standing suggestion that the southward spread of the Pitted Ware Culture to Denmark represents a re-expansion of hunter-gatherer populations from the north has been supported by a genomic analysis of ancient DNA samples from Pitted Ware skeletons from Gotland (Haak et al., 2015; Skoglund et al., 2014, 2012), which showed continuity from Late Mesolithic to PWC samples, and that they all belonged to a group of Mesolithic populations characteristic of northern Europe but with a small amount of farmer admixture. Despite the evidence for the adoption of some farming and herding in suitable locations as groups of the PWC moved south, the subsistence, settlement and genetic evidence all indicate a strong degree of separation between them and the TRB population. The fact that it was possible for PWC groups to expand their range, to some degree at the expense of farming groups, may be a confirmation of deteriorating conditions for farming and improving conditions for marine exploitation at this time, as a long-term cooling trend set in the Baltic area after c.5500 BP (Hinz, 2015; Warden et al., 2017), seen also in north German lake sediments (Dreibrodt et al., 2012).

Population gradually decreases in the Danish islands in the first half of the 5th millennium BP. In contrast, Jutland sees a new demographic upturn from c.4900/4800 BP. This corresponds to the appearance in the western part of Jutland, peripheral to the TRB, of the Single Grave Culture, one of the group of Corded Ware cultures that spread from the east across broad areas of the North European Plain as far as the Netherlands and into some of the areas to the south, including the eastern part of the Alpine foreland lake village region. The nature of this expansion, and whether it represents the expansion of a set of new practices among existing populations or of people bringing those new practices, has been discussed since early in the 20th century, not least in relation to explanations of the spread of Indo-European languages in Europe. Recent aDNA work has demonstrated that expansion of groups from the steppes north of the Black Sea indeed played a major role in the Corded Ware expansion (Allentoft et al., 2015; Haak et al., 2015; Mittnik et al., 2017). It is now possible to see that the demographic decline in parts of northern Germany and southern Scandinavia at the end of the 6th millennium BP left space into which it was possible for these incoming groups to infiltrate. There are signs of similar patterns of low late 6th-millennium TRB populations followed by rising Corded Ware numbers further east, in Poland (Timpson et al., 2014: fig 3). Areas such as the Danish islands, on the other hand, with their dense TRB populations were less easy to infiltrate. Indeed, the radiocarbon population proxy may underestimate the population here since there is considerable evidence for greater settlement nucleation in the late TRB (e.g. Nielsen, 2004). The fact that, both here and in neighbouring Scania in south-west Sweden, small defensive palisaded enclosures occur dated to the period c.5100–4800 BP, with both late TRB and Corded Ware (known as the Battle Axe Culture in Sweden) associations may well indicate conflict between the incomers and the native inhabitants, not to mention PWC groups as well (Iversen, 2016). There are suggestions of a similar situation in central Germany at the same time, with the fortifications of the Bernburg Culture. These early third millennium developments mark massive changes in the cultures, economies and societies of prehistoric Europe and are beyond the scope of this book.

SUMMARY AND CONCLUSION

As in all the other areas we have seen, farming was introduced to southern Scandinavia by a process of population expansion represented by the TRB Culture, c.6000 BP, leading to a demographic boom. The eastern side of the Baltic was not reached by this expansion and farming was not adopted by the local populations of hunter-fisher-gatherers. Here it did not occur until a further wave of population expansion after c.5000 BP, when groups of Corded Ware ancestry moved into the region. Genome analysis of further samples is required to establish whether or not there was admixture with local foragers in southern Scandinavia beyond that which had already occurred between TRB ancestors and foragers further south in Central Europe. Farmer expansion was rapid and must have had a major seaborne coastal element. There is evidence that it occurred when it did because climatic warming moved the frontier for successful farming further north than it had previously been. The immigrants brought a full agricultural package of cereals and domestic animals with them, including the skills to manage them successfully, not least the knowledge and ability to manipulate annual cattle reproduction to get two birth seasons a year to ensure a continuous supply of milk. However, they also exploited marine resources to a significant degree, raising the question of how they acquired the relevant expertise and how difficult this really was. The earliest farming may not have been a mobile slash-and-burn system but it certainly involved burning and the creation of secondary forest, with a strong element of animal, especially cattle, keeping. By 5600 BP or so it was being replaced by the ard-based cultivation of fields using animal traction.

It is unclear whether long barrow burial was an ancestral practice present from the start but flint mining, exploiting the outstanding flint resources of Denmark and Scania certainly was. In any case, long barrows were certainly being constructed by 5800 BP, marking the beginning of a process of tomb-building, first long barrows then dolmens and to a lesser extent passage graves, that is unparalleled in its intensity elsewhere in Europe, especially in the EN II period, c. 5500–5300 BP. Large numbers of enclosures are also constructed at this time and it is hard to avoid the conclusion that the high rate of monument construction is an indicator of exceptionally intense competition for good farming resources.

In the last centuries of the 6th millennium BP there are indications of a population decline in north Germany, Jutland and Scania, reflected in evidence for forest regeneration in pollen diagrams, but in the Danish islands this does not occur until after 5000 BP. At the same time Pitted Ware forager groups of Mesolithic ancestry expand southwards from central Sweden, apparently taking advantage of the farming decline, while shortly afterwards Corded Ware farming groups of mixed steppe and European Middle Neolithic ancestry began to infiltrate the whole of the Baltic region.

CHAPTER 8

THE FARMING COLONISATION OF BRITAIN AND IRELAND

The expansion of farming into Britain and Ireland occurs immediately before and after 6000 BP, at almost exactly the same time as in southern Scandinavia, and it is therefore hard to avoid the idea that in some way the two processes were connected (cf. Rowley-Conwy, 2011). We will return to this question below but first we need to look at the evidence for early farming in Britain and Ireland and the processes responsible for its arrival, to assess whether or not it fits into the pattern that has been emerging.

IMMIGRATION OR DIFFUSION?

As in all the other regions examined so far, the key issue that has attracted most discussion is whether or not agriculture was introduced by colonising farmers. However, perhaps more so than in other regions, the broad theoretical commitments of researchers have influenced these debates, because in Britain the Neolithic period has been the main single substantive focus in the development of post-processual archaeology, with its emphasis on the impact of modern ideologies on interpreting the past. Thus, to suggest farming was introduced by colonists rather than being locally adopted is to assume that foragers lacked agency, with the imputation that this represents a residue of colonialist ideas about the capacity of native peoples. Taking this sort of perspective leads Thomas (2013: 425), for example, to the view that the complete lack of evidence for mixed Mesolithic and Neolithic assemblages, rather than pointing to lack of continuity from one to the other, is the result of conscious decisions by Mesolithic communities all over the land to decisively reject their past and consciously 'become Neolithic', having sent apprentices across the English Channel to pick up the relevant skills together with the crops and animals. Much has also been made of the possibility that Mesolithic groups *could* have been using sea routes to establish contact with farmer communities in northern France and Brittany (Garrow and Sturt, 2011). However, the sheer lack of indications of contact is striking when we compare it to the extensive evidence of contact between the Mesolithic groups of southern Scandinavia and the farming groups to the south that we saw in the previous chapter. The one exception to this is the site of Ferriter's Cove in south-west Ireland (see map, Fig 8.1, for all sites mentioned in this chapter), where the presence of cattle bone and a sheep tooth in a Mesolithic context dated to the second half of the 7th millennium BP points to contact with continental Europe (Woodman et al., 1999). Sheridan (2010) considers that this represents the theft of animals from an unknown early farming settlement, which certainly seems more probable than foragers sailing to France and bringing back the animals; moreover, isotope analyses from human bones at the site point to a diet dominated by marine resources and therefore in keeping with Mesolithic patterns (Schulting, 1999, cited in Pailler and Sheridan, 2009). Certainly, there is no reason why such voyages should not have occurred occasionally and this may be one of those rare instances where we find one of the very earliest examples of something, against all the odds. However, like all isolated observations that do not (yet) conform to a pattern, the Ferriter's Cove evidence remains hard to evaluate.

Since at least the middle of the last century the key evidence for the continental connections of the British Neolithic, apart from the domesticates themselves, has been the pottery, in particular what is now known as the 'Carinated Bowl' tradition (Sheridan, 2007), which has strong similarities with the Chasséen and Michelsberg of northern France and Belgium discussed in Chapter 6. The problem for many scholars has been that there has been no exact match between British assemblages and those from specific known sites on the European mainland. However, the likelihood of finding specific ancestral sites is small. Moreover, as David Clarke long ago pointed out, archaeological entities such as cultures are 'polythetic'; site assemblages are never identical – they are linked by family resemblances, sharing some features and not others. Indeed, Vander Linden and Bradley (2011: 36) specifically point out the 'constantly changing' nature of Chasséen assemblages and 'the polythetic character of groups responsible for the recolonisation of the sandy and clayey areas of Belgium' at this time. Finally, in the case of the colonisation of new regions, as we saw with the LBK, it is highly likely that founder effects and drift would have been operating in any groups that crossed the Channel. That is to say, specific founder communities would only have produced some fraction of the range of forms present in their ancestors, and that initial range itself would have been subject to the vagaries of individual choices and preferences over subsequent years and generations (cf. the discussion in Whittle et al., 2011: 859–861). What was certainly transferred across the Channel, on the other hand, was the level of expertise to produce the high-quality pottery characteristic of the British and Irish Early Neolithic.

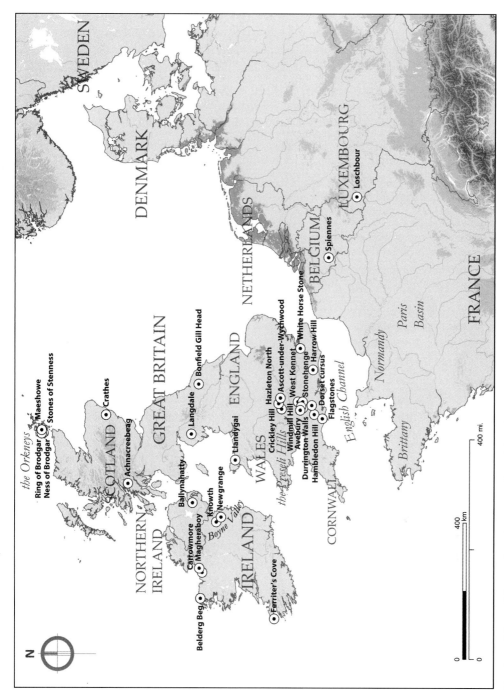

Fig 8.1. Map of sites and regions mentioned in Chapter 8.

SWEDEN

DENMARK

NETHERLANDS

BELGIUM

LUXEMBOURG
• Loschbour

Spiennes •

FRANCE

Normandy

Paris Basin

Brittany

English Channel

CORNWALL

Flagstones

Durrington Walls
Hambledon Hill

Avebury
West Kennet
Stonehenge
Dorset cursus

Windmill Hill
Crickley Hill

the Preseli Hills

WALES

Ascott-under-Wychwood
Hazleton North

White Horse Stone
Harrow Hill

ENGLAND

GREAT BRITAIN

Bonfield Gill Head

Langdale •

Llandygai •

SCOTLAND

Crathes •

Achnacreebeag •

the Orkneys
Maeshowe
Ring of Brodgar •
Ness of Brodgar •
Stones of Stenness

NORTHERN IRELAND

Ballynahatty

Knowth
Newgrange
Boyne Valley

IRELAND

Carrowmore
Magheraboy

Belderg Beg •

Ferriter's Cove

N

0   400 km
0   400 mi.

185

The Genetic Evidence

However, as the debates of the last 50 years in both Britain and the other regions examined have shown, arguments on the question of demic versus cultural diffusion based on material culture associations will by their nature never be conclusive. To resolve this issue, we need direct evidence from the people themselves, and this is now forthcoming. The genome of a Middle Neolithic woman dated 5343–5020 cal BP from a megalithic grave at Ballynahatty in Northern Ireland (Cassidy et al., 2016) fits in with that of the other MN individuals from western Europe that have been discussed in previous chapters, with a majority of Anatolian–Aegean farmer ancestry and evidence of a greater degree of hunter-gatherer introgression, c.40% in her case, than their Early Neolithic ancestors. The closest affinities of the Ballynahatty female were with MN individuals from Spain and Sweden, while the hunter-gatherer component was, unsurprisingly, closest to the Western Hunter Gatherer group (Haak et al., 2015), and in particular to the individual from Loschbour in Luxembourg. At the moment it is impossible to say whether this hunter-gatherer component was acquired within Ireland or somewhere along the way. But we can make inferences about relevant ancestral population sizes by analysing *runs of homozygosity* (ROH) in the genome. These are areas of the genome where the copies inherited from both parents are identical; if they are identical it is because both parents inherited them from a common ancestor. Longer runs imply a smaller population, where the sharing of a recent common ancestor is more probable. The Loschbour hunter-gatherer individual has very high ROH levels indicating that its ancestral population size was small, while those of the Ballynahatty individual were much lower. The inference to be drawn from this is that she was a descendant not of a small pioneering group but of large-scale Neolithic migration.

The Ballynahatty evidence has since been confirmed by a more extensive study that included a number of Early Neolithic skeletons from Britain, mainly from Scotland (Olalde et al., 2017). Like the Irish individual, all fall within the central and west European Middle Neolithic group that we have seen in the last three chapters, descendants of Anatolian–Aegean farmers who had mixed with local Western Hunter Gatherers in western and Central Europe in the course of the 7th millennium BP. Somewhat surprisingly at first sight, both the Ballynahatty individual and those from Britain have a closer affinity to the Mediterranean Cardial and Impressed Ware early famers than to the LBK early farmers of Central Europe and are close to Middle Neolithic individuals from southern France. Nevertheless, as we saw in Chapter 6, mtDNA evidence from the early 7th-millennium cemetery of Gurgy in the Yonne valley on the south-eastern side of the Paris Basin (Rivollat et al., 2015) indicates that mixing had already been going on between individuals of Mediterranean and Central European farmer descent, as well as with indigenous hunter-gatherers.

Moreover, this is in keeping with the archaeological evidence for north–south contacts in France, starting already at the end of the 8th millennium. However, most of the British samples come from western and northern Scotland and it may be that future samples from south-east England will reveal individuals of entirely Central European farmer descent.

THE PROCESS OF COLONISATION

There are two rather different current views of how farming and farmers spread into Britain and Ireland. Sheridan (e.g. Pailler and Sheridan, 2009) suggests that there were three different routes and movements, one starting from Brittany in the local MN II c.6300–6000 BP and going north via the Irish Sea, indicated by specific types of collective tombs including closed polygonal chambers and simple passage graves, found on the west coasts of Wales and Scotland and associated in two cases with pottery that apparently resembles the late Castellic pottery of Brittany, for example from the site of Achnacreebeag in Scotland. The second, referred to as the 'Cross-Channel West' route, dates to the first quarter of the 6th millennium BP, and links Normandy with south and south-west England, again indicated by the presence of specific burial monument types that are covered with small circular mounds and confirmed now by similarities in pottery technology (Pioffet, 2017). Finally, there is the 'Cross-Channel East' route, represented by the so-called Carinated Bowl Neolithic, mentioned above, which has more extensive evidence, not just the specific pottery with its Michelsberg and Chasséen antecedents but also settlement sites with domestic plants and animals; evidence of its arrival in large parts of Britain and Ireland dates to the period 6000–5800 BP. Olalde et al. (2017) suggest that the Mediterranean connections indicated by the British EN genomes may be indicative of the proposed early movement from Brittany, which is certainly possible, but the Gurgy mtDNA results imply that there was an input from individuals of southern origin across the whole of northern France, so at the moment it appears that it could be associated with any of Sheridan's proposed streams.

Whittle et al. (2011) take a rather different view of the pattern of colonisation on the basis of their Bayesian analyses of the sequences of radiocarbon dates from their ground-breaking dating programme. Their results suggest that the earliest occupation occurred in south-east England during the 61st century BP but they do not assume that farming simply spread overland from there. As Fig 8.2 shows, they envisage further continental movements from northern France, Belgium and Brittany over the following two centuries as well as coastal movements within Britain, especially on the eastern side.

The speed of the spread is worth emphasising. The analysis by Bocquet-Appel et al. (2012) of the speed of expansion of the different regional cultures

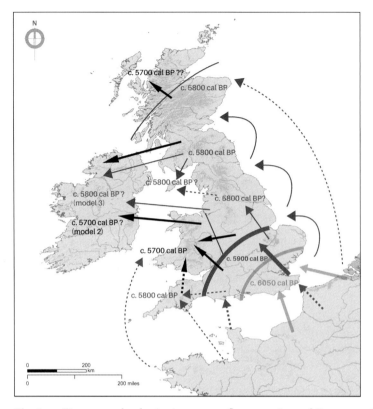

Fig 8.2. Contact and colonisation routes from continental Europe to Britain. Reproduced from fig 15.8 in Whittle, A.W.R. et al., *Gathering Time: Dating the Early Neolithic of Southern Britain and Ireland*, 2011, Oxbow Books, with permission from the author and Oxbow.

associated with the spread of farming shows that the rate of expansion of the Carinated Bowl tradition is only matched by the seaborne spread of the western Mediterranean Impressa, thus supporting the idea of a coastal expansion; the average rate of spread is three times as fast as the LBK. By c. 5800 BP, if not earlier (Sheridan, 2017), farming and pottery, of the Carinated Bowl tradition, had reached Ireland and northern Scotland. Clearly this implies that the same sort of leapfrog or long-distance movement pattern that is apparent in the west Mediterranean was operating in the case of the colonisation of Britain and Ireland as well, with rapid movements into new territories by fissioning groups long before there was any question of local carrying capacity limits being reached. As we have seen, in the case of the western Mediterranean, and indeed the LBK, there is no evidence that the speed of spread can be explained by the adoption of farming by local forager groups, and the same is true in the case of Britain. However, this does not exclude the absorption of what must have generally been low-density Mesolithic groups into Neolithic communities.

Why did the farming colonisation of Britain and Ireland not take place sooner, given that farmers had reached the Normandy coast by 7000 BP and that the Villeneuve-St-Germain Culture continued to expand rapidly westwards into Brittany in the early centuries of the 7th millennium BP? In the case of the expansion into southern Scandinavia we saw that it probably resulted from the development of a new farming system in west-central Europe in the Michelsberg phase in the late 7th millennium, but also from rising temperatures that increased the northern range of effective cereal-growing and might have had negative effects on marine resources. Although a climatic explanation has been suggested for Britain as well (Bonsall et al., 2002), the evidence is currently weak (Woodbridge et al., 2014). However, it seems likely that the development of the expansive MN II Chasséen-Michelsberg farming system of the late 5th millennium was relevant, as in southern Scandinavia. We have already seen in Chapter 6 how it was associated with a re-occupation of the areas abandoned after the LBK and a big extension of the settled area into areas of sandy soils in the Low Countries. The radiocarbon population proxy curve for western France (Fig 6.3b) indicates that the population reached a peak c.6200 BP, and then declined to a trough at c.5700 BP. Similarly, the Paris Basin proxy (Fig 6.3a) rises to a Middle Neolithic peak c.5800 BP before decreasing to a trough at 5500 BP. It is thus at least plausible to see the population peak as an indicator of population pressure that could have prompted a colonisation movement to Britain, and the subsequent decrease as evidence that a significant part of the population did indeed leave.

POPULATION BOOM AND BUST IN BRITAIN AND IRELAND

In the same way as we have seen already for other regions, the demographic patterns inferred from summed radiocarbon probabilities reflect the impact of the arrival of farming. This was first demonstrated by Collard et al. (2010), who showed that there was a very marked increase in population size from c.6000 to 5600 BP, followed by an even more rapid decrease in the period to c.5300 BP, to a level less than half that of the peak. The low level lasted to c.4500–4400 BP before rising continuously to 4000 BP, at which point the date series stops. Removing from the dataset those dates from highly visible Neolithic monuments made no difference to the EN pattern of dramatic population rise and fall although of course the peak was lower. As Collard et al. pointed out, the rapid population increase synchronous with the arrival of domesticated plants is not consistent with a slow indigenous uptake of farming, and the recent ancient DNA results described above have confirmed this. Subsequent more rigorous analyses (Shennan et al., 2013; Timpson et al., 2014) (Fig 8.3) using the methodology described in previous chapters have confirmed that the population patterns are statistically significant, with a dramatic rise to a peak over the period 6000–5600 BP, followed by a drop of 50% or more from

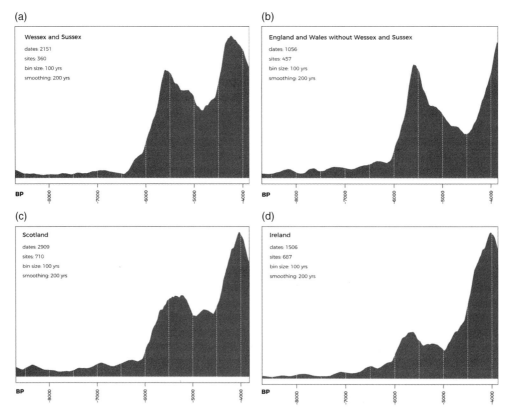

Fig 8.3. Radiocarbon population proxies for Britain and Ireland. a) Wessex and Sussex; b) Rest of England and Wales; c) Scotland; d) Ireland. b) and d) Data from EUROEVOL project; a) and c) Data from EUROEVOL project, updated by Professor A. Bevan.

the peak over the next 200–300 years. In other words, as in most of the other areas we have seen, the arrival of farming is followed by a population boom and then a bust, which in Britain and Ireland is especially marked.

In the light of suggestions that the summed radiocarbon probabilities cannot be considered a valid representation of population, Woodbridge et al. (2014) compared the radiocarbon data for Britain with an independent proxy for human population: human impact on the environment as reflected in pollen diagrams. Fig 8.4 shows pollen-inferred land cover through time divided into three categories: deciduous woodland, semi-open arboreal and semi-open pasture, at a resolution of 200 years, plotted against the radiocarbon demography proxy. It can be seen that between 6000 and 5500 BP the proportion of woodland decreases and semi-open arboreal landscapes increase in correspondence with the population boom as primary forest is cleared. The reverse occurs between c.5500 and 5300 as the population goes down and woodland increases again. The proportion of woodland remains high until c.4500 BP when population levels rise and open environments expand once more, with a substantial

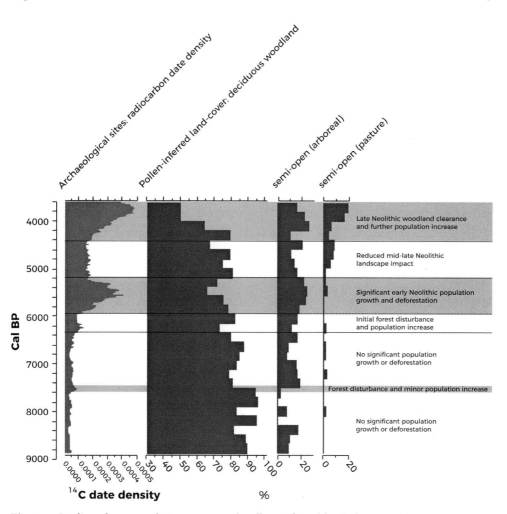

Fig 8.4. Radiocarbon population proxy and pollen-inferred land clearance history for Neolithic Britain. Reprinted from fig 5 in *Journal of Archaeological Science* 51, Woodbridge, J. et al., The impact of the Neolithic agricultural transition in Britain: a comparison of pollen-based land-cover and archaeological 14C date-inferred population change, pp. 216–224, copyright 2014, with permission from Elsevier.

decrease in woodland from c.4000 BP. In other words, the pollen evidence confirms the boom–bust pattern. The idea that there was some sort of Middle Neolithic downturn, indicated by forest regeneration and decreased settlement evidence, has often been suggested in the past (e.g. Bradley, 1978), and linked by some to a shift to a more mobile pastoralist economy, but Whittle's (1978) perceptive suggestion that this involved a population downturn as a result of over-exploitation of resources was largely forgotten.

In Ireland too, the boom and bust pattern seen in the demographic proxy has been confirmed by other evidence (Whitehouse et al., 2014). Although there is some indication of Neolithic activity in the EN I period, c.6000–5750

BP, it really takes off in EN II, c.5750–5600. It turns out that the great majority of the rectangular Neolithic houses known from Ireland fall into a so-called 'house horizon' within this period of peak population in the radiocarbon proxy, with an estimated start date c.5720–5680 BP and an end date of 5640–5620 BP. There is some indication of clearance in the pollen record in the EN II phase and extensive evidence from studies of plant macro-remains of cereal cultivation and consumption (McClatchie et al., 2014).

MN I in Ireland (c.5600–5400 BP) sees major changes. While houses seem to disappear, settlement evidence in the form of complexes of pits and post-holes continues, up until at least 5515–5460 BP, but, overall, levels of activity seem to be lower. This phase also overlaps with the beginning of a period of less intensive land use and reafforestation documented in the pollen record, the so-called '*Plantago* gap', that apparently starts c.5500 BP in the north but much later in the west. In MN II (c.5400–5100) the pollen record shows a continuation of decreased land-use intensity (Ghilardi and O'Connell, 2013; Whitehouse et al., 2014), and this inference is confirmed by results of an analysis of the beetle evidence (Whitehouse and Smith, 2010), pointing to a widespread period of forest regeneration from c.5500 BP until c.5000.

EARLY NEOLITHIC SUBSISTENCE PATTERNS

The evidence for EN subsistence patterns and their associated practices in Britain and Ireland corresponds with what we have seen elsewhere and fits entirely with the picture of initial large-scale immigration and demographic expansion rather than local adoption. As we saw in Chapter 6, there is a model for what the adoption of farming by forager groups looks like, in the Swifterbant Culture of the coastal Netherlands, with its gradual piecemeal adoption of domestic animals and crops. In contrast, in Britain and Ireland, with the exception of Ferriter's Cove as we have seen, there are no bone assemblages with domestic animals prior to the beginning of the Neolithic at c.6000 BP and the proportion of domestic animals in the British EN (5900–5300 BP) is over 90% (Manning, unpublished analysis). It is notable that the same high proportion, well over 90%, is seen in the faunal assemblages of the Paris Basin in the period 6400–5800 BP. Moreover, Tresset (e.g. 2003: fig 3.2) has shown that the relative proportions of the different domestic animals at EN sites in southern England are matched by those at sites in Normandy and the Paris Basin, while analyses of the sizes of domestic cattle show that these are also very similar. In other words, the pattern is consistent with the introduction of a set of established practices by colonists from adjacent parts of continental Europe rather than their gradual adoption over time, as in the case of the Swifterbant Culture.

This picture of an introduced set of subsistence practices has been confirmed in recent years by increasing numbers of isotope studies. Analyses of stable carbon and nitrogen isotopes in human skeletons showed that that there was a very marked shift in the diets of communities at coastal sites from a heavy reliance on marine protein sources at Mesolithic sites to dependence on largely terrestrial resources at Neolithic sites, a pattern that occurs throughout Britain albeit with some minor variations (summary in Schulting, 2013). These studies have been increasingly confirmed by ceramic residue analyses, which have also shown the same fundamental importance of dairying and milk processing in EN economies and societies that we have seen elsewhere. Thus, Cramp et al.'s (2014a) study of residues from over 300 vessels dating from the Early to Late Neolithic from coastal sites in northern Britain, including the Scottish islands, found virtually no evidence for their use for processing marine products; these were found in less than 1% of vessels from over 40 sites, a major difference from southern Scandinavia. In contrast, around 80% of the EN and MN vessels with residues showed traces of dairy fats, with the remainder coming from ruminant carcass fats, a proportion that increased in the Late Neolithic. Since wild animals make up only a small proportion of the animal bone assemblages, it follows that the carcass fats too must come from domestic animals. The evidence from northern Britain is paralleled by that from the rest of Britain and Ireland, with similarly high proportions of dairy residues, a situation that continues into the MN, although in southern England the proportion of carcass fat residues increases to over 30%. Interestingly, the Late Neolithic pattern suggests the appearance of some regional specialisation, with increasing proportions of meat fats in some regions and an overwhelming predominance of dairy fats in others, notably Ireland, though the number of samples here is small (Cramp et al., 2014a: fig 1, g–i).

One of the mainstays of the view that farming was adopted by local foragers was the belief that it took place very gradually, with a long initial phase when cereals were present but relatively little used, perhaps only on special ceremonial occasions, while the main plant resource exploited continued to be hazelnut (e.g. Thomas, 2003). This idea was undermined by Jones and Rowley-Conwy (2007), who emphasised the importance of taphonomic factors in accounting for the differences in representation of cereals versus hazelnuts on sites: hazelnut shells are waste and as such are more likely to be deliberately thrown on to fires than cereal grains, which are consumed and thus only burned as a result of accidental spillage; if allowances are made for this disparity the evidence suggests that cereals were the major plant food source. At the same time a study of directly dated cereal grains (Brown, 2007) showed that they were actually more frequent in the earlier than the later Neolithic of Britain. In keeping with Brown's argument that the only reliable source of data for the incidence of particular species is directly radiocarbon-dated samples of plant remains, Stevens and Fuller (2012) took this study further on the basis of an updated database of directly dated remains from the Early Mesolithic through to the post-Medieval period in Britain and Ireland. Their results indicated that cereals were introduced c.5950–5850 BP and the summed probabilities of the dated samples rose extremely rapidly

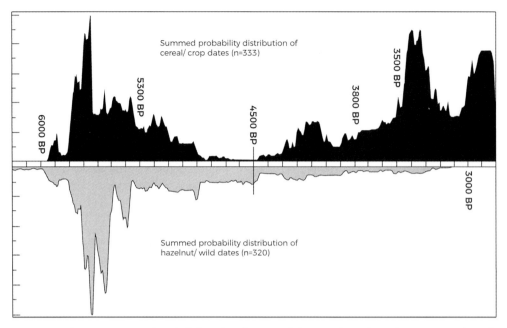

Fig 8.5. Summed probability distribution of direct radiocarbon dates on cereals and wild plant remains through time in Neolithic and Bronze Age Britain. Reproduced, with permission, from fig 3 in *Antiquity* 86, Stevens, C.J. and Fuller, D.Q., Did Neolithic farming fail? The case for a Bronze Age agricultural revolution in the British Isles, pp. 707–722, 2012.

after that date (see Fig 8.5). As they pointed out, this seems an extremely unlikely pattern if cereal agriculture spread through adoption by indigenous groups because it implies that they acquired not only the crops but more importantly all the knowledge required to grow them successfully, virtually instantaneously, a knowledge that embodies years if not generations of transmitted practice. Apparently more surprising in the light of the argument that has been made so far is the fact that numbers of directly dated samples of wild foods, in particular hazelnut shells, increased dramatically in tandem with the cereals. At first sight it might be thought that this is evidence in favour of the continuity of forager traditions. In fact, it reflects the creation of secondary woodland, of which hazel, as an early coloniser of cleared ground, is a key constituent that was no doubt further encouraged for its food value. This is clearly demonstrated in Tipping et al.'s (2009) high-resolution study of pollen from the site of the Early Neolithic so-called 'hall' at Crathes in north-east Scotland. This showed that cereal cultivation was dominant in the immediate environs, with indications that it was intermixed with stands of secondary woodland dominated by hazel, a situation that we have seen already in post-LBK Central Europe.

The earlier Neolithic farming systems in Britain and Ireland seem to have been very similar to one another (Jones and Rowley-Conwy, 2007;

McClatchie et al., 2014, 2016). The range of crops was narrow, comprising emmer and to a lesser extent barley as the main crops, with very little evidence of einkorn or free-threshing wheat (the latter a contrast with central and northern Europe) and no evidence of pulses; the genetic diversity of the crops that did reach Britain may have been similarly impoverished (Fuller and Lucas, 2017). The great majority of the weed species recovered are characteristic of disturbed ground rather than woodland and the proportions of annual and perennial weeds are roughly equal. This latter pattern is more or less the same as that for the LBK and in both cases the weed data are interpreted as evidence of farming plots that would have been in use for at least ten years, rather than slash-and-burn farming. As we have seen, the argument has been further developed by Bogaard and colleagues (e.g. 2013) in recent years on the basis of patterns of nitrogen enrichment in cereal grains that suggests the use of manuring. Evidence for this practice is also found in the British earlier Neolithic, albeit with variation in the intensity of manuring from site to site. Nevertheless, the farming system as a whole was not unchanged since the LBK. As we saw in Chapter 6, in Central Europe, even if intensive working of small fields continued, it was accompanied by a new forest-based dimension, perhaps associated with the creation of forest pasture for cattle, that led to the creation of extensive areas of secondary forest. It is this sort of system that characterises the first farming in southern Scandinavia and probably Britain and Ireland as well. High-resolution pollen analysis of a core from the site of Bonfield Gill Head in the North York Moors (Innes et al., 2013), admittedly an upland area, led to the conclusion that an Early Neolithic phase of clearance activity lasting c.100 years indicated 'forest farming', probably focussed on stock-keeping. Tree girdling would have produced 'stump-sprout woodland' good for cattle-grazing for a number of years. This would have been followed by a phase of cereal-growing in the resulting clearing, with conditions improved by the burning of dead wood, succeeded by a period of coppice-woodland management. Strontium isotope analyses of skeletons from the EN long cairn of Hazleton North in the Cotswold region are in keeping with this sort of activity pattern. The majority have values that are not consistent with permanent sedentism in the region where they were buried but point to regular movement to a region with a different geology, at least 40 km away, possibly as part of a transhumant cycle since cattle share the same isotope pattern as people (Neil et al., 2016).

MIDDLE NEOLITHIC SUBSISTENCE AND THE POPULATION 'BUST'

Regardless of the nature of the farming system, what is striking is the fact that, according to Stevens and Fuller's data, after increasing rapidly to a peak c.5700–5600 BP the numbers of directly dated wild plant foods and cereals in

Britain both decline quite rapidly, with cereals showing an initial sharp fall from c.5600 BP and wild plant foods from c.5400. An almost identical pattern in the chronological distribution of directly dated cereal and hazelnut remains has now been found in Ireland (McClatchie et al., 2016), with a rapid rise to a peak from c.5750 BP and a virtual disappearance of both from c.5300 BP. It is immediately apparent that Stevens and Fuller's cereal date pattern matches the Great Britain population curve and also the forest clearance pattern documented by Woodbridge et al. (2014), including the upturn in population and evidence for clearance seen at the end of the sequence in the late 5th millennium BP. The hazelnut curve is very similar although it does not show the same late upturn, and as such is in accordance with the pollen evidence that the landscape was becoming increasingly open. The Irish plant macro-remains pattern, too, largely matches both the population picture for Ireland and the pollen evidence for forest regeneration from c.5500 BP onwards seen above (Whitehouse et al., 2014), though the records deviate from one another from c.4500 BP, when the population curve shows another major upturn that is not visible in the directly dated macro-remains.

Although Stevens and Fuller's evidence and their inference of a decline in the importance of cereals has been questioned, especially for Scotland (Bishop, 2015), they show in a further analysis that their argument can in fact be sustained (Stevens and Fuller, 2015). In northern England and mainland Scotland both emmer wheat and barley are cultivated during the population peak but after 5600 BP wheat largely disappears from the record while barley, the more resilient cereal, continues, until it too almost entirely disappears c.5000 BP; at the same time hazelnut frequencies increase, a pattern that continues until c.4300 BP (Fig 8.6). The Scottish islands are different, however, as Stevens and Fuller had already pointed out. Here the cereal peak runs from 5500 to 4800 BP, and coincides with major monument construction in the Orkneys (see below). The northern islands seem to have had a different population and subsistence trajectory from the rest of Britain, booming in the period from c.5500 to c.4900 BP when the rest of Britain was in decline.

Current work comparing the population trajectories for Britain and Ireland as a whole with the chronological distribution of directly dated plant macro-remains using a massively increased dataset (Bevan et al., 2017) confirms these patterns and the correlation between them. Here again the Initial Neolithic boom is associated with a high proportion of wheat species. As population decreases this goes down, to virtually zero by 5200 BP, and the proportion of both barley and hazelnuts rises. The former reaches a peak by the same date and then also declines to virtually zero, so that by 4500 BP hazelnut makes up virtually 100% of the dated plant remains. In other words, it is not simply that there were far fewer people and therefore far less subsistence activity overall, but its nature had changed. Wheat was replaced by barley, which can flourish in worse conditions but produces lower yields, but then even this was largely abandoned

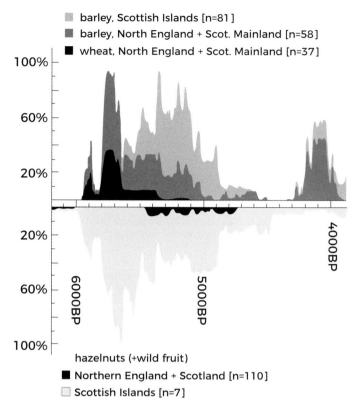

Fig 8.6. Summed probability distribution of direct radiocarbon dates on identified crops, indicating the relative contribution of dates on wheat from northern England and mainland Scotland, barley from northern England and mainland Scotland, and barley from the Scottish islands; inverted in grey and black is the SPD for direct dates on hazelnut shell and other wild foods. Reproduced from fig 3 in *World Archaeology* 47(5), Stevens, C.J. and Fuller, D.Q., Alternative strategies to agriculture: the evidence for climatic shocks and cereal declines during the British Neolithic and Bronze Age (a reply to Bishop), pp. 856–875, 2015. Taylor & Francis Ltd. www.informaworld.com. With permission.

for an ever-increasing reliance on wild plant resources, reaching a peak c.4500 BP, after which there is a rapid renewed increase in the proportion of barley.

It is clear from what we have seen that the agricultural system brought to Britain and Ireland by the first farmers was initially successful, but it could not be sustained, hence the boom and bust. Cultivation of wheat gave way to less productive but more robust barley, which was then itself virtually abandoned; the question is why? Worsening climatic conditions for cereal-growing, for which there is extensive evidence in the later 6th millennium (e.g. Ghilardi and O'Connell, 2013), were probably one of the reasons, and would certainly account for the shift to barley. In Ireland the period c.5600–5400 BP sees a decline in the bog-oak record that has been taken to indicate increasingly cool and wet climatic conditions, which continue down to c.5100 BP. Verrill and Tipping's (2010) study of farming at Belderg Beg in north-west Ireland found evidence that local farming ceased in the late 6th millennium BP and they linked this, together with other evidence in the region for decline, to a shift to a 'more oceanic climate', while acknowledging that local soil conditions could have had an impact on precisely when abandonment occurred. An alternative explanation may be declining crop productivity resulting from soil degradation, which again would account for a shift from wheat to barley. However, climate deterioration and soil degradation resulting from initial farming using up centuries of accumulated soil fertility could easily have interacted with one another. Nevertheless, not all areas fit into this pattern, for reasons that remain unclear. As noted above, in the Scottish islands, much further north than southern Britain and Ireland, a substantial decline in farming does not take place until early in the following millennium, c.4900–4800 BP.

In contrast to some of the other regions we have seen, in Britain and Ireland population levels remained far lower than their earlier peak for hundreds of years and the archaeobotanical results show why. The shift to barley would have decreased carrying capacities and when even this declined and was largely replaced by a reliance on wild plant resources they would have decreased still further. However, this was not a return to a Mesolithic way of life. As Bevan et al. (2017) show, it was a subsistence based on cattle pastoralism, which would have supported a much lower population than cereal agriculture. This system lasted far longer than the climatic downturn that may have been an/the initiating factor. In the language of complex systems (Downey et al., 2016 and see Chapter 9 for further discussion) it can be seen as a 'phase shift' in the system from one equilibrium to another at a much lower density.

SOCIAL AND CULTURAL CHANGE

So far the focus has been on the demographic and subsistence aspects of the appearance of the first farmers with their domestic crops and animals in Britain and Ireland, though attention has been drawn to the 'family resemblances' in the pottery assemblages on both sides of the English Channel, but of course many other novel phenomena were also introduced, just as in the case of southern Scandinavia. These include long barrow burial mounds, megalithic tombs, rectangular post-built houses, flint mines and causewayed enclosures. They all have predecessors in continental north-west Europe although, with the possible exception of the flint mines and causewayed enclosures, the similarities are generic rather than specific and cannot be readily tied down to a single area. In some cases it remains unclear whether the innovations result from ongoing interaction with continental Europe or descent from a common cultural ancestor.

However, recent work, especially Whittle et al.'s (2011, see e.g. fig 14.140) monumental study, has now made it possible to clarify the chronology of the beginning and end dates of most of the EN site and artefact types, and in doing so has shown that the majority were relatively short-lived. As in southern Scandinavia, where flint mining was already beginning at the Scanian site of Södra Sallerup by 6000 BP (see Fig 7.1), mines exploiting the flint in the southern English chalk in Sussex, such as Harrow Hill, are among the earliest Neolithic features, with dates going back to 6000 BP, if not before, contemporary with similar developments going on across the Channel, for example at the site of Spiennes. Rectangular houses, such as at White Horse Stone in Kent, which may have continued in use for over 200 years, also begin to be constructed at the same time. Until recently very few EN houses were known in Britain but new fieldwork is now revealing increasing numbers and pointing to a settlement pattern of individual houses and small hamlets (see e.g. Barclay and Harris, 2017), again as in southern Scandinavia.

The first earthen long barrows had also appeared by c.5800 BP. It is clear though that the great majority of the various types of sites and monuments in both Britain and Ireland were constructed and mainly used between c.5750 BP and c.5500. This makes an interesting contrast with southern Scandinavia where, though farmers arrived at the same time, the construction peak was in the local EN II phase, c.5500–5300 BP, 250 years later than in Britain. The EN house boom in Ireland has already been mentioned. At the same time the earliest circular megalithic passage tombs in Ireland were constructed at the site of Carrowmore (Bergh and Hensey, 2013), while the earliest megalithic so-called court tombs in their trapezoid mounds begin only slightly later (Schulting et al., 2012). In Britain the construction and use of Cotswold-Severn chambered tombs, such as Ascott-under-Wychwood and West Kennet, also took place at this time and the large rectangular timber buildings found in Scotland, such as Crathes, mentioned earlier, were also built, as were the causewayed enclosures of southern Britain, for example the well-known site of Windmill Hill. In addition, there is evidence of extensive exchange. Beginning c.5800 BP the quarries in Langdale in northern England were producing thousands of axes that were distributed over large areas of England and Scotland, as well as across the sea to Ireland.

By c.5600 BP the currency of Carinated Bowls as well as of the Scottish 'halls' had come to an end; from c.5500 to 5400 BP we see the end of the Sussex flint mines, of digging new ditch circuits at causewayed enclosures, of stone axe exchange networks, and then groundstone axes themselves. By c.5300 BP the southern British enclosures are no longer used, though long barrows and cairns, linear monuments and the miscellaneous category of diverse and small monuments continue later. In Ireland the house phase is finished by c.5600 BP, while pit complexes seem to end or decline massively in frequency shortly after c.5500 during MN I. The construction of court tombs also appears to cease although their use continued. In contrast, however, the building of passage graves, which had begun during the EN II settlement boom not only continued but apparently peaked during the MN II phase, c.5400–5100 BP with the construction of the major tombs such as Knowth and Newgrange in the Boyne Valley.

Of course, what links the various comings and goings together is their connection to the pattern of population booms and busts in Britain and Ireland that we have seen earlier in the chapter. They appear as the population begins to rise and they largely disappear as it declines. The reasons for the coincidence of the beginnings and endings of these varied phenomena with the population boom and bust are likely to have been varied. Innovations like the new pottery types that appeared early in the 4th millennium quite possibly simply increased and then decreased with the population while random processes of innovation and drift could have led to the emergence of new types, such as Middle Neolithic Peterborough Ware (Ard and Darvill, 2015). Exchange networks of stone axes, involving production far beyond local needs, were no doubt responding to the demand created by a large population for both clearance tools and ritual/prestige objects. The larger population might also have resulted in an increased demand for social distinction which exotic artefacts would have met. The same may be true of burial monuments, since, just as in southern Scandinavia, only a small proportion of the population were buried in them. However, these would also have been a response to the need of local groups to assert claims to territory as population grew, and their varied styles of monumentality are clearly about much more than just burial.

The peak of construction of causewayed enclosures in southern England occurs during the period of the population peak, beginning c.5700 BP. Whittle et al. (2011: fig 14.20) (see Fig 8.7) show that the majority of the ditch construction for the enclosures they examine in detail occurs in the 57th century BP, with a subsidiary peak in the 56th century. By 5500 BP construction is effectively over and they are almost all out of use by c.5300 BP. The previous two chapters have shown that the immediate origin of the enclosures lies in adjacent areas of continental Europe in the mid–late 7th millennium, following patterns that arose in the LBK, and that they plausibly represent the largest collectively acting group. In southern Britain, as we have just seen, they only occur from c.5700 BP, after c.300 years of farming occupation. Whittle et al. (2011: 894–898) suggest that their construction is associated with intergroup competition. When we see the relationship between enclosure construction and the population pattern it becomes clear why that would be the case. As with the agricultural colonisation of southern Scandinavia, the reason they were not constructed initially was because there was no need for them during the period of initial colonisation when no pressure existed. Initial settlement would have followed the ideal-free distribution and it

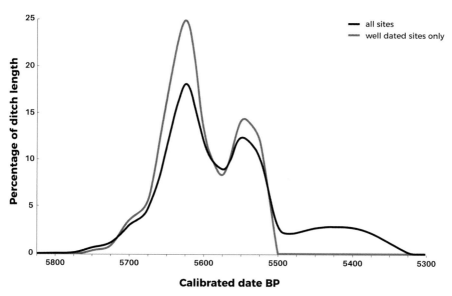

Fig 8.7. Chronology of causewayed enclosure building in Britain. Reproduced from fig 14.20 in Whittle, A.W.R. et al., *Gathering Time: Dating the Early Neolithic Enclosures of Southern Britain and Ireland*, 2011, Oxbow Books, Oxford, with permission from the author and Oxbow.

was undertaken by individual households and small groups, evident in the dispersed pattern and small scale of early settlements. But we then have to suppose either that some knowledge of the relevant practices was transmitted through perhaps 8–12 generations without being put to use, or that contact was maintained with the adjacent continental groups from which they came and which had continued the enclosure tradition because populations there were high and competition was prevalent; perhaps groups continued to come to Britain for 200–300 years, or interaction continued. If transmission was based on continuing contact between south-east England and the adjacent continent, then, as Whittle et al. suggest, that could help to explain the lack of enclosures in Scotland, where, as we have seen, the population boom–bust also occurs.

As in late 7th-millennium BP continental west-central Europe and in southern Scandinavia, their construction should be seen as the result of costly signalling of group strength and thus a discouragement to attack, as regional population rose to a peak and competition increased. As elsewhere, it seems entirely likely that it was such competition that caused the creation of the higher level social-political entities represented by the enclosures in the first place (cf. Zimmermann, 2012), the construction of the enclosures perhaps itself being part of the process that created the new entities. At the same time, the high population resulting from the successful farming economy also provided the labour to make construction possible. In other words, if, as we have argued earlier, increased population in prehistory was an index of economic growth, then the period of enclosure construction shows that at this point in time the new economy was providing the resources not only for population increase but also for significant production beyond subsistence to invest in construction and in the feasting that went with it. As we have seen though, population almost immediately peaked and began to decline as barley and wild plant resources increased in importance at the expense of wheat, lowering the carrying capacity and coinciding with the end of enclosure construction; these fell out of use over the next 200–300 years (Whittle et al., 2011: fig 14.30) as population declined.

Indications of violence in the archaeological record of southern Britain (Whittle et al., 2011: fig 14.36) support the scenario which has been outlined. They increase markedly from c.5700 BP and include evidence of attacks on causewayed enclosures, for example at the site of Crickley Hill, where the enclosure was protected by a palisade, probably c.5400 BP, at a time when population was declining but the enclosures remained in primary use. The enclosure at Hambledon Hill, which was also the subject of attack, had seen extensive palisade and earthwork construction around the same time (Bayliss et al., 2017). Nevertheless, although population was declining and enclosures being abandoned, the period from c.5500 to 5200 seems to be the main period of construction of so-called cursus monuments, linear features made up of a pair of parallel banks and ditches often around 100 m apart. The largest, the Dorset cursus, is made of two such monuments, each c.5 km in length, placed end to end. In what ways these were a response to the decline of the enclosures and what scale of effort they involved at any given time remains unclear. In any case, these too had ceased to be constructed by c.5200 BP (Bayliss et al., 2017: fig 17.14).

In the context just described, the enclosure at Magheraboy in north-west Ireland presents a widely recognised anomaly. Under all the possible current models for its construction date, it belongs to the beginning of the Neolithic colonisation of Ireland, shortly after population began to rise and not as it was nearing its peak, as in Britain (Whittle et al., 2011: 665–666). Sheridan (2017) plausibly sees it as an indication of early 'Carinated Bowl' settlement that had arrived in Ireland from the north, via Scotland, and there are now some other early dates for occupation material that would support this. It is as if the need for an enclosure was assumed to exist by the first settlers, on the basis of the situation prevailing where they came from, even though the competitive conditions that had led to enclosure building did not exist at this time in Ireland, and its initial irrelevance meant that enclosure building was never taken up on any scale. In any case, Scotland and Ireland both demonstrate that enclosure construction and the practices that went on there were not necessary responses to local population increase and inter-group competition.

AFTER THE CRASH

As we have seen, the end of the population boom led, for a variety of reasons, to the demise of the many earlier Neolithic traditions, practices and organisational features identified by Whittle et al. as ceasing in the period 5500–5300 BP. Demand for resources exploited for exchange declined, transmission chains for artefact traditions were disrupted and the socio-political entities responsible for enclosure construction were collapsing, making for increased insecurity. All this was taking place in the context of a probable climatic downturn and a change in the staple cereal from wheat to barley, more resilient but less productive, that probably helped to cause the population decline. By 5000 BP even barley had declined in importance and been replaced by an emphasis on cattle pastoralism and the use of wild plant resources.

In such a situation we might expect greatly increased local innovation responding to the failure of the previous system, but also potentially the infiltration of new ideas and features from any area that had survived the crash. Given that the new subsistence system was based on cattle pastoralism rather than cereal agriculture, we can also expect there would have been changes in value systems and social institutions. It is in this context that the first stage of Stonehenge was constructed c.5000 BP or shortly after, consisting of a ditch with internal and external banks, and the circle of so-called Aubrey Holes, containing the famous bluestones imported from the Preseli Hills in south-west Wales, as well as cremation burials (Darvill et al., 2012). There were also stone and post features in alignment with the midsummer sunrise and the northern major moonrise. Nor was Stonehenge the only site of its kind being constructed at this time. Similar large 'henge monuments' with evidence of stones and cremations, slightly earlier in date, have been found at Llandygai in north Wales and at Flagstones in Dorchester, which is 50 miles to the south of Stonehenge and at the centre of another major group of Neolithic monuments (Parker Pearson, 2012: 316–319). Similar but smaller cremation enclosures of roughly the same date are now known quite widely from southern England to Scotland.

However, arguably the most impressive monuments constructed in Britain around 3000 BC are to be found in the Orkney Islands in northern Scotland, in the context of the major ritual and settlement complex on and around the Ness of Brodgar, which seems to have been a centre for the whole of the Orkney Islands. The monuments include the Stones of Stenness henge monument and stone circle, as well as the Ring of Brodgar and the monumental stone buildings of the recently discovered Ness of Brodgar site (www.orkneyjar.com/archaeology/nessofbrodgar/), apparently a walled ceremonial centre, which began to be constructed c.5200 BP, as well as the Maeshowe-type passage tombs, which borrow features from the Irish Boyne Valley tombs, such as the orientation of the passage on the mid-winter solstice found at

Maeshowe itself. Moreover, finely carved stone balls and maceheads plausibly suggested to be 'symbols of power' also occur at these sites (details summarised in Sheridan, 2017). As we have seen, the Scottish islands do not show a marked drop in the incidence of dated cereals until c.4850 BP, in contrast to mainland Britain, where it occurs c.5350, in parallel with the population crash we have seen above. In other words, the Scottish islands in general and Orkney in particular seem to have continued to flourish and develop new and exceptional monumental, ritual and social forms at a time when there was decline elsewhere, and were widely emulated subsequently as a result. Thus, the Stones of Stenness remains the earliest 'true' henge, that is to say a circular monument with a bank outside the ditch, though it is uncertain at present whether these monuments originated in Orkney and spread south from there given the wide distribution of similar monuments across Britain at the end of the 6th millennium BP. On the other hand, it does seem clear that Grooved Ware pottery had its origin there, perhaps by c.5200 BP (Brophy and Sheridan, 2012: 68) and subsequently spread to the rest of Britain and to Ireland, where it is mainly found in ceremonial/monumental contexts. It was prevalent across Scotland by 5000 BP and had already spread to southern England by 4800 BP (Parker Pearson, 2012: 330). In Ireland it occurs in the Boyne Valley passage tomb cemeteries, beginning c.5000 BP and continuing down to c.4500/4400 BP (Sheridan, 2004), as it did in Britain, but this is after their construction and initial use in the late 4th millennium. The construction of the great Boyne Valley passage tombs in Ireland precedes those in Orkney, which used features from them, as we have seen, and occurred at the end of the population crash in Ireland.

What is abundantly clear is that developments in Britain from the end of the 6th to the late 5th millennium BP were very different from those that preceded them. The likelihood that subsistence was now based on cattle pastoralism fits in with the evidence for exceptionally extensive long-distance contacts within the British Isles that involved novel ritual and social developments, at a time when contacts with continental Europe had largely if not entirely ceased. It is difficult to imagine the sorts of social and economic arrangements that made it possible to move the bluestones from south-west Wales to Stonehenge, while the evidence that some cattle were being brought from as far away as Scotland in connection with the feasting evidenced at the site of Durrington Walls during the period of the massive second phase of construction at Stonehenge, c.4570–4430 BP is also striking (Viner et al., 2010). It is hard not to see all this as indicative of a growing capacity to centralise power that is evidenced earlier in the Boyne Valley tombs and the monuments of Orkney. Parker Pearson (2012: 331) suggests that, 'The work of moving the bluestones was not that of a small devoted sect but entailed the mobilization of an entire society, possibly a growing political domain or kingdom', which also attempted to unify cosmic as well as human forces on an unprecedented scale, a scale that was taken even further 500 years later with the second phase of construction at the site. It is all the more striking that these extraordinary enterprises and the novel social developments they reflect were taking place at a time when population was low and the role of cereal agriculture minimal, *contra* the usual models of social evolution.

From c.4500 BP, however, the proportion of barley in the record increases rapidly, and the activities at the major monuments began to be transformed with the renewed contacts with mainland Europe represented by the appearance of Bell Beakers, associated with new burial rituals and the beginnings of copper and gold metallurgy. We now know that this was the result of a large-scale infiltration of new groups of people, with a mixed ancestry that included the pre-existing Middle Neolithic population of western and Central Europe and the steppe populations of the 6th millennium BP (Olalde et al., 2017), arriving just as Grooved Ware monument construction at such centres as Stonehenge and Avebury was at its height. Just as southern Scandinavia saw the arrival of such groups with the Corded Ware Culture after 5000 BP, so later descendants reached the far west more than 500 years later. Perhaps the low populations of the Middle and Late Neolithic once again made Britain and Ireland a viable target for migration and a renewed agricultural adaptation, just as the low forager populations of the Mesolithic had done over 1500 years earlier.

SUMMARY AND CONCLUSION

All the evidence points to the remarkably speedy introduction of a well-established farming subsistence economy, including cereal agriculture and an emphasis on dairying, and no doubt the values and beliefs that went with it, by colonising groups from adjacent areas of continental Europe in the 200–300 years after c.6100 BP. It may have been prompted by population pressure but the colonisation of Britain and Ireland was far too rapid to be considered the result of a gradual wave of advance – there was settlement in Scotland and Ireland long before there is any suggestion of a population peak further south – so, once again, we see evidence of leapfrog migration. The result of the expansion was a massive increase in population over the next 300–400 years, which was accompanied by the building of burial and other monuments such as causewayed enclosures, forms that had their origin in adjacent continental Europe. Interestingly, monument construction reached a peak in Britain earlier than it did in southern Scandinavia though it appears never to have been so intense. After this initial expansion phase that lasted until c.5600–5500 BP there was a crash in population over the following centuries, culminating in a low point at c.5000 BP, associated with the failure of the agricultural system, whether as a result of climate change, soil degradation or some combination of the two. The result was the emergence of a new system based on cattle pastoralism associated with new forms of monument on a massive scale that was to last for hundreds of years, before the arrival of Bell Beaker immigrants after 4500 BP.

CHAPTER 9

CONCLUSION: EVOLUTIONARY PATTERNS AND PROCESSES

Although the particular long-term history that this book has described is unique, we can recognise within it the action of a number of general evolutionary processes operating at different timescales.

The origin of farming in south-west Asia should be seen in terms of the interaction between payoffs to hunter-gatherers at the day-to-day scale and those at the generational scale. As long as higher day-to-day payoffs could be obtained by focussing on the exploitation of low-density mobile animal resources there was no possibility of regional population increasing beyond a low level, because the carrying capacity of this mode of subsistence was low; increased fertility would not be rewarded with successful recruitment to the next generation. If such resources decline, for whatever reason, then the rate at which people encounter them will drop and people will broaden their subsistence activities to include resources with lower return rates that are encountered more frequently and thus increase return rates overall. If the resources that are then introduced are both dense and sustainable then people will become more sedentary. In these circumstances the previous population ceiling will be lifted; more children can be born and raised successfully and population will increase up to the limit of the new resources. In the case of the Late Pleistocene Fertile Crescent, spatial distributions of resources were constantly changing as a result of climatic fluctuations and the evidence suggests that more sedentary subsistence systems came and went in response. However, in the 1500 or so years before the beginning of the Holocene, including the Younger Dryas, modelling of the available data suggests that conditions in both the northern and southern Levant were sufficiently stable and benign that populations relying on dense and sustainable locally available plant resources could increase to the unprecedented level observed in the radiocarbon population proxy. At this point the beginning of the Holocene introduced exceptionally good conditions for plant growth in terms of both temperature and precipitation. It may have been the ensuing expansion of woodland that led people to cultivate to ensure continued access to sustainable grass/cereal crops, which themselves were changing their distribution in response to the new conditions. This raised the sustainable carrying capacity at which births and deaths were in balance still further, especially when the mutualistic relationship of cultivation between plants and people led to high-yielding domesticated forms. Nevertheless, fluctuations in local limits continued to occur, no doubt at least partly for climatic reasons.

Already at the beginning of the Holocene, when cultivation had barely begun, we see people trying to come to terms with the consequences of the previous 1500 years of increasing population density and more sedentary ways of life. One response was the colonisation of Cyprus; another was the appearance of new forms of ritual, symbolism, monumentality and settlement, which were taken to Cyprus as well. These innovations continued through the Pre-Pottery Neolithic and spread from one region to another through links evidenced, for example, by the movement of obsidian. In adaptive radiations, when a new environment or energy source opens up, it is unclear what its possibilities are and which ones are viable, so all sorts of different possibilities may be tried in a process of 'breadth-first' search; this seems to be what is evidenced in the extraordinary social and symbolic developments during the Pre-Pottery Neolithic. It is only later that the less successful ones are winnowed out. In contrast to new technologies or subsistence practices, where the relative success of different options can emerge relatively quickly, it may take much longer to establish whether some social arrangements are more successful than others, and for whom. One likely arena of change in these unprecedented situations is around property rights and the potential for social inequality. When hunting mobile animals is the main focus of subsistence, fluctuations in day-to-day returns as well as over different stages of the lifespan mean that sharing is the best means of insurance for evening things out. However, once returns start to depend more on the effort put in, then they are increasingly restricted to immediate dependents, while the fact that members of a community are effectively stuck in one place means that they all vulnerable to the same natural disasters. The evidence for increased crop storage within houses is probably a reflection of such changes in property rights and the relative autonomy of individual households in this respect. However, it seems likely that household autonomy would have been in tension with the growth of the so-called 'mega-sites', settlements with populations in the low thousands at the top end, some of which, such as Çatalhöyük, lasted for a millennium. These must have had special institutional arrangements to keep them together, all the more so given the lack of evidence for warfare, which is generally one of the main reasons for settlement nucleation and the overcoming of centrifugal social forces.

In contrast to the innovative developments of the Pre-Pottery Neolithic, the story of the expansion of farming into and across Europe is one of conservatism. It represents the success of one version of the many social, cultural and economic variants that had flourished in south-west Asia. That version was based on small groups of autonomous households lacking much of the symbolic elaboration of the core area and with a rather stereotyped subsistence pattern based on the integration of crops and animals (M. Özdoğan, 2010). This new niche was highly portable, based as it was on annual cereal crops that were harvested every year and could be re-sown somewhere different, as well as on mobile domestic animals. It turned out to be remarkably successful, in that it created possibilities for population growth and expansion that enabled its possessors to take advantage of the existence of vast areas that were very well-suited to the new subsistence system but only very thinly occupied by hunter-gatherers, because of the low carrying capacity that their terrestrial wild resources afforded.

While they have had relatively little impact so far on understandings of the processes involved in the origins of agriculture, recent studies of whole-genome ancient DNA data using new methods have had a major effect on understanding the European spread. These studies have settled decades of inconclusive debate by showing that farming spread across Europe as a result of the spread of successive generations of descendants of farmers originally from south-east Anatolia. In other words, farmers passed on farming knowledge, practices and the plant and animal resources themselves to their children, through the generations, in a process of vertical transmission that enabled them to successfully colonise new areas. On the edge of the spread, with endless dispersal opportunities, increased fertility would have been an option that gave a fitness advantage to those that made use of it.

The tight linkage of people, niche and culture by vertical transmission over several thousand years would have created possibilities of gene-culture co-evolution that we still know very little about, though it seems increasingly unlikely that lactase persistence was part of this initial complex since it does not reach noticeable frequencies until the Bronze Age (Olalde et al., 2017). Such transmission also means that all aspects of culture and practice, as well as the adaptive environment, were being transmitted together, representing a coherent cultural core, not separate packages with different histories, tightly connected by common descent to the genes. Some of these practices and resources were those which gave these people their selective advantage, especially the domesticated plants and animals and the knowledge to turn them into food while ensuring their continuing reproduction. We still need to know more about the factors affecting the transmission of such features as monumental burial traditions or the LBK house, but particular social institutions and practices were probably also key to the success of these expansions. Others would simply have been 'hitchhiking', carried along with the expanding population, for example the language they spoke.

In fact, there is remarkably little evidence of foragers adopting farming as a result of cultural diffusion, though the Pitted Ware Culture of southern Scandinavia seems to have eventually adopted some farming elements from the TRB Culture and the Swifterbant Culture of the wetlands of the Low Countries may be another example. This in itself is telling us that it would not have been simple to adopt. It was a way of life that had been put together and then modified for local circumstances over thousands of years. This point is confirmed by the evidence for the later spread of farming into the east Baltic c.5000 BP. Here too it was introduced by immigrants, in this case by Corded Ware-Battle Axe groups of steppe descent, not as a result of its diffusion and adoption by the local foragers (Mittnik et al., 2017). It is worth noting that there is even less evidence of farmers becoming foragers: this is not simply a matter of more or less hunting but commitment to a completely different set of values and priorities. Paradoxically, it has been those most in favour of cultural diffusion explanations of the spread of farming who think that people can easily change their culture on the basis of an assessment of costs and benefits of different ways of life. Rather, foragers were incorporated, albeit at low rates, into farming communities. Recent work (e.g. Lipson et al., 2017) is beginning to tell us in some cases when this incorporation might have occurred and the extent to which it was a result of major pulses at certain times or a gradual process over longer periods. How low or high these rates of incorporation were remains unclear. If they were occurring at the farming frontier they could have been extremely low. The process of 'surfing on the wave of advance', discussed in Chapter 4, means that those versions of genes present in a population at the point where it is expanding have a high probability of reaching significant frequencies purely by chance, because the number of individuals there is small but they are likely to be successful. Thus the proportion of forager genetic admixture in a population may give an exaggerated picture of the extent of interaction, though the picture we see at the Blätterhöhle in the 6th millennium BP shows it could be close.

The process of strongly vertical cultural transmission from parents to children documented by the close link between genes and culture has a further consequence. It is inherently conservative, because it leaves little scope for the adoption of innovations from outside the local group that challenge existing practices. This is most clearly seen in the LBK, in everything from the crops to the houses and the decoration on the pottery, and results in strong path dependence. In other words, once a particular set of knowledge and practices has been established as something that works, it becomes the basis for decisions that are made in the future, because it defines the range of options that can be envisaged. For example, once a number of criteria have been established for what represents a good place to establish a new settlement, other possibilities will be ignored. It is in keeping with this idea that two contexts in which innovation does occur are cases where different traditions meet. One is Lepenski Vir, where the striking cultural phenomena of the Transition Phase result from the interaction of farmer immigrants and indigenous hunter-fisher-gatherers, though they are short-lived. The other is the meeting of the descendants of the

Mediterranean and Central European farming streams in France, which seems to result in changed farming systems and novel monuments. This is something we need to know far more about, as we do indeed for the Mediterranean expansion more generally, which is far less well documented than the Central European one, especially for aspects other than subsistence.

The fact that farming expansion stalls for centuries in certain places – central Anatolia, the northern Aegean, the Middle Danube region and north-west/northern Europe – may be an indication of the difficulty of making innovations in a world of mainly vertical transmission. Environmental factors, including adverse climate conditions and lack of success in growing cereals in more northerly latitudes until genetic modifications had taken place, may well be relevant in some of these cases, but 'technological lock-in' that made it impossible for people to imagine doing things in different ways from what they had been doing may also be a factor. In the case of the LBK it has been suggested that it was a combination of drift and innovation in small semi-isolated communities that enabled change to occur and a new adaptation to be established. In the case of the spread of farming to Britain and Scandinavia, climatic factors may have been relevant to the delay but it is also clear that it depended on changes to the farming system that overcame its previous restriction to a very narrow range of soil, temperature and precipitation conditions that did not occur until a millennium after the initial farming arrival in Central Europe. What we can certainly conclude is that, despite being on the edge of new areas to colonise, there were periods when people were not prepared to take the risk.

This takes us to the much-reviled 'wave of advance' model. In my view it remains a useful framework for thinking about and modelling the factors behind the range expansion of farming and farmers, though it is misleading as a descriptive model of the expansion from south-west Asia to north-west Europe as a whole. This is because of the pauses that have just been discussed. When expansion does occur it is very fast, a point that has long been recognised by the introduction of the concept of 'leapfrog migration', but it is important to note that the new genetic evidence now excludes the alternative possibility that the speed could be accounted for by the diffusion of farming to foragers. Given that we now know it was migration we need a principled way of explaining the rapid spread episodes. During these episodes movement occurs long before local farming landscapes fill to their carrying capacity and far faster than the Gaussian distribution of movement distances generally used in the model would predict, but that does not mean we should give up using the model as a tool. Some combination of advection, moving along a gradient of preferred movement, and a Lévy flight model of dispersal distances that incorporates a certain probability of long distance moves, seems more appropriate and has some ecological justification. The need to continue to explore general models of range expansion, rather than simply stating that such models do not work, is emphasised when we realise that the speed of the spread of farming during the expansion episodes is not unique. In fact, it seems likely to be the rule rather than the exception, as such examples as the Lapita colonisation of the Pacific and the human occupation of the New World indicate; there is some general process at work here. In any case, in all these examples, the risks of going long distances into the unknown in the face of Allee effects were clearly considered worth taking and must have paid off much of the time.

The preceding summary has focussed on the expansion and its payoffs, and the predicted increase in regional populations after farming arrives has been shown to be visible in the radiocarbon proxy measure of population that has been used throughout this book. However, one of the most striking features that has come out of the use of this proxy is that the population booms set off when farmers arrived in new areas favourable to their subsistence system did not last, but were followed by busts or slower population declines. Britain and Ireland, for example, go from the arrival of farming to the start of a bust in c. 300–400 years and many other regions are similar, though in central Germany, one of the largest areas of fertile loess soils in Europe, it is the best part of a millennium from the arrival of the LBK to the demographic decline in the later 7th millennium BP. Downey et al. (2016) showed that the population trajectories of many of these regions are characterised by statistical indicators of declining resilience in advance of the impending busts, but it is not obvious why the apparent ceilings in the different regions were what they were.

The reasons for the busts also remain unclear. In some cases, for example the decline in most of Britain and Ireland after 5500 BP, it is likely that the known onset of cooler and wetter conditions at this time had a negative effect on cereal-growing conditions (Stevens and Fuller 2015; Bevan et al., 2017), but for some reason the Scottish islands do not seem to be affected in the same way until 500 years later. Similarly, in southern Scandinavia, both Jutland and Scania show a population decline from c. 5500 BP, but in the Danish islands, situated between these two regions, population levels carry on rising for another 200–300 years. In other words, there seem to be different patterns in regions that are close together and share similar conditions, so other factors must be at work as well. Conversely, the boom–bust pattern is not restricted to those regions where farming arrived at 6000 BP. It also occurs in areas where farming began at 7500 BP or shortly after, with a decline after 7000/6900 BP in the western part of the LBK distribution but also in the Kuyavia region of Poland. A very similar pattern is visible in Iberia, obviously a very different climatic region, while in the Apulia region of south-east Italy decline seems to begin c. 7500 BP, just before the onset of arid conditions, after 500 years of farming. In other words, even if the impact of climate change cannot be excluded in these cases too, the pattern raises the question of whether the arrival of farming sets off an intrinsically cyclical phenomenon, in which population increases rapidly, on the basis of the exploitation of thousands of years of accumulated soil fertility, and then exceeds local carrying capacities. Peters and Zimmermann (2017) make a similar argument for the presence of cultural cycles in the Central European Neolithic from the perspective of resilience theory.

Such a boom–bust process is in keeping with the 'invisible cliff' model of population growth in farming societies when they settle a new habitat, developed by Puleston et al. (2014), which builds on the work of Wood (1998) on the operation of Malthusian processes described in Chapter 1. The model includes the population size and its age-sex distribution, environmental factors affecting yield, taking into account available labour, the food needs of the population given its size and age distribution, and the impact on fertility and mortality of the food available. The interactions of these factors produce new fertility and mortality rates which in turn produce a changed population size and age distribution. Puleston et al. show that the model leads to a characteristic three-phase population trajectory. In the first so-called 'copial' phase, rates of fertility and mortality remain unchanged, there is a food surplus and population increases. If the area available is large and yields are high then this can last a considerable time. It is followed by a short transition phase when fertility decreases and mortality increases as a result of food shortages. This phase in turn is succeeded by 'a Malthusian phase of indefinite length in which vital rates and quality of life are depressed, sometimes strikingly so' (Puleston et al., 2014: 1). The key point about the processes embodied in the model is that while food availability goes down gradually, its effect on life expectancy, probability of survival to age five and women's completed fertility rate (TFR) are sudden and dramatic (Fig 9.1). In effect, one minute everything is going fine, next there is disaster, hence the invisible cliff. Moreover, the better the copial phase conditions in terms of resource yield and fertility rate, the shorter the transition interval will be and the worse the effect of the transition to the Malthusian equilibrium, where births and deaths balance one another. These are circumstances conducive to increased social competition, and we have seen evidence for this in the regional records as populations reach their peak, including increased violence.

It is important to emphasise that all the processes are endogenous to the model; they do not involve any outside forces such as climate deterioration, but such forces, or others like disease, can obviously make things much worse. Indeed, if the population is at the Malthusian equilibrium it may not take much to tip it downwards. If the external force is short-lived then in principle we might expect population to bounce back accordingly, but this will not necessarily happen; such forces may lead to 'critical transitions' or 'regime shifts' if environmental changes interact with other processes that are going on, like population growth (Downey et al., 2016). Thus, to take the example of Britain and Ireland again, the mid-6th-millennium BP climatic downturn was relatively short-lived, but the population decline at that time was not immediately reversed, with a rise to previous levels. On the contrary, there was a 'regime

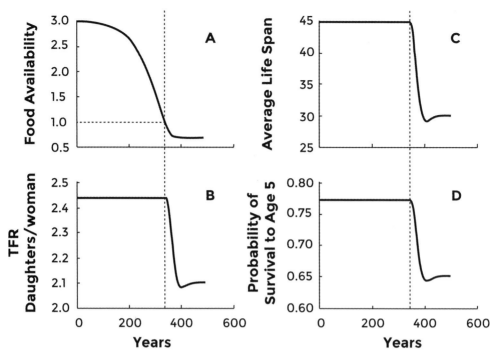

Fig 9.1. The invisible cliff: modelled Malthusian transition interval and quality of life demographic variables as food availability decreases. Reproduced from fig 3 in *PLoS ONE* 9(1): e87541, Puleston, C. et al., The Invisible Cliff: Abrupt Imposition of Malthusian Equilibrium in a Natural-Fertility, Agrarian Society, 2014. doi:10.1371/journal.pone.0087541. Creative Commons license.

shift'. It was about 800 years before population started increasing again and we know that during this period a shift occurred from wheat to barley cultivation and then to an emphasis on cattle pastoralism that produced a population equilibrium at a lower level. This adaptation itself was only ended by renewed immigration from continental Europe, re-introducing cereal cultivation.

This development makes the point that the general processes that have been emphasised in this book interact to produce the contingencies of history. There is no incompatibility between the two. The down phases of regional population fluctuations, for example, potentially make those regions attractive for populations with new adaptations that can exploit them more successfully, just as we saw with the immigration of farmers into Europe in the first place. Bell Beaker immigration into Britain in the late 5th millennium BP was the result of the success of a new adaptation that enabled populations from the steppe regions of eastern Europe to expand into central and western Europe and to intermix with the existing Neolithic populations, resulting in the creation of a novel set of long-lasting cultural practices and traditions that superseded those established by the first farmers whose history this book has described.

NOTES

CHAPTER 1 INTRODUCTION: POPULATION, RESOURCES AND LIFE HISTORIES

1 In the earlier periods covered by this book the general convention is to use Before Present for dates while in European prehistory from the Neolithic onwards the usual convention is to quote dates as BC or BCE (Before Christian Era). To avoid confusion I decided, after much thought, to use BP throughout, with apologies to those who prefer BCE. The present is taken as CE 2000, so BC dates are easily obtained by subtracting this. In the relatively small number of cases where I have cited specific radiocarbon dates I have taken the BCE date given in the source and added 2000 to it, rather than the usual convention of adding 1950.

CHAPTER 2 THE ORIGINS OF AGRICULTURE IN SOUTH-WEST ASIA

1 That is to say, their grains are enclosed in husks known as glumes that require pounding for their removal, another handling cost. This was characteristic of all the ancestral wild cereals and would have helped protect the grains in the soil from predators.
2 This is the DNA from the mitochondria in cells, not the nucleus, and is passed on through the maternal line because only the egg, not the sperm, contains mitochondria. Importantly mtDNA only represents a single gene lineage and is therefore relatively limited in what it can us tell us. The same is true of Y chromosome DNA, a single lineage passed on to males only, through the paternal line. The individual variants in mtDNA or Y DNA are known as haplotypes; groups of similar haplotypes are haplogroups.

REFERENCES

Ackland, G.J., Signitzer, M., Stratford, K., Cohen, M.H., 2007. Cultural hitchhiking on the wave of advance of beneficial technologies. *Proceedings of the National Academy of Sciences* 104, 8714–8719.

Ahlström, T., 2009. *Underjordiska Dödsriken. Humanosteologiska Studier av Neolitiska Kollektivgravar.* Institutionen för Arkeologi, Göteborgs Universitet, Göteborg.

Alberti, G., 2014. Modeling group size and scalar stress by logistic regression from an archaeological perspective. *PLOS ONE* 9, e91510.

Alenius, T., Mökkönen, T., Lahelma, A., 2013. Early farming in the northern Boreal zone: reassessing the history of land use in southeastern Finland through high-resolution pollen analysis. *Geoarchaeology* 28, 1–24.

Allaby, R.G., Fuller, D.Q., Brown, T.A., 2008. The genetic expectations of a protracted model for the origins of domesticated crops. *Proceedings of the National Academy of Sciences* 105, 13982–13986. doi:10.1073/pnas.0803780105.

Allaby, R.G., Kitchen, J.L., Fuller, D.Q., 2016. Surprisingly low limits of selection in plant domestication. *Evol Bioinform Online* 11, 41–51. doi:10.4137/EBO.S33495.

Allard, P., 2014. *5000 Ans Avant JC, Archéologie Rurale de la Vallée de l'Aisne: Premières Fermes, Premiers Champs, la Vie Quotidienne au Néolithique.* Association pour le sauvetage archéologique de la vallée de l'Aisne, Soissons.

Allentoft, M.E., Sikora, M., Sjögren, K.-G. et al., 2015. Population genomics of Bronze Age Eurasia. *Nature* 522, 167–172. doi:10.1038/nature14507.

Amkreutz, L., Vanmontfort, B., 2008. Diverging trajectories? Forager-farmer interaction in two adjacent regions, in: Hofmann, D., Bickle, P. (Eds.), *Creating Communities: New Advances in Central European Neolithic Research.* Oxbow, Oxford, pp. 11–31.

Amkreutz, L., Vanmontfort, B., De Bie, M., Verbeek, C., 2010. Bowls of contention: Mesolithic sites with pottery in the lower Rhine area, in: Vanmontfort, B., Louwe Kooijmans, L., Amkreutz, L., Verhart, L. (Eds.), *Pots, Farmers and Foragers: Pottery Traditions and Social Interaction in the Earliest Neolithic of the Lower Rhine Area.* Leiden University Press, Leiden, pp. 15–26.

Ammerman, A.J., Cavalli-Sforza, L.L., 1973. A population model for the diffusion of early farming in Europe, in: Renfrew, C. (Ed.), *The Explanation of Culture Change; Models In Prehistory.* Duckworth, London, pp. 343–357.

Andersen, N.H., 2008. Die Region um Sarup im Südwesten der Insel Fünen (Dänemark) im 3. Jahrtausend v. Chr., in: Dörfler, W., Müller, J. (Eds.), *Umwelt – Wirtschaft – Siedlungen im Dritten Vorchristlichen Jahrtausend Mitteleuropas und Südskandinaviens.* Offa-Beihefte. na, Kiel, pp. 35–48.

Andersson, M., Artursson, M., Brink, K., 2016. Early Neolithic Landscape and Society in Southwest Scania: new results and perspectives. *Journal of Neolithic Archaeology* 18, 23–114.

Anthony, D., 1997. Prehistoric migration as a social process, in: Chapman, J., Hamerow, H. (Eds.), *Migration and Invasions in Archaeological Explanation.* BAR International Series. 664. Archaeopress, Oxford, pp. 21–32.

Antolín, F., Jacomet, S., Buxó, R., 2015. The hard knock life. Archaeobotanical data on farming practices during the Neolithic (5400–2300 cal BC) in the NE of the Iberian Peninsula. *Journal of Archaeological Science* 61, 90–104.

Araus, J.L., Ferrio, J.P., Voltas, J., Aguilera, M., Buxó, R., 2014. Agronomic conditions and crop evolution in ancient Near East agriculture. *Nature Communications* 5, 3953.

Arbuckle, B.S., 2013. The late adoption of cattle and pig husbandry in Neolithic Central Turkey. *Journal of Archaeological Science* 40, 1805–1815.

Arbuckle, B.S., Atici, L., 2013. Initial diversity in sheep and goat management in Neolithic south-western Asia. *Levant* 45, 219–235.

Arbuckle, B.S., Kansa, S.W., Kansa, E. et al., 2014. Data sharing reveals complexity in the westward spread of domestic animals across Neolithic Turkey. *PLOS ONE* 9, e99845.

Ard, V., Darvill, T., 2015. Revisiting old friends: the production, distribution and use of Peterborough Ware in Britain. *Oxford Journal of Archaeology* 34, 1–31.

Artursson, M., Earle, T., Brown, J., 2016. The construction of monumental landscapes in low-density societies: new evidence from the Early Neolithic of Southern Scandinavia (4000–3300BC) in comparative perspective. *Journal of Anthropological Archaeology* 41, 1–18.

Ashraf, Q., Galor, O., 2011. Dynamics and stagnation in the Malthusian epoch. *The American Economic Review* 101, 2003–2041.

Asouti, E., Fuller, D.Q., 2012. From foraging to farming in the southern Levant: the development of Epipalaeolithic and Pre-Pottery Neolithic plant management strategies. *Vegetation History and Archaeobotany* 21, 149–162.
2013. A contextual approach to the emergence of agriculture in Southwest Asia: reconstructing Early Neolithic plant-food production. *Current Anthropology* 54, 299–345.

Atakuman, Ç., 2014. Architectural discourse and social transformation during the early Neolithic of southeast Anatolia. *Journal of World Prehistory* 27, 1–42.

Baird, D., 2014. Origins of caprine herding. *Proceedings of the National Academy of Sciences* 111, 8702–8703.

Baird, D., Fairbairn, A., Martin, L., Middleton, C., 2012. The Boncuklu Project: the origins of sedentism, cultivation and herding in central Anatolia, in: Özdogan, M., Başgelen, N., Kuniholm, P. (Eds.), *The Neolithic in Turkey: New Excavations and New Research*. Archaeology and Art Publications, Istanbul, pp. 219–244.

Bandy, M.S., Fox, J.R., 2010. Becoming villagers: the evolution of early village societies, in: Bandy, M.S., Fox, J.R. (Eds.), *Becoming Villagers: Comparing Early Village Societies*. University of Arizona Press, Tucson, pp. 1–16.

Bánffy, E., 2004. *The 6th Millennium BC Boundary in Western Transdanubia and its Role in the Central European Neolithic Transition: The Szentgyörgyvölgy-Pityerdomb Settlement*. Archaeological Institute of the Hungarian Academy of Sciences, Budapest.

Bánffy, E., Osztás, A., Oross, K. et al., 2016. The Alsónyék story: towards the history of a persistent place. *Bericht der Römisch-Germanischen Kommission* 94, 283–318.

Banning, E.B., Akkermans, P., Baird, D. et al., 2011. So fair a house: Göbekli Tepe and the identification of temples in the Pre-Pottery Neolithic of the Near East. *Current Anthropology* 52, 619–660.

Barclay, A.J., Harris, O.J., 2017. Community building: houses and people in Neolithic Britain, in: Bickle, P., Cummings, V., Hofmann, D., Pollard, J. (Eds.), *The Neolithic of Europe: Papers in Honour of Alasdair Whittle*. Oxbow, Oxford, pp. 222–233.

Barth, F., 1971. Tribes and intertribal relations in the Fly headwaters. *Oceania* 41, 171–191.

Bar-Yosef, O., 1998. The Natufian culture in the Levant, threshold to the origins of agriculture. *Evolutionary Anthropology: Issues, News, and Reviews* 6, 159–177.

Baum, T.G., 2014. Models of wetland settlement and associated land use in South-West Germany during the fourth millennium BC. *Vegetation History and Archaeobotany* 23, 67–80.

Bayliss, A., Brock, F., Farid, S., Hodder, I., Southon, J., Taylor, R.E., 2015. Getting to the bottom of it all: a Bayesian approach to dating the start of Çatalhöyük. *Journal of World Prehistory* 28, 1–26.

Bayliss, A., Cartwright, C., Cook, G.T. et al., 2017. Rings of fire and Grooved Ware settlement at West Kennet, Wiltshire, in: Bickle, P., Cummings, V., Hofmann, D., Pollard, J. (Eds.), *The Neolithic of Europe*. Oxbow, Oxford, pp. 249–277.

Beau, A., Rivollat, M., Réveillas, H. et al., 2017. Multi-scale ancient DNA analyses confirm the western origin of Michelsberg farmers and document probable practices of human sacrifice. *PLOS ONE* 12, e0179742.

Bell, A.V., Winterhalder, B., 2014. The population ecology of despotism. *Human Nature* 25, 121–135.

Bender, B., 1978. Gatherer-hunter to farmer: A social perspective. *World Archaeology* 10, 204–222.

Bentley, R.A., Bickle, P., Fibiger, L. et al., 2012. Community differentiation and kinship among Europe's first farmers. *Proceedings of the National Academy of Sciences* 109, 9326–9330.

Berger, J.-F., 2005. Sédiments, dynamique du peuplement et climat au Néolithique ancien, in: Guilaine, J. (Ed.), *Populations Néolithiques et Environnements*. Errance, Paris, pp. 153–214.

Berger, J.-F., Guilaine, J., 2009. The 8200calBP abrupt environmental change and the Neolithic transition: A Mediterranean perspective. *Quaternary International* 200, 31–49.

Berger, J.-F., Metallinou, G., Guilaine, J., 2014. Vers une révision de la transition méso-néolithique sur le site de Sidari (Corfou, Grèce): nouvelles données géoarchéologiques et radiocarbone, évaluation des processus post-dépositionnels, in: Manen, C., Perrin, T., Guilaine, J. (Eds.), *La Transition Néolithique En Méditerranée*. Errance/Archives d'Écologie Préhistorique, Arles/Toulouse, pp. 213–232.

Bergh, S., Hensey, R., 2013. Unpicking the chronology of Carrowmore. *Oxford Journal of Archaeology* 32, 343–366.

Bernabeu Aubán, J., Köhler, T.O., Castillo, A.D., Puche, M.G., Hernández, F.J.M., 2003. Mas d'Is (Penàguila, Alicante): aldeas y recintos monumentales del Neolítico Inicial en el valle del Serpis. *Trabajos de Prehistoria* 60, 39–59.

Bernabeu Aubán, J., Balaguer, L.M., Castillo, A.D., Köhler, T.O., 2006. Inequalities and power. Three millennia of prehistory in Mediterranean Spain (5600–2000 cal BC), in: Díaz-del-Río, P., García Sanjuán, L. (Eds.), *Social Inequality in Iberian Late Prehistory*. Archaeopress, Oxford, pp. 97–116.

Bernabeu Aubán, J., Molina, L., Esquembre, M.A., Ortega, J.R., Boronat, J., 2009. La cerámica impresa mediterránea en el origen del Neolítico de la península Ibérica, in: *De Méditerranée et d'Ailleurs. Melanges Offerts à Jean Guilaine*. Archives d'Écologie Préhistorique, Toulouse, pp. 83–95.

Bernabeu Aubán, J., García-Puchol, O., Pardo, S., Barton, M., McClure, S.B., 2014. Socioecological dynamics at the time of Neolithic transition in Iberia. *Environmental Archaeology* 19, 214–225.

Bernabeu Aubán, J., Barton, C.M., Gordó, S.P., Bergin, S.M., 2015. Modeling initial Neolithic dispersal. The first agricultural groups in West Mediterranean. *Ecological Modelling* 307, 22–31.

Bernabeu Aubán, J., Manen, C., Pardo-Gordó, S., 2017. Spatial and temporal diversity during the Neolithic spread in western Mediterranean. The first pottery productions, in: García-Puchol, O., Salazar-García, D.C. (Eds.), *Times of Neolithic Transition along the Western Mediterranean*. Fundamental Issues in Archaeology. Springer, Cham, pp. 373–398.

Berrocal, M.C., 2012. The Early Neolithic in the Iberian Peninsula and the Western Mediterranean: a review of the evidence on migration. *Journal of World Prehistory* 25, 123–156.

Bertemes, F., Meller, H. (Eds.), 2012. *Neolithische Kreisgrabenanlagen in Europa: Internationale Arbeitstagung 7.-9. Mai 2004 in Goseck (Sachsen-Anhalt).* Tagungen des Landesmuseums für Vorgeschichte Halle. Landesamt für Denkmalpflege und Archäologie in Sachsen-Anhalt, Landesmuseum für Vorgeschichte, Halle (Saale).

Bettinger, R.L., 2006. Agriculture, archaeology, and human behavioral ecology, in: Kennett, D.J., Winterhalder, B. (Eds.), *Behavioral Ecology and the Transition to Agriculture*. University of California Press, Berkeley, pp. 304–322.

Bevan, A., Colledge, S., Fuller, D. et al., 2017. Holocene fluctuations in human population demonstrate repeated links to food production and climate. *Proceedings of the National Academy of Sciences*, published online ahead of print November 20, 2017. doi: 10.1073/pnas.1709190114.

Biagi, P., Shennan, S., Spataro, M., 2005. Rapid rivers and slow seas. New data for the radiocarbon chronology of the Balkan peninsula, in: Nikolova, L., Higgins, J. (Eds.), *Prehistoric Archaeology and Anthropological Theory and Education*. Reports of Prehistoric Research Projects 6–7. Karlovo, Salt Lake City, pp. 43–51.

Billard, C., Bostyn, F., Hamon, C., Meunier, K., 2014. *L'Habitat du Néolithique Ancien de Colombelles 'Le Lazzaro' (Calvados)*. Mémoire de la Société Préhistorique Française 58. Société Préhistorique Française, Paris.

Binford, L.R., 1968. Post-pleistocene adaptations, in: Binford, L.R., Binford, S.R. (Eds.), *New Perspectives in Archaeology*. Aldine, Chicago, pp. 313–342.

2001. *Constructing Frames of Reference: An Analytical Method for Archaeological Theory Building using Ethnographic and Environmental Data Sets*. University of California Press, Oakland.

Binford, L., Chasko, W., 1976. Nunamiut demographic history: a provocative case, in: Zubrow, E. (Ed.), *Demographic Anthropology: Quantitative Approaches*. University of New Mexico Press, Albuquerque, pp. 63–143.

Bird, D.W., O'Connell, J.F., 2006. Behavioral ecology and archaeology. *Journal of Archaeological Research* 14, 143–188. doi:10.1007/s10814-006-9003-6.

Bird, D.W., Bird, R.B., Codding, B.F., 2009. In pursuit of mobile prey: Martu hunting strategies and archaeofaunal interpretation. *American Antiquity* 74, 3–29.

Bird, D.W., Bliege Bird, R., Codding, B.F., 2016. Pyrodiversity and the anthropocene: the role of fire in the broad spectrum revolution. *Evolutionary Anthropology: Issues, News, and Reviews* 25, 105–116.

Bishop, R.R., 2015. Did Late Neolithic farming fail or flourish? A Scottish perspective on the evidence for Late Neolithic arable cultivation in the British Isles. *World Archaeology* 47, 834–855.

Bliege Bird, R., 2015. Disturbance, complexity, scale: new approaches to the study of human-environment interactions. *Annual Review of Anthropology* 44, 241–257.

Bliege Bird, R., Smith, E., 2005. Signaling theory, strategic interaction, and symbolic capital. *Current Anthropology* 46, 221–248.

Bocquet-Appel, J.-P., 2002. Paleoanthropological traces of a Neolithic demographic transition. *Current Anthropology* 43, 637–650.

2008. Explaining the Neolithic demographic transition, in: Bocquet-Appel, J.-P., Bar-Yosef, O. (Eds.), *The Neolithic Demographic Transition and Its Consequences*. Springer, New York, pp. 35–55.

2011. When the world's population took off: the springboard of the Neolithic Demographic Transition. *Science* 333, 560–561.

Bocquet-Appel, J.-P., Naji, S., Vander Linden, M., Kozlowski, J., 2012. Understanding the rates of expansion of the farming system in Europe. *Journal of Archaeological Science* 39, 531–546.

Bocquet-Appel, J.-P., Moussa, R., Dubouloz, J., 2015. Multi-agent modelling of the Neolithic LBK, in: Giligny, F., Djindjian F., Costa L. (Eds.), *Proceedings of the 42nd Annual Conference on Computer Applications and Quantitative Methods in Archaeology*. Archaeopress, Oxford, pp. 611–622.

Boelicke, U., Lüning, J., Stehli, P., 1994. *Die Bandkeramik im Merzbachtal auf der Aldenhovener Platte*. Rheinland-Verlag/Habelt, Cologne/Bonn.

Bofinger, J., Lechterbeck, J., Merkl, M., Rösch, M., Schlichtherle, H., Hald, J., 2012. Die ersten Bauern zwischen Hegau und westlichem Bodensee. Eine archäologische und vegetationsgeschichtliche Untersuchung zur Besiedlungsdynamik während der Jungsteinzeit. *Denkmalpflege in Baden-Württemberg–Nachrichtenblatt der Landesdenkmalpflege* 41, 245–250.

Bogaard, A., 2004a. The nature of early farming in central and south-east Europe. *Documenta Praehistorica* 31, 49–58.

2004b. *Neolithic Farming in Central Europe: An Archaeobotanical Study of Crop Husbandry Practices*. Routledge, London/New York.

2005. 'Garden agriculture' and the nature of early farming in Europe and the Near East. *World Archaeology* 37, 177–196.

Bogaard, A., Isaakidou, V., 2010. From megasites to farmsteads: community size, ideology and the nature of early farming landscapes in Western Asia and Europe, in: Finlayson, B., Warren, G. (Eds.), *Landscapes in Transition: Understanding Hunter-Gatherer and Farming Landscapes in the Early Holocene of Europe and the Levant*. Oxbow, Oxford, pp. 192–207.

Bogaard, A., Charles, M., Twiss, K.C. et al., 2009. Private pantries and celebrated surplus: storing and sharing food at Neolithic Çatalhöyük, Central Anatolia. *Antiquity* 83, 649–668.

Bogaard, A., Krause, R., Strien, H.-C., 2011. Towards a social geography of cultivation and plant use in an early farming community: Vaihingen an der Enz, south-west Germany. *Antiquity* 85, 395–416.

Bogaard, A., Fraser, R., Heaton, T.H. et al., 2013. Crop manuring and intensive land management by Europe's first farmers. *Proceedings of the National Academy of Sciences* 110, 12589–12594.

Bogucki, P., 1993. Animal traction and household economies in Neolithic Europe. *Antiquity* 67, 492–503.

2011. How wealth happened in Neolithic central Europe. *Journal of World Prehistory* 24, 107.

Bogucki, P., Nalepka, D., Grygiel, R., Nowaczyk, B., 2012. Multiproxy environmental archaeology of Neolithic settlements at Osłonki, Poland, 5500–4000 BC. *Environmental Archaeology* 17, 45–65.

Bohannan, P., 1954. The migration and expansion of the Tiv. *Africa* 24, 2–16.

Bollongino, R., Burger, J., Powell, A., Mashkour, M., Vigne, J.-D., Thomas, M.G., 2012. Modern taurine cattle descended from small number of Near-Eastern founders. *Molecular Biology and Evolution* 29, 2101–2104.

Bollongino, R., Nehlich, O., Richards, M.P. et al., 2013. 2000 years of parallel societies in Stone Age Central Europe. *Science* 342, 479–481.

Bonsall, C., Macklin, M.G., Anderson, D.E., Payton, R.W., 2002. Climate change and the adoption of agriculture in north-west europe. *European Journal of Archaeology* 5, 9–23. doi:10.1179/eja.2002.5.1.9.

Bonsall, C., Mlekuž, D., Bartosiewicz, L., Pickard, C., 2013. Early farming adaptations of the northeast Adriatic Karst, in: Colledge, S., Conolly, J., Dobney, K., Manning, K., Shennan, S. (Eds.), *The Origins and Spread of Domestic Animals in Southwest Asia and Europe.* Left Coast Press, Walnut Creek, CA, pp. 145–160.

Bonsall, C., Macklin, M.G., Boroneanţ, A. et al., 2015. Holocene climate change and prehistoric settlement in the lower Danube valley. *Quaternary International, Climate impact on ecosystem changes and human responses during the Last Glacial and Early Holocene: a contribution to the INTIMATE (INTegration of Ice-core, MArine and TErrestrial records) COST Action ES0907* 378, 14–21. doi:10.1016/j.quaint.2014.09.031.

Boone, J.L., Kessler, K.L., 1999. More status or more children? Social status, fertility reduction, and long-term fitness. *Evolution and Human Behavior* 20, 257–277.

Borić, D., 2011. Adaptations and transformations of the Danube Gorges foragers (c. 13,000–5500 cal. BC): an overview, in: Krauss, R. (Ed.), *Beginnings – New Research in the Appearance of the Neolithic between Northwest Anatolia and the Carpathian Basin.* Verlag Marie Leidorf, Rahden, pp. 157–203.

Borić, D., Price, T.D., 2013. Strontium isotopes document greater human mobility at the start of the Balkan Neolithic. *Proceedings of the National Academy of Sciences* 110, 3298–3303. doi:10.1073/pnas.1211474110.

Borrell, F., Junno, A., Barceló, J.A., 2015. Synchronous environmental and cultural change in the emergence of agricultural economies 10,000 years ago in the Levant. *PLOS ONE* 10, e0134810.

Boserup, E., 1965. *The Conditions of Agricultural Growth. The Economics of Agrarian Change under Population Pressure.* Allen and Unwin, London. 1981. *Population and Technological Change.* University of Chicago Press, Chicago.

Boulestin, B., Zeeb-Lanz, A., Jeunesse, C., Haack, F., Arbogast, R.-M., Denaire, A., 2009. Mass cannibalism in the linear pottery culture at Herxheim (Palatinate, Germany). *Antiquity* 83, 968–982.

Bowles, S., Choi, J.-K., 2013. Coevolution of farming and private property during the early Holocene. *Proceedings of the National Academy of Sciences* 110, 8830–8835. doi:10.1073/pnas.1212149110.

Bradley, R., 1978. *The Prehistoric Settlement of Britain.* Routledge, London.

Bramanti, B., Thomas, M.G., Haak, W. et al., 2009. Genetic discontinuity between local hunter-gatherers and Central Europe's first farmers. *Science* 326, 137–140.

Brami, M.N., 2015. A graphical simulation of the 2,000-year lag in Neolithic occupation between Central Anatolia and the Aegean basin. *Archaeological and Anthropological Sciences* 7, 319–327.

Branch, N.P., Black, S., Maggi, R., Marini, N.A., 2014. The Neolithisation of Liguria (NW Italy): An environmental archaeological and palaeoenvironmental perspective. *Environmental Archaeology* 19, 196–213.

Bréhard, S., Beeching, A., Vigne, J.-D., 2010. Shepherds, cowherds and site function on middle Neolithic sites of the Rhône valley: an archaeozoological approach to the organization of territories and societies. *Journal of Anthropological Archaeology* 29, 179–188.

Broodbank, C., 2013. *The Making of the Middle Sea: A History of the Mediterranean from the Beginning to the Emergence of the Classical World.* Thames and Hudson, London.

Brophy, K., Sheridan, A., 2012. *Neolithic Scotland. ScARF Panel Report. ScARF Summary Neolithic Panel Document [WWW Document]*. Scottish Archaeological Research Framework: Society of Antiquaries of Scotland. www.tinyurl.com/d73xkvn.

Broushaki, F., Thomas, M.G., Link, V. et al., 2016. Early Neolithic genomes from the eastern Fertile Crescent. *Science* 353, 499–503.

Brown, A., 2007. Dating the onset of cereal cultivation in Britain and Ireland: the evidence from charred cereal grains. *Antiquity* 81, 1042–1052.

Burmeister, S., 2012. Der Mensch lernt fahren–Zur Frühgeschichte des Wagens. *Mitteilungen der Anthropologischen Gesellschaft in Wien* 142, 81–100.

Çakırlar, C., 2013. Rethinking Neolithic subsistence at the gateway to Europe with new archaeozoological evidence from Istanbul, in: Groot, M., Lentjes, D., Zeiler, J. (Eds.), *The Environmental Archaeology of Subsistence, Specialisation and Surplus Food Production*. Sidestone Press, Leiden, pp. 59–79.

Cappers, R.T., Raemaekers, D.C., Barker, G. et al., 2008. Cereal cultivation at Swifterbant? Neolithic wetland farming on the North European Plain. *Current Anthropology* 49, 385–402.

Carter, T., 2016. Obsidian consumption in the Late Pleistocene–Early Holocene Aegean: contextualising new data from Mesolithic Crete. *Annual of the British School at Athens* 111, 13–34.

Carter, T., Saarikko, R., Niemi, K., et al., 1996. Assessing the risks and uncertainties of regional crop potential under a changing climate in Finland. *Agricultural and Food Science in Finland* 5, 329–350.

Carvalho, A.F., 2010. Chronology and geography of the Mesolithic-Neolithic transition in Portugal, in: Armbruester, T., Hegewisch, M. (Eds.), *On Pre- and Earlier History of Iberia and Central Europe. Studies in Honour of Philine Kalb*. Habelt, Bonn, pp. 45–62.

Carvalho, A.F., Gibaja, J.F., Cardoso, J.L., 2013. Insights into the earliest agriculture of Central Portugal: sickle implements from the Early Neolithic site of Cortiçóis (Santarém). *Comptes Rendus Palevol* 12, 31–43.

Cassen, S., de Labriffe, P.-A., Menanteau, L., 2008. Washing and heating on the Neolithic shores of Western Europe. An archaeological hypothesis on the production of sea salt, in: Weller, O., Dufraisse, A., Pétrequin, P. (Eds.), *Sel, Eau et Forêt. D'hier à Aujourd'hui. Cahiers de La MSH Ledoux*. Presses Universitaires de Franche-Comté, pp. 175–204.

Cassen, S., Boujot, C., Dominguez Bella, S., et al., 2012. Dépôts bretons, tumulus carnacéens et circulations à longue distance, in: Pétrequin, P., Cassen, S., Errera, M., Klassen, L., Sheridan, A., Pétrequin, A.-M. (Eds.), *Jade. Grandes Haches Alpines Du Néolithique Européen. Ve et IVe Millénaires Av. J.-C.* Presses Universitaires de Franche-Comté, pp. 918–994.

Cassidy, L.M., Martiniano, R., Murphy, E.M. et al., 2016. Neolithic and Bronze Age migration to Ireland and establishment of the insular Atlantic genome. *Proceedings of the National Academy of Sciences* 113, 368–373.

Catt, J.A., 2001. The agricultural importance of loess. *Earth-Science Reviews* 54, 213–229.

Cauvin, J., 1994. *Naissance des divinités, naissance de l'agriculture: la révolution des symboles au Néolithique*. CNRS Éditions, Paris.

Chambon, P., Thomas, A., 2010. The first monumental cemeteries of western Europe: the 'Passy type' necropolis in the Paris basin around 4500 BC. *Journal of Neolithic Archaeology* (special issue: Megaliths and Identities). www.jna.uni-kiel.de/index.php/jna/article/view/37. doi: 10.12766/jna.2010.37.

Chenal, F., Perrin, B., Barrand-Emam, H., Boulestin, B., 2015. A farewell to arms: a deposit of human limbs and bodies at Bergheim, France, c. 4000 BC. *Antiquity* 89, 1313–1330.

Childe, V.G., 1928. *The Most Ancient East: The Oriental Prelude to European Prehistory*. Kegan Paul, London.

Çilingiroğlu, C., 2010. The appearance of impressed pottery in the Neolithic Aegean and its implications for maritime networks in the eastern Mediterranean. *Tüba-Ar* 13, 9–22.

Çilingiroğlu, Ç., 2017. The Aegean before and after 7000 BC dispersal: defining patterning and variability. *Neo-Lithics* 1/16, 32–41.

Cladders, M., 2001. *Die Tonware der Ältesten Bandkeramik: Untersuchung zur Zeitlichen und Räumlichen Gliederung*. Habelt, Bonn.

Cladders, M., Stäuble, H., 2003. Das 53. Jahrhundert v. Chr.: Aufbruch und Wandel, in: Eckert, J., Eisenhauer, U., Zimmermann, A. (Eds.), *Archäologische Perspektiven. Analysen* und *Interpretationen im Wandel. Festschrift für Jens Lüning Zum 65en Geburtstag.* Verlag Marie Leidorf, Rahden, pp. 491–503.

Cladders, M., Stäuble, H., Tischendorf, T., Wolfram, S., 2012. Zur linien- und stichbandkeramischen Besiedlung von Eythra, Lkr. Leipzig, in: Smolnik, R. (Ed.), *Siedlungsstruktur und Kulturwandel in Der Bandkeramik, Arbeits- und Forschungsberichte zur Sächsischen Bodendenkmalpflege.* Landesamt für Archäologie, Dresden, pp. 146–159.

Cohen, M.N., 1977. *The Food Crisis in Prehistory: Overpopulation and the Origins of Agriculture.* Yale University Press, New Haven, Connecticut.

Colas, C., Manolakakis, L., Thevenet, C. et al., 2007. Le monument funéraire Michelsberg ancien de Beaurieux 'la Plaine' (Aisne, France), in: Besse, M. (Ed.), *Sociétés Néolithiques. Des Faits Archéologiques aux Fonctionnements Socio-Économiques, Actes du 27e Colloque Interrégional Sur le Néolithique (Neuchâtel, 1 et 2 Octobre 2005),* Cahiers d'Archéologie Romande, Lausanne, pp. 329–334.

Collard, M., Edinborough, K., Shennan, S., Thomas, M.G., 2010. Radiocarbon evidence indicates that migrants introduced farming to Britain. *Journal of Archaeological Science* 37, 866–870.

Colledge, S.M., 1998. Identifying Pre-domestication cultivation using multivariate analysis, in: Damania, A.B., Valkoun, J., Willcox, G., Qualset, C.O. (Eds.), *The Origins of Agriculture and Crop Domestication.* International Center for Agricultural Research in the Dry Areas, Aleppo, Syria, pp. 121–131.

2001. *Plant Exploitation on Epipalaeolithic and Early Neolithic Sites in the Levant.* British Archaeological Reports International Series 986. Archaeopress, Oxford.

Colledge, S., Conolly, J., 2007. A review and synthesis of the evidence for the origins of farming on Cyprus and Crete, in: Colledge, S., Conolly, J. (Eds.), *The Origins and Spread of Domestic Plants in Southwest Asia and Europe.* Left Coast Press, Walnut Creek, CA, pp. 53–74.

2010. Reassessing the evidence for the cultivation of wild crops during the Younger Dryas at Tell Abu Hureyra, Syria. *Environmental Archaeology* 15, 124–138.

2014. Wild plant use in European Neolithic subsistence economies: a formal assessment of preservation bias in archaeobotanical assemblages and the implications for understanding changes in plant diet breadth. *Quaternary Science Reviews* 101, 193–206.

Colledge, S., Conolly, J., Shennan, S., 2004. Archaeobotanical evidence for the spread of farming in the Eastern Mediterranean. *Current Anthropology* 45, S35–S58.

2005. The evolution of Neolithic farming from SW Asian origins to NW European limits. *European Journal of Archaeology* 8, 137–156.

Colominas, L., Edwards, C.J., Beja-Pereira, A. et al., 2015. Detecting the T1 cattle haplogroup in the Iberian Peninsula from Neolithic to medieval times: new clues to continuous cattle migration through time. *Journal of Archaeological Science* 59, 110–117.

Conolly, J., Colledge, S., Shennan, S., 2008. Founder effect, drift, and adaptive change in domestic crop use in early Neolithic Europe. *Journal of Archaeological Science* 35, 2797–2804.

Conolly, J., Colledge, S., Dobney, K., Vigne, J.-D., Peters, J., Stopp, B., Manning, K., Shennan, S., 2011. Meta-analysis of zooarchaeological data from SW Asia and SE Europe provides insight into the origins and spread of animal husbandry. *Journal of Archaeological Science* 38, 538–545.

Conolly, J., Manning, K., Colledge, S., Dobney, K., Shennan, S., 2012. Species distribution modelling of ancient cattle from early Neolithic sites in SW Asia and Europe. *The Holocene* 22, 997–1010.

Coşkun, A., Benz, M., Rössner, C. et al., 2012. New results on the Younger Dryas occupation at Körtik Tepe. *Neo-Lithics* 1, 25–32.

Coudart, A., 1998. *Architecture et Société Néolithique: L'unité et la Variance de la Maison Danubienne.* Éditions de la maison des sciences de l'homme, Paris.

Craig, O.E., Forster, M., Andersen, S.H. et al., 2007. Molecular and isotopic demonstration of the processing of aquatic products in northern European prehistoric pottery. *Archaeometry* 49, 135–152.

Craig, O.E., Steele, V.J., Fischer, A. et al., 2011. Ancient lipids reveal continuity in culinary practices across the transition to agriculture in Northern Europe. *Proceedings of the National Academy of Sciences* 108, 17910–17915.

Cramp, L.J.E., Jones, J., Sheridan, A. et al., 2014a. Immediate replacement of fishing with dairying by the earliest farmers of the northeast Atlantic archipelagos. *Proceedings of the Royal Society B: Biological Sciences* 281 (1780), 20132372.

Cramp, L.J.E., Evershed, R.P., Lavento, M. et al., 2014b. Neolithic dairy farming at the extreme of agriculture in northern Europe. *Proceedings of the Royal Society B: Biological Sciences* 281 (1781), 20140819–20140819. doi:10.1098/rspb.2014.0819.

Crema, E.R., Habu, J., Kobayashi, K., Madella, M., 2016. Summed probability distribution of 14C dates suggests regional divergences in the population dynamics of the Jomon period in eastern Japan. *PLOS ONE* 11, e0154809.

Crombé, P., Vanmontfort, B., 2007. The neolithisation of the Scheldt basin in western Belgium, in: Whittle, A., Cummings, V. (Eds.), *Going Over: The Mesolithic-Neolithic transition in North-West Europe*. Proceedings of the British Academy 144, Oxford University Press, Oxford, pp. 263–285.

Crombé, P., Sergant, J., Perdaen, Y., Meylemans, E., Deforce, K., 2015. Neolithic pottery finds at the wetland site of Bazel-Kruibeke (Flanders, Belgium): evidence of long-distance forager-farmer contact during the late 6th and 5th millennium cal BC in the Rhine-Meuse-Scheldt area. *Archäologisches Korrespondenzblatt* 45, 21–39.

Crosby, A.W., 1986. *Ecological Imperialism: The Biological Expansion of Europe, 900–1900*. Cambridge University Press, Cambridge.

Cubas, M., Altuna, J., Alvarez-Fernández, E. et al., 2016. Re-evaluating the Neolithic: the impact and the consolidation of farming practices in the Cantabrian Region (Northern Spain). *Journal of World Prehistory* 29, 79–116.

Cucchi, T., Vigne, J., Auffray, J., Croft, P., Peltenburg, E., 2002. Passive transport of the house mouse (Mus musculus domesticus) to Cyprus at the Early Preceramic Neolithic (late 9th and 8th millennia cal. BC). *Comptes Rendus Palevol* 1, 235–241.

Czerniak, L., 2012. After the LBK. Communities of the 5th millennium BC in north-central Europe, in: Gleser, R., Becker, V. (Eds.), *Mitteleuropa im 5. Jahrtausend vor Christus*. Lit, Berlin, pp. 151–174.

Darvill, T., Marshall, P., Pearson, M.P., Wainwright, G., 2012. Stonehenge remodelled. *Antiquity* 86, 1021–1040.

Davison, K., Dolukhanov, P., Sarson, G.R., Shukurov, A., 2006. The role of waterways in the spread of the Neolithic. *Journal of Archaeological Science* 33, 641–652.

de Groot, B.G., 2016. *Ceramic Assemblages as Evidence of Social Interaction in Neolithic Anatolia, the Aegean, and the Balkans*. Unpublished Ph.D. thesis, University College London.

de Klerk, P., Couwenberg, J., Joosten, H., 2015. Pollen and macrofossils attributable to Fagopyrum in western Eurasia prior to the Late Medieval: An intercontinental mystery. *Palaeogeography, Palaeoclimatology, Palaeoecology* 440, 1–21.

Delhon, C., Thiébault, S., Berger, J.-F., 2009. Environment and landscape management during the Middle Neolithic in Southern France: evidence for agro-sylvo-pastoral systems in the Middle Rhone Valley. *Quaternary International* 200, 50–65.

Demirci, S., Baştanlar, E.K., Dağtaş, N.D. et al., 2013. Mitochondrial DNA diversity of modern, ancient and wild sheep (Ovis gmelinii anatolica) from Turkey: new insights on the evolutionary history of sheep. *PLOS ONE* 8, e81952.

Demján, P., Dreslerová, D., 2016. Modelling distribution of archaeological settlement evidence based on heterogeneous spatial and temporal data. *Journal of Archaeological Science* 69, 100–109.

Denaire, A., Lefranc, P., Wahl, J. et al., 2017. The cultural project: Formal chronological modelling of the Early and Middle Neolithic sequence in Lower Alsace. *Journal of Archaeological Method and Theory*, 1–78.

Dietrich, O., Heun, M., Notroff, J., Schmidt, K., Zarnkow, M., 2012. The role of cult and feasting in the emergence of Neolithic communities. New evidence from Göbekli Tepe, south-eastern Turkey. *Antiquity* 86, 674–695.

Discamps, E., 2014. Ungulate biomass fluctuations endured by Middle and Early Upper Paleolithic societies (SW France, MIS 5–3): The contributions of modern analogs and cave hyena paleodemography. *Quaternary International* 337, 64–79.

Douka, K., Efstratiou, N., Hald, M.M., Henriksen, P.S., Karetsou, A., 2017. Dating Knossos and the arrival of the earliest Neolithic in the southern Aegean. *Antiquity* 91, 304–321.

Downey, S.S., Haas, W.R., Shennan, S.J., 2016. European Neolithic societies showed early warning signals of population collapse.

Proceedings of the National Academy of Sciences 113, 9751–9756.

Drake, B.L., Blanco-González, A., Lillios, K.T., 2017 Regional demographic dynamics in the Neolithic transition in Iberia: results from summed calibrated date analysis. *Journal of Archaeological Method and Theory* 24/3, 796–812.

Dreibrodt, S., Lubos, C., Terhorst, B., Damm, B., Bork, H.-R., 2010. Historical soil erosion by water in Germany: Scales and archives, chronology, research perspectives. *Quaternary International, Quaternary Landscape Evolution and Morphodynamics of Terrestrial Ecosystems* 222, 80–95. doi:10.1016/j.quaint.2009.06.014.

Dreibrodt, S., Zahrer, J., Bork, H.-R., Brauer, A., 2012. Witterungs- und Umweltgeschichte während der norddeutschen Trichterbecherkultur – rekonstruiert auf Basis mikrofazieller Untersuchungen an jahresgeschichteten Seesedimenten, in: Hinz, M., Müller, J. (Eds.), *Siedlung, Grabenwerk, Großsteingrab.* Frühe Monumentalität und Soziale Differenzierung 2. Habelt, Bonn, pp. 145–158.

Dubouloz, J., 2008. Impacts of the Neolithic demographic transition on Linear Pottery Culture settlement, in: Bocquet-Appel, J.-P., Bar-Yosef, O. (Eds.), *The Neolithic Demographic Transition and Its Consequences.* Springer, pp. 207–235.
2012. À propos d'implantation, de démographie et de scission villageoises au Néolithique rubané. *Les Nouvelles de l'Archéologie* 127, 30–34.

Dubreuil, L., Nadel, D., 2015. The development of plant food processing in the Levant: insights from use-wear analysis of Early Epipalaeolithic ground stone tools. *Philosphical Transactions of the Royal Society B* 370, 20140357.

Dunbar, R.I., 1993. Coevolution of neocortical size, group size and language in humans. *Behavioral and Brain Sciences* 16, 681–694.

Düring, B.S., 2013. Breaking the bond: investigating the Neolithic expansion in Asia Minor in the seventh millennium BC. *Journal of World Prehistory* 26, 75–100. doi:10.1007/s10963-013-9065-6.

Düring, B.S., Marciniak, A., 2005. Households and communities in the central Anatolian Neolithic. *Archaeological Dialogues* 12, 165–187.

Dyson, T., 2010. *Population and Development: the Demographic Transition.* Zed Books Ltd, London/New York.

Dyson-Hudson, R., Smith, E.A., 1978. Human territoriality: an ecological reassessment. *American Anthropologist* 80, 21–41. doi:10.1525/aa.1978.80.1.02a00020.

Eckmeier, E., Gerlach, R., Tegtmeier, U., Schmidt, M.W.I., 2008. Charred organic matter and phosphorus in black soils in the Lower Rhine Basin (Northwest Germany) indicate prehistoric agricultural burning, in: Fiorentino, G., Magri, D. (Eds.), *Charcoals from the Past: Cultural and Palaeoenvironmental Implications.* Archaeopress, Oxford, pp. 93–103.

Edmonds, C.A., Lillie, A.S., Cavalli-Sforza, L.L., 2004. Mutations arising in the wave front of an expanding population. *Proceedings of the National Academy of Sciences of the United States of America* 101, 975–979.

Edwards, C.J., Bollongino, R., Scheu, A. et al., 2007. Mitochondrial DNA analysis shows a Near Eastern Neolithic origin for domestic cattle and no indication of domestication of European aurochs. *Proc Biol Sci* 274, 1377–1385. doi:10.1098/rspb.2007.0020.

Ehrmann, O., Rösch, M., Schier, W., 2009. Experimentelle Rekonstruktion eines jungneolithischen Wald-Feldbaus mit Feuereinsatz: ein multidisziplinäres Forschungsprojekt zur Wirtschaftsarchäologie und Landschaftsökologie. *Prähistorische Zeitschrift* 84, 44–72.

Eisenhauer, U., 1994. Mittelhessen zwischen Bandkeramik und Michelsberg. Zur Siedlungsgeschichte des hessischen Mittelneolithikums, in: Beier, H.J. (Ed.), *Der Rössener Horizont in Mitteleuropa.* Beier & Beran, Wilkau-Hasslau, pp. 93–108.

Ellison, P.T., Panter-Brick, C., Lipson, S.F., O'Rourke, M.T., 1993. The ecological context of human ovarian function. *Human Reproduction* 8, 2248–2258.

Eriksson, G., Linderholm, A., Fornander, E. et al., 2008. Same island, different diet: cultural evolution of food practice on Öland, Sweden, from the Mesolithic to the Roman Period. *Journal of Anthropological Archaeology* 27, 520–543.

Ervynck, A., Hongo, H., Dobney, K., Meadow, R., 2001. Born free? New evidence for the status of *Sus scrofa* at Neolithic Cayönü Tepesi (southeastern Anatolia, Turkey). *Paléorient* 27/2, 47–73.

Evershed, R.P., Payne, S., Sherratt, A.G. et al., 2008. Earliest date for milk use in the Near

East and southeastern Europe linked to cattle herding. *Nature* 455, 528.

Excoffier, L., Ray, N., 2008. Surfing during population expansions promotes genetic revolutions and structuration. *Trends in Ecology and Evolution* 23, 347–351.

Fedele, F., 2006. La traction animale au Val Camonica et en Valteline pendant le Néolithique et le Chalcolithique (Italie), in: Pétrequin, P., Arbogast, R.-M., Pétrequin, A.-M., van Willigen, S., Bailly, M. (Eds.), *Premiers Chariots, Premiers Araires: La Diffusion de La Traction Animale En Europe Pendant Les IVe et IIIe Millénaires Avant Notre Ère*. CNRS Editions, Paris, pp. 47–61.

Feeser, I., Furholt, M., 2014. Ritual and economic activity during the Neolithic in Schleswig-Holstein, northern Germany: An approach to combine archaeological and palynological evidence. *Journal of Archaeological Science* 51, 126–134.

Feeser, I., Dörfler, W., Averdieck, F.-R., Wiethold, J., 2012. New insight into regional and local land-use and vegetation patterns in eastern Schleswig-Holstein during the Neolithic, in: Hinz, M., Müller, J. (Eds.), *Siedlung, Grabenwerk, Großsteingrab*. Frühe Monumentalität und Soziale Differenzierung 2. Habelt, Bonn, pp. 159–190.

Ferguson, R.B., 2013. The prehistory of war and peace in Europe and the Near East, in: Fry, D.P. (Ed.), *War, Peace, and Human Nature: The Convergence of Evolutionary and Cultural Views*. Oxford University Press, Oxford, pp. 191–240.

Feynman, J., Ruzmaikin, A., 2007. Climate stability and the development of agricultural societies. *Climatic Change* 84, 295.

Fiorentino, G., Caldara, M., De Santis, V. et al., 2013. Climate changes and human–environment interactions in the Apulia region of southeastern Italy during the Neolithic period. *The Holocene* 23, 1297–1316.

Fischer, A., Olsen, J., Richards, M., Heinemeier, J., Sveinbjörnsdóttir, Á.E., Bennike, P., 2007. Coast: inland mobility and diet in the Danish Mesolithic and Neolithic: evidence from stable isotope values of humans and dogs. *Journal of Archaeological Science* 34, 2125–2150.

Flannery, K., 1969. Origins and ecological effects of early domestication in Iran and the Near East, in: Ucko, P.J., Dimbleby, G.W. (Eds.), *The Domestication and Exploitation of Plants and Animals*. Duckworth, London, pp. 73–100.

Forenbaher, S., Miracle, P., 2014. Transition to Farming in the Adriatic: a View from the Eastern Shore, in: Manen, C., Perrin, T., Guilaine, J. (Eds.), *La Transition Néolithique en Méditerranée*. Errance/Archives d'Écologie Préhistorique, Arles/Toulouse, pp. 233–242.

Fort, J., Pujol, T., Vander Linden, M., 2012. Modelling the Neolithic transition in the Near East and Europe. *American Antiquity* 77, 203–219.

Fraser, R.A., Bogaard, A., Schäfer, M., Arbogast, R., Heaton, T.H., 2013. Integrating botanical, faunal and human stable carbon and nitrogen isotope values to reconstruct land use and palaeodiet at LBK Vaihingen an der Enz, Baden-Württemberg. *World Archaeology* 45, 492–517.

Freeman, J., Anderies, J.M., 2015. A comparative ethnoarchaeological analysis of corporate territorial ownership. *Journal of Archaeological Science* 54, 135–147.

Friederich, S., 2012. Siedlungs- und Landschaftsarchäologie zwischen Heilbronn und der Schwäbischen Alb. Eine Fallstudie für das Mittelneolithikum: mit einem Ausblick auf Mitteldeutschland, in: Gleser, R., Becker, V. (Eds.), *Mitteleuropa im 5. Jahrtausend vor Christus*. Lit, Berlin, pp. 267–290.

Fritsch, B., Furholt, M., Hinz, M. et al., 2010. Dichtezentren und lokale Gruppierungen: eine Karte zu den Großsteingräbern Mittel- und Nordeuropas. www.jungsteinsite.de. (Version produced 20.10.2010).

Fuller, D.Q., Lucas, L., 2017. Adapting crops, landscapes and food choices: patterns in the dispersal of domesticated plants across Eurasia, in: Boivin, N., Crassard, R., Petraglia, M. (Eds.), *Human Dispersal and Species Movement: From Prehistory to the Present*. Cambridge University Press, Cambridge, pp. 304–331.

Fuller, D.Q., Willcox, G., Allaby, R.G., 2011. Early agricultural pathways: moving outside the 'core area' hypothesis in Southwest Asia. *Journal of Experimental Botany* 63, 617–633.

Furholt, M., 2012. Monuments and Durable Landscapes in the Neolithic of Southern Scandinavia and Northern Central Europe, in: Furholt, M., Hinz, M., Mischka, D. (Eds.), *As Time Goes By? Monumentality, Landscapes and the Temporal Perspective*. Habelt, Bonn, pp. 115–132.

Gallagher, E., n.d. Evolutionary models for the origins of agriculture. Unpublished PhD thesis, University College London.

Gallagher, E.M., Shennan, S.J., Thomas, M.G., 2015. Transition to farming more likely for small, conservative groups with property rights, but increased productivity is not essential. *Proceedings of the National Academy of Sciences* 112, 14218–14223. doi:10.1073/pnas.1511870112.

Gamba, C., Jones, E.R., Teasdale, M.D. et al., 2014. Genome flux and stasis in a five millennium transect of European prehistory. *Nature Communications* 5, 5257.

García-Puchol, O., Castillo, A.A.D., Pardo-Gordó, S., 2017. Timing the Western Mediterranean last hunter-gatherers and first farmers, in: García-Puchol, O., Salazar-García, D.C. (Eds.), *Times of Neolithic Transition along the Western Mediterranean*, Fundamental Issues in Archaeology. Springer, Cham, pp. 69–99. doi:10.1007/978-3-319-52939-4_4.

Garrow, D., Sturt, F., 2011. Grey waters bright with Neolithic argonauts? Maritime connections and the Mesolithic–Neolithic transition within the 'western seaways' of Britain, c. 5000–3500 BC. *Antiquity* 85, 59–72. doi:10.1017/S0003598X00067430.

Gerritsen, F.A., Özbal, R., Thissen, L.C., 2013. The earliest neolithic Levels at Barcın Höyük, Northwestern Turkey. *Anatolica* 39, 53–92.

Geschwinde, M., Raetzel-Fabian, D., Gehrt, E., 2009. *EWBSL: Eine Fallstudie zu den jungneolithischen Erdwerken am Nordrand der Mittelgebirge*. Verlag Marie Leidorf, Rahden.

Ghilardi, B., O'Connell, M., 2013. Fine-resolution pollen-analytical study of Holocene woodland dynamics and land use in north Sligo, Ireland. *Boreas* 42, 623–649.

Gibson, M.A., 2014. How development intervention drives population change in rural Africa: a case study of applied evolutionary anthropology, in: Gibson, M.A., Lawson, D.W. (Eds.), *Applied Evolutionary Anthropology*. Springer, pp. 59–81.

Gillespie, D.O.S., Russell, A.F., Lummaa, V., 2008. When fecundity does not equal fitness: evidence of an offspring quantity versus quality trade-off in pre-industrial humans. *Proceedings of the Royal Society of London B: Biological Sciences* 275, 713–722. doi:10.1098/rspb.2007.1000.

Gleser, R., 2012. Zeitskalen, stilistische Tendenzen und Regionalität des 5. Jahrtausends in den Altsiedellandschaften zwischen Mosel und Morava, in: Gleser, R., Becker, V. (Eds.), *Mitteleuropa im 5. Jahrtausend vor Christus*. Lit, Berlin, pp. 35–104.

Goldstein, L., 1981. One-dimensional archaeology and multi-dimensional people: spatial organization and mortuary analysis, in: Chapman, R.W. (Ed.), *The Archaeology of Death*. Cambridge University Press, Cambridge, pp. 53–69.

Gomart, L., 2014. *Céramique au Néolithique Ancien: Traditions Techniques et Production [Étude de Huit Sites Rubanés du Nord Est de la France et de Belgique]*. Sidestone Press, Leiden.

Gomart, L., Hachem, L., Hamon, C., Giligny, F., Ilett, M., 2015. Household integration in Neolithic villages: A new model for the Linear Pottery Culture in west-central Europe. *Journal of Anthropological Archaeology* 40, 230–249.

Goody, J., 1976. *Production and Reproduction: A Comparative Study of the Domestic Domain*. Cambridge University Press, Cambridge.

Goring-Morris, N., Belfer-Cohen, A., 2010. 'Great Expectations', or, the Inevitable Collapse of the Early Neolithic in the Near East., in: Bandy, M.S., Fox, J.R. (Eds.), *Becoming Villagers: Comparing Early Village Societies*. University of Arizona Press, Tucson, pp. 62–77.

Grifoni Cremonesi, R., Radi, G., 2014. Du Mésolithique au Néolithique ancien en Italie centrale et méridionale, in: Manen, C., Perrin, T., Guilaine, J. (Eds.), *La Transition Néolithique en Méditerranée*. Errance/Archives d'Écologie Préhistorique, Arles/Toulouse, pp. 243–267.

Gron, K.J., Montgomery, J., Rowley-Conwy, P., 2015. Cattle management for dairying in Scandinavia's earliest Neolithic. *PLOS ONE* 10, e0131267.

Gronenborn, D., Strien, H.-C., Dietrich, S., Sirocko, F., 2014. 'Adaptive cycles' and climate fluctuations: a case study from Linear Pottery Culture in western Central Europe. *Journal of Archaeological Science* 51, 73–83.

Guilaine, J., 2003. *De la Vague à la Tombe: La Conquête Néolithique de la Méditerranée, 8000–2000 avant J.-C.* Seil, Paris.

Guilaine, J., Freises, A., Montjardin, R., 1984. *Leucate-Corrège*. Centre d'Anthropologie des Sociétés Rurales, Toulouse.

Gurova, M., Bonsall, C., 2014. 'Pre-Neolithic' in Southeast Europe: a Bulgarian perspective. *Documenta Praehistorica* 41, 95–109. doi:10.4312/dp.41.5.

Haak, W., Lazaridis, I., Patterson, N. et al., 2015. Massive migration from the steppe was a source for Indo-European languages in Europe. *Nature* 522, 207–211.

Hage, F., 2016. *Büdelsdorf/Borgstedt: Eine Trichterbecherzeitliche Kleinregion.* Habelt, Bonn.

Halstead, P., 1995. Plough and power: the economic and social significance of cultivation with the ox-drawn ard in the Mediterranean. *Bulletin on Sumerian Agriculture* 8, 11–22.

2006. Sheep in the garden: the integration of crop and livestock husbandry in early farming regimes of Greece and Southern Europe, in: Serjeantson, D., Field, D. (Eds.), *Animals in the Neolithic of Britain and Europe.* Oxbow, Oxford, pp. 42–55.

Halstead, P., Isaakidou, V., 2013. Early stock-keeping in Greece, in: Colledge, S., Conolly, J., Dobney, K., Manning, K., Shennan, S. (Eds.), *The Origins and Spread of Domestic Animals in Southwest Asia and Europe.* Left Coast Press, Walnut Creek, CA, pp. 129–144.

Halstead, P., O'Shea, J., 1989. Introduction: cultural responses to risk and uncertainty, in: Halstead, P., O'Shea, J. (Eds.), *Bad Year Economics: Cultural Responses to Risk and Uncertainty.* Cambridge University Press, Cambridge, pp. 1–7.

Hamilton, M.J., Lobo, J., Rupley, E., Youn, H., West, G.B., 2016. The ecological and evolutionary energetics of hunter-gatherer residential mobility. *Evolutionary Anthropology* 25, 124–132. doi:10.1002/evan.21485.

Hansen, J.M., 1991. *The Palaeoethnobotany of Franchthi Cave.* Indiana University Press, Bloomington, IN.

Hayden, B., 1990. Nimrods, piscators, pluckers, and planters: the emergence of food production. *Journal of Anthropological Archaeology* 9, 31–69.

Helle, S., Brommer, J.E., Pettay, J.E., Lummaa, V., Enbuske, M., Jokela, J., 2014. Evolutionary demography of agricultural expansion in pre-industrial northern Finland. *Proceedings of the Royal Society of London B: Biological Sciences* 281, 20141559.

Helmer, D., Gourichon, L., Monchot, H., Peters, J., Segui, M.S., 2005. Identifying early domestic cattle from Pre-Pottery Neolithic sites on the Middle Euphrates using sexual dimorphism, in: *The First Steps of Animal Domestication: New Archaeobiological Approaches.* Oxbow, Oxford, pp. 86–95.

Hill, K.R., Hurtado, A.M., 1996. *Ache Life History: The Ecology and Demography of a Foraging People.* Aldine de Gruyter, New York.

Hillman, G.C., Davies, M.S., 1990a. Measured domestication rates in wild wheats and barley under primitive cultivation, and their archaeological implications. *Journal of World Prehistory* 4, 157–222.

1990b. Domestication rates in wild-type wheats and barley under primitive cultivation. *Biological Journal of the Linnean Society* 39, 39–78.

Hinz, M., 2015. Growth and decline? Population dynamics of Funnel Beaker societies in the 4th millennium BC, in: Brink, K., Hydén, S., Jennbert, K., Larsson, L., Olausson, D. (Eds.), *Neolithic Diversities. Perspectives from a Conference in Lund, Sweden.* Acta Archaeologica Lundensia 8/65. Department of Archaeology and Ancient History, Lund University, Lund, pp. 43–51.

Hinz, M., Feeser, I., Sjögren, K.-G., Müller, J., 2012. Demography and the intensity of cultural activities: an evaluation of Funnel Beaker Societies (4200–2800 cal BC). *Journal of Archaeological Science* 39, 3331–3340.

Hodder, I., 1990. *The Domestication of Europe.* Blackwell, Oxford.

Hodder, I., Meskell, L., 2011. A 'Curious and Sometimes a Trifle Macabre Artistry'. Some Aspects of Symbolism in Neolithic Turkey. *Current Anthropology* 52, 235–263.

Hofmanová, Z., Kreutzer, S., Hellenthal, G. et al., 2016. Early farmers from across Europe directly descended from Neolithic Aegeans. *Proceedings of the National Academy of Sciences* 113, 6886–6891.

Hongo, H., Pearson, J., Öksüz, B., Ilgezdi, G., 2009. The process of ungulate domestication at Çayönü, Southeastern Turkey: a multidisciplinary approach focusing on Bos sp. and Cervus elaphus. *Anthropozoologica* 44, 63–78.

Horejs, B., Milić, B., Ostmann, F., Thanheiser, U., Weninger, B., Galik, A., 2015. The Aegean in the early 7th millennium BC: maritime networks and colonization. *Journal of World Prehistory* 28, 289–330.

Huisman, D.J., Raemaekers, D.C.M., 2014. Systematic cultivation of the Swifterbant wetlands (The Netherlands). Evidence from Neolithic tillage marks (c. 4300–4000 cal. BC). *Journal of Archaeological Science* 49, 572–584.

Ibáñez, J.J., Ortega, D., Campos, D., Khalidi, L., Méndez, V., 2015. Testing complex networks of interaction at the onset of the Near Eastern Neolithic using modelling of obsidian exchange. *Journal of the Royal Society Interface* 12 (107), 20150210.

Ibáñez-Estévez, J.J., Gassin, B., Mazzucco, N., Gibaja Bao, J.F., 2017. Paths and rhythms in the spread of agriculture in the western Mediterranean: the contribution of the analysis of harvesting technology, in: García-Puchol, O., Salazar-García, D.C. (Eds.), *Times of Neolithic Transition along the Western Mediterranean*. Fundamental Issues in Archaeology. Springer, Cham, pp. 339–371.

Innes, J.B., Blackford, J.J., Rowley-Conwy, P.A., 2013. Late Mesolithic and early Neolithic forest disturbance: A high resolution palaeoecological test of human impact hypotheses. *Quaternary Science Reviews* 77, 80–100.

Isaakidou, V., 2006. Ploughing with cows: Knossos and the secondary products revolution, in: Serjeantson, D., Field, D. (Eds.), *Animals in the Neolithic of Britain and Europe*. Oxbow Books, Oxford, pp. 95–112.

2008. The fauna and economy of Neolithic Knossos revisited, in: Isaakidou, V., Tomkins, P. (Eds.), *Escaping the Labyrinth. The Cretan Neolithic in Context. Sheffield Studies in Aegean Archaeology*. Oxbow, Oxford, pp. 90–114.

Isaksson, S., Hallgren, F., 2012. Lipid residue analyses of Early Neolithic funnel-beaker pottery from Skogsmossen, eastern Central Sweden, and the earliest evidence of dairying in Sweden. *Journal of Archaeological Science* 39, 3600–3609.

Isern, N., Fort, J., Carvalho, A.F., Gibaja, J.F., Ibáñez, J.J., 2014. The Neolithic transition in the Iberian Peninsula: data analysis and modeling. *Journal of Archaeological Method and Theory* 21, 447–460.

Isern, N., Zilhão, J., Fort, J., Ammerman, A.J., 2017. Modeling the role of voyaging in the coastal spread of the Early Neolithic in the West Mediterranean. *Proceedings of the National Academy of Sciences* 114, 897–902.

Iversen, R., 2010. The Pitted Ware complex in a large scale perspective. *Acta Archaeologica* 81, 5–43.

2016. Arrowheads as indicators of interpersonal violence and group identity among the Neolithic Pitted Ware hunters of southwestern Scandinavia. *Journal of Anthropological Archaeology* 44, 69–86.

Iversen, R., Larsson, M., Debert, J., 2013. Beyond the Neolithic transition – the 'de-Neolithisation' of South Scandinavia, in: Larsson, M., Debert, J. (Eds.), *NW Europe in Transition. The Early Neolithic in Britain and South Sweden*. Archaeopress, Oxford, pp. 21–27.

Jacomet, S., Ebersbach, R., Akeret, Ö. et al., 2016. On-site data cast doubts on the hypothesis of shifting cultivation in the late Neolithic (c. 4300–2400 cal. BC): Landscape management as an alternative paradigm. *The Holocene* 26, 1858–1874.

Jakucs, J., Bánffy, E., Oross, K. et al., 2016. Between the Vinča and Linearbandkeramik worlds: the diversity of practices and identities in the 54th–53rd centuries cal BC in Southwest Hungary and beyond. *Journal of World Prehistory* 29, 267–336.

Jeunesse, C., 2006. Les sépultures de paires de bovins dans le Néolithique final de l'Est de l'Europe centrale, in: Petrequin, P., Arbogast, R.-M., Pétrequin, A.-M., van Willigen, S. (Eds.), *Premiers Chariots, Premiers Araires: La Diffusion de La Traction Animale en Europe Pendant Les IVe et IIIe Millénaires Avant Notre Ère*. CNRS Editions, Paris, pp. 247–258.

1997. *Pratiques funéraires au néolithique ancien: sépultures et nécropoles des sociétés danubiennes (5500–4900 av. J.-C.)*. Editions Errance, Paris.

1998. Pour une origine occidentale de la culture de Michelsberg? *Materialhefte zur Archäologie in Baden-Württemberg* 43, 29–45.

2010. Die Michelsberger Kultur, in: *Jungsteinzeit im Umbruch: Die 'Michelsberger Kultur' und Mitteleuropa vor 6000 Jahren. [Katalog Zur Ausstellung im Badischen Landesmuseum Schloss Karlsruhe, 20.11.2010–15.5.2011]*. Primus-Verlag, Darmstadt, pp. 46–55.

Jeunesse, C., Seidel, U., 2010. Die Erdwerke, in: *Jungsteinzeit im Umbruch: Die 'Michelsberger Kultur' und Mitteleuropa vor 6000 Jahren. [Katalog Zur Ausstellung im Badischen Landesmuseum Schloss Karlsruhe, 20.11.2010–15.5.2011]*. Primus-Verlag, Darmstadt, pp. 58–61.

Johannsen, N.N., 2006. Draught cattle and the South Scandinavian economies of the 4th millennium BC. *Environmental Archaeology* 11, 35–48.

Johannsen, N., Laursen, S., 2010. Routes and wheeled transport in late 4th–early 3rd millennium funerary customs of the Jutland peninsula: regional evidence and European context. *Praehistorische Zeitschrift* 85, 15–58.

Johnson, G.A., 1982. Organizational structure and scalar stress, in: Renfrew, C., Rowlands, M.J., Segraves, B.A. (Eds.), *Theory and Explanation in Archaeology*. Academic Press, New York, pp. 389–421.

Jones, G., Rowley-Conwy, P., 2007. On the importance of cereal cultivation in the British Neolithic, in: Colledge, S., Conolly, J. (Eds.), *The Origins and Spread of Domestic Plants in Southwest Asia and Europe*. Left Coast Press, Walnut Creek, CA, pp. 391–419.

Jones, G., Charles, M.P., Jones, M.K. et al., 2013. DNA evidence for multiple introductions of barley into Europe following dispersed domestications in Western Asia. *Antiquity* 87, 701–713. doi:10.1017/S0003598X00049401.

Jones, J.H., 2009. The force of selection on the human life cycle. *Evolution and Human Behavior* 30, 305–314.
2015. Resource transfers and human life-history evolution. *Annual Review of Anthropology* 44, 513–531.

Jones, J.H., Bliege Bird, R., 2014. The marginal valuation of fertility. *Evolution and Human Behavior* 35, 65–71.

Jones, J.H., Tuljapurkar, S., 2015. Measuring selective constraint on fertility in human life histories. *Proceedings of the National Academy of Sciences* 112, 8982–8986.

Jones, J.R., 2012. Using gazelle dental cementum studies to explore seasonality and mobility patterns of the Early-Middle Epipalaeolithic Azraq Basin, Jordan. *Quaternary International* 252, 195–201.

Jordà, G.P., Peña-Chocarro, L., Mateos, J.M., 2011. Neolithic Agriculture in Andalusia: Seeds and Fruits. *Menga* 02, 231–236.

Jordan, P., Gibbs, K., Hommel, P., Piezonka, H., Silva, F., Steele, J., 2016. Modelling the diffusion of pottery technologies across Afro-Eurasia: emerging insights and future research. *Antiquity* 90, 590–603.

Juan-Cabanilles, J., Oliver, B.M., 2017. New approaches to the Neolithic transition: the last hunters and first farmers of the Western Mediterranean, in: García-Puchol, O., Salazar-García, D.C. (Eds.), *Times of Neolithic Transition along the Western Mediterranean*. Fundamental Issues in Archaeology. Springer, Cham, pp. 33–65.

Kaczanowska, M., Kozłowski, J., 2014. The Origin and Spread of the Western Linear Pottery Culture: between Forager and Food Producing Lifeways in Central Europe. *Archaeologiai Értesítő* 139, 293–318.

Kadowaki, S., Nishiaki, Y., 2016. New Epipalaeolithic assemblages from the middle Euphrates and the implications for technological and settlement trends in the northeastern Levant. *Quaternary International* 396, 121–137.

Kalis, A.J., 2010. Umwelt, Klima und Landnutzung im Jungneolithikum, in: *Jungsteinzeit im Umbruch: Die Michelsberger Kultur und Mitteleuropa vor 6.000 Jahren*. Primus-Verlag, Darmstadt, pp. 37–43.

Kanstrup, M., Holst, M.K., Jensen, P.M., Thomsen, I.K., Christensen, B.T., 2014. Searching for long-term trends in prehistoric manuring practice. δ 15 N analyses of charred cereal grains from the 4th to the 1st millennium BC. *Journal of Archaeological Science* 51, 115–125.

Kaplan, H., 1996. A theory of fertility and parental investment in traditional and modern human societies. *American Journal of Physical Anthropology* 101, 91–135.

Kaplan, D., 2000. The darker side of the 'original affluent society'. *Journal of Anthropological Research* 56, 301–324.

Kaplan, H., Hill, K., Lancaster, J., Hurtado, A.M., 2000. A theory of human life history evolution: Diet, intelligence, and longevity. *Evolutionary Anthropology*. 9, 156–185.

Karamitrou-Mentessidi, G., Efstratiou, N., Kozłowski, J.K., et al., 2013. New evidence on the beginning of farming in Greece: the Early Neolithic settlement of Mavropigi in western Macedonia (Greece). *Antiquity* 87. www.antiquity.ac.uk/projgall/mentessidi336/.

Kerig, T., 2003. Von Gräbern und Stämmen: Zur Interpretation bandkeramischer Erdwerke, in: Veit, U., Kienlin, T.L., Kümmel, C., Schmidt, S. (Eds.), *Spuren und Botschaften: Interpretationen Materieller Kultur*. Waxmann, Münster, pp. 225–244.
2007. 'Als Adam grub…'. Vergleichende Anmerkungen zu landwirtschaftlichen Betriebsgrössen in prähistorischer Zeit. *Ethnographisch-Archäologische Zeitschrift* 48, 375–402.

2008. *Hanau-Mittelbuchen. Siedlung und Erdwerk der bandkeramischen Kultur. Materialvorlage-Chronologie-Versuch einer Handlungstheoretischen Interpretation.* Habelt, Bonn.

2013. Introducing economic archaeology: examples from Neolithic agriculture and Hallstatt princely tombs, in: Kerig, T., Zimmermann, A. (Eds.), *Economic Archaeology: From Structure to Performance in European Archaeology,* Universitätsforschungen zur Prähistorischen Archäologie 237. Habelt, Bonn, pp. 13–28.

Kirleis, W., Fischer, E., 2014. Neolithic cultivation of tetraploid free threshing wheat in Denmark and Northern Germany: implications for crop diversity and societal dynamics of the Funnel Beaker Culture. *Vegetation History and Archaeobotany* 23, 81–96.

Kılınç, G.M., Omrak, A., Özer, F. et al., 2016. The demographic development of the first farmers in Anatolia. *Current Biology* 26, 2659–2666.

Klassen, L., 2000. *Frühes Kupfer im Norden: Untersuchungen zu Chronologie, Herkunft und Bedeutung der Kupferfunde der Nordgruppe der Trichterbecherkultur.* Aarhus University Press, Aarhus.

2014. *Along the Road: Aspects of Causewayed Enclosures in South Scandinavia and Beyond.* Aarhus University Press, Aarhus.

Klatt, S., 2009. Die neolithischen Einhegungen im westlichen Ostseeraum. Forschungsstand und Forschungsperspektiven, in: Terberger, T. (Ed.), *Neue Forschungen Zum Neolithikum im Ostseeraum. Archäologie und Geschichte im Ostseeraum.* Verlag Marie Leidorf, Rahden, pp. 7–134.

Knipper, C., 2011. *Die Räumliche Organisation der Linearbandkeramischen Rinderhaltung: Naturwissenschaftliche und Archäologische Untersuchungen.* Archaeopress, Oxford.

Knoche, B., 2008. *Die Erdwerke von Soest (Kr. Soest) und Nottuln-Uphoven (Kr. Coesfeld): Studien zum Jungneolithikum in Westfalen.* Verlag Marie Leidorf, Rahden.

Kolář, J., Kuneš, P., Szabó, P. et al., 2016. Population and forest dynamics during the Central European Eneolithic (4500–2000 BC). *Archaeological and Anthropological Sciences* 1–12.

Končelová, M., 2012. The settlement structure of the Linear Pottery Culture in East Bohemia – geographical patterns and cultural continuity, in: Smolník, R. (Ed.), *Siedlungsstruktur und Kulturwandel in der Bandkeramik. Arbeits- und Forschungsberichte zur Sächsischen Bodendenkmalpflege.* Landesamt für Archäologie, Dresden, pp. 190–197.

Kramer, K.L., Boone, J.L., 2002. Why intensive agriculturalists have higher fertility: a household energy budget approach. *Current Anthropology* 43, 511–517. doi:10.1086/340239.

Kramer, K.L., Greaves, R.D., 2007. Changing patterns of infant mortality and maternal fertility among Pumé foragers and horticulturalists. *American Anthropologist* 109, 713–726.

Kramer, K.L., McMillan, G.P., 2006. The effect of labor-saving technology on longitudinal fertility changes. *Current Anthropology* 47, 165–172. doi:10.1086/499550.

Krause-Kyora, B., Makarewicz, C., Evin, A. et al., 2013. Use of domesticated pigs by Mesolithic hunter-gatherers in northwestern Europe. *Nature Communications* 4, 2348.

Krauss, R., Elenski, N., Weninger, B., Lee, C., Çakırlar, C., Zidarov, P., 2014. Beginnings of the Neolithic in Southeast Europe: the Early Neolithic sequence and absolute dates from Džuljunica-Smărdeš (Bulgaria). *Documenta Praehistorica* 41, 51–77.

Krauss, R., Marinova, E., De Brue, H., Weninger, B., 2017. The rapid spread of early farming from the Aegean into the Balkans via the Sub-Mediterranean-Aegean Vegetation Zone. *Quaternary International.* doi.org/10.1016/j.quaint.2017.01.019.

Kreuz, A., 2012. Die Vertreibung aus dem Paradies? Archäobiologische Ergebnisse zum Frühneolithikum im westlichen Mitteleuropa. *Bericht der Römisch-Germanischen Kommission* 91, 23–196.

Kreuz, A., Marinova, E., Schäfer, E., Wiethold, J., 2005. A comparison of early Neolithic crop and weed assemblages from the Linearbandkeramik and the Bulgarian Neolithic cultures: differences and similarities. *Vegetation History and Archaeobotany* 14, 237–258.

Kreuz, A., Märkle, T., Marinova, E. et al., 2014. The Late Neolithic Michelsberg culture–just ramparts and ditches? A supraregional comparison of agricultural and environmental data. *Praehistorische Zeitschrift* 89, 72–115.

Kuijt, I., 2000. People and space in early agricultural villages: exploring daily lives, community size, and architecture in the Late Pre-Pottery Neolithic. *Journal of Anthropological Archaeology* 19, 75–102.

2008. Demography and storage systems during the southern Levantine Neolithic demographic transition, in: Bocquet-Appel, J.-P., Bar-Yosef, O. (Eds.), *The Neolithic Demographic Transition and Its Consequences*. Springer, pp. 287–313.

2009. Population, socio-political simplification, and cultural evolution of Levantine Neolithic villages, in: Shennan, S. (Ed.), *Pattern and Process in Cultural Evolution*. University of California Press, Berkeley, pp. 315–328.

Kuijt, I., Finlayson, B., 2009. Evidence for food storage and predomestication granaries 11,000 years ago in the Jordan Valley. *Proceedings of the National Academy of Sciences* 106, 10966–10970.

Lake, M.W., Venti, J., 2009. Quantitative analysis of macroevolutionary patterning in technological evolution, in: Shennan, S. (Ed.), *Pattern and Process in Cultural Evolution*. University of California Press, Berkeley, pp. 147–174.

Lambert, P.M., 2009. Health versus fitness: competing themes in the origins and spread of agriculture? *Current Anthropology* 50, 603–608. doi:10.1086/605354.

Lang, C., Peters, J., Pöllath, N., Schmidt, K., Grupe, G., 2013. Gazelle behaviour and human presence at early Neolithic Göbekli Tepe, south-east Anatolia. *World Archaeology* 45, 410–429.

Larsen, C.S., Hillson, S.W., Boz, B. et al., 2015. Bioarchaeology of Neolithic Çatalhöyük: lives and lifestyles of an early farming society in transition. *Journal of World Prehistory* 28, 27–68.

Larson, G., Albarella, U., Dobney, K. et al., 2007. Ancient DNA, pig domestication, and the spread of the Neolithic into Europe. *Proceedings of the National Academy of Sciences* 104, 15276–15281.

Larsson, L., Broström, S.-G., 2011. Meeting for transformation. *Current Swedish Archaeology* 19, 183–201.

Last, J., 2013. The end of the longhouse, in: Hofmann, D., Smyth, J. (Eds.), *Tracking the Neolithic House in Europe*. Springer, pp. 261–282.

Lazaridis, I., Nadel, D., Rollefson, G. et al., 2016. Genomic insights into the origin of farming in the ancient Near East. *Nature* 536, 419–424.

Lechterbeck, J., Edinborough, K., Kerig, T., Fyfe, R., Roberts, N., Shennan, S., 2014. Is Neolithic land use correlated with demography? An evaluation of pollen-derived land cover and radiocarbon-inferred demographic change from Central Europe. *The Holocene* 24, 1297–1307. doi:10.1177/0959683614540952

Lee, R., 1986. Malthus and Boserup: A dynamic synthesis, in: Coleman, D., Schofield, R. (Eds.), *The State of Population Theory: Forward from Malthus*. Blackwell, Oxford, pp. 96–130.

Lefranc, P., Jeunesse, C., 2012. Deux enceintes de type de 'Rosheim' de la seconde moitié du Ve millénaire à Entzheim 'Les Terres de la Chapelle' et Dutzenheim 'Frauenabwand' (Bas Rhin). Premiers résultats, in: Gleser, R., Becker, V. (Eds.), *Mitteleuropa im 5. Jahrtausend vor Christus: Beiträge zur Internationalen Konferenz in Münster 2010*. Lit, Berlin, pp. 229–252.

Lehe, R., Hallatschek, O., Peliti, L., 2012. The rate of beneficial mutations surfing on the wave of a range expansion. *PLoS Computational Biology* 8, e1002447.

Lelli, R., Allen, R., Biondi, G. et al., 2012. Examining dietary variability of the earliest farmers of South-Eastern Italy. *American Journal of Physical Anthropology* 149, 380–390.

Lemercier, O., 2010. La transition du Néolithique moyen au Néolithique final dans le sud-est de la France: Recherches, données et scenarii, in: Lemercier, O., Furestier, R., Blaise, E. (Eds.), *La Transition du Néolithique Moyen au Néolithique Final Dans Le Sud-Est de La France: Recherches, Données et Les Régions Voisines. Monographies d'Archéologie Méditerranéenne*. UMR 5140 du CNRS/ADAL, Lattes, pp. 305–321.

Lenneis, E., 2008. Perspectives on the beginnings of the earliest LBK in east-central Europe, in: Whittle, A., Hofmann, D., Bailey, D.W. (Eds.), *Living Well Together? Settlement and Materiality in the Neolithic of South-East and Central Europe*. Oxbow Books, Oxford, pp. 164–178.

Lewis, J.P., Ryves, D.B., Rasmussen, P. et al., 2016. The shellfish enigma across the Mesolithic-Neolithic transition in southern Scandinavia. *Quaternary Science Reviews* 151, 315–320.

Lightfoot, E., Boneva, B., Miracle, P.T., Šlaus, M., O'Connell, T.C., 2011. Exploring the Mesolithic and Neolithic transition in Croatia through isotopic investigations. *Antiquity* 85, 73–86.

Link, T., 2012. Stilwandel contra Siedlungskontinuität–Zum Übergang von der Linien-zur Stichbandkeramik in Sachsen, in: Gleser, R., Becker, V. (Eds.), *Mitteleuropa im 5. Jahrtausend vor Christus.* Lit, Berlin, pp. 115–232.

Lipson, M., Szécsényi-Nagy, A., Mallick, S. et al., 2017. Parallel ancient genomic transects reveal complex population history of early European farmers. *bioRxiv,* 114488. doi: 10.1101/114488.

Löhr, H., 1994. Linksflügler und Rechtsflügler in Mittel- und Westeuropa. Der Fortbestand der Verbreitungsgebiete asymmetrischer Pfeilspitzenformen als Kontinuitätsbeleg zwischen Meso- und Neolithikum. *Trierer Zeitschrift für Geschichte und Kunst des Trierer Landes und seiner Nachbargebiete* 57, 9–127.

Loubier, J.-C., Burri, E.M.E., 2011. Modélisation spatiale de la dynamique de peuplement du Plateau Suisse au Néolithique. *M@ppemonde* 101/04.

Lucas, L., Colledge, S., Simmons, A., Fuller, D.Q., 2012. Crop introduction and accelerated island evolution: archaeobotanical evidence from 'Ais Yiorkis and Pre-Pottery Neolithic Cyprus. *Vegetation History and Archaeobotany* 21, 117–129.

Lüning, J. 1988. Frühe Bauern in Mitteleuropa im 6. und 5. Jahrtausend v. Chr. *Jahrbuch Römisch-Germanischen Zentralmuseums Mainz* 35, 27–93.

MacArthur, R.H., Pianka, E.R., 1966. On Optimal Use of a Patchy Environment. *The American Naturalist* 100, 603–609.

Maeda, O., Lucas, L., Silva, F., Tanno, K.-I., Fuller, D.Q., 2016. Narrowing the harvest: Increasing sickle investment and the rise of domesticated cereal agriculture in the Fertile Crescent. *Quaternary Science Reviews* 145, 226–237.

Maher, L.A., Banning, E.B., Chazan, M., 2011. Oasis or mirage? Assessing the role of abrupt climate change in the prehistory of the southern Levant. *Cambridge Archaeological Journal* 21, 1–30.

Maher, L.A., Richter, T., Macdonald, D., Jones, M.D., Martin, L., Stock, J.T., 2012. Twenty thousand-year-old huts at a hunter-gatherer settlement in eastern Jordan. *PLOS ONE* 7, e31447. doi:10.1371/journal.pone.0031447.

Maher, L.A., Macdonald, D.A., Allentuck, A., Martin, L., Spyrou, A., Jones, M.D., 2016. Occupying wide open spaces? Late Pleistocene hunter-gatherer activities in the Eastern Levant. *Quaternary International* 396, 79–94.

Maier, U., 1996. Morphological studies of free-threshing wheat ears from a Neolithic site in southwest Germany, and the history of the naked wheats. *Vegetation History and Archaeobotany* 5, 39–55. doi:10.1007/BF00189434.

Malone, C., 2003. The Italian Neolithic: a synthesis of research. *Journal of World Prehistory* 17, 235–312.

Manen, C., 2014. Dynamiques spatio-temporelles et culturelles de la Néolithisation Ouest-Méditerranéenne, in: Manen, C., Perrin, T., Guilaine, J. (Eds.), *La Transition Néolithique en Méditerranée.* Errance/Archives d'Écologie Préhistorique, Arles/Toulouse, pp. 405–418.

Manen, C., Convertini, F., 2012. Neolithization of the Western Mediterranean: pottery productions, circulation and recombination. *Rubricatum: Revista del Museu de Gavà* 5, 363–368.

Manen, C., Sabatier, P., 2003. Chronique radiocarbone de la néolithisation en Méditerranée nord-occidentale. *Bulletin de la Société Préhistorique Française* 479–504.

Manning, K., Conolly, J., Stopp, B. et al., 2013a. Animal exploitation in the early Neolithic of the Balkans and central Europe, in: Colledge, S., Conolly, J., Dobney, K., Manning, K., Shennan, S. (Eds.), *The Origins and Spread of Domestic Animals in Southwest Asia and Europe.* Left Coast Press, Walnut Creek, CA, pp. 237–252.

Manning, K., Downey, S.S., Colledge, S. et al., 2013b. The origins and spread of stock-keeping: the role of cultural and environmental influences on early Neolithic animal exploitation in Europe. *Antiquity* 87, 1046–1059.

Marchand, G., 2007. Neolithic fragrances: Mesolithic-Neolithic interactions in western France, in: Whittle, A., Cummings, V. (Eds.), *Going Over: The Mesolithic-Neolithic transition in North-West Europe.* Proceedings of the British Academy 144, Oxford University Press, Oxford, pp. 225–242.

Marcigny, C., Ghesquiere, E., Juhel, L., Charraud, F., 2010. Entre Néolithique ancien et Néolithique moyen en Normandie et dans les îles anglo-normandes. Parcours chronologique, in: Billard, C., Legris, M. (Eds.), *Premiers Néolithiques de l'Ouest. Cultures, Réseaux, Échanges des Premières Sociétés Néolithiques à leur Expansion,* pp. 117–62.

Marciniak, A., 2013. Origin of stock-keeping and the spread of animal exploitation strategies in the early and middle Neolithic of the North European Plain, in: Colledge, S., Conolly, J., Dobney, K., Manning, K., Shennan, S. (Eds.), *The Origins and Spread of Domestic Animals in Southwest Asia and Europe*. Left Coast Press, Walnut Creek, CA, pp. 221–236.

Marciniak, A., Barański, M.Z., Bayliss, A. et al., 2015. Fragmenting times: interpreting a Bayesian chronology for the late Neolithic occupation of Çatalhöyük East, Turkey. *Antiquity* 89, 154–176.

Marshall, F.B., Dobney, K., Denham, T., Capriles, J.M., 2014. Evaluating the roles of directed breeding and gene flow in animal domestication. *Proceedings of the National Academy of Sciences* 111, 6153–6158.

Martin, L., Edwards, Y., 2013. Diverse Strategies: evaluating the appearance and spread of domestic caprines in the southern Levant, in: Colledge, S.M., Conolly, J., Dobney, K., Manning, K., Shennan, S. (Eds.), *The Origins and Spread of Domestic Animals in Southwest Asia and Europe*. Left Coast Press, Walnut Creek, CA, pp. 49–82.

Mathieson, I., Roodenberg, S.A., Posth, C. et al., 2017. The genomic history of southeastern Europe. *bioRxiv,* 135616. doi: 10.1101/135616.

Mayr, E., 1954. Change of genetic environment and evolution, in: Huxley, J., Hardy, A.C., Ford, E.B. (Eds.), *Evolution as a Process*. Allen and Unwin, London, pp. 157–180.

McClatchie, M., Bogaard, A., Colledge, S. et al., 2014. Neolithic farming in north-western Europe: archaeobotanical evidence from Ireland. *Journal of Archaeological Science* 51, 206–215.

McClatchie, M., Bogaard, A., Colledge, S. et al., 2016. Farming and foraging in Neolithic Ireland: an archaeobotanical perspective. *Antiquity* 90, 302–318.

Meadows, J.R., Cemal, I., Karaca, O., Gootwine, E., Kijas, J.W., 2007. Five ovine mitochondrial lineages identified from sheep breeds of the Near East. *Genetics* 175, 1371–1379.

Meyer, C., Lohr, C., Gronenborn, D., Alt, K.W., 2015. The massacre mass grave of Schöneck-Kilianstädten reveals new insights into collective violence in Early Neolithic Central Europe. *Proceedings of the National Academy of Sciences* 112, 11217–11222.

Milić, M., 2014. PXRF characterisation of obsidian from central Anatolia, the Aegean and central Europe. *Journal of Archaeological Science* 41, 285–296.

Mischka, D., 2011. The Neolithic burial sequence at Flintbek LA 3, north Germany, and its cart tracks: a precise chronology. *Antiquity* 85/329, 742–758.

Mischka, D., Roth, G., Struckmeyer, K., 2015. Michelsberg and Oxie in contact next to the Baltic Sea, in: Brink, K., Hydén, S., Jennbert, K., Larsson, L., Olausson, D. (Eds.), *Neolithic Diversities: Perspectives from a Conference in Lund, Sweden*. Acta Archaeologica Lundensia 8/65. Department of Archaeology and Ancient History, Lund University, Lund, pp. 241–250.

Mithen, S.J., Finlayson, B., Smith, S., Jenkins, E., Najjar, M., Maričević, D., 2011. An 11 600 year-old communal structure from the Neolithic of southern Jordan. *Antiquity* 85, 350–364.

Mittnik, A., Wang, C.-C., Pfrengle, S., et al., 2017. The Genetic History of Northern Europe. *bioRxiv,* 113241. doi: 10.1101/113241.

Morales, J., Jordà, G.P., Peña-Chocarro, L. et al., 2016. The introduction of South-Western Asian domesticated plants in North-Western Africa: an archaeobotanical contribution from Neolithic Morocco. *Quaternary International* 412, 96–109.

Mordant, D., 2008. En France du Nord, in: Tarrete, J., Le Roux, C.-T. (Eds.), *Archéologie de La France. Le Néolithique*. Picard, Paris, pp. 120–142.

Morris, I., 1991. The archaeology of ancestors: the Saxe/Goldstein hypothesis revisited. *Cambridge Archaeological Journal* 1, 147–169.

Müller, J., 2001. *Soziochronologische Studien zum Jung- und Spätneolithikum im Mittelelbe-Saale-Gebiet (4100–2700 v. Chr.)*. Verlag Marie Leidorf, Rahden.

Müller, J., 2011. *Megaliths and Funnel Beakers: Societies in Change 4100–2700 BC*. Stichting Nederlands Museum voor Anthropologie en Praehistorie, Amsterdam.

Munro, N., Bar-Oz, G., Dayan, T. et al., 2004. Zooarchaeological measures of hunting pressure and occupation intensity in the Natufian: implications for agricultural origins. *Current Anthropology* 45, S5–S34.

Munro, N.D., Stiner, M.C., 2015. Zooarchaeological evidence for early neolithic colonization at Franchthi cave (Peloponnese, Greece). *Current Anthropology* 56, 596–603.

Neil, S., Evans, J., Montgomery, J., Scarre, C., 2016. Isotopic evidence for residential mobility of farming communities during the transition to agriculture in Britain. *Royal Society Open Science* 3, 150522.

Neiman, F.D., 1997. Conspicuous consumption as wasteful advertising: a Darwinian perspective on spatial patterns in Classic Maya terminal monument dates. *Archeological Papers of the American Anthropological Association* 7, 267–290.

Nielsen, P.O., 2004. Causewayed camps, palisade enclosures and central settlements of the Middle Neolithic in Denmark. *Journal of Nordic Archaeological Science* 14, 19–33.

Nikolov, V., 2010. Salt and gold: Provadia-Solnitsata and the Varna Chalcolithic cemetery. *Archäologisches Korrespondenzblatt* 40, 487–501.

Nisbet, R., 2008. Environment and agriculture in the early Neolithic of Arene Candide (Liguria), in: Fiorentino, G., Magri, D. (Eds.), *Charcoals from the Past: Cultural and Palaeoenvironmental Implications. Proceedings of the Third International Meeting of Anthracology, Cavallino-Lecce (Italy), June 28th–July 1st 2004.* British Archaeological Reports International Series 1807. Archaeopress, Oxford, pp. 193–198.

North, D.C., 1981. *Structure and Change in Economic History.* Norton, New York.

Nowak, K., 2012. Silexrohmaterialversorgung im Mittelneolithikum – ein Fallbeispiel aus dem Rheinland., in: Becker, V., Gleser, R. (Eds.), *Mitteleuropa im 5. Jahrtausend v. Chr. Beiträge zur Internationalen Konferenz in Münster 2010.* Lit, Berlin, pp. 409–420.

Odling-Smee, F.J., Laland, K.N., Feldman, M.W., 2003. *Niche Construction: The Neglected Process in Evolution (MPB-37).* Princeton University Press, Princeton.

Olalde, I., Brace, S., Allentoft, M.E. et al., 2017. The Beaker phenomenon and the genomic transformation of northwest Europe. *bioRxiv*, 135962. doi: 10/1101/135962.

Olalde, I., Schroeder, H., Sandoval-Velasco, M. et al., 2015. A common genetic origin for early farmers from Mediterranean Cardial and Central European LBK cultures. *Molecular Biology and Evolution* 32, 3132–3142.

Olea, L., San Miguel-Ayanz, A., 2006. The Spanish dehesa. A traditional Mediterranean silvopastoral system linking production and nature conservation, in: Loveras, A., González-Rodriguez, A., Vázquez-Yañez, O. (eds.), *Proceedings of the 21st General Meeting of the European Grassland Federation, Badajoz (Spain), April 2006*, pp. 1–15.

Oms, F.X., Martín, A., Esteve, X. et al., 2016. The Neolithic in Northeast Iberia: Chronocultural Phases and 14 C. *Radiocarbon* 58, 291–309.

Orton, D., 2012. Herding, settlement, and chronology in the Balkan Neolithic. *European Journal of Archaeology* 15, 5–40.

Orton, D., Gaastra, J., Vander Linden, M., 2016. Between the Danube and the Deep Blue Sea: zooarchaeological meta-analysis reveals variability in the spread and development of Neolithic farming across the Western Balkans. *Open Quaternary* 2.

Ottoni, C., Girdland Flink, L., Evin, A. et al., 2012. Pig domestication and human-mediated dispersal in western Eurasia revealed through ancient DNA and geometric morphometrics. *Molecular Biology and Evolution* 30, 824–832.

Özdoğan, E., 2015. Current research and new evidence for the Neolithization process in Western Turkey. *European Journal of Archaeology* 18, 33–59.

Özdoğan, M., 2010. Westward expansion of the Neolithic way of life: Sorting the Neolithic package into distinct packages, in: Matthiae, P., Pinnock, F., Nigro, L., Marchetti, N. (Eds.), *Proceedings of the 6th International Congress on the Archaeology of the Ancient Near East.* Harrassowitz Verlag, Wiesbaden, pp. 883–897.

Özdoğan, M., 2011. Archaeological evidence on the westward expansion of farming communities from eastern Anatolia to the Aegean and the Balkans. *Current Anthropology* 52, S415–S430.

Özdoğan, M., 2016. The earliest farmers of Europe. Where did they come from?, in: Bacvarov, K., Gleser, R. (Eds.), *Southeast Europe and Anatolia in Prehistory: Essays in Honor of Vassil Nikolov on His 65th Anniversary.* Habelt, Bonn, pp. 51–57.

Page, A.E., Viguier, S., Dyble, M. et al., 2016. Reproductive trade-offs in extant hunter-gatherers suggest adaptive mechanism for the Neolithic expansion. *Proceedings of the National Academy of Sciences* 113, 4694–4699.

Pailler, Y., Sheridan, A., 2009. Everything you always wanted to know about... la néolithisation de la Grande-Bretagne et de l'Irlande. *Bulletin de la Société Préhistorique Française* 106 (1), 25–56.

Pailler, Y., Marchand, G., Blanchet, S., Guyodo, J.-N., Hamon, G., 2008. Le Villeneuve-Saint-Germain dans la péninsule armoricaine: Les débuts d'une enquête, in: Ilett, M., Burnez-Lanotte, L., Allard, P. (Eds.), *Fin Des Traditions Danubiennes Dans Le Néolithique Du Bassin Parisien et de La Belgique (5100–4700 Avant J.-C.). Autour Des Recherches de Claude Constantin.* Mémoire de La Société Préhistorique Française 44. Société Préhistorique Française/ Presses Universitaires de Namur, pp. 91–111.

Palomo, A., Piqué, R., Terradas, X. et al., 2014. Prehistoric occupation of Banyoles lakeshore: results of recent excavations at La Draga site, Girona, Spain. *Journal of Wetland Archaeology* 14, 58–73.

Parker Pearson, M., 2012. *Stonehenge: Exploring the Greatest Stone Age Mystery*. Simon and Schuster, London.

Pechtl, J., 2009. A monumental prestige patch-work, in: Hofmann, D., Bickle, P. (Eds.), *Creating Communities: New Advances in Central European Neolithic Research*. Oxbow, Oxford, pp. 186–201.

2012. Stephansposching, Lkr. Deggendorf, und die Linienbandkeramik des Isarmündungsgebietes. Überlegungen zu Siedlungsstrukturen und zur Bevölkerungsabschätzung, in: Wolfram, S., Stäuble, H. (Eds.), *Siedlungsstruktur und Kulturwandel in der Bandkeramik. Beiträge der Internationalen Tagung 'Neue Fragen zur Bandkeramik oder Alles beim Alten?!'*, Landesamt für Archäologie, Dresden, pp. 130–140.

Peltenburg, E., Colledge, S., Croft, P., Jackson, A., McCartney, C., Murray, M.A., 2001. Neolithic dispersals from the Levantine corridor: a Mediterranean perspective. *Levant* 33, 35–64.

Pennington, R.L., 1996. Causes of early human population growth. *American Journal of Physical Anthropology* 99, 259–274.

Pérez-Jordà, G., Peña-Chocarro, L., Mateos, J.M., Zapata, L., 2017. Evidence for early crop management practices in the Western Mediterranean: latest data, new developments and future perspectives, in: García-Puchol, O., Salazar-García, D.C. (Eds.), *Times of Neolithic Transition along the Western Mediterranean*. Fundamental Issues in Archaeology. Springer, Cham, pp. 171–197.

Pérez-Losada, J., Fort, J., 2011. Spatial dimensions increase the effect of cultural drift. *Journal of Archaeological Science* 38, 1294–1299.

Perlès, C., 2001. *The early Neolithic in Greece: The First Farming Communities in Europe.* Cambridge University Press, Cambridge.

Perlès, C., 2012. Quand 'diffusion' ne veut pas dire 'interaction'. *Rubricatum: Revista del Museu de Gavà* 5, 585–590.

Perlès, C., Quiles, A., Valladas, H., 2013. Early seventh-millennium AMS dates from domestic seeds in the Initial Neolithic at Franchthi Cave (Argolid, Greece). *Antiquity* 87, 1001–1015.

Perrin, T., 2003. Mesolithic and Neolithic cultures coexisting in the upper Rhône valley. *Antiquity* 77, 732–739.

Perrin, T., Binder, D., 2014. Le Mésolithique à trapèzes et la néolithisation de l'Europe sud-occidentale, in: Manen, C., Perrin, T., Guilaine, J. (Eds.), *La Transition Néolithique En Méditerranée.* Errance/Archives d'Écologie Préhistorique, Arles/Toulouse, pp. 271–281.

Peters, J., Buitenhuis, H., Grupe, G., Schmidt, K., Pöllath, N., 2013. The long and winding road: ungulate exploitation and domestication in early Neolithic Anatolia (10,000–7,000 cal BC), in: Colledge, S., Conolly, J., Dobney, K., Manning, K., Shennan, S. (Eds.), *The Origins and Spread of Domestic Animals in Southwest Asia and Europe.* Left Coast Press, Walnut Creek, CA, pp. 83–108.

Peters, R., Zimmermann, A., 2017. Resilience and cyclicity: towards a macrohistory of the Central European Neolithic. *Quaternary International* 446, 43–53.

Petrasch, J., 2001. 'Seid Fruchtbar und Mehret euch und Füllet die erde und Machet sie euch Untertan': Überlegungen zur Demographischen Situation der Bandkeramischen Landnahme. *Archäologisches Korrespondenzblatt* 31, 13–25.

2010. Demografischer Wandel während der neolithisierung in Mitteleuropa, in: Gronenborn, D., Petrasch, J. (Eds.), *Die Neolithisierung Mitteleuropas/The Spread of the Neolithic to Central Europe.* Römisch-Germanischen Zentralmuseum, Mainz, pp. 351–363.

2012. Die mittelneolithischen Kreisgraben-anlagen in Zentraleuropa: Forschungsstand und Interpretationstheorien zu Funktion und Bedeutung, in: Bertemes, F., Meller, H.

(Eds.), *Neolithische Kreisgrabenanlagen in Europa*. Landesmuseum für Vorgeschichte, Halle (Saale), pp. 41–66.

2015. Central European enclosures, in: Fowler, C., Harding, J., Hofmann, D. (Eds.), *The Oxford Handbook of Neolithic Europe*. Oxford University Press, Oxford, pp. 763–778.

Pétrequin, P., Pétrequin, A.-M., 2015. *Clairvaux et le Néolithique Moyen Bourguignon, Vol. 1 et 2*. Presses Universitaires de Franche-Comté.

Pétrequin, P., Magny, M., Bailly, M., 2005. Habitat lacustre, densité de population et climat. L'exemple du Jura français, in: Della Casa, Ph., Trachsel, M. (Eds.), *WES'04 – Wetland Economies and Societies. Proceedings of the International Conference in Zürich, 10–13 March 2004*. Collectio Archæologica 3. Chronos, Zürich, pp. 143–68.

Pétrequin, P., Martineau, R., Nowicki, P., Gauthier, E., Schaal, C., 2009. La poterie Hoguette de Choisey (Jura), les Champins. Observations techniques et insertion régionale. *Bulletin de la Société Préhistorique Française* 106/3, 491–515.

Pétrequin, P., Cassen, S., Errera, M. et al., 2012a. Les haches en 'jades alpins' en Bulgarie, in: Pétrequin, P., Cassen, S., Errera, M., Klassen, L., Sheridan, A., Pétrequin, A.-M. (Eds.), *Jade. Grandes Haches Alpines Du Néolithique Européen. V e et IV e Millénaires Av. J.-C.* Presses Universitaires de Franche-Comté, pp. 1231–1279.

Pétrequin, P., Cassen, S., Gauthier, E., Klassen, L., Pailler, Y., Sheridan, A., 2012b. Typologie, chronologie et répartition des grandes haches alpines en Europe occidentale, in: Pétrequin, P., Cassen, S., Errera, M., Klassen, L., Sheridan, A., Pétrequin, A.-M. (Eds.), *Jade. Grandes Haches Alpines Du Néolithique Européen. V e et IV e Millénaires Av. J.-C.*, Presses Universitaires de Franche-Comté, pp. 574–727.

Pétrequin, P., Cassen, S., Klassen, L., Fábregas Valcarce, R., 2012c. La circulation des haches carnacéennes en Europe occidentale, in: Pétrequin, P., Cassen, S., Errera, M., Klassen, L., Sheridan, A., Pétrequin, A.-M. (Eds.), *Jade. Grandes Haches Alpines Du Néolithique Européen. V e et IV e Millénaires Av. J.-C.* Presses Universitaires de Franche-Comté, pp. 1015–1045.

Pétrequin, P., Pétrequin, A.-M., Cassen, S., Errera, M., Gauthier, E., Prodeo, F., Vaquer, J., 2015a. Les grandes haches polies en jades alpins, in: *Signes de Richesse, Inégalités au Néolithique. 27 Juin 2015–15 Novembre 2015. Musée de Préhistoire, Les Eyzies-de-Tayac 27 Juin–15 Novembre 2015, Musée Des Confluences, Lyon, 1er Décembre 2015–17 Avril 2016*, Musée national de la Préhistore des Eyzies de Tayac et Réunion des Musées nationaux -Grand Palais, pp. 43–54.

Pétrequin, P., Sheridan, J.A., Gauthier, E., Cassen, S., Errera, M., Klassen, L., 2015b. Projet JADE 2. 'Object-signs' and social interpretations of Alpine jade axeheads in the European Neolithic: theory and methodology, in: Kerig, T., Shennan, S. (Eds.), *Connecting Networks: Characterising Contact by Measuring Lithic Exchange in the European Neolithic*. Archaeopress, Oxford, pp. 83–102.

Pilaar Birch, S.E., Vander Linden, M., 2017. A long hard road… Reviewing the evidence for environmental change and population history in the eastern Adriatic and western Balkans during the Late Pleistocene and Early Holocene. *Quaternary International* 30, 1–15.

Piličiauskas, G., Kisielienė, D., Piličiauskienė, G., 2017. Deconstructing the concept of Subneolithic farming in the southeastern Baltic. *Vegetation History and Archaeobotany* 26, 183–193. doi:10.1007/s00334-016-0584-9.

Pioffet, H., 2017. Societies and identities during the Early Neolithic of Britain and Ireland in their west European context: characterisation and comparative analyses of pottery production between Channel, Irish Sea and North Sea. *PAST* 87, 5–7.

Piperno, D.R., Weiss, E., Holst, I., Nadel, D., 2004. Processing of wild cereal grains in the Upper Palaeolithic revealed by starch grain analysis. *Nature* 430, 670.

Porčić, M., Nikolić, M., 2016. The Approximate Bayesian Computation approach to reconstructing population dynamics and size from settlement data: demography of the Mesolithic-Neolithic transition at Lepenski Vir. *Archaeological and Anthropological Sciences* 8, 169–186.

Preece, C., Livarda, A., Wallace, M. et al., 2015. Were Fertile Crescent crop progenitors higher yielding than other wild species that were never domesticated? *New Phytologist* 207, 905–913.

Preece, C., Livarda, A., Christin, P.-A. et al., 2017. How did the domestication of Fertile

Crescent grain crops increase their yields? *Functional Ecology* 31, 387–397.

Price, T.D., Bar-Yosef, O., 2010. Traces of inequality at the origins of agriculture in the ancient Near East, in: Price, T.D., Feinman, G.M. (Eds.), *Pathways to Power: New Perspectives on the Origins of Social Inequality*. Springer, pp. 147–168.

Puleston, C., Tuljapurkar, S., Winterhalder, B., 2014. The invisible cliff: abrupt imposition of Malthusian equilibrium in a natural-fertility, agrarian society. *PLOS ONE* 9, e87541. doi:10.1371/journal.pone.0087541.

Purugganan, M.D., Fuller, D.Q., 2011. Archaeological data reveal slow rates of evolution during plant domestication. *Evolution* 65, 171–183.

Pyzel, J., 2012. Kuyavian settlements from the Linear Pottery Culture to the Brześć Kujawski Culture – the question of continuity, tradition and cultural memory in the 5th millennium BC, in: Gleser, R., Becker, V. (Eds.), *Mitteleuropa im 5. Jahrtausend vor Christus, Beiträge zur Internationalen Konferenz in Münster 2010*. Lit, Berlin, pp. 175–182.

Quinlan, R.J., 2007. Human parental effort and environmental risk. *Proceedings of the Royal Society of London B: Biological Sciences* 274, 121–125.

Raichlen, D.A., Wood, B.M., Gordon, A.D., Mabulla, A.Z., Marlowe, F.W., Pontzer, H., 2014. Evidence of Lévy walk foraging patterns in human hunter-gatherers. *Proceedings of the National Academy of Sciences* 111, 728–733.

Read, D., LeBlanc, S., 2003. Population growth, carrying capacity, and conflict. *Current Anthropology* 44, 59–85.

Reed, K., 2015. From the field to the hearth: plant remains from Neolithic Croatia (ca. 6000–4000 cal BC). *Vegetation History and Archaeobotany* 24, 601–619.

Reingruber, A., 2011. Early Neolithic settlement patterns and exchange networks in the Aegean. *Documenta Praehistorica* 38, 291.

Revelles, J., Cho, S., Iriarte, E. et al., 2015. Mid-Holocene vegetation history and Neolithic land-use in the Lake Banyoles area (Girona, Spain). *Palaeogeography, Palaeoclimatology, Palaeoecology* 435, 70–85.

Richards, M.P., Price, T.D., Koch, E., 2003. Mesolithic and Neolithic subsistence in Denmark: new stable isotope data. *Current Anthropology* 44, 288–295. doi:10.1086/367971.

Richerson, P.J., Boyd, R., 2001. Institutional evolution in the Holocene: the rise of complex societies, in: Runciman, W.G. (Ed.), *The Origin of Human Social Institutions*. Proceedings of the British Academy 110, Oxford University Press, Oxford, pp. 197–234.

Richerson, P.J., Boyd, R., Bettinger, R.L., 2001. Was agriculture impossible during the Pleistocene but mandatory during the Holocene? A climate change hypothesis. *American Antiquity* 66, 387–411.

2009. Cultural innovations and demographic change. *Human Biology* 81, 211–235.

Richter, T., Maher, L.A., Garrard, A.N., Edinborough, K., Jones, M.D., Stock, J.T., 2013. Epipalaeolithic settlement dynamics in southwest Asia: new radiocarbon evidence from the Azraq Basin. *Journal of Quaternary Science* 28, 467–479.

Rick, J.W., 1987. Dates as data: an examination of the Peruvian preceramic radiocarbon record. *American Antiquity* 52, 55–73.

Rigaud, S., d'Errico, F., Vanhaeren, M., 2015. Ornaments reveal resistance of North European cultures to the spread of farming. *PLOS ONE* 10, e0121166.

Rindos, D., 1984. *The Origins of Agriculture: An Evolutionary Perspective*. Academic Press, New York.

Rivollat, M., Mendisco, F., Pemonge, M.-H. et al., 2015. When the waves of European neolithization met: first paleogenetic evidence from early farmers in the southern Paris Basin. *PLOS ONE* 10, e0125521.

Rivollat, M., Rottier, S., Couture, C. et al., 2017. Investigating mitochondrial DNA relationships in Neolithic Western Europe through serial coalescent simulations. *European Journal of Human Genetics* 25, 388–392.

Robb, J., 2007. *The Early Mediterranean Village: Agency, Material Culture, and Social Change in Neolithic Italy*. Cambridge University Press, Cambridge.

Roberts, N., Woodbridge, J., Bevan, A., Palmisano, A., Shennan, S., Asouti, E., 2017. Human responses and non-responses to climatic variations during the Last Glacial: interglacial transition in the eastern Mediterranean. *Quaternary Science Reviews*. doi.org/10.1016/j.quascirev.2017.09.011.

Robinson, E., Sergant, J., Crombé, P., 2013. Late Mesolithic armature variability in the southern North Sea Basin: implications for forager-Linearbandkeramik contact models of the transition to agriculture in Belgium and the southern Netherlands. *European Journal of Archaeology* 16, 3–20.

Robinson, S.A., Black, S., Sellwood, B.W., Valdes, P.J., 2006. A review of palaeoclimates and palaeoenvironments in the Levant and Eastern Mediterranean from 25,000 to 5000 years BP: setting the environmental background for the evolution of human civilisation. *Quaternary Science Reviews* 25, 1517–1541.

Rösch, M., Lechterbeck, J., 2016. Seven Millennia of human impact as reflected in a high resolution pollen profile from the profundal sediments of Litzelsee, Lake Constance region, Germany. *Vegetation History and Archaeobotany* 25, 339–358.

Rösch, M., Biester, H., Bogenrieder, A. et al., 2017. Late Neolithic agriculture in temperate Europe – a long-term experimental approach. *Land* 6, 11.

Roscoe, P., 2009. Social signaling and the organization of small-scale society: the case of contact-era New Guinea. *Journal of Archaeological Method and Theory* 16, 69–116.

Rosen, A., 2013. Natufian foragers and the 'Monocot Revolution': A Phytolith perspective, in: Bar-Yosef, O., Valla, F.R. (Eds.), *Natufian Foragers in the Levant: Terminal Pleistocene Social Changes in Western Asia*. International Monographs in Prehistory, Ann Arbor, pp. 638–648.

Rosen, A.M., Rivera-Collazo, I., 2012. Climate change, adaptive cycles, and the persistence of foraging economies during the late Pleistocene/Holocene transition in the Levant. *Proceedings of the National Academy of Sciences* 109, 3640–3645.

Rosenberg, M., 1994. Pattern, process, and hierarchy in the evolution of culture. *Journal of Anthropological Archaeology* 13, 307–340.

Rottoli, M., Pessina, A., 2007. Neolithic agriculture in Italy: an update of archaeobotanical data with particular emphases on northern settlements, in: Colledge, S., Conolly, J. (Eds.), *The Origins and Spread of Domestic Plants in Southwest Asia and Europe*. Left Coast Press, Walnut Creek, CA, pp. 141–154.

Rowley-Conwy, P., 1984. The laziness of the short-distance hunter: the origins of agriculture in western Denmark. *Journal of Anthropological Archaeology* 3, 300–324.

2011. Westward Ho! The spread of agriculture from Central Europe to the Atlantic. *Current Anthropology* 52, S431–S451.

2013. North of the frontier: Early domestic animals in northern Europe, in: Colledge, S., Conolly, J., Dobney, K., Manning, K., Shennan, S. (Eds.), *The Origins and Spread of Domestic Animals in Southwest Asia and Europe*. Left Coast Press, Walnut Creek, CA, pp. 283–312.

Rowley-Conwy, P., Gourichon, L., Helmer, D., Vigne, J.D., 2013. Early domestic animals in Italy, Istria, the Tyrrhenian islands and Southern France, in: Colledge, S., Conolly, J., Dobney, K., Manning, K., Shennan, S. (Eds.), *The Origins and Spread of Domestic Animals in Southwest Asia and Europe*. Left Coast Press, Walnut Creek, CA, pp. 161–194.

Russell, K.W., 1988. *After Eden: The Behavioral Ecology of Early Food Production in the Near East and North Africa*. British Archaeological Reports International Series 391, Oxford.

Sahlins, M., 1972. The original affluent society, in: *Stone Age Economics*. Aldine, Chicago, pp. 1–40.

Sahlins, M.D., 1961. The segmentary lineage: an organization of predatory expansion. *American Anthropologist* 63, 322–345.

Salavert, A., 2011. Plant economy of the first farmers of central Belgium (Linearbandkeramik, 5200–5000 BC). *Vegetation History and Archaeobotany* 20, 321–332.

Salazar-García, D.C., Aura, J.E., Olària, C.R., Talamo, S., Morales, J.V., Richards, M.P., 2014. Isotope evidence for the use of marine resources in the Eastern Iberian Mesolithic. *Journal of Archaeological Science* 42, 231–240.

Salque, M., Radi, G., Tagliacozzo, A. et al., 2012. New insights into the Early Neolithic economy and management of animals in Southern and Central Europe revealed using lipid residue analyses of pottery vessels. *Anthropozoologica* 47, 45–62.

Salque, M., Bogucki, P.I., Pyzel, J. et al., 2013. Earliest evidence for cheese making in the sixth millennium BC in northern Europe. *Nature* 493, 522–525.

Saña, M., 2013. Domestication of animals in the Iberian Peninsula, in: Colledge, S., Conolly, J., Dobney, K., Manning, K., Shennan, S. (Eds.), *The Origins and Spread of Domestic Animals in Southwest Asia and Europe*. Left Coast Press, Walnut Creek, CA, pp. 195–220.

Sánchez, M.C., Espejo, F.J.J., Vallejo, M.D.S. et al., 2012. The Mesolithic–Neolithic transition in southern Iberia. *Quaternary Research* 77, 221–234.

Sattenspiel, L., Harpending, H., 1983. Stable populations and skeletal age. *American Antiquity* 48, 489–498.

Saulieu, G. de, 2004. *Gravures Rupestres et Statues Menhirs dans les Alpes. Des Pierres et des Pouvoirs (3000–2000 av. J.-C.).* Paris, Errance.

Savard, M., Nesbitt, M., Jones, M.K., 2006. The role of wild grasses in subsistence and sedentism: new evidence from the northern Fertile Crescent. *World Archaeology* 38, 179–196.

Saxe, A., 1970. *Social Dimensions of Mortuary Practices.* University of Michigan, Ann Arbor.

Scarre, C., 2001. Modeling prehistoric populations: the case of Neolithic Brittany. *Journal of Anthropological Archaeology* 20, 285–313.

2011. *Landscapes of Neolithic Brittany.* Oxford University Press Oxford.

Schade, C.C., 2004. *Die Besiedlungsgeschichte der Bandkeramik in der Mörlener Bucht/Wetterau. Zentralität und Peripherie, Haupt- und Nebenorte, Siedlungsverbände.* Universitätsforschungen zur Prähistorischen Archäologie 105. Habelt, Bonn.

Schade-Lindig, S., Schade, C., 2010. Woher kommt Flomborn? Keramikimporte und Nachahmungen in der bandkeramischen Siedlung Bad Nauheim – Nieder-Mörlen 'auf dem Hempler,' in: Gronenborn, D., Petrasch, J. (Eds.), *Die Neolithisierung Mitteleuropas/ The Spread of the Neolithic to Central Europe.* Römisch-Germanischen Zentralmuseum, Mainz, pp. 461–474.

Scheu, A., Powell, A., Bollongino, R. et al., 2015. The genetic prehistory of domesticated cattle from their origin to the spread across Europe. *BMC Genetics* 16, 54.

Schier, W., 2009. Extensiver Brandfeldbau und die Ausbreitung der neolithischen Wirtschaftsweise in Mitteleuropa und Südskandinavien am Ende des 5. *Jahrtausends v. Chr. Praehistorische Zeitschrift* 84, 15–43.

Schier, W., Ehrmann, O., Rösch, M. et al., 2013. The economics of Neolithic swidden cultivation. Results of an experimental long-term project in Forchtenberg (Baden-Württemberg, Germany), in: Kerig, T., Zimmermann, A. (Eds.), *Economic Archaeology: From Structure to Performance in European Archaeology.* Universitätsforschungen zur Prähistorischen Archäologie 237. Habelt, Bonn, pp. 97–106.

Schlichtherle, H., 2006. Chemins, roues et chariots: Innovations de la fin du Néolithique dans le sud-ouest de l'Allemagne, in: Pétrequin, P., Arbogast, R.-M., Pétrequin, A.-M., van Willigen, S., Bailly, M. (Eds.), *Premiers Chariots, Premiers Araires.* CNRS Editions, Paris, pp. 165–178.

2010. Kultbilder in den Pfahlbauten des Bodensees, in: Lichter, C. (Ed.), *Jungsteinzeit im Umbruch. Die Michelsberger Kultur und Mitteleuropa vor 6000 Jahren.* Badischen Landesmuseum Karlsruhe/Primus-Verlag, Darmstadt, pp. 266–277.

Schlichtherle, H., Herbig, C., Maier, U., 2010. Endneolithische Häuser Räder und jede Menge botanische Funde im Olzreuter Ried: Bad Schussenried-Olzreute, Kreis Biberach. *Archäologische Ausgrabungen in Baden-Württemberg* 2010, 94–97.

Schlumbaum, A., Neuhaus, J.-M., Jacomet, S., 1998. Coexistence of tetraploid and hexaploid naked wheat in a Neolithic lake dwelling of Central Europe: evidence from morphology and ancient DNA. *Journal of Archaeological Science* 25, 1111–1118.

Schmidt, B., Gruhle, W., Rück, O., 2004. Klimaextreme in bandkeramischer Zeit (5300 bis 5000 v. Chr.): Interpretation dendrochronologischer und archäologischer Befunde. *Archäologisches Korrespondenzblatt* 34, 303–307.

Schoop, U.-D., 2005. The late escape of the Neolithic from the central Anatolian plain, in: Lichter, C. (Ed.), *How Did Farming Reach Europe? Anatolian-European Relations from the Second Half of the 7th through to the First Half of the 6th Millennium Cal BC, Proceedings of the International Workshop Istanbul, 20–22 May 2004.* Ege Yayinlari, Istanbul, pp. 41–58.

Schulting, R.J., 1999. Radiocarbon dates, in: Woodman, P.C., Anderson, E., Finlay, N. (Eds.), *Excavations at Ferriter's Cove, 1983–95: Last Foragers, First Farmers in the Dingle Peninsula.* Wordwell, Bray, p. 219.

Schulting, R., 2013. On the northwestern fringes: earlier Neolithic subsistence in Britain and Ireland as seen through faunal remains and stable isotopes, in: Colledge, S., Conolly, J., Dobney, K., Manning, K., Shennan, S. (Eds.), *The Origins and Spread of Domestic Animals in*

Southwest Asia and Europe. Left Coast Press, Walnut Creek, CA, pp. 313–38.

Schulting, R.J., Murphy, E., Jones, C., Warren, G., 2012. New dates from the north and a proposed chronology for Irish court tombs. *Proceedings of the Royal Irish Academy. Section C: Archaeology, Celtic Studies, History, Linguistics, Literature* 112, 1–60.

Schweizer, A., 2003. Archäopalynologische Untersuchungen zur Neolithisierung der Wetterau (Hessen), in: Eckert, J., Eisenhauer, U., Zimmermann, A. (Eds.), *Archäologische Perspektiven: Analysen und Interpretationen im Wandel*. Verlag Marie Leidorf, Rahden, pp. 243–250.

Sear, R., Lawson, D.W., Kaplan, H., Shenk, M.K., 2016. Understanding variation in human fertility: what can we learn from evolutionary demography? *Philosophical Transactions of the Royal Society B* 371, 20150144. doi: 10.1098/rstb.2015.0144.

Seidel, U., 2010. Satelliten der Erdwerke? Die unbefestigten Siedlungen der Michelsberger Kultur, in: *Jungsteinzeit im Umbruch: Die 'Michelsberger Kultur' und Mitteleuropa vor 6000 Jahren. [Katalog zur Ausstellung im Badischen Landesmuseum Schloss Karlsruhe, 20.11.2010–15.5.2011]*. Primus-Verlag, Darmstadt, pp. 82–87.

Shennan, S., 2002. *Genes, Memes and Human History*. Thames and Hudson, London.

2008. Population processes and their consequences in early Neolithic central Europe, in: Bocquet-Appel, J.-P., Bar-Yosef, O. (Eds.), *The Neolithic Demographic Transition and Its Consequences*. Springer, New York, pp. 315–329.

2011. Property and wealth inequality as cultural niche construction. *Philosophical Transactions of the Royal Society of London B: Biological Sciences* 366, 918–926. doi:10.1098/rstb.2010.0309.

Shennan, S., Downey, S.S., Timpson, A. et al., 2013. Regional population collapse followed initial agriculture booms in mid-Holocene Europe. *Nat Commun* 4, 2486. doi:10.1038/ncomms3486.

Sheridan, A., 2007. From Picardie to Pickering and Pencraig Hill? New information on the 'Carinated Bowl Neolithic' in northern Britain, in: Whittle, A., Cummings, V. (Eds.), *Going Over: The Mesolithic-Neolithic Transition in North-West Europe*. Proceedings of the

British Academy 144, Oxford University Press, Oxford, pp. 441–492.

2017. Interdigitating pasts: the Irish and Scottish Neolithics, in: Bickle, P., Cummings, V., Hofmann, D., Pollard, J. (Eds.), *The Neolithic in Europe*. Oxbow, Oxford, pp. 298–313.

Sheridan, J.A., 2004. Going round in circles? Understanding the Irish Grooved Ware 'complex' in its wider context, in: Coles, J., Grogan, E., Raftery, B. (Eds.), *From Megaliths to Metals: Essays in Honour of George Eogan*. Oxbow, Oxford, pp. 26–37.

2010. The Neolithisation of Britain and Ireland: the big picture, in: Finlayson, B., Warren, G. (Eds.), *Landscapes in Transition*. Oxbow, Oxford, pp. 89–105.

Sherratt, A., 1981. Plough and pastoralism: aspects of the secondary products revolution, in: Hodder, I., Isaac, G., Hammond, N. (Eds.), *Pattern of the Past: Studies in Honour of David Clarke*. Cambridge University Press, Cambridge, pp. 261–305.

Sidéra, I., 2010. De mains méridionales en mains septentrionales. *Mélanges de la Casa de Velázquez Tome* 40, 17–32.

Simmons, A., 2011. Re-writing the colonisation of Cyprus: tales of hippo hunters and cow herders, in: Phoca-Cosmetatou, N. (Ed.), *The First Mediterranean Islanders: Initial Occupation and Survival Strategies*. University of Oxford School of Archaeology, Oxford, pp. 55–75.

2012. Mediterranean island voyages. *Science* 338, 895–897.

Skoglund, P., Malmström, H., Raghavan, M. et al., 2012. Origins and Genetic Legacy of Neolithic Farmers and Hunter-Gatherers in Europe. *Science* 336, 466–469. doi:10.1126/science.1216304.

Skoglund, P., Malmström, H., Omrak, A. et al., 2014. Genomic diversity and admixture differs for Stone-Age Scandinavian foragers and farmers. *Science* 344, 747–750. doi:10.1126/science.1253448.

Smits, L., van der Plicht, H., 2009. Mesolithic and Neolithic human remains in the Netherlands: physical anthropological and stable isotope investigations. *Journal of Archaeology in the Low Countries* 1, 55–85.

Snir, A., Nadel, D., Groman-Yaroslavski, I. et al., 2015. The origin of cultivation and protoweeds, long before Neolithic farming. *PLOS ONE* 10, e0131422.

Soltis, J., Boyd, R., Richerson, P.J., 1995. Can group-functional behaviors evolve by cultural group selection? An empirical test. *Current Anthropology* 36, 473–494.

Sommer, U., 2001. 'Hear the instruction of thy father, and forsake not the law of thy mother'. Change and persistence in the European early Neolithic. *Journal of Social Archaeology* 1, 244–270.

Sørensen, L., 2014. *From Hunter to Farmer in Northern Europe: Migration and Adaptation During the Neolithic and Bronze Age*. Acta Archaeologica 85.1. Wiley, Oxford.

Sørensen, L., Karg, S., 2014. The expansion of agrarian societies towards the north: new evidence for agriculture during the Mesolithic/Neolithic transition in Southern Scandinavia. *Journal of Archaeological Science (The World Reshaped: Practices and Impacts of Early Agrarian Societies)* 51, 98–114. doi:10.1016/j.jas.2012.08.042.

Sørensen, M., Rankama, T., Kankaanpää, J., et al., 2013. The first eastern migrations of people and knowledge into Scandinavia: evidence from studies of mesolithic technology, 9th–8th Millennium BC. *Norwegian Archaeological Review* 46, 19–56.

Spataro, M., 2010. The Neolithisation of the Central Balkans: leapfrogging diffusion and cultural transmission, in: Gronenborn, D., Petrasch, J. (Eds.), *Die Neolithisierung Mitteleuropas/The Spread of the Neolithic to Central Europe*. Römisch-Germanischen Zentralmuseum, Mainz, pp. 79–90.

Spiteri, C.D., Gillis, R.E., Roffet-Salque, M., et al., 2016. Regional asynchronicity in dairy production and processing in early farming communities of the northern Mediterranean. *Proceedings of the National Academy of Sciences* 113, 13594–13599.

Spiteri, C., Muntoni, I.M., Craig, O.E., 2017. Dietary practices at the onset of the Neolithic in the Western Mediterranean revealed using a combined biomarker and isotopic approach, in: García-Puchol, O., Salazar-García, D.C. (Eds.), *Times of Neolithic Transition along the Western Mediterranean*. Fundamental Issues in Archaeology. Springer, Cham, pp. 253–279.

Stadler, P., 2005. Settlement of the Early Linear ceramics culture at Brunn am Gebirge, Wolfholz site. *Documenta Praehistorica* 32, 269–278.

Starkovich, B.M., Stiner, M.C., 2009. Hallan Çemi Tepesi: high-ranked game exploitation alongside intensive seed processing at the Epipaleolithic-Neolithic transition in Southeastern Turkey. *Anthropozoologica* 44, 41–61.

Starling, N.J., 1983. Neolithic settlement patterns in Central Germany. *Oxford Journal of Archaeology* 2, 1–11. doi:10.1111/j.1468-0092.1983.tb00092.x.

Stäuble, H., Wolfram, S., 2013. Bandkeramik und Mesolithikum: Abfolge oder Koexistenz, in: Hansen, S., Meyer, M. (Eds.), *Parallele Raumkonzepte*. de Gruyter, Berlin, pp. 105–134.

Steele, J., 2009. Human dispersals: mathematical models and the archaeological record. *Human Biology* 81, 121–140.

Sterelny, K., Watkins, T., 2015. Neolithization in Southwest Asia in a context of niche construction theory. *Cambridge Archaeological Journal* 25/3, 673–705.

Stevens, C.J., Fuller, D.Q., 2012. Did Neolithic farming fail? The case for a Bronze Age agricultural revolution in the British Isles. *Antiquity* 86, 707–722.

2015. Alternative strategies to agriculture: the evidence for climatic shocks and cereal declines during the British Neolithic and Bronze Age (a reply to Bishop). *World Archaeology* 47/5, 856–875.

Stika, H.-P., 2005. Early Neolithic agriculture in Ambrona, Provincia Soria, central Spain. *Vegetation History and Archaeobotany* 14, 189–197.

Stiner, M.C., Munro, N.D., 2002. Approaches to prehistoric diet breadth, demography, and prey ranking systems in time and space. *Journal of Archaeological Method and Theory* 9, 181–214.

Stiner, M.C., Buitenhuis, H., Duru, G. et al., 2014. A forager–herder trade-off, from broad-spectrum hunting to sheep management at Aşıklı Höyük, Turkey. *Proceedings of the National Academy of Sciences* 111, 8404–8409.

Stordeur, D., Der Aprahamian, G., Brenet, M., Roux, J.-C., 2000. Les bâtiments communautaires de Jerf el Ahmar et Mureybet horizon PPNA (Syrie). *Paléorient* 26, 29–44.

Stutz, A.J., Munro, N.D., Bar-Oz, G., 2009. Increasing the resolution of the Broad Spectrum Revolution in the Southern Levantine Epipaleolithic (19–12 ka). *Journal of Human Evolution* 56/3, 294–306.

Styring, A., Maier, U., Stephan, E., Schlichtherle, H., Bogaard, A., 2016. Cultivation of choice: new insights into farming practices at Neolithic lakeshore sites. *Antiquity* 90, 95–110.

Sutherland, W.J., 1996. *From Individual Behaviour to Population Ecology*. Oxford University Press.

Tallavaara, M., Pesonen, P., Oinonen, M., Seppä, H., 2014. The mere possibility of biases does not invalidate archaeological population proxies – response to Teemu Mokkonen. *Fennoscandia Archaeologica* 31, 135–140.

Tanno, K., Willcox, G., Muhesen, S., Nishiaki, Y., Kanjo, Y., Akazawa, T., 2013. Preliminary results from analyses of charred plant remains from a burnt Natufian building at Dederiyeh Cave in northwest Syria, in: Bar-Yosef, O., Valla, F.R. (Eds.), *Natufian Foragers in the Levant: Terminal Pleistocene Social Changes in Western Asia*. International Monographs in Prehistory, Ann Arbor, pp. 83–87.

Tarrús, J., 2008. La Draga (Banyoles, Catalonia), an Early Neolithic Lakeside Village in Mediterranean Europe. *Catalan Historical Review* 1, 17–33.

Terradas, X., Piqué, R., Palomo, A. et al., 2017. Farming Practices in the Early Neolithic According to Agricultural Tools: Evidence from La Draga Site (Northeastern Iberia), in: García-Puchol, O., Salazar-García, D.C. (Eds.), *Times of Neolithic Transition along the Western Mediterranean*. Fundamental Issues in Archaeology. Springer, Cham, pp. 199–220.

Teschler-Nicola, M., Gerold, F., Kanz, F., Lindenbauer, K., Spannagl, M., 1996. Anthropologische Spurensicherung: Die traumatischen und postmortalen Veränderungen an den linearbandkeramischen Skelettresten von Asparn/Schletz. *Archäologie Österreichs* 7, 4–12.

Thomas, A., Chambon, P., Murail, P., 2011. Unpacking burial and rank: the role of children in the first monumental cemeteries of Western Europe (4600–4300 BC). *Antiquity* 85, 772–786.

Thomas, J., 2003. Thoughts on the 'repacked' Neolithic revolution. *Antiquity* 77, 67–74.
2013. *The Birth of Neolithic Britain: An Interpretive Account*. Oxford University Press, Oxford.

Timpson, A., Colledge, S., Crema, E. et al., 2014. Reconstructing regional population fluctuations in the European Neolithic using radiocarbon dates: a new case-study using an improved method. *Journal of Archaeological Science* 52, 549–557. doi:10.1016/j.jas.2014.08.011.

Tinevez, J.-Y., Hamon, G., Querré, G. et al., 2015. Les vestiges d'habitat du Néolithique ancien de Quimper, Kervouyec (Finistère). *Bulletin de la Société Préhistorique Française* 112, 269–316.

Tipping, R., Bunting, M.J., Davies, A.L., Murray, H., Fraser, S., McCulloch, R., 2009. Modelling land use around an early Neolithic timber 'hall' in north east Scotland from high spatial resolution pollen analyses. *Journal of Archaeological Science* 36, 140–149.

Tresset, A., 2003. French connections II: of cows and men, in: Armit, I., Murphy, E.M., Nelis, E., Simpson, D. (Eds.), *Neolithic Settlement in Ireland and Western Britain*. Oxbow, Oxford, pp. 18–30.

Tveito, O.E., Førland, E.J., Alexandersson, H., et al., 2001. *Nordic Climate Maps. Report No. 06/01. KLIMA. DNMI Report*. Norwegian Meteorological Institute.

van Andel, T.H., Runnels, C.N., 1995. The earliest farmers in Europe. *Antiquity* 69, 481–500.

van der Velde, P., 1990. Bandkeramik social inequality – a case study. *Germania* 68, 19–38.

Vander Linden, M., 2011. To tame a land: archaeological cultures and the spread of the Neolithic in western Europe, in: Roberts, B.W., Vander Linden, M. (Eds.), *Investigating Archaeological Cultures*. Springer, New York, pp. 289–319.

Vander Linden, M., Bradley, R., 2011. Identification et définition du plus ancien Néolithique dans les îles britanniques: nouvelles données et implications pour les contacts trans-Manche. *Revue Archéologique de Picardie*. Numéro spécial 28, 31–40.

Vanmontfort, B., 2008. Forager–farmer connections in an 'unoccupied' land: first contact on the western edge of LBK territory. *Journal of Anthropological Archaeology* 27, 149–160. doi:10.1016/j.jaa.2008.03.002.

Verrill, L., Tipping, R., 2010. Use and abandonment of a Neolithic field system at Belderrig, Co. Mayo, Ireland: evidence for economic marginality. *The Holocene* 20, 1011–1021.

Vigne, J.-D., 2007. Exploitation des animaux et néolithisation en Méditerranée nord-occidentale, in: Guilaine, J., Manen, C., Vigne, J.-D. (Eds.), *Pont de Roque-Haute. Nouveaux Regards sur la Néolithisation de La*

France Méditerranéenne. Archives d'Écologie Préhistorique, Toulouse, pp. 221–301.

2014. Nouveaux éclairages chypriotes sur les débuts de la domestication des animaux et sur la néolithisation au Proche-Orient, in: Manen, C., Perrin, T., Guilaine, J. (Eds.), *La Transition Néolithique en Méditerranée*. Errance/ Archives d'Écologie Préhistorique, Arles/ Toulouse, pp. 125–140.

Vigne, J.-D., Helmer, D., 2007. Was milk a 'secondary product' in the Old World Neolithisation process? Its role in the domestication of cattle, sheep and goats. *Anthropozoologica* 42, 9–40.

Vigne, J.-D., Zazzo, A., Saliège, J.-F., Poplin, F., Guilaine, J., Simmons, A., 2009. Pre-Neolithic wild boar management and introduction to Cyprus more than 11,400 years ago. *Proceedings of the National Academy of Sciences* 106, 16135–16138.

Vigne, J.-D., Carrere, I., Briois, F., Guilaine, J., 2011. The early process of mammal domestication in the Near East: new evidence from the Pre-Neolithic and Pre-Pottery Neolithic in Cyprus. *Current Anthropology* 52, S255–S271.

Vigne, J.-D., Briois, F., Zazzo, A. et al., 2012. First wave of cultivators spread to Cyprus at least 10,600 y ago. *Proceedings of the National Academy of Sciences* 109, 8445–8449.

Vigne, J.-D., Zazzo, A., Cucchi, T., Carrère, I., Briois, F., Guilaine, J., 2014. The transportation of mammals to Cyprus sheds light on early voyaging and boats in the Mediterranean Sea. *Eurasian Prehistory* 10, 157–176.

Viner, S., Evans, J., Albarella, U., Pearson, M.P., 2010. Cattle mobility in prehistoric Britain: strontium isotope analysis of cattle teeth from Durrington Walls (Wiltshire, Britain). *Journal of Archaeological Science* 37, 2812–2820.

Vitzthum, V.J., 2009. The ecology and evolutionary endocrinology of reproduction in the human female. *American Journal of Physical Anthropology* 140, 95–136. doi:10.1002/ajpa.21195.

Voland, E., 1995. Reproductive decisions viewed from an evolutionary informed historical demography, in: Dunbar, R.I.M. (Ed.), *Human Reproductive Decisions, Studies in Biology, Economy and Society*. Palgrave, London, pp. 137–159. doi:10.1007/978-1-349-23947-4_7.

Voland, E., 1998. Evolutionary ecology of human reproduction. *Annual Review of Anthropology* 27/1, 347–374.

Vosteen, M.U., 1999. *Urgeschichtliche Wagen in Mitteleuropa: Eine Archäologische und Religionswissenschaftliche Untersuchung Neolithischer bis Hallstattzeitlicher Befunde*. Verlag Marie Leidorf, Rahden.

Wahl, J., Konig, H.G., Biel, J., 1987. Anthropologisch-traumatologische Untersuchung der menschlichen Skelettreste aus dem bandkeramischen Massengrab bei Talheim, Kreis Heilbronn. *Fundberichte aus Baden-Württemberg* 12, 65–193.

Walker, R.S., Hill, K.R., 2014. Causes, consequences, and kin bias of human group fissions. *Human Nature* 25, 465–475.

Warden, L., Moros, M., Neumann, T. et al., 2017. Climate induced human demographic and cultural change in northern Europe during the mid-Holocene. *Scientific Reports* 7/ 1, 15251.

Weiss, E., Zohary, D., 2011. The Neolithic Southwest Asian founder crops: their biology and archaeobotany. *Current Anthropology* 52, S237–S254.

Weninger, B., Lee, C., Gerritsen, F. et al., 2014. Neolithisation of the Aegean and Southeast Europe during the 6600–6000 cal BC period of Rapid Climate Change. *Documenta Praehistorica* 41, 1–31.

Whitehouse, N.J., Smith, D., 2010. How fragmented was the British Holocene wildwood? Perspectives on the 'Vera' grazing debate from the fossil beetle record. *Quaternary Science Reviews* 29, 539–553.

Whitehouse, N.J., Schulting, R.J., McClatchie, M. et al., 2014. Neolithic agriculture on the European western frontier: the boom and bust of early farming in Ireland. *Journal of Archaeological Science* 51, 181–205.

Whittle, A.W.R., 1978. Resources and population in the British Neolithic. *Antiquity* 52, 34–42.

Whittle, A.W.R., Healy, F.M.A., Bayliss, A., 2011. *Gathering Time: Dating the Early Neolithic Enclosures of Southern Britain and Ireland*. Oxbow Books, Oxford.

Wiessner, P.W., Tumu, A., Pupu, N., 1998. *Historical Vines: Enga Networks of Exchange, Ritual, and Warfare in Papua New Guinea*. Smithsonian Inst Press, Washington DC.

Willcox, G., 2004. Measuring grain size and identifying Near Eastern cereal domestication: evidence from the Euphrates valley. *Journal of Archaeological Science* 31, 145–150.

2012. Searching for the origins of arable weeds in the Near East. *Vegetation History and Archaeobotany* 21, 163–167.

Willcox, G., Stordeur, D., 2012. Large-scale cereal processing before domestication during the tenth millennium cal BC in northern Syria. *Antiquity* 86, 99–114.

Willcox, G., Buxo, R., Herveux, L., 2009. Late Pleistocene and early Holocene climate and the beginnings of cultivation in northern Syria. *The Holocene* 19, 151–158.

Winterhalder, B., Goland, C., 1993. On Population, Foraging Efficiency, and Plant Domestication. *Current Anthropology* 34, 710–715. doi:10.1086/204214.

Winterhalder, B., Kennett, D.J., 2006. Behavioral ecology and the transition from hunting and gathering to agriculture, in: Kennett, D.J., Winterhalder, B. (Eds.), *Behavioral Ecology and the Transition to Agriculture*. University of California Press, Berkeley, pp. 1–21.

Winterhalder, B., Leslie, P., 2002. Risk-sensitive fertility: the variance compensation hypothesis. *Evolution and Human Behavior* 23, 59–82.

Winterhalder, B., Puleston, C., Ross, C., 2015. Production risk, inter-annual food storage by households and population-level consequences in seasonal prehistoric agrarian societies. *Environmental Archaeology* 20, 337–348.

Wood, J.W., 1998. A theory of preindustrial population dynamics: demography, economy, and well-being in Malthusian systems. *Current Anthropology* 39, 99–135.

Woodbridge, J., Fyfe, R.M., Roberts, N., Downey, S., Edinborough, K., Shennan, S., 2014. The impact of the Neolithic agricultural transition in Britain: a comparison of pollen-based land-cover and archaeological 14C date-inferred population change. *Journal of Archaeological Science (The World Reshaped: Practices and Impacts of Early Agrarian Societies)* 51, 216–224. doi:10.1016/j.jas.2012.10.025.

Woodburn, J., 1982. Egalitarian societies. *Man* 17, 431–451.

Woodman, P.C., Anderson, E., Finlay, N., 1999. *Excavations at Ferriter's Cove, 1983–95: Last foragers, First Farmers in the Dingle Peninsula*. Wordwell, Bray.

Wright, K.I., 1994. Ground-stone tools and hunter-gatherer subsistence in south-west Asia: implications for the transition to farming. *American Antiquity* 59, 238–263.

Yeshurun, R., Bar-Oz, G., Weinstein-Evron, M., 2014. Intensification and sedentism in the terminal Pleistocene Natufian sequence of el-Wad Terrace (Israel). *Journal of Human Evolution* 70, 16–35.

Zapata, L., Peña-Chocarro, L., Pérez-Jordá, G., Stika, H.-P., 2004. Early neolithic agriculture in the Iberian Peninsula. *Journal of World Prehistory* 18, 283–325.

Zeder, M.A., 2006. Central questions in the domestication of plants and animals. *Evolutionary Anthropology: Issues, News, and Reviews* 15, 105–117.

2011. The origins of agriculture in the Near East. *Current Anthropology* 52, S221–S235.

Zeder, M.A., Spitzer, M.D., 2016. New insights into broad spectrum communities of the Early Holocene Near East: The birds of Hallan Çemi. *Quaternary Science Reviews* 151, 140–159.

Zilhão, J., 2001. Radiocarbon evidence for maritime pioneer colonization at the origins of farming in west Mediterranean Europe. *Proceedings of the National Academy of Sciences* 98, 14180–14185.

Zimmermann, A., 1995. *Austauschsysteme von Silexartefakten in der Bandkeramik Mitteleuropas*. Habelt, Bonn.

2002. Landschaftsarchäologie I. Die Bandkeramik auf der Aldenhovener Platte. *Bericht der Römisch-Germanischen Kommission* 83, 17–38.

2012. Cultural cycles in Central Europe during the Holocene. *Quaternary International* 274, 251–258.

Zimmermann, A., Richter, J., Frank, T., Wendt, K.P., 2004. Landschaftsarchäologie II: Überlegungen zu Prinzipien einer Landschaftsarchäologie. *Bericht der Römisch-Germanisches Kommission* 85, 85, 37–95.

Zimmermann, A., Hilpert, J., Wendt, K.P., 2009a. Estimations of population density for selected periods between the Neolithic and AD 1800. *Human Biology* 81/2–3, 357–380.

Zimmermann, A., Wendt, K.P., Frank, T., Hilpert, J., 2009b. Landscape archaeology in central Europe. *Proceedings of the Prehistoric Society* 75. Cambridge University Press, Cambridge, pp. 1–53.

Zohary, D., 2004. Unconscious selection and the evolution of domesticated plants. *Economic Botany* 58, 5–10.

Zvelebil, M., Rowley-Conwy, P., 1984. Transition to farming in Northern Europe: a hunter-gatherer perspective. *Norwegian Archaeological Review* 17, 104–128.

INDEX